The Great Demarcation

The Great Demarcation

The French Revolution and the Invention of Modern Property

RAFE BLAUFARB

OXFORD
UNIVERSITY PRESS

OXFORD
UNIVERSITY PRESS

Oxford University Press is a department of the University of Oxford. It furthers
the University's objective of excellence in research, scholarship, and education
by publishing worldwide. Oxford is a registered trade mark of Oxford University
Press in the UK and certain other countries.

Published in the United States of America by Oxford University Press
198 Madison Avenue, New York, NY 10016, United States of America.

© Oxford University Press 2016

Library of Congress Cataloging-in-Publication Data
Names: Blaufarb, Rafe, author.
Title: The great demarcation: the French Revolution and the invention of
modern property / Rafe Blaufarb.
Description: New York: Oxford University Press, 2016. | Includes
bibliographical references and index.
Identifiers: LCCN 2015042357 | ISBN 978-0-19-977879-9 (hardcover: alk. paper)
Subjects: LCSH: Property—France—History. | Public domain—France—History.
| France—History—Revolution, 1789–1799
Classification: LCC KJV1130.3 .B53 2016 | DDC 344.44/02509033—dc23 LC record available at
http://lccn.loc.gov/2015042357

1 3 5 7 9 8 6 4 2
Printed by Sheridan, USA

To David D. Bien (1930–2015)

CONTENTS

Acknowledgments   ix
Note on the Use of French Technical Vocabulary   xiii

Introduction   1

1. Talking Property before 1789   15

2. Loyseau's Legacy: The Night of August 4th and the First Abolition
   of Feudalism   48

3. The Death and Rebirth of the Direct Domain: The Second
   Feudal Abolition   82

4. The Invention of the National Domain   119

5. Emptying the Domain: The Problem of *Engagements*   148

6. When the Nation Became a Lord: Feudal Dues as
   Biens Nationaux   175

Epilogue   208

Glossary   223
Notes   227
Bibliography   259
Index   271

ACKNOWLEDGMENTS

This book is dedicated to David D. Bien, my doctoral advisor and mentor. When I entered the graduate program at the University of Michigan in September 1989, I was overconfident and intellectually hasty (which is to say, lazy). The rigors of the program and brilliance of my fellow students chipped away at the overconfidence. I am fortunate that this was so, for David Bien was too gentle and gracious a man to derive any pleasure from taking a cocky 22-year-old down a peg. He never saw that as the role of graduate advisor. What Bien did—and did so well, as any of his other students will attest—was to teach the craft of history. He did this more through the example of his own research and written work than by precept. In his seminars he naturally told us what historians should do—develop good questions, make them capacious and flexible, remain open to seeing the unexpected, do not impose prefabricated interpretations on the evidence, and, above all, archives, archives, archives. But in his articles, he showed us how all this could come together in a piece of historical writing. For many years, I would start the process of writing my own articles by reading and re-reading the introductions to his own ("The Army in the French Enlightenment" was my favorite model). His introductions exemplify how the historian can frame questions in such a way as to guide the reader into a work and explain its historical significance. Bien was a consummate craftsman, and his masterpieces have lost none of their sparkle.

Not all of his colleagues in the Michigan history department appreciated his genius. It was the late 1980s/early 1990s, the time when the wave of what was initially called "deconstruction" was sweeping through the department. By the time I received my doctorate in 1996, this movement had changed somewhat and acquired a new name, "the linguistic turn." Some of the professors who most eagerly embraced explicitly theoretical approaches may have regarded their older colleague as an anachronism, as a mere craftsman who "did" history without thinking critically about the discourses that structured it. But I have never met a historian more attuned to the constructed nature of language than David Bien. For him, it was self-evident that the meaning of words changed over time. He conveyed to his students that it was through these shifts in meaning that one could get a glimpse of the ideas and assumptions of an earlier time. For Bien, the real veins of gold in old documents were the points where seemingly familiar words were being used in strange and unexpected ways. He had taken the "linguistic turn" decades before the phrase was coined. For him, it was an obvious and necessary part of the historical craft.

David D. Bien died last Friday and is no longer here to see this book. Had he lived to read it, I hope it would have met his high standard and made him proud.

Many other people helped me with this project. My research assistant and doctoral student, Richard Siegler, deserves first mention. Without his tireless and efficient help, it would not have been possible to finish the manuscript in a timely fashion. Special thanks are also due to William Sewell (who offered incisive criticism of the entire manuscript), Suzanne Desan (whose challenging comments led me to reconceptualize the second chapter), Darrin McMahon (who gave me helpful feedback on the introduction and first chapter), Jonathan Shovlin and Liana Vardi (who read the first chapter and commented on its discussion of physiocracy), Nina Kushner (who shared her thoughts on the conclusion), and the readers of the Oxford University Press. My editor there, Susan Ferber, was an invaluable guide and critic. Her tough assessment prompted me to rewrite the introduction, for which I am grateful. Ambrogio Caini and Munro Price read chapter 7 which, through no fault of their own, ended up on the cutting room floor.

At different points in the project, I turned to experts for advice. I thank Rebecca Spang, David Andress, Gabe Paquette, Valérie Piétri, and Lourdes Garcia-Navarro for furnishing such prompt answers to my sometimes-frantic queries. And I am especially grateful to Professors Danaya C. Wright and John H. Baker for helping me understand the basic contours of English land law. This led me to reconceptualize the system of property-holding in early modern France as a tenurial system, a move which gave me a way of encompassing feudal and non-feudal property relations within a single frame.

I have had the opportunity to test some of my arguments at different conferences and seminars. These include the Newberry Library seminar on comparative early modern legal history (2011), the early modern history seminar at the University of Oxford (2011), and the Institut sur l'histoire de la Révolution française (2014). I would like to thank the organizers of these events for giving me the opportunity to present my work. They are, Tamar Herzog and Richard J. Ross, David Parrott, and Pierre Serna, respectively. I would also like to thank my co-panelists, Hannah Callaway, Allan Greer, Rebecca Spang, and Christine

Zabel, who participated in a panel on property in early modern and revolutionary France at the annual meeting of the Western Society for French History
in 2014.

This book required a great deal of archival research in France. This would not
have been possible without the generous support of the Ben Weider endowment and the Weider Foundation. Additional help came from a number of
French research institutions: the École des Hautes Études en Sciences Sociales,
the Institut National de la Recherche Agronomique, and French universities
(Besançon, Bordeaux, Grenoble, Limoges, Montpellier, and Rouen) which
hosted me as a visiting professor.

Finally, I thank my wife, Claudia, for her reading and commenting on multiple drafts of this work, as well as discussing with me the ideas it contains. I would
also like to thank Peggy Bien, for her moral support and, above all, her example.

R.B.

Tallahassee

Sunday, 27 September 2015

NOTE ON THE USE OF FRENCH
TECHNICAL VOCABULARY

Throughout this book, I use the French technical vocabulary of the time to discuss the forms of property that existed during the Old Regime. I decided not to obscure these variations under the generic term "property" for several reasons. First, the meaning of property itself was the principal stake in the debates this book follows. The term "property" was an empty signifier, a battleground, not a solid concept with a fixed definition. Second, the term does not reflect the legal and institutional complexity of the many types of property in Old Regime France.

I seriously considered using early modern English common-law vocabulary, but ultimately chose not to. The terms of that legal tradition often have meanings just as obscure as those in the French tradition—take, for example, the term "copyhold," the English term for what in Old Regime France would have been called a *censive*. Other terms, such as "estate in land," have no French equivalents. Moreover, the English terms have remained in constant usage, which has obscured their early modern meanings. An example is the term "fee simple" which is used in the United States to describe the typical form of homeownership, but which originally meant "a simple fief." Finally, as J. G. A. Pocock has shown, some of the common-law language of property itself originated in the French law faculties of the sixteenth century, from which it was transplanted to Scotland and then spread to England.[1]

One thing I have borrowed from the common-law tradition is the concept of tenurial holding. This refers to the still-vigorous English doctrine that all land is "held" of some superior (and ultimately the monarch), rather than owned

---

[1] *The Ancient Constitution and the Feudal Law* (Cambridge: Cambridge University Press, 1957), 1–90.

outright. It describes well how early modern French jurists thought about the nature of rights in both feudal and non-feudal property (with the sole exception of a kind of property called the *allod*, for which there is no English equivalent). Thus, throughout this book, I distinguish carefully between the tenurial system of property-*holding* that prevailed before 1789 and the ideal of property-*ownership* that triumphed thereafter.

In addition to these technical considerations, I prefer the original French terms because their very unfamiliarity illustrates just how radical the Revolution's transformation of property really was. Among the many changes it wrought, the French Revolution consigned an entire legal vocabulary to the dustbin of history. A glossary is thus provided, both to help the reader understand these unfamiliar terms as well as to provide a kind of homage to a vanished conceptual world.

The Great Demarcation

Introduction

> The French Revolution will seem as but a shadow to those who would
> restrict their view to that event alone. We must seek out the only light
> which can illuminate it in the times which led up to it.
> —Alexis de Tocqueville, *The Ancien Régime and the Revolution*

The French Revolution remade the system of property-holding that had existed in France before 1789.[1] This book engages with the French revolutionary transformation of property not from an economic or social perspective, but from the perspective of laws and institutions. This transformation destroyed the conceptual basis of the Old Regime, laid the foundation of France's new constitutional order, and crystallized modern ways of thinking about polities and societies. This revolution in property brought about a Great Demarcation: a radical distinction between the political and the social, state and society, sovereignty and ownership, the public and private. How the revolutionary transformation of Old Regime property produced such profound change is the subject of this book.

The revolutionary remaking of property had such important consequences because there was no clear distinction in Old Regime France between the regime of property and the constitutional order. Before 1789, French notions of property differed in two crucial ways from what is now understood by the term "property." The first was that public administrative, judicial, and sovereign powers could be owned as hereditable, vendible possessions. The second was that real estate, such as land and buildings, was rarely owned independently and completely by a single person. Instead, any given piece of real estate had multiple, partial owners who stood in legally enforced relations of superiority and dependence toward one another.

The first of these differences, the private ownership of public power, is the most alien feature of the pre-revolutionary French regime of property. At first glance, it does not seem all that different from the way things are today. After all, ownership of property—and, indeed, wealth of all kinds—still brings

disproportionate access to power. But it does so indirectly, through the opportunities and influence it can buy. In contrast, before 1789 public functions could
be purchased directly and owned as private property. The two most common
proprietary manifestations of public power were saleable public offices (hereinafter referred to as venal offices) and jurisdictional lordships (hereinafter designated by their French name, *seigneuries*). Both were found throughout France.

Venal office was a relatively recent creation of the absolutist monarchy. In the
course of the sixteenth century, the customary royal practice of raising revenue
through the sale of offices was expanded, routinized, and given a solid basis in
law.[2] During the seventeenth century, thousands of public offices were created
and sold. They enjoyed the legal status of real estate. Like land, they circulated
in a kingdom-wide market, provided collateral for loans, helped constitute
dowries, and entered into inheritance arrangements. Far from withering away
with the growth of the bureaucratic state, venality of office grew increasingly
entrenched. By the end of the seventeenth century, it had become the backbone
of the monarchy's administrative, judicial, and military apparatus and an essential component of royal fiscal policy.[3]

Venal offices were also the key to social mobility in Old Regime France. The
most prestigious offices gave their owners hereditary noble status as well as
public function. By purchasing such offices, the cream of the bourgeoisie (in its
eighteenth-century sense of wealthy non-nobles) rose steadily into the nobility.
"A noble," a scholar of this phenomenon observed, was "nothing but a successful
bourgeois."[4] The most desirable offices were those of King's Secretaries, which
ennobled more rapidly than any other, and judgeships in the highest law courts
of the land. These coveted offices have garnered the lion's share of scholarly
attention.[5] But most venal offices were more modest and did not ennoble. They
included masterships in the guilds, intermediate positions in the legal profession
such as notary and bailiff, and offices in all branches of municipal government.
Each town had dozens of offices of this kind. Cities could have a hundred or
more. For example, Lyon, one of France's largest cities, had over 125 different
types of municipal office.[6] Whether eminent or modest, venal office was ubiquitous.[7] Through this institution, thousands of people, ranging from the kingdom's
greatest aristocrats to urban workers, owned public power as private property.

The second way one could own formal public power was by acquiring a *seigneurie*. Numbering about 70,000, *seigneuries* covered almost the entire surface
of France. Although usually linked to a landed estate, called a fief, the *seigneurie* proper consisted in the right to exercise civil and criminal justice over the
inhabitants of a specific area. This jurisdiction generally corresponded to the
geographical boundaries of the fief with which the *seigneurie* was associated.
For almost all the kingdom's inhabitants, seigneurial justice was the first rung of
the judicial hierarchy, the *seigneur's* (lord's) court the tribunal of first instance.

The justice it was authorized to render was classified as either low, medium, or high, depending on the gravity of the cases it could hear. *Seigneuries* with high justice had once been empowered to judge the most heinous crimes and hand down the death penalty, but the Crown had stripped them of this power long ago. Nonetheless, *seigneurs* with the right of high justice (called *seigneurs hauts-justiciers*) retained the right of erecting gallows before their chateau, as a symbol of the eminent legal jurisdiction they possessed.

Like venal offices, *seigneuries* were fully transmissible, whether by sale, gift, or inheritance. Traditionally, they were closely associated with the nobility. But their transformation into objects of commerce had made them accessible to any individual—and any corporate entity—with enough money to purchase one. Among the owners of *seigneuries* were women (both noble and non-noble), rich commoners, towns and villages, guilds, and the Church. In fact, the Church was the largest single owner of *seigneuries* in the kingdom, a state of affairs that complicated the Revolution's nationalization of ecclesiastical property in 1789. A further complicating factor was that a *seigneurie* could be sold apart from its associated fief, either in its entirety or subdivided into smaller parcels of justice. Because of this, many *seigneuries* were shared by multiple owners whose fractions of justice were broken into days (1/365), hours (1/24), or even ounces (1/16).[8] To style oneself a lord before 1789, all one had to do was purchase a sliver of lordly jurisdiction. Yet *seigneuries* remained intimately connected to the nobility, in both the social imaginary and actual social composition of seigneurial ownership.[9] This link was enshrined in law through the *droit de franc fief*, an indemnity non-nobles had to pay when they purchased *seigneuries*. This hated burden stood as a permanent reminder of the divide between nobles and the rest of society.[10]

The private ownership of public power was just one of the distinctive features of Old Regime property. The other was the hierarchical, divided ownership of real estate. Almost all lands, buildings, and many forms of annuities and rents were held by multiple owners standing in relations of domination and subordination to one another. What the makers of the Napoleonic Code would call "absolute property"—that is, property owned fully and independently by a single person—existed nowhere in France before the Revolution. Instead, property rights over any given piece of real estate were split, generally between the actual possessor-occupier (hereinafter referred to as the tenant) and the lord who had originally conceded the land. The former enjoyed the right to use the land and appropriate its fruits. The latter retained the right to collect dues from and exercise certain kinds of authority over the tenant. Neither tenant nor lord had a complete claim to the parcel. If ownership is defined as the exclusive right to something, the right to call something entirely one's own, it is misleading to speak of ownership at all when describing property in the Old Regime.

The French property regime before 1789 is better described as a tenurial system, a system of holding, rather than a system of ownership.[11] Under it, the actual occupiers of land held their parcels from superiors who retained distinct rights over the properties they had conceded. The relations that arose formed a complex hierarchy of tenure. At its base was the mass of modest urban and rural tenants who were purely dependent and had no tenants below them. Above these were multiple strata of lords who were simultaneously the proprietary superiors of those tenants (and often their seigneurial judges as well) and the dependents of even higher lords from whom they held their own lands. At the summit of the pyramid was the Crown, which asserted that its sovereignty gave it a general right of proprietary superiority, a kind of universal lordship, over the land of the entire kingdom. By conflating sovereignty and property rights in what amounted to a hereditary, public office, the Crown incarnated the confusion of power and property that was the defining characteristic of the Old Regime.

This regime of property-holding is generally called the feudal system. It had once enmeshed much of Europe's population in a web of authority, duty, and obligation. By the eighteenth century, however, most of the original conditions of personal service (whether military, labor, or formal serfdom) under which lands had been granted to tenants by their lords had lapsed or been converted into monetary equivalents. These were often heavy and were generally accompanied by an array of perpetual dues and rents. A few vestiges remained of the original personal dimension of the feudal tie. The ceremonies of homage and fealty, symbolizing the reciprocal man-to-man obligations of tenant and lord, continued to be observed in transactions involving the transfer of property. Every time a new lord entered into possession of a fief, the tenants had to acknowledge that they held their properties from their new master by recognizing the fact on bended knee in a public ceremony. Finally, lords exercised over their tenants regulatory powers (tellingly known in French as *police*) that varied widely from fief to fief. Thus, although feudalism was no longer the full-fledged mode of government it may have been at the time of the knights, the tenurial system continued to inject notions of lordly superiority and personal servitude into the world of real estate.[12] Built on dependence and hierarchy, this system of property was incompatible with the cardinal principles of the new revolutionary order—liberty and equality. To refound the polity on the basis of these principles required the replacement of divided, hierarchical tenure with a system of full, individual ownership.

To be sure, there were many non-feudal tenures as well, particularly in the southern provinces of the kingdom. But while non-feudal in a strict legal sense, they were just as tenurial as their feudal counterparts. Like the feudal tenures, these non-feudal arrangements bound inferior properties to superior ones in perpetuity and subjected them to the payment of similar types of dues and rents.

In fact, some of the same legal vocabulary was used to describe both the feudal and non-feudal tenures, making clear the extent to which the latter partook of the same hierarchical spirit as the former. Tenant holdings of both the feudal and non-feudal type were said to "depend" on the superior estates from which they had been "dismembered." The possessor-occupiers of these inferior tenures were required to "serve" various dues and rents in recognition of the "right of superiority" reserved by the dominant property from which they had "sprung." Thus, whether formally feudal or not, nearly all real estate in Old Regime France embodied hierarchical relations of domination and dependence.

The Old Regime conception of property was both more and less capacious than that which prevailed after 1789. It was broader because it encompassed public powers, such as the right of justice, which have since lost the status of property. At the same time, it was more limited than the modern concept of property because it did not permit full, unshared ownership by a single person. In both ways, Old Regime property incarnated values at odds with revolutionary ideals. It shattered the unity of sovereignty by allowing thousands of people to own fragments of public power as private property. It undermined liberty and equality because it bound together property-holders into perpetual hierarchies of domination and dependence. To build a new constitutional order based on national sovereignty, liberty, and equality, the revolutionaries had to pry apart power and property and replace tenurial landholding with absolute, individual ownership. To do this, they created modern property.

To flesh out this summary of the Old Regime system of property, a description of how it actually worked may be useful. The city of Aix-en-Provence, the medium-sized capital of Provence, and its rural hinterland offer ample illustrations. The first thing to note is the proliferation of venal offices in this administrative, judicial, and religious center. Like other cities of its size, Aix had a large complement of guild masterships. But as a provincial capital, it had an even greater concentration of royally created municipal offices. These ranged from the prestigious positions of mayor and town councilor (called at different times *échevin, consul, capitoul,* and *jurat*) to the lowly offices of herald, porter, city-hall doorman, and crier for the dead. In addition, because the city funded itself by entry tolls and market fees, there were many offices associated with municipal finance and commerce. These included weighers and measurers, butchery inspectors, inspectors and testers of oil, and a wide range of officers charged with searching carts and collecting fees at the town's gates.

To squeeze money out of existing bodies of officers, the Crown often established new offices whose functions encroached on their privileges. By doing this, it hoped to induce the threatened officers to extinguish the unwelcome new offices by purchasing them themselves.[13] The Crown repeatedly employed this fiscal tactic on the town clerks of Aix by creating the new and redundant offices of municipal clerks (1634), secretary-clerks (1690), hereditary clerks (1697), controllers of clerks (1704), and alternative and triennial clerks (1709). All of these unwelcome offices were bought up and quashed by the original clerks. The market officers were subject to similar fiscal manipulation. For example, the pork sellers of the Aix meat market had to buy up the offices of sworn seller of pork (1704), visitor of swine (1704), sworn inspector of pork (1707), and controller of hogs (1707) in order to protect their privileges. These examples show how fiscal motives drove the proliferation of new offices whose functions touched nearly every aspect of local political and economic life.

Not all venal offices in Aix were so trivial or blatantly fiscal in origin. As a provincial capital, the town contained three sovereign courts—a supreme provincial court (*parlement*) and two high financial courts (a *cour des comptes* and a *bureau des trésoriers-généraux*). Together they counted about 200 magistrates, all of whose offices were venal and very expensive. They ranged in value from 30,000 to 150,000 *livres* (Old Regime French pounds).[14] These prestigious magisterial offices were ennobling, although many of their aristocratic owners were already of distinguished lineage. In fact, the urban elite of Aix was dominated by noble families who had achieved their status generations earlier through the purchase of these offices, but continued to pass them down from father to son as a family tradition. A typical example of an Aixois magisterial aristocrat is Esprit-Hiacinthe-Bernard d'Albert.[15] In 1765, at the age of 32, he inherited the office of president in the *cour des comptes* that had been held by his father and grandfather before him. Sometimes established families of the magisterial nobility who needed money sold their offices to up-and-coming plutocrats, often mercantile families from nearby Marseille who had made their fortunes in Mediterranean or Atlantic commerce. Esprit-Hiacinthe-Bernard found a different way of rejuvenating his family's fortune. In 1769 he married Suzanne de l'Enfant de la Patriere, whose family had recently acquired nobility and riches through venal offices in the upper-level financial and military administration. By marrying into the d'Alberts, one of the leading families of the Provençal nobility, she helped complete her own family's impressive social ascension.

Suzanne brought into her marriage not only wealth but also a prestigious fief and *seigneurie*, the Barony of Bormes, that her grandfather had purchased twenty years earlier. Through the alliance, Esprit-Hiacinthe-Bernard thus added a seigneurial lordship to his presidency in the *cour des comptes*. Simultaneous ownership of magisterial offices, *seigneuries*, and fiefs was common among the Aixois elite. Although most preferred to live in their opulent townhouses in the provincial capital, they regarded ownership of a rural fief/*seigneurie* ensemble as an essential part of their identity. This made the Aixois elites lords in the double sense of exercising both seigneurial legal jurisdiction and feudal proprietary superiority over their rural tenants. Esprit-Hiacinthe-Bernard was typical in all these respects. Like his peers, he lived in Aix; indeed, the chateau of Bormes had long ago fallen into ruins and was entirely uninhabitable. But as *seigneur haut-justicier* of Bormes, he maintained a court there to exercise his jurisdiction. And as feudal lord of Bormes, he enjoyed further powers and privileges. These included the right to collect various dues from his tenants and the right of first refusal over their property transactions.

Compared to other feudal lords, however, his prerogatives were limited. This is because the original lord of Bormes, Henry de Grasse, had long ago sold to the villagers most of his dues, together with his seigneurial *banalités* (milling, baking, and butchering monopolies), in exchange for an annual cash payment. By eliminating these potential sources of friction, this arrangement helped maintain harmonious relations between the barons of Bormes and their tenants through 1789 and beyond. This was rarely the case in fiefs where the lords had retained their prerogatives and insisted on exercising them. One such fief was Cuges, a theater of permanent conflict between the villagers and their lord, Gabrielle-Charlotte de Gautier de Girenton.[16] From the moment she inherited the fief in 1772 until her death in 1812, she waged a legal battle against her tenants to enforce her many prerogatives. These included her olive press and bread-baking monopolies, control of the villagers' wood-gathering activities in the local forest, exclusive access to the communal wash basin on certain days, regulation of violin playing in the village, exemptions from various taxes, a charitable bequest of clothing for the village poor, and supervision of the elected municipal council. The villagers responded with countersuits. This legal war of attrition lasted until 1792, when the exasperated villagers took direct action by sacking the seigneurial chateau.[17] When "order" returned with the Napoleonic regime, litigation resumed. It only ended in 1865 when Gautier de Girenton's descendants sold off their last properties in Cuges. In contrast, there were no lawsuits to embitter relations between the baron of Bormes and his community, let alone any acts of violence. This somewhat atypical state of affairs may help explain why Esprit-Hiacinthe-Bernard accepted the Revolution in 1789, declined to emigrate, and was able to defuse denunciations by Aixois radicals with testimonials to his patriotism and humanity from his former tenants. Bormes was an exception that proves the rule.

Seigneurialism and tenurial landholding were everywhere in the countryside. But it would be a mistake to imagine that the reach of lordship stopped at the gates of the city. Within Aix, all real estate was held in the same divided, hierarchical manner as in the countryside. But there were some differences, notably that the principal lord in Aix, as in most other French cities, was not the nobility, but the Church. Almost all land and buildings had been conceded by ecclesiastical establishments and were held under their superiority. Because of this, the great dynasties of the Aixois elite, who all owned fiefs in the countryside, found themselves in the position of dependent tenurial tenants when residing in their townhomes. Perhaps they chafed at this. D'Albert certainly seems to have done so. On 22 August 1790, he became one of the first people in Aix to avail himself of the revolutionary abolition of feudalism to free his urban dwelling from the lordship of the Archbishop of Aix.[18]

The example of Aix and its hinterland illustrates the pervasive intertwining of property and power that was the essence of the Old Regime. The ownership of public power as private property structured the justice system, formed the armature of local administration, defined the mechanisms of social mobility and hierarchy, and characterized the monarchy itself. The vertical division of property rights in real estate, per the tenurial schema discussed above, not only reinforced traditional social hierarchies in rural France, but also permeated the urban space. The revolutionaries saw these features of Old Regime property as utterly incompatible with the kind of polity they wanted to create. To eliminate these obstacles to the new constitutional order, they effected a revolution in property.

The men of 1789 understood what they were doing as part of a wider European movement toward the destruction of the feudal order. They were well aware of the other countries that had already begun this process. England had abolished feudal land tenure during its Civil War, but had left intact the non-feudal instances of the tenurial system—and they were many.[19] After independence, the United States had gone farther, abolishing most (although not all) forms of proprietary tenure.[20] On the European continent, the Grand Duchy of Tuscany had achieved the gradual, compensated abolition of most feudal dues in the middle of the eighteenth century, and the Kingdom of Piedmont was in the midst of a similar operation when the French Revolution occurred.[21] Great change was clearly afoot. But no country had attempted such a rapid and total dismantling of the tenurial structure of property in all of its manifestations, feudal and non-feudal alike, as the French revolutionaries did in 1789. When contemplating their work two decades later, one Prussian reformer was gripped by a powerful sense of inevitability. He remarked that "our times . . . demand changes in the nature of the ownership of land. These are changes which no human power can arrest."[22] Those who lived through the years of the French Revolution grasped the unprecedented magnitude of the transformation it had undertaken and recognized it as the beginning of a new stage of human existence.

Many subsequent commentators shared their view, the most influential of whom was Karl Marx. But Marx understood feudalism quite differently from the revolutionaries themselves. Instead of seeing it as a constitutional form (as they had), he redefined it in economic terms, as a mode of production and social organization.[23] Marx's recasting of feudalism as an economic system powerfully influenced scholarship on the French Revolution.[24] The resulting Marxist interpretation held that 1789 was a bourgeois revolution that had overthrown the feudal socioeconomic structure and inaugurated the capitalist system. During the first half of the twentieth century, this became the dominant way of comprehending the Revolution's historical significance. In the 1960s, however, revisionist research challenged the Marxist interpretation by arguing that the Revolution had not been engineered by the bourgeoisie and that it had produced no fundamental change in the structure of the French economy. Far from liberating the nascent bourgeois economy from its feudal shackles, the revisionists claimed, the Revolution damaged the capitalist industries that had been ascendant in the decades before 1789. Its principal economic impact, they argued, was to set French growth back decades. With the triumph of revisionism, the understanding of 1789 as an anti-feudal bourgeois revolution fell into disfavor. Despite renewed attention to the experience of the mercantile bourgeoisie, the rise of capitalism, and the destabilizing effects of consumer culture on the traditional society of orders, the notion of 1789 as a bourgeois revolution remains marginal in the historiography.[25]

The notion of feudalism the revisionists had in their sights when taking aim at the Marxist interpretation was the same economic one advanced by Marx in the nineteenth century. The men of 1789, however, had not seen feudalism in primarily economic terms and had not been seeking economic transformation when they abolished it. Instead, the French revolutionaries conceived of feudalism—which they also called "feudal government"—as a constitutional form based on the twin pillars of privately owned public power and hierarchical landholding.[26] Their understanding of feudalism derived from a juristic critique of the "feudal constitution" first articulated by the founding generation of absolutist legal humanists in the sixteenth century.[27] According to this critique, feudal government was illegitimate because it had arisen through the lordly usurpation of royal lands and the king's sovereign justice. The former had become fiefs, the latter *seigneuries,* and the two had fused together to form the hereditable, vendible fief-*seigneurie* ensemble that blanketed the territory of France and much of Western Europe. The resulting confusion of landed property and public power had shaped the course of European history and had caused most of France's problems. In part, the jurists' account of the rise of feudal government was a reflection on the origin of property, for all real estate in France was either a fief, had been dismembered from a fief, or could become a fief. But because seigneurial jurisdiction had become so closely linked to the fief, discussion of feudal origins was also a way of reflecting on political power, sovereignty, and the government of the kingdom. As long as property and power remained entangled conceptually, linguistically, and institutionally, property talk was constitutional talk.[28] Since many revolutionaries were lawyers by training and profession, they were well acquainted with the absolutist jurists' thought. It shaped their understanding of feudalism as an undesirable mode of government founded on the confusion of property and power. It taught them that the feudal order could be undone by dispelling this confusion. The men of 1789 purposefully set out to do this by making a radical distinction between private property and public power.

This was the Great Demarcation. It was the Revolution's fundamental act, the stake in the Old Regime's heart, and the basis of all of its other reforms. The revolutionaries committed themselves to this program of demarcation on the Night of August 4th 1789. For it was then that they abolished the *seigneurie*, venal office, and tenurial property-holding in a single decree. Although these measures were partly intended to propitiate the peasantry, then swept up in a wave of violent rural panic known as the Great Fear, they were more than an emergency response to an immediate crisis. Taken together, the abolitions of the Night of August 4th outlined a comprehensive program to dismantle the complex of institutions that fostered the Old Regime's confusion of property and power. Among those institutions figured the feudal and seigneurial prerogatives against which the peasants were revolting. But they also included other things, such as venal office, which were of no concern to the peasantry and were neither historically nor legally feudal. Even insofar as they affected landholding, the abolitions of August 4th extended beyond feudal property, for they explicitly sought to transform all forms of tenure—non-feudal as well as feudal, urban as well as rural—into independent, individual ownership. The label "abolition of feudalism"—which historians usually apply in a narrowly economic and rural sense to the measures adopted on the Night of August 4th—does not convey the breadth of the transformation the revolutionaries were attempting. Nor does it express the purposeful, forward-looking thrust of their action. The term "Great Demarcation" is better suited to describing the transformation the revolutionaries were striving for on August 4th, for it simultaneously evokes the confusion they were seeking to dispel and the fundamental principle that would order the new polity. This principle was the separation in idea and practice between the sphere of private property, on the one hand, and public power, on the other.

By putting an end to the tenurial model of property-holding and the private ownership of public power, the Great Demarcation made possible a new constitution based on citizenship and elective government. The first of these measures, the replacement of dependent, proprietary tenure with a system of full, independent ownership, was the necessary precondition for free and equal citizenship. If left intact, the perpetual ties of proprietary hierarchy would impinge upon the citizen's freedom and make him the inferior of his lord. By keeping him in a state of dependence on his proprietary superior, the bond of tenure would thus render liberty and equality empty words. The second of these measures, the abolition of the private ownership of public power, was necessary to gather together the many fragments of public power held in private hands as offices and *seigneuries* and reunite them as a single, undivided, national sovereignty. Without this step, election-based representative government could not function. If the scattered parcels of public power remained private properties, their owners would occupy public function by right. Had this situation persisted, there would have been no point in holding elections, representative government could not have existed, and national sovereignty would have been a hollow concept. The abolition of tenurial property-holding and the private ownership of public office were the sine qua non of citizenship, national sovereignty, and the new constitution.

The Great Demarcation was the underlying framework of the new polity. But, as experience soon showed, it did not necessarily produce a democratic or even liberal form of government. Napoleon's rule demonstrated this most clearly. While his regime preserved and in some ways strengthened the separation between property and power, notably through the Napoleonic Code, it reduced the participatory practices introduced by the Revolution to insignificance. Political liberty evaporated. Within a decade or so, the Great Demarcation had proven to be perfectly compatible with authoritarian government. Perhaps this should have come as no surprise, given its intellectual roots in the absolutist legal tradition of sixteenth-century France.[29]

The legacy of the Great Demarcation was thus not the triumph of a specific political form. Rather, it bequeathed to subsequent generations the conceptual matrix within which modern political forms would be built and understood. From the Great Demarcation of power and property flowed some of the key distinctions that constitute political modernity: between the political and the social, state and society, sovereignty and ownership, the public and the private. In recent decades, historians of the French Revolution have debated whether 1789 was a political or a social revolution. Identifying the Revolution's fundamental achievement as the Great Demarcation offers a way of transcending this debate. Rather than being either a social or a political revolution, 1789 was the moment that clarified the very distinction between the concepts of "social" and "political" which structures historical scholarship and the social sciences more generally.

The revolutionaries' vision of this distinction was clear. But to make it a reality, they had to craft and enact an array of nuts-and-bolts reforms. Contested, traumatic, and sometimes sloppy, these reforms remade the Church, justice system, financial administration, local government, and the Crown itself. All were necessary consequences of the Great Demarcation. After a first chapter discussing the early modern legal-historical debates that helped inform the revolutionaries' aims, the remainder of the book concentrates on how the men of 1789 and their successors struggled to implement this program. This was a difficult task, for the commitment made on the Night of August 4th required the revolutionaries to rework the concept, laws, and institutional structure of "property" as a whole. This book does not offer a comprehensive treatment of every aspect of French

Revolutionary property reforms; for that, the classic study published in 1953 by Marcel Garaud remains definitive.[30] Rather, it focuses on several especially problematic types of property that highlight the two main challenges encountered by the revolutionaries after 1789 as they sought to realize the Great Demarcation.

The first of these challenges, to excise formal public power from the sphere of private property, is the subject of chapters 2 and 3. To accomplish this, the revolutionaries had to abolish the forms of property that directly conveyed public powers (principally *seigneuries* and venal office), as well as the tenurial model of landholding that injected perpetual relations of domination and dependence into the domain of real estate. In abolishing seigneurial justice and venal office, they encountered surprisingly little resistance. But in dismantling the tenurial system, they ran into difficulties. These were largely of their own making, for they were determined to make tenants indemnify their former lords for the proprietary superiorities they were abolishing. As lawyers and landowners, the revolutionaries believed that these superiorities (represented principally by perpetual dues and rents) had been integral parts of the real estate regime before 1789 and thus insisted that they be respected. This policy provoked substantial popular opposition. At the same time, the task of making a clear legal distinction between legitimate and illegitimate dues proved more difficult than they had expected. And since the State itself possessed many of these dues and rents, the revolutionaries found themselves torn between their commitment to abolishing them and the temptation of using them to pay down the national debt. For these reasons, the transition from a system of real estate based on hierarchical tenure to one based on independent ownership dragged on long after 1789.

Chapters 4 and 5 treat the second major challenge the revolutionaries faced in realizing the separation of power and property. This was to remove all proprietary rights and possessions from the new sovereign, the nation. The first step in this process required deciding what to do with the royal domain—the lands, buildings, and property rights of the Crown. Driven by fiscal pressures as well as their commitment to constructing a purely sovereign, non-proprietary State, the revolutionaries took over the Crown's domain and transformed it into a new, national domain. Unlike the royal domain, which had been legally inalienable (unable to be transferred by sale or gift), this new domain was designed by the revolutionaries to be sold off piece by piece to individual citizen-purchasers. This would reduce the national debt and transform the quasi-public holdings of the Crown into private property. The revolutionaries also realized that the national domain would be an ideal mechanism for converting lands confiscated from political opponents, the Church, and other suppressed corporations into individual holdings. With time, the revolutionaries expected, the national domain would sell off as a private property everything it had absorbed. This would empty the domain, cleanse the State of its proprietary taint, and ensure that whatever was susceptible of private ownership found its way into individual hands. The new national domain was more than a fiscal expedient. It was an instrument for making the separation of public power and private property a reality.

In the actual event, the revolutionary expropriation and sale of the nationalized properties did not proceed smoothly. These operations spawned political opposition, speculation, and many other problems that historians have amply cataloged.[31] More fundamentally, the revolutionaries encountered unexpected conceptual and legal difficulties in distinguishing what had been domanial from what had been individual property before 1789. The problems arose from the pervasive imbrication of property and power they had inherited from the Old Regime, an imbrication especially pronounced in everything connected with the royal domain. In their reform of domanial legislation, therefore, the revolutionaries were not simply liquidating an archaic relic of the monarchy, but were contending with an institution that had sustained the Old Regime's confusion of property and power. Their successors were still trying to unravel this historical entanglement well into the nineteenth century.

The final chapter, chapter 6, examines an overlooked aspect of the revolutionary transformation of property that brings into a single frame these two major challenges. This was the problem of what to do with the dues and rents, many of feudal origin, that the revolutionary state had acquired when it took over the royal domain and the properties of the Church. The name under which they were originally known, "feudal dues belonging to the nation," eloquently expresses the dual legal status of these politically awkward properties. Simultaneously feudal and domanial, they forced the revolutionaries to confront in a single effort the two fundamental challenges raised by the creation of the new regime of property.

Despite the turbulent context of the Revolution, the men of 1789 and their successors succeeded in transforming property and, by doing so, remade the polity. They abolished venal office and the *seigneurie*, converted tenure into individual ownership, recast the State's relationship to this new kind of property by transforming the royal domain into a national one, and eliminated the proprietary superiorities the new domain had unexpectedly absorbed. No longer would some possess public function as private property. No longer would ownership of a piece of land convey supremacy, jurisdiction, and other public powers over one's fellow citizens. These changes simultaneously ended the Old Regime and provided the blueprint for the constitutional order that would take its place. The abolition of the ownership of public power set the stage for popular sovereignty by prying public offices from private hands and making them available to election. The dismantling of tenure made possible free and equal citizenship by breaking down traditional hierarchies that had been sustained by the perpetual bonds of proprietary domination and dependence. The reform of property was the key act of the Revolution, the act required to make its core principles concrete realities. It was the act on which the revolutionary dream of a New Regime depended. But it was even more than this. By ending the conceptual confusion and institutional imbrication of property and power, it enacted a Great Demarcation that still shapes the way polities are understood today.[32] By honing the set of distinctions—between the political and social, state and society, sovereignty and ownership, the public and private—through which the world is perceived and acted upon, the Great Demarcation left a legacy that extends far beyond the history of the French Revolution. It created a distinctly modern way of seeing.[33]

1

Talking Property before 1789

They [the revolutionaries] kept from the Old Regime most of the sentiments, habits, and even ideas with whose aid they carried out the Revolution which destroyed it and, without realizing it, used its debris to build the new society.
—Alexis de Tocqueville, *The Ancien Régime and the Revolution*

An essential part of the French revolutionaries' "regeneration" of the nation was the transformation of property. "In a free state, properties must be as free as persons," proclaimed the draft of a preamble to their decree on feudal abolition.[1] Where did the revolutionaries' ideas about property come from? What can an understanding of these sources of thought tell us about the constitutional work the revolution in property was intended to accomplish? Many historians concerned with the sources of revolutionary thinking about property have looked no further than John Locke's *Second Treatise* (1689).[2] Thomas Kaiser is an exception. He has convincingly argued that the revolution in property of 1789 is "better envisaged as the product of a wider application of certain elements of Old Regime jurisprudence than of a violent Lockean assault from without."[3] For Kaiser, an important inspiration for the Revolution's ideal of absolute, individual property came not from Locke, but rather from seventeenth-century debates over the French approximation of "freehold," the *allod*.[4] Kaiser's specific point about the *allod* is on the mark, but his observation that a rich tradition of French juristic thought informed the revolutionaries' thinking about property is even more important, for it suggests a whole new avenue of approach to the subject.

The early modern jurists' discussion of property often took the form of debate over the historical origins of the fief. This deceptively antiquarian quarrel broadened over the course of the sixteenth and seventeenth centuries to encompass the issues of property right, public power, and, above all, their relationship. Insofar as he articulated his notion of natural property against Filmer's patriarchal model of political power, Locke himself could be considered one of its participants. Over the course of the eighteenth century, the debate moved beyond the world of the lawyers to involve a diverse range of thinkers: absolutists and their aristocratic opponents, philosophers of all stripes, and physiocrats. The concepts it honed and, perhaps even more important, the aspirations and sensitivities it nourished exerted significant influence on the men of 1789 as they confronted the problem of property and polity.

The debate over the origins of the fief is well-known—but not by historians of eighteenth-century France and the Revolution.[5] Rather, the scholars who have engaged with it have been historians of ideas, particularly those associated with the Cambridge School.[6] They have produced brilliant analyses of this debate, but their interest lies primarily with the elaboration of modern historiography and constitutionalism in the Anglophone world. Only tangentially do they address how the question of property fits into these strands of thought and practice.[7] And they have as yet not carried their investigations up to—much less past—the French Revolution. Yet by highlighting the problematic relationship between property and power, the debate over the origin of the fief informed the revolutionaries' approach to the problem of property and polity.

Legal Humanism and the Feudal Origins of the French Constitution

In the early sixteenth century, a movement began to stir in the French law faculties. Known to historians of ideas as legal humanism, it had originated in Italy at least a century earlier. Its distinctive methodology emphasized textual and etymological analysis of historical documents, both Roman and Medieval. In the course of their studies, the Italian legal humanists had discovered a text which would stimulate centuries of debate. This was the *Libri Feudis* (Books of Fiefs), an eleventh-century Lombard writing which described how the fief had evolved from a precarious, conditional grant into patrimonial (heritable and vendible) property. When the Italian scholar, André Alciato, took a position at the University of Bourges in 1518, he brought with him his historical-legal perspective, his sensitivity to words, and his interest in the history of the fief. The spread of legal humanism to Northern Europe in general and France in particular, J. G. A. Pocock has observed, marked the beginning of modern historiography.[8]

Alciato's students hewed closely to his scholarly approach. But in one key way, French legal humanism made an important break. Whereas the Italians believed that the fief derived from Roman precedents, the French jurists argued that it originated in the Frankish conquest of Roman Gaul. By the end of the sixteenth century, this so-called Germanist thesis had become dominant in France, although Romanism reappeared in the eighteenth century.[9] Of more significance than the Germanist/Romanist split were disputes within the Germanist camp itself, often over seemingly arcane issues such as the precise moment when fiefs became heredi-tary. These were not antiquarian indulgences. Rather, such controversies reflected competing efforts to construct useable historical pasts. The ideological stakes could be high. For example, the French move from a Romanist to a Germanist theory of feudal origins was a political move, a way of asserting royal sovereignty against both the Papacy and the Holy Roman Empire. Seen in this light, historical minutiae had enormous significance. The domestic French stakes were even higher.

For the Germanists the key moment in the history of France was the Frankish conquest. Often described by them as a "revolution," they saw it as the found-ing event of the nation. In their view it had given France its authentic attributes and set it on its distinct historical trajectory. The many histories of the conquest which appeared from the sixteenth through the eighteenth centuries indirectly aired some of the most burning issues of the day. Competing accounts of how the Frankish warriors interacted with the Gaulish natives, such as those of Boulainviliers and Dubos, were thinly veiled interventions in the debate over the respective place of nobles and commoners in French society. Mably's glorifi-cation of the conquerors' deliberative assemblies hinted at a republican past that might become a republican present. While dismissed by medievalists today as useless for understanding the reality of medieval feudalism,[10] these histories were critical interventions in early modern political debates. Through them, French scholars and polemicists critiqued their present and offered suggestions for their future. When he observed in 1767 that "justices are *at present* patrimonial and hereditary," the sometime-contributor to the *Encyclopédie*, Antoine-Gaspard Boucher d'Argis, was not only indicating that this controversial institution was a historical construction; he was also evoking a future without it.[11]

In hinting at a world without seigneurial justice, Boucher was touching upon the central problem raised by the debate over the origin of fiefs: the confusion of public power and private property. This debate raised a set of loaded ques-tions about the "patrimoniality of public power," which was "the distinctive and indelible characteristic" of the French polity.[12] How did the Franks distribute the lands of Gaul? How did their original, conditional tenures evolve into a more durable form of property, the fief? How did public authority (military, politi-cal, judicial) become attached to the fief? How did this ensemble—the fief and the quasi-sovereign power embedded in it—become the patrimonial property known as the *seigneurie*? The answers the jurists and philosophers offered varied widely, reflecting their divergent political assumptions, emphases, and predi-lections. Some said that Clovis had unilaterally allocated the conquered lands. Others said the national assembly of all the Franks had done so. Some said the Franks had usurped the property of their fiefs through violence. Others said that this had occurred consensually. Despite the varying weight they placed on spe-cific episodes in their respective accounts of the "origin of fiefs," the participants in this debate shared an overriding concern with a single core issue: the entwining of private property and public power in the French constitution. Lefevre de la Planche, a noted eighteenth-century *domaniste* (an expert in the law of the royal domain), stated this with exceptional clarity: "the confusion of property with public power is the key to the history of our public law."[13]

To talk about property, therefore was to talk about power. The relationship between them, many believed, determined a nation's constitution—monarchical or feudal, sovereign or proprietary, free or despotic. For the *abbé* de Fleury, who wrote to educate princes, liberty depended on separating power from property. "There is liberty," he wrote, "where the individual enjoys the entire disposition of private law; and the Sovereign and his Officers the entire exercise of public law, whether this Sovereign be the whole People as a body, or a certain assembly, or a single man." Under the Franks and during the Middle Ages, there was "confusion of public authority and private property," and "subjects were proprietors of public power." But the strong Renaissance monarchs and their successors had largely undone these "usurpations" so that almost all "public power has returned to the King."[14] For Fleury this meant liberty because lords no longer had the power to oppress their subjects and because the monarchy, content with the exclusive exercise of sovereignty, would leave the realm of property alone.

However, not everybody had such confidence in absolutism. The jurist Bouquet was concerned because the same historical process (the Frankish conquest) that had "made [seigneurial] justices patrimonial in France" had "produced the same effect on the sovereign justice in Clovis's hand." "Sovereign public power" had thus been "annexed to the Crown" by the same dynamic which had "incorporated subaltern public power into the *seigneuries*."[15] Could the latter be abolished without undermining the former? Even Lefevre de la Planche had doubts. He felt that "the unity of the instant" that had created fiefs and hereditary monarchy, meant that property and power "could not be separated without the entire dissolution of society."[16] Others, however, saw their marriage as cause for celebration. Montesquieu famously asserted the interdependence of monarchy and nobility (for whom he believed ownership of *seigneuries* to be the defining characteristic) and saw as a key to moderate government the very confusion of property and power Fleury had condemned. A significant constitutional debate thus coalesced around the question of their entanglement.

Pioneering Reflections: Dumoulin and Bodin

The confusion of property and power exercised the most important legal-historical writers of the sixteenth century: Charles Dumoulin, Jean Bodin, and

Charles Loyseau. Dumoulin and Bodin delimited the field on which subsequent thinkers would stake out their positions. Their intellectual heir, Loyseau, would build upon their work to construct a new vocabulary that future theoreticians and practitioners would use to engage with property, power, and their problematic relationship.

Charles Dumoulin was the first jurist to address the problem systematically. Active in the first half of the sixteenth century, he gained fame as a codifier and defender of customary law. Although he produced no explicitly political or constitutional manifestos, as would Bodin, his commentaries offer a theory of monarchical power—a theory of particular significance because it led Dumoulin to consider the respective property rights of King and subject in their relation to sovereignty. A Calvinist in the first half of the sixteenth century (thus before the horrors of the Wars of Religion), Dumoulin was a Gallican absolutist who defended the preeminence of French custom over Roman law. His belief in the paramountcy of the Crown was uncompromising. The King, he argued, held both "proprietary overlordship and supreme jurisdiction over the universality of the kingdom."[17] In this particular elaboration, Dumoulin presented absolutist power as the conjoining of proprietary right (which he understood in feudal terms) and sovereignty (which he understood as the power to judge in last resort). But in most of his *oeuvre*, Dumoulin departed from this mixed model of royal power in favor of a purely jurisdictional or sovereign one. He argued that royal sovereignty was more potent than the king's proprietary overlordship because it transcended the feudal hierarchy to attain the very base of the social order.[18] Thus secondary and even tertiary vassals, who held fiefs from individual lords rather than directly from the Crown, nonetheless owed fidelity to the King as sovereign—even to the point of going to war against their immediate feudal superiors on the monarch's behalf. This would not have been permitted within a feudal-proprietary conception of kingship.

Making royal power purely sovereign had the effect of outlining a purely proprietary realm distinct from the state. We can see this in Dumoulin's defense of allodial property. One might have expected this firm absolutist to have condemned allodiality and asserted that the King had a universal feudal property right over all lands not subordinate to a particular lord. But no. Dumoulin instead held that allodiality did not weaken the King's sovereign jurisdiction. By removing proprietors from the intermediate screen of particular lordship and exposing them to direct royal sovereignty, free property actually favored absolutism. As Quentin Skinner has observed, its effect was to assign all members of society "undifferentiated legal status" as royal subjects rather than the hierarchical standing of suzerains, lords, and vassals.[19]

Dumoulin was thus one of the first French jurists to undermine the imbrication of property and power. But his ability—or desire—to make a clear-cut conceptual demarcation had limits. When considering the *seigneurie*—property in the right of justice, usually linked to real estate (the fief)—Dumoulin ran into trouble. The jurist frowned on this institution which he saw as usurpation of the King's sovereign jurisdiction. In a fateful phrase, he asserted that "fief and jurisdiction have nothing in common," for a fief was just a landholding that did "not confer any jurisdiction."[20] The Custom of Paris had long made this distinction, but Dumoulin elevated it to a kingdom-wide maxim. His point was radical: the fief was a form of property, while the *seigneurie* was a form of power. The two were not just separable; they were qualitatively different phenomena.

This theory implied a radical separation of property and power, and some of Dumoulin's successors made this explicit. But Dumoulin himself did not. His solution to the problem of seigneurial justice even tightened the knot that bound fief and *seigneurie*, property and power. To subordinate the *seigneurie* to royal power, Dumoulin assimilated the lord's right of justice to an incorporeal fief, granted by the King under the same conditions as a landed feudal domain. While this solution afforded the King some immediate leverage over the *seigneuries* in his direct grant, it subverted the conceptual distinction Dumoulin had made by admitting that lords could have property in sovereign power. It also reinforced the feudal-proprietary nature of the monarchy itself. As with many other absolutists both before and after him, the temptation of proprietary overlordship proved hard to resist.

In the end, Dumoulin's attempt to subordinate seigneurial justice by making it a fief and placing it under royal feudal overlordship reintroduced the confusion of property and power he had elsewhere tried to dispel. It subverted the radical implications of the point from which he had started—fief and justice have nothing in common—without really resolving the problem of the *seigneurie*. Recast as a fief, the *seigneurie* became a piece of property like any other. It could be inherited, sold, and divided. And it could be conceded by its lordly proprietor as a sub-fief to a subordinate lord. This would shelter it from the King's feudal reach by a screen of intermediate lordship. Dumoulin's feudal solution to the problem of *seigneuries* would have thereby removed some privately held jurisdictions from direct royal oversight. It would be uncharitable to conclude that Dumoulin's thinking was ambiguous, self-contradictory, or confused. Rather, it reflected a pioneering effort to construct a new theory of power and property within a discursive and institutional context that tended to blend what we now see as two distinct concepts.

Perhaps Dumoulin ultimately reached for royal property right to rein in the *seigneurie* because he conceived of sovereignty in jurisdictional terms, as the highest form of *seigneurie*—a term for lordly justice that also carried strong proprietary implications. It was only with the publication of Jean Bodin's *Six Books of the Republic* in 1576 that a concept of sovereignty distinct from feudal (proprietary) and seigneurial (jurisdictional) models became readily available.[21] Bodin was Dumoulin's ideological heir—an absolutist committed to indivisible royal authority. But his understanding of sovereignty was new. Bodin believed that the essence of sovereignty lay in the absolute right to make law, not in the power to judge nor still less in proprietary right. In his work, justice figures as an essential attribute of sovereignty, but it is not sovereignty itself.

The importance of Bodin's thought has been widely recognized.[22] Yet, despite the attention it has received, more can be said about his theory of sovereignty. By abandoning the older understanding of the sovereign as judge, with its links to the notion of *seigneurie*, Bodin avoided the implicit comparisons of the King to a feudal overlord and his kingdom to a fief. This distanced royal sovereignty from property and more sharply distinguished the King from his subjects. Sovereignty was no longer just the preeminent form of something—jurisdiction—that thousands owned as *seigneuries*. Rather, it was something unique to the Crown, something incapable of being alienated to the subjects and fundamentally different from their properties. Moreover, Bodin envisioned sovereignty as distinct from the prince himself, as something he "exercised in the form of a loan or precarious possession" (222). This depersonalization of sovereignty, Skinner has noted, encouraged an abstract, "modern" conception of "the State as a locus of power."[23] This imagining of the state *in abstracto* also began to make it possible to imagine the state's counterpart—society.

The tendency to demarcate state and society pervades the *Six Books*. For Bodin, sovereignty defines the former, property the latter. This is clear from the very first page, where Bodin writes that a commonwealth is the "right government of several families" (1). The heads of families, the constituent parts of society, have "power over their own things." Government must respect this by abandoning to them "natural liberty and property of goods" (11 and 279). Bodin reinforces his distinction between sovereign state and proprietary society through his typology of monarchies. He contrasts seigneurial monarchy, in which "the prince makes himself lord of both goods and persons," with royal monarchy, in which the sovereign leaves "the property of goods to the subjects" (273). Seigneurial monarchy, Bodin observed, was alien to Europe. Lordship in any form was unknown to the Romans, and the concept of *seigneurie* is absent from their codes. They even let conquered peoples retain their lands "in pure property." It was only in imitation of the Huns that the German, Lombard, and Frankish monarchs began to style themselves "lords of all things." But these pretentions, just a pale simulacrum of the genuine article, faded with the advance of "humanity" and "good laws." All that remained was "seigneurial monarchy's shadow and image" (275).

In contrast, Bodin cannot praise royal monarchy highly enough. Respecting its subjects' properties, it is happy and just. Deriving its supremacy from sovereignty alone, it is majestic beyond compare. In Bodin's rendering, even the royal domain—the Crown's property rights and landholdings—was not really the king's, but rather belonged to the "people."[24] Freed from the temptations and constraints of property, Bodin's king ceases to be lord-of-lords to become a sovereign, a unique being subject only to divine and natural law. Bodin thus rejects the notion, which had informed Dumoulin's approach to *seigneuries*, that property right could enhance royal power. Although an absolutist through and through—and, indeed, because of it—Bodin states categorically that the sovereign "cannot take another's property" (156-57).[25] He even took this to a conclusion which would be surprising were it not for Bodin's conviction that true sovereignty required a strict demarcation between power and property: he believed that the King could not impose taxes without consent.[26] In the final analysis, it was the sovereign's relationship to property that determined the character of the State. "The difference between monarchs," Bodin wrote, lay in "their means of government"—through property right or sovereignty (289).

Bodin's evacuation of proprietary right from royal sovereignty was a bold theoretical move. But how did he deal with concrete institutions that embodied the confusion of property and power? Although trained as a lawyer, his approach to seigneuries and venal office shows his mind to have inclined more toward the formulation of theory than its application to real-life situations. He devoted little of his treatise to discussing practical matters of any sort. When he did, his approach was pedestrian. Bodin thus added his voice to a chorus of critics denouncing the sale of offices.[27] And as many had also done before him, he bemoaned the lordly usurpation of royal sovereignty (214). On these points, Bodin was not original. And he occasionally contradicted himself. For example, when addressing the question of whether a king in vassalage to another king was truly sovereign, he even forgot his distinction between proprietary and sovereign right. Bodin reasoned that a vassal-king could not be "absolutely sovereign" because only a monarch "holding nothing from another" could have this preeminent quality. This position contradicted Bodin's own theoretical innovation by positing that a feudal-proprietary relationship not only existed on the same plane as sovereignty, but could even trump it. When applying his theory to specific cases, which he rarely did, Bodin displayed an unsteady grasp of his distinction between property and power.

Bodin's misstep in relation to vassal-kings is telling. It illustrates the difficulty even a brilliant thinker like Bodin had in making the conceptual demarcation between property and power. And it reflects a more serious problem that pervades the *Six Books*, a problem not specific to Bodin. Despite his determination to write property out of the realm of sovereignty, the linguistic tools at his disposal constantly reintroduce the confusion he is trying to dispel. As Herbert Rowen put it, "Bodin was driven to use the concept of property to make his point."[28] Tellingly, the density of property language increases the more intently Bodin focuses on the concept of sovereignty. There are multiple, striking examples of this in his chapter "On Sovereignty" (Book I, Chapter 8). There Bodin defines the sovereign prince as a "proprietor [*propriétaire*] formally possessed of [*saisi de*] sovereignty."[29] In contrast, the magistrate is "neither proprietor [*propriétaire*], nor possessor [*possesseur*] of it and holds nothing except on deposit [*en dépôt*]" (225). Bodin uses a technical vocabulary reminiscent of a notarial lease drawn up between a lord and tenant to characterize a king with lifetime tenure. Such a monarch is truly sovereign, he concludes, "because the people has let go of [*s'est desaisi*] and stripped [*depouillé*] itself of its sovereign power in order to grant him formal possession [*l'ensaisiner*] and invest [*investir*] him with it; and transfer [*transporte*] to him all of its power, authority, prerogatives, and sovereignties, like he who gives [*donne*] the possession [*possession*] and property [*propriété*] of that which belongs to him [*luy appartenoit*]" (227). It is extremely significant that we find the language of property cropping up to such an extent in Bodin's discussion of sovereignty. This illustrates how language itself was a source of the confusion between property and power and that the eventual demarcation of these concepts required a linguistic solution.

Loyseau and the Linguistic Separation of Property and Power

Charles Loyseau was the first jurist to address the confusion of property and power at the heart of legal language.[30] This aspect of his work has rarely been appreciated. This is because most scholars have focused on his *Treatise of Orders and Plain Dignities* (1610).[31] The *Orders*, however, was the final volume in a three-volume series that Loyseau conceived as a whole. The first two tomes, the *Treatise on Seigneuries* (1608) and the *Treatise on Offices* (1610), focus on the two principal manifestations of the private ownership of public power. Together, they analyze the historical, linguistic, and institutional entanglement of property and power in the institutions of *seigneuries* and venal offices with the aim of distinguishing between those two concepts. While Loyseau's treatment of public power owed much to Bodin, he went beyond his predecessor's calls for separation of sovereignty and property to offer a sustained reflection on the historical origins of their confusion and to craft a set of conceptual-linguistic tools to pry them apart. Loyseau's new vocabulary quickly became the definitive way of talking about fiefs, *seigneuries*, and offices.[32]

In *Seigneuries*, Loyseau tackles the problem of language head-on.[33] He recognizes that the confusion of property and power derived to no small extent from the translation of the Latin term *dominium*, used in Roman law texts and early modern notarial contracts to denote property, by the French word *seigneu-rie*. The use of this word was problematic because it meant not only property, but power as well. Taken in the former sense, *seigneurie* drew its meaning from *sien* (one's own). But Loyseau was skeptical that this was the primary root of *seigneurie*. He believed that the Latin *senior* (an elderly person) communicated its meaning even more powerfully to the French term *seigneurie*. In "almost all nations" throughout history, he observed, "people of age and experience" were the public officers. Thus, in all ancient languages (Hebrew, Greek, etc.), a single word was used to signify "the elder and the officer, old age and the office" (4).[34] *Seigneur* referred to the magistrate and *seigneurie* to his office.

This had been so in ancient France. Citing Caesar's commentaries on the Gallic Wars, Loyseau noted that the Gauls had been ruled by *seigneurs* whose authority "resided as a true office in their persons, not in their lands" (3-5). In its original meaning, therefore, the concept of *seigneurie* had everything to do with public power and nothing whatsoever to do with property. But *seigneurie* had acquired proprietary connotations and become "the term most commonly used to signify property of something" (6). This was the result of a historical process that Loyseau considered the defining moment in French history. Exploiting the weakness of the early Frankish kings, lords had gradually converted their *sei-gneuries*, "which had originally been offices" (6), into patrimonial property and linked them to their feudal landholdings. This lordly "usurpation" (19) was the origin of the modern *seigneurie*.[35] Like an office, it conveyed public power. But unlike an office, it had become a form of heritable, vendible property—thereby giving institutional expression to the linguistic ambiguity already present in the etymology of *seigneurie*.

Like Dumoulin and Bodin, Loyseau deplored this entanglement. Yet unlike them he was acutely aware that this confusion permeated language itself. To talk about property, one had to use the word *seigneurie* which, by equating ownership to lordship, connoted a hierarchical, tenurial relationship of power. Conversely, when talking about power, one had to employ *seigneurie*, which, as the French translation of the Latin *dominium*, implied proprietary right. Loyseau's contribution was to disentangle this linguistic knot by constructing a new vocabulary to expose the two meanings of *seigneurie*. He did so by positing two distinct types of *seigneurie*, one private and one public. Private *seigneurie* (*seigneurie privée*) meant property. Expressing the concepts of "yours" and "mine," this proprietary form of *seigneurie* was "real and entirely apparent" (1). It was, in short, property right itself: "the true property and actual enjoyment of something . . . the right that each individual has in his thing" (7). As the qualification "private" indicated, this *seigneurie* conveyed no "public power" over people, only ownership of things.[36] In contrast, public *seigneurie* meant formal power, specifically the right of justice, over people (8). It was an "intellectual right," a kind of "authority" which could not be "made visible." Abstract and immaterial, it could not become legitimate property. Moreover, "from their inception, *seigneuries* had been established in confusion, by force and usurpation." Because of the chaotic, discreditable origins of public *seigneurie*, "it has been almost impossible to bring order to this confusion, assign a right to this force, and regulate its usurpation according to reason" (1). For Loyseau the *seigneurie* that had actually arisen in France (what he called, the *seigneurie in concreto*) was the unholy fusion of the two different orders of *seigneurie*—private and public, property and power—into a single entity. By splitting the concept of *seigneurie* into public and private types, Loyseau took an important step toward the dissociation of property and power.

Loyseau made a further distinction within each of his new categories. The first had arisen within the category of private *seigneurie* through the historic circumstances of the Frankish conquest. After their victory, the Franks had taken all the "lands of Gaul" and "given their State both *seigneuries* [public and private] over them" (13).[37] After reserving some of these lands for "the domain of their Prince," the rest were distributed to "the principal chiefs and captains." These warrior elites did not, however, enjoy full *seigneurie* over their grants. First, the State retained the totality of public *seigneurie*, creating for itself a monopoly of public power which the absolutist Loyseau saw as the proper state of affairs. Second, the warriors did not hold their land grants as hereditary property, but only for the duration of their military service. Over time, however, they took advantage of weak monarchs to expand the conditions of their tenure bit by bit, until their grants had become hereditable.

The transformation of the original, conditional grants into full property took place gradually, through a series of distinct stages on whose progression the jurists essentially agreed. First, the service-based grants were converted into lifetime tenures, regardless of whether or not their beneficiaries were still performing military duties. Then they became hereditary in the male line. After that they became vendible, and soon thereafter women and girls were allowed to inherit and possess them. This last transformation signaled the definitive transformation of the grants into true property.[38] For the jurists, the historical rise of property in France was predicated upon female ownership.

But this property was not complete. Because of the conditional tenure under which the warriors' original grants had originally been made, the state still retained a proprietary interest in them. This had the effect of dividing private *seigneurie* into a superior and inferior type of property right. The State's superior right, which Loyseau termed *seigneurie directe*, was a new "degree of private *seigneurie*" (13-14). As for the property right enjoyed by the Frankish captains, Loyseau called it *seigneurie utile* (useful *seigneurie*) (19). Over time, this hierarchical division of property right was repeated, as the captains distributed a portion of their lands to their military retainers, and they, in turn, did the same. At the base of this nascent hierarchy, the vanquished Gauls received land to farm.[39] But unlike the hierarchy of Frankish lords and vassals, who held their grants in exchange for military service, those at the bottom of the hierarchy had to pay an annual rent, called the *cens* after the former Roman tribute *census*, to the proprietary superior from whom they held their land. These tenures came to be called *censives*, and those granted for military service fiefs.

Loyseau equated the two degrees of private *seigneurie* to the *dominium directum* and *dominium utile* familiar to Renaissance jurists. Working with the raw material of Roman law, especially the hierarchically divided tenure known as emphyteusis, humanist legal scholars had gradually constructed these gradations of property to express the superior and inferior tiers of feudal land tenure. By the end of the fourteenth century, this concept of property right, generally referred to as "divided domain," was already entrenched in France.[40] Loyseau was the first to translate its terminology from Latin into French, but this was not his only claim to fame. By confining the concepts of *seigneurie directe/dominium directum* and *seigneurie utile/dominium utile* to his new category of private *seigneurie*, he underlined the purely proprietary nature of the hierarchical relationship—the division of *dominium*—they expressed. Before Loyseau (and sometimes after), jurists would confuse the proprietary superiority of *seigneurie directe/dominium directum* with the formal power of public *seigneurie*. This resulted in their equating ownership of a fief with jurisdiction over the people living within its boundaries. This was to assimilate fief and justice to one another. It was against this equation that Loyseau's linguistic deconstruction of *seigneurie* took aim.

Originally the Frankish captains did not own public *seigneurie*, which was entirely at the disposition of the "state" or "sovereign prince" (16). But as long as they remained in office, their captaincies conferred on them the exercise of two kinds of public power (*puissance publique*): command of their soldiers and jurisdiction over the inhabitants of their districts. The captains thus had a dual obligation. The first was a public one attached to the functions of their office. The second was a private, purely personal one of service and fidelity to the superior from whom they had received their land. The "charges of captains" were thus "offices and fiefs together" (17). They tended to become indistinguishable over time. Once this fusion had been accomplished, all that remained to complete their transformation into the modern fief/*seigneurie* ensemble, the *seigneurie in concreto*, was their conversion into hereditable property. For Loyseau, this historical "usurpation" (19) led to the patrimonialization of both the original conditional land grants and the public functions attached to the captaincies. This was the great revolution that had given the French polity its specific character. The heredity of fiefs divided private *seigneurie* into two distinct domains—the *directe* and the *utile*. The heredity of the public authority attached to the captains' charges divided public *seigneurie* in a similar way—into the original, supreme

Table 1.1 **Loyseau's deconstruction of *Seigneurie***

Seigneurie			
Seigneurie privée (Private Property)		*Seigneurie publique* (Public Power)	
Seigneurie. directe (Tenurial Superiority)	*Seigneurie utile* (Possession and Use)	*Souveraineté* (Sovereignty)	*Puissance publique* (Subordinate Public Power)

form of public *seigneurie* (which Loyseau termed "sovereignty") still retained by the Crown and a subordinate public power attached to the fief (19).

Throughout his treatise, Loyseau assumed the stance of an impartial observer objectively describing *seigneurie*. His deconstruction of the concept, however, was anything but neutral. There are hints in the text that Loyseau was uncomfortable with the division of private *seigneurie* into a superior direct and subordinate useful domain Although in principle a purely proprietary relationship between two parcels of land, this hierarchical division produced effects similar to (and was often confused with) public *seigneurie*. Tenurial and thus hierarchical, it subjected the holder of the useful *seigneurie* to the power of *seigneur directe* (19).[41] Loyseau envisioned an alternative to it. This appears in several passages where he comments on the word *sieurie*, a term which had once signified the full "property of something" without any suggestion of divided rights or hierarchy.[42] It corresponded to the Roman concept of property, which "did not recognize the *dominium directum et utile* produced by our fiefs and *censives*" (20). The hierarchical system of divided domain, Loyseau observed, tended to produce confusion between property right and public power because of the "great affinity and resemblance between the private direct *seigneurie* of a feudal lord and the public *seigneurie* of a lord with high justice" (20). Unfortunately, however, *sieurie* had fallen out of use and now seemed old-fashioned and rustic (6). It could no longer serve as the basis of a non-hierarchical language of property. Moreover, Loyseau was well aware that any attack on divided domain would be enormously disruptive. Since nearly all landed property in France was linked into great tenurial chains of fiefs and *censives*, to overthrow the distinction between *seigneurie directe/dominium directum* and *seigneurie utile/dominium utile* would plunge everything into turmoil and threaten the existence of property itself. These practical considerations were a powerful restraint on Loyseau, who kept his critique of the divided-domain model of property relatively muted.

He displayed no such restraint when it came to public *seigneurie*. Loyseau flatly denounced the lordly appropriation of the right of seigneurial justice as usurpation founded in violence and lords themselves as "tyrants" and "thieves" (257). At points in the *Treatise on Seigneuries*, he comes close to calling for the return of seigneurial justice to the undivided body of royal sovereignty from which it had been dismembered. The method he considers for doing this was the outright abolition of *seigneuries* (227). But he stops short, recognizing that seigneurial justice is so ubiquitous and deeply entrenched that it could not be dismantled. Instead, he claims, his goal is more modest: to "order . . . and regulate by reason" *seigneurie* as it actually existed (1).

Loyseau's disclaimer is not entirely convincing. He was certainly too pragmatic to demand the abolition of *seigneurie*. This would have been revolutionary, for it would have abolished feudalism and seigneurialism and required both a new order of property and a new system of justice. Yet, Loyseau's deconstruction of *seigneurie* was subversive nonetheless, for it conjured up the image of just such a change and created a vocabulary for articulating it. Although the *Treatise on Seigneuries* eschewed overt prescription, its analysis of how the Frankish past produced the French present beckoned toward a radically transformed future. Once their historical origins and contingent nature were exposed, the hierarchies of fief and *censive* could give way to undivided, equal property. Once seigneurial jurisdiction was revealed as the fruit of lordly usurpation, the Crown could reclaim its rights and reconstitute its original monopoly of sovereignty. Since the nobility's preeminence was founded in large part on its ownership of fiefs and seigneurial jurisdiction, this would have revolutionized the social order. Although he never explicitly called for such radical change, Loyseau's historicization and deconstruction of *seigneurie* made it possible to imagine a great transformation that would undo the "revolutions" of Frankish times and fundamentally remake the polity.

The Question of Allodiality

Since Loyseau never directly mentioned the royal domain (the properties and rights attached to the Crown) nor addressed the question of how Crown property fit into his theory, it is not possible to know what he thought of a proprietary State. The few indications we have of his views on the matter are ambiguous. On the one hand, there are signs that he was uncomfortable with the idea of a domanial state. At one point, he describes sovereignty as the "true *seigneurie* of the state," not private *seigneurie* or property (25). At another, he asserted that "feudalism diminishes sovereignty" (35). Moreover, his definition (borrowed from Bodin) of "seigneurial monarchs" (proprietary kings) as despots who enslaved their subjects and took their possessions also supports this assumption (*Seigneuries*, 36-37).[43] Yet, his account of the division of the conquered Gaulish lands, which made the King the source of all property in France, furnished ample material with which to construct a powerful justification of royal property right. Shortly after Loyseau's death in 1627, theorists of the royal domain and officers in the domanial administration seized upon his account of the origin of fiefs to assert a royal lordship over all French territory. Their efforts undermined the jurists' attempt to separate property and power.

Little was written about the royal domain before the seventeenth century.[44] The few works on the subject tended to classify as domanial a hodge-podge of physical and incorporeal properties, as well as a collection of rights that would today be considered sovereign. As constructed by these early writers, the royal domain placed the confusion of property and power at the heart of the monarchy itself. For René Choppin (1537-1606), the first author to consider the domain seriously, the king was "from the very beginning seigneurial sovereign of all things." Although he had "given and abandoned" many of his possessions "under the title and condition of fief," he had "retained and reserved" an overarching property right. As a result, the King had "domain and sovereignty . . . over all things in his kingdom."[45] Choppin's enumeration of the royal domain's components—"lands and *seigneuries*," "tolls," "entry duties," "dues on merchandise," "sovereign rights," "fealty and homage," "confiscated goods," "shipwrecks," "vacant successions," "the successions of foreigners" and "bastards," and "offices"—further the confusion. He even saw taxes as the "sacred patrimony of the King."[46] Subsequent *domanistes* would differ with Choppin (and each other) over the precise composition and nature of the domain's holdings: Were they inherent to sovereignty or not? Domanial by nature or custom? Susceptible to individual ownership or inherently public? Saleable or not? Physical or incorporeal?[47] Yet they all agreed that the Crown's domain consisted of a mix of property and sovereign rights.[48]

Considered by many as the fundamental law of the kingdom, the Edict of Moulins (February 1566) affirmed the proprietary character of the monarchy. Its first article, called the Salic Law, pronounced the royal succession hereditary by male primogeniture. Its second article declared that the royal domain was inalienable.[49] Although governed by special laws, not the general successoral regime, the hereditary nature of the Crown suggested a parallel with patrimonial property.[50] And when coupled with Loyseau's account of the origin of fiefs, the doctrine of inalienability implied that all properties had once belonged to the royal domain, that they had been granted only conditionally, and that the King could revoke them and reunite them to his domain. This laid the groundwork for a theory of universal royal property right by assimilating the monarchy to a great, constitutionally inalienable fief from which all lesser fiefs had sprung and upon which they still depended. On this, the *domaniste* Lefevre de la Planche was explicit: "in its entirety, the domain is nothing but a grand fief."[51]

This paved the way for a campaign to impose a universal royal *directe* (proprietary superiority). It began in 1629, two years after Loyseau's death, and continued until 1789.[52] The opening shot was Article 383 of the Code Michau (1629) by which the King declared that "all holdings not dependent upon other *seigneurs* are considered to depend upon us."[53] The claim was reiterated throughout the seventeenth and eighteenth centuries, most forcefully by Louis XIV.[54] By his Edict of August 1692 he asserted his "feudal superiority [*mouvance*] and universal *directe* over all the lands of the kingdom."[55] This is significant because, in encompassing "all the lands of the kingdom," it subjected *allods* to direct royal lordship. This amounted to the extension of the principle "no land without a lord" (*nulle terre sans seigneur*) to all real estate in the kingdom and would have abolished allodiality. But for those who already held fiefs, sub-fiefs, and *censives*, nothing would have changed. Nor would it have affected those provinces (half of the total) which already recognized the maxim *nulle terre sans seigneur*. But in provinces which observed the opposite principle—*nul seigneur sans titre* (no lord without title)—it would have recast proprietary relationships along feudal lines by converting *allods* into immediate royal fiefs.

The Crown offered little theoretical justification for the universal royal *directe*. Even Auguste Galland, the *domaniste* commissioned in 1629 to craft an argument for it, did little more than denounce the *allod*-owners' "imaginary liberty."[56] Eight years later, after public protest and the resistance of law courts had stalled the domanial offensive, Galland returned with a more ample justification.[57] In the original state of nature, he admitted, properties were available for the "common usage of all men"; there were no "particular *seigneurs*." But soon "the most powerful" took what they wanted, and "holy equality" was destroyed.[58] To exploit their holdings efficiently, the powerful gave portions to the "most feeble" in exchange for dues (creating *censives*) or personal service (creating fiefs). The result was the feudal hierarchy which, in Galland's account, was the inevitable outcome of human nature. He conceded that a few lands may have been granted "without any charge, submission, or recognition [of dependence]." But these were so rare that their allodial status would have to be proven by title.

Galland's was the only published justification of the 1629 measure. Why such theoretical poverty? In large measure it reflects the fact that the campaign for the universal royal *directe* was a fiscal initiative, driven by the Crown's consuming need for funds and implemented by bureaucrats and sub-contracting financiers rather than jurists. Moreover, its true aim was not really to impose a royal *directe* and collect feudal dues for the King. Rather, it was to extort from the owners of *allods* a confirmation fee—one year's worth of revenue—to preserve their lands' liberty. Money, not legal principle, was the motive force behind the initiative. But it was no less pressing for that.

The advocates of allodiality fiercely defended their cause with a tidal wave of judicial remonstrations and published tracts that soon forced the royal government to suspend its attempts at implementation.[59] *Parlements* whose jurisdiction extended over allodial provinces—those of Dijon, Grenoble, Toulouse, Bordeaux, and Paris—protested against the 1629 Edict and refused to register it. And affected provinces commissioned pamphlets to defend their rights. The first, written by Pierre de Casaneuve for the Estates of Languedoc, appeared in 1640. The last, written for the Estates of Navarre by Etienne Polverel (better-known for helping abolish slavery in revolutionary Saint-Domingue) appeared in 1784.

Throughout its long history, the pro-allodial campaign deployed a stable set of arguments. First, the pamphleteers presented historical evidence showing regional variation in the Germanic conquest and appropriation of Gaulish lands. This challenged the undifferentiated, bare-bones account of Loyseau and others. Second, they claimed that allodiality was not merely compatible with royal power, but actually increased the Crown's dignity. Arguing that "pure" property, decoupled from public authority and freed from the hierarchical chains of feudal tenure, would increase the state's sovereign power, the allodialists made an important contribution to the ideology of proprietary liberty available in 1789.[60]

They used history to show that Loyseau's account did not apply to certain provinces. The most important exceptions to Loyseau's schema were the provinces of southern and eastern France, which had not been conquered by the Franks, but had fallen under the sway of the Goths and Burgundians, respectively. In the case of southern France (Languedoc, Navarre, Roussillon, and parts of Aquitaine), there had been no conquest at all.[61] Instead the Romans had voluntarily transferred those provinces to the Goths. In return, the Goths had promised to respect the laws, liberties, and properties of the Gallo-Roman inhabitants. As there had been neither conquest nor land redistribution, the existing properties had retained their original Roman allodiality. These provinces had eventually come under Frankish control—but, once again, not by conquest. Instead, when its Gothic rulers had embraced the Arian heresy, Languedoc had revolted and invited in the orthodox Franks. Consequently, the new rulers had no right of conquest over their new subjects; on the contrary, they were morally indebted to their piety.

The historical argument for the allodiality of eastern France was similar. Pamphleteers for Burgundy, Franche-Comté, Dauphiné, and parts of Champagne admitted that their provinces had been conquered—but by Burgundians, not Franks.[62] Unlike the Franks, these conquerors did not take all the lands, but let the inhabitants retain a portion and continue to own them as Roman-law *allods*. Many of these had eventually become fiefs. But this had occurred gradually, as weaker property-owners sought the protection of the powerful in exchange for fealty and service. Feudalism had thus arisen organically and voluntarily on a case-by-case basis. In consequence, the feudal status of lands in these provinces could not be presumed.

The Gothic and Burgundian exceptions furnished the principal historical arguments for allodiality. But there were many smaller localities that claimed histories favorable to their allodial status. One example is the town of Aurillac in the mountainous province of Auvergne in central France.[63] According to local legend, the town had been founded like Rome itself by a Trojan refugee (Francus, son of Hector). This common ancestry was recognized by the Romans who, after vanquishing the rest of Gaul, allowed Aurillac to retain its liberty. Honorary Romans, the people of Aurillac naturally embraced Christianity early and fervently—long before the barbarian Franks. But when Clovis converted, Aurillac voluntarily placed itself under his rule. Since there had been neither conquest nor land redistribution, there could be no royal *directe*. Fiefs did not arise until much later, in the Middle Ages, when the people of Aurillac began placing their *allods* under the feudal domination of the local Church as living pious bequests. The only lords the town had ever known were the clergy.

The main claim of the allodialist argument was that allodiality and royal sovereignty were not merely compatible, but actually complementary. To show that allodiality did not mean independence from royal sovereignty, the allodialists turned to the sixteenth-century jurists' distinction between sovereign and proprietary right. Although "there is no land in the kingdom not subject to the sovereign rights of the prince," Dumoulin had noted, "the King is not entitled to call himself universal proprietor or *seigneur* of individuals' things."[64] Drawing on the venerable jurist's distinction, the town of Saint-Quentin-en-Vermandois assured that "allodiality, such as we enjoy, is compatible with universal regalian *seigneurie*." In a similar invocation of Dumoulin's (and Loyseau's) distinction between fief and justice, the province of Dauphiné reminded that the "*directe* and jurisdiction have always been considered separate and different rights."[65] Some allodialists went further, arguing that allodiality actually enhanced the Crown's prestige and power. Caseneuve was particularly eloquent in this regard.[66] As sovereign, the King was "unique," but as feudal lord he was just one among many. Juxtaposition to "so many *seigneurs* . . . took something away" from the dignity of the Crown. As sovereign, however, the King "inherited the power of the Roman Emperors . . . the grandest, most potent, and most triumphant princes ever to wear a Crown." Allodiality did not diminish royal power, rather the contrary. "Kings are just as much sovereign over lands held allodially as those held in fief; indeed, they are even more powerful [over the former] in that *allods* recognize no other *seigneur*." For Caseneuve, feudal property right was undignified compared to sovereignty. "Like the Sun, whose light is all the more beautiful when it is alone and when no other stars share its splendor," sovereignty was the most glorious attribute, the only one worthy of a French king.

The *domanistes* were hard-pressed to combat such arguments. By the second half of the eighteenth century, many even seem to have given up the fight. A prime example is the influential Lefevre de la Planche. In his massive, two-volume work, he never even mentioned the universal royal *directe*. And much of its content is even pro-allodial. Rejecting Loyseau's account of the conquest, Lefevre wrote that the Frankish kings "reserved for themselves only sovereignty" and that "allo-diality was [thus] the general state of all the kingdom's properties." The present-day *allods* were therefore not usurpations, but rather the "residue of that [original] universal liberty."[67] Of course, most lands had become feudal. But this had not occurred through the imposition of a royal *directe*, but rather through a variety of historical circumstances, many involving the voluntary renunciation by the owners of *allods* of their lands' independence. As the weak placed themselves and their lands under the protection of the strong, a chain of fidelity and property—the feudal hierarchy—took shape.[68] Ultimately, even great lords sought the pro-tection of the greatest lord of all, the King, lending plausibility to what Lefevre's editor (a *domaniste* himself!) termed "the fiction that assumes all lands to have been dismembered from the ancient patrimony of the Crown."[69] A more damning comment on the domanial offensive of 1629 and 1692 can hardly be imagined. With defenders like this, the universal royal *directe* hardly needed enemies.

Expansive royal property right finally found a spokesman in 1769. This was Edmé de la Poix de Fréminville, a *feudiste* (a legal specialist who asserted feudal rights for *seigneurs*) who decided to ply his trade on a kingdom-wide stage.[70] He began by embracing Loyseau's version of the conquest and the origin of fiefs. The King possessed "the sole, grand, and general fief of the kingdom, upon which all portions are feudally subordinate, either directly or indirectly . . . without excep-tion" (1:559). Having "possession and property. . . . of the whole," the King was therefore the "universal *seigneur*, grantor of all holdings in the kingdom" (1:401 and 406). Poix rejected the notion that certain provinces had historical claims to allodiality. "Roman laws" might favor the liberty of property, but these laws were now irrelevant. To claim that provincial custom trumped royal authority, moreover, was seditious "license" (1:340). When it came to property, "the law of fiefs is the same in written law lands [those which observed Roman law] as in ones governed by custom" (1:559). The King certainly had the power to grant his lands as *allods*, but such allodiality had to be proven. *Allods* lacking royal title had almost certainly been usurped—whether by fraud, conniving, or sei-gneurial weakness. Poix bolstered his case by invoking domanial inalienability. Usurped *allods* violated this principle because, in diminishing the particular fief from which they had been carved, they ultimately diminished the royal domain, source of all fiefs. *Allods* granted by individual lords without royal consent were thus illegal dismemberments of the "inalienable, sovereign domain" (1:599).

Poix's use of the phrase "sovereign domain" is significant, for it illustrates the persistent confusion of the two concepts—property and power—the jurists had been struggling to separate. For many *domanistes*, however, this confusion was the foundation upon which the royal domain and the Crown—as well as their professions—rested. Poix stated it explicitly. The King had "two sovereign powers." The first, consisting of the power of war and peace, justice in last resort, the granting of dignities, supreme military command, and the right of taxation, is recognized today as an attribute of sovereignty. However, the second, universal proprietary superiority, is not. Derived from the conception of the King "as grand feudal lord . . . of all the kingdom's fiefs and sub-fiefs," this made property right a pillar of the monarchy (2:417). In Poix's rendering, the royal domain effaced the line between property and sovereignty and elevated their confusion to the status of constitutional principle.

Poix's, however, was a lone voice. From the mid-eighteenth century, a wide range of authors began to extend their rejection of the universal royal *directe* to the principle of domanial inalienability itself and called for the elimination of property right from the Crown's prerogatives. The influential German jurist Puffendorf, whose theories were widely disseminated in France, restricted the sovereign's right over his subjects' lands to establishing the basic laws of property, levying taxes for the common good, and invoking eminent domain (with compensation for the dispossessed) in case of emergency. He made no allowance for a royal domain of any sort.[71] Puffendorf's restriction of royal property right gained special relevance in the middle of the century, when opponents of increased taxation deployed his arguments against fiscal innovations of all sorts. Writers from such diverse social and ideological backgrounds as Jansenist *parlementaires* and aristocratic republicans found these ideas appealing. Representatives of the former group, the *abbé* Mey and his *parlementaire* colleagues asserted the "total difference between public power and domain or property." They stated categorically that "sovereignty, public power, does not give the Supreme Magistrate the domain or property of the lands or goods of the citizens."[72] The republican *marquis* d'Argenson adopted a similar stance. A truly royal king, he wrote, "considers less his right of property than the good of the state he governs." Urging the King to give up his domain altogether, he asked rhetorically why a monarch needed "suzerainty over all the fiefs" when he exercised "such decided sovereignty over all [his] subjects?" This sovereignty could be enhanced, he urged, if feudalism itself were abolished and all properties were "free, exempt from all dues and servitudes just as they were when first cleared by our forefathers." Concluding with a call for universal allodiality, he urged that the kingdom "ought to be nothing but a non-noble *allod*."[73]

D'Argenson's appeal was taken up shortly before the Revolution by Polverel in defense of Navarese allodiality. Although commissioned to defend only his native province, Polverel took the opportunity to make a sweeping attack against not only feudalism, but all forms of tenurial property-holding. He began by asserting that property was free and absolute by nature; what one man owns, he owns fully, without any division of property right. From this assertion of the primacy of exclusive, individual ownership, Polverel proceeded to attack the royal domain's claims to tenurial superiority over the lands of France. The members of a nation might decide collectively to grant the nation itself the *seigneurie directe* or even the full property of their individual possessions. However, for "a single man . . . to reserve for himself *seigneurie* of the lands . . . of an entire nation" was outrageous. At odds with the "laws of nature" and "the most basic notions of natural reason," such an arrangement could only be mandated by a "primitive convention . . . between all the members of a nation." Until that "single man" (obviously the King) offered proof of that original contract, "each individual would recover the rights of nature" and "everything he possessed would belong to him personally, freely, and absolutely and, following the technical expression of the modern peoples of Europe, allodially." "Universal allodiality," Polverel concluded, was "the common law of all of France."[74] Within five years Polverel's vision of free property became a constitutional principle, his requirement that would-be lords be forced to prove their rights or lose them the law of the Republic.

By the end of the Old Regime, the allodialists appeared to have won the ideological battle—at least they had swept the opposition, such as it was, from the field. But argument alone could not prevail against fiscal necessity. Thus, efforts to squeeze money from the royal domain continued through 1789. Indeed, as will be seen in chapters 4, 5, and 6, the temptation to raise money through the domain (re-baptized "national" in 1789-90) proved difficult to resist. The national debt and the intense pressure it exerted on nearly every aspect of revolutionary policy hampered the efforts to liquidate feudal, domanial, and other doubtful categories of property that offered financial resources to the State. Because of this, domanial and allodial counter-claims were still being hurled back and forth in lawsuits in the 1830s and sometimes beyond.[75]

Even though the Old Regime's battle over domanial property right was inconclusive, it was significant because it made the entanglement of power and property a central concern of constitutional debate. Those who had not already been sensitized by Dumoulin, Bodin, and Loyseau to the problematic relationship between property and power were forced to confront it by the debate over allodiality.[76]

The *Thèse Seigneuriale*

Domanial claims thus provoked an allodial reaction that widened the conceptual gap between sovereignty and property. But the domanial offensive also helped spark a seigneurial backlash that opposed absolutist pretentions by asserting the constitutional necessity of the fusion of property and power. This movement, which emerged during the waning years of Louis XIV's reign, came into the open only after the monarch's death. Scholars have described the movement's position as a *thèse nobiliaire* (noble thesis) and claimed special significance for its Germanist historical approach, one going so far as to call Germanism "the fundamental instrument of anti-absolutist critique."[77] Both characterizations are misleading. As we have seen, Germanism had already triumphed in the sixteenth century, when it provided a historiographical foundation for absolutism. And it is more accurate to describe the *thèse nobiliaire* as a *thèse seigneuriale* (seigneurial thesis), for the counterweight it opposed to royal despotism was not the noble order per se, but rather private ownership of public power—primarily in the form of the *seigneurie*.

The first major proponent of the *thèse seigneuriale* was Henry de Boulainviliers, a noble of an ancient seigneurial family.[78] Although his works were only published posthumously, beginning in the late 1720s, he had earlier circulated manuscript versions.[79] Although his argument shifted over time toward a fullthroated defense of the fief, he was never a doctrinaire reactionary. On one fundamental point, however, he never wavered: his rejection of Loyseau's account of the historical origin of fiefs. Boulainvilliers denied that the original Frankish landholdings had been distributed by either king or state.[80] Rather, the victorious Franks met in a great assembly and distributed most of the conquered lands among themselves as lifetime grants. They set aside a smaller portion to form the "domain of the state." After this initial distribution, some land still remained, and this was left to the original inhabitants, albeit on condition that they pay the conquerors various dues and submit to their authority. The Frankish warriors thus acquired with their land grants responsibility for exercising public power over the natives and, in compensation, the right to collect dues from them. The *seigneurie* had thus arisen from the very inception of the kingdom and had done so without royal intervention.

Two salient points emerge from Boulainvilliers's history. The first is that the assembled nation, not the King, was the source of all property in France. Although he never stated it explicitly, Boulainvilliers meant to deny the universal royal *directe*. The second point, even more significant for the debate over the relationship between property and sovereignty, is that Boulainvilliers believed that landownership and public authority were originally and inherently linked. His rejection of Loyseau's account of the conquest thus provided historical grounds to reject the maxim, "fief and justice have nothing in common." For Boulainvilliers, property and power had been entwined from their inception.

Boulainvilliers's second argument concerned the historical evolution of the Franks' lifetime grants into patrimonial fiefs. On this point, his thinking evolved over time. In his earliest work he described this process in conventional terms, as usurpation legitimized by the passage of time.[81] But he eventually developed a more positive account without, however, entirely shedding his ambivalence.

He eventually "feudalized"[82] the original grants by describing them as the product of a mutual "convention" between the kings and nobility.[83] These fiefs would prove their worth—and secure their legitimacy—by protecting the people from Norman and Hungarian incursions. In Boulainvilliers's revised account, the fief thus became the original Frankish form of property, the fruit of a social contract, and a force for the common good.

But the fief was not without drawbacks, for it offered kings a means of corrupting the nation and arrogating power. By distributing new fiefs from their personal lands and the "domain of the state," they were able to gain new supporters willing to give up their liberty for land. Charles Martel's expropriation of Church lands, which he redistributed as fiefs, further increased royal power. By the time of Hugues Capet, corruption had triumphed, and Frankish liberty was no more. In the final analysis (for this was Boulainvilliers's last word on the subject), there were two histories of feudal origins—an initial one redolent with quasi-republican virtue and a later one marked by greed, servility, and tyranny. For a supposedly uncompromising defender of aristocracy and the feudal order, Boulainvilliers's account of the fief's origins was remarkably ambivalent.

Boulainvilliers's work created a stir, but not everyone welcomed his views. Although the memory of Louis XIV was a dark one for many and although fear of royal despotism was rising as the middle of the eighteenth century approached, Boulainvilliers's Gothic remedies were not to everybody's taste. A counterblast appeared in 1734, in the form of the Abbé Dubos's *Histoire critique de l'établissement de la monarchie françoise dans les Gaules*.[84] He based his argument against feudal government on a refurbished Romanist account of France's historical origins. Denying the reality of the conquest, Dubos argued that the Franks had already established themselves in Gaul under the Romans, who treated them like "natural subjects" (3). Of all the barbarians, they were the most civilized and Christian to boot. As the Empire tottered, power shifted organically from the Romans to the Franks, beginning with Clovis's appointment as consul and culminating in Justinian's formal transfer of sovereignty to the Frankish kings. There was thus neither conquest nor land redistribution. Fiefs had only arisen much later, as the fruit of naked usurpation by unscrupulous strongmen (120). To justify their crimes, they had fabricated the myth of the conquest, a dangerous lie which Dubos denounced as "the source of [all] errors concerning the origin and nature of fiefs." It had led to the false maxim—no lands without lords—"so contrary to natural liberty" and so subversive of royal authority because it put the "feudal *seigneur*" in the place of the "sovereign" (52).

Dubos's argument won plaudits from a variety of authors—the *comte* de Buat, François de Paule Lagarde, and the *abbé* Mably.[85] But it also elicited a hostile response from a lord and president of the Bordeaux *parlement*—Charles-Louis de Secondat, Baron de la Brède et de Montesquieu. This, of course, was

De l'Esprit des lois.[86] Although appreciated from the moment of its publication (and still today) as an eloquent statement of liberalism, it can be (and was) also read as an elaboration of Boulainvilliers. Against this view, many have noted Montesquieu's criticism of Boulainvilliers's work as "a conspiracy against the Third Estate" (758). But the specific issue which provoked this comment was minor: Boulainvilliers's lack of historical evidence for the Franks' oppression of the Gauls. This was Montesquieu's only complaint; he presumably approved of the rest of what Boulainvilliers had had to say. In contrast, *De l'Esprit des lois* is full of attacks on Dubos, who at that time was the most prominent French critic of feudalism and aristocracy (770). Although Montesquieu distanced himself from both men, the imbalance is telling. Without diminishing his work's contribution to liberal political thought, one must recognize how much it borrowed from Boullainvillier's seigneurial thesis. Among its many qualities, *De l'Esprit des Lois* offered the most influential version of the *thèse seigneuriale* ever elaborated.[87]

From the moment it appeared, *De l'Esprit des lois* was praised for its insight that moderate government could be achieved by separating the sovereign powers and entrusting them to intermediate bodies.[88] But this was just one component of Montesquieu's recommendation. Although celebrated for its liberal theory of the separation of powers, *De l'Esprit des lois* culminated with a historical account of the origin of fiefs designed to show that the *confusion of property and power* was just as necessary as the *separation of powers* to restrain the monarchy's tendency toward despotism. For Montesquieu and other advocates of the seigneurial order, the very confusion denounced by legal humanists, absolutists, and republicans was actually an indispensable rampart of constitutionality.

This relatively neglected aspect of the work is the main argument of its concluding, historical books. Already in the eighteenth century, many readers saw them as, at best, an eccentric excursion into erudition, irrelevant to the abstract, earlier chapters.[89] At worst, they appeared at odds with the liberal thrust of the work as a whole.[90] Voltaire was the most prominent contemporary appalled by its defense of seigneurialism and venality of office.[91] In his *Commentaires sur l'Esprit des lois*, he denounced the feudal system which Montesquieu valued so highly as a "vestige of anarchy" (388). He also attacked venality of office, which Montesquieu considered a necessary guarantee of judicial independence, as a "vice," "strange abuse," and "monster."[92] Although more recent commentators have noted Montesquieu's "ambivalence about liberal politics,"[93] they have not sufficiently emphasized the extent to which his recipe for moderate monarchy depended upon the private ownership of public power.

Given this, it is surprising that Montesquieu had as much influence on the revolutionaries as he apparently did.[94] *De l'Esprit des lois* defends everything that would be abolished on the Night of August 4th: seigneurial justice, the feudal structure of property, ecclesiastical, noble, and municipal privilege, and venality of office (535 and 555). Nor was Montesquieu particularly subtle when it came to expressing his attachment to these institutions. "If you abolish in a monarchy the prerogatives of the *seigneurs*, clergy, nobility, and cities," he warned on the very first page of his work, "you will soon have a popular or despotic state" (535). Above all, Montesquieu admired the "beautiful spectacle" (756) of seigneurialism. He sought to defend it in the most orthodox of ways, by a history of the origin of fiefs. In fact, his treatment of the subject was even more of an attack on Loyseau (often cited by name) than on Dubos, from whose account of a peaceful transfer of power from Romans to Franks Montesquieu liberally borrowed.

Montesquieu dismissed Loyseau's notion of a conquest, along with its key consequences—the Frankish redistribution of Gallic lands and the reduction of the Gallo-Romans to servitude. Instead, he claimed that the Franks took only a portion of the land, leaving the rest to the natives as Roman-style *allods*. And along with Boulainvilliers, Montesquieu emphasized that the conquerors did not receive their grants from the King. Had they done so "the King would have disposed continually of the fiefs, which is to say all property, [and] would have had a power as arbitrary as the Sultan of Turkey," the Old Regime's favorite example of despotic seigneurial monarchy (757). Having denied conquest, expropriation, subjection, and royal property right, Montesquieu thus cleared the way for legitimizing the institution of fiefs. In his analysis, they are not the result of violent usurpation, but rather Frankish "moderation" (757).

The second institution legitimated by the historical books of *De l'Esprit des lois* is seigneurial justice. The original Frankish landholders were required to provide military service. To fund this was the purpose of their land grants. According to the fundamental principles of monarchy, Montesquieu claimed, military power carried with it the exercise of civil jurisdiction.[95] Consequently, the Franks had always had the right of both justice and administration over their inhabitants. Fief, military power, and civil jurisdiction thus arose simultaneously and integrally with the original distribution of lands among the Franks. The point of this historical account was to rebut Dumoulin's and Loyseau's maxim "fief and justice have nothing in common." In case the implication was too subtle, Montesquieu made it explicit, stating that "justice" was "a right inherent in the fief," a right that had always been "patrimonial in France" (768). Seigneurial justice was thus a legitimate property inherent in the fief, not a usurpation of sovereignty.

The final move in Montesquieu's rehabilitation of the fief/*seigneurie* ensemble was his defense of its hereditability. Originally, Montesquieu admitted, the Frankish land grants were precarious and revocable. Gradually these were converted into hereditable holdings—but by royal decree, not usurpation (789-91). Since it had been accorded by the Crown, the hereditability of the fief/*seigneurie* was not illegitimate, as Loyseau and others had claimed.

Voluntarism also characterizes Montesquieu's account of the transformation of *allods* into fiefs. Not violence, but the desire of *allod*-owners to acquire
advantages enjoyed by fief-holders, including noble status, drove this process.
Most donated their *allods* to the King who returned them as fiefs under royal
lordship. Since as *allods* they had been heritable, they retained that status when
converted to fiefs (779-80 and 789). Montesquieu thus tried to replace the dominant narrative of usurpation with a picture of a royally sanctioned, voluntary
metamorphosis.

For Montesquieu, the hereditability of the fief was the culmination of a historical process which had given the French constitution its fundamental attribute—
the fusion of property and power. Others like Poix de Fréminville stated this
more bluntly, but in the final chapter of *De l'Esprit des lois* it becomes clear that
upholding this position has been the central purpose of its historical books. When
fiefs were precarious "military obligations," Montesquieu writes, they "belonged
only to the [realm of] political laws." "But once they became hereditary" and "a
type of good in commerce," they acquired a civil existence as well. Partaking of
both spheres—the political and civil, the realms of power and property—the
fief embodied the confusion that Montesquieu considered essential to moderate
government. Applauding this salutary blurring of the "political" and the "civil," he
closes his work with the words of Aeneas and his fellow refugees as they finally
reached their destination. "Italiam! Italiam! I finish the treatise on fiefs where
most authors start" (795). Whereas Loyseau had begun his work by disentangling the confusion of property and power in order to clear the way for a new
organization of the French polity, Montesquieu concludes his work by praising
that very confusion as the pinnacle of French constitutional evolution.

The Physiocrats

Montesquieu provides a sharp contrast with one of the most important intellectual currents of the Old Regime, physiocracy.[96] His thinking was in almost every
way its antithesis. This can be clearly seen in the criticisms offered by the central
figure of the movement, the royal physician François Quesnay, of the *marquis* de
Mirabeau's *Traité de la monarchie*. Mirabeau had first gained fame in the 1750s
as the author of the wildly popular *L'Ami des hommes*. In that work, the *marquis*
had praised "feudal laws" and "ancient chivalry," comparing them favorably to
"modern philosophy," and had also described seigneurial justice as "admirable
for a thousand reasons."[97] Encouraged by his book's success, Mirabeau embarked
upon a more ambitious work intended to reinforce and improve upon *De l'Esprit
des lois*.[98] It was on a draft of this work, the future *Traité de la monarchie*, that he
asked his friend Quesnay to comment.

In this initial draft, Mirabeau hewed closely to Montesquieu's line. He defended the constitutional necessity of intermediate corps, describing them as the bulwark of royal majesty and warning the sovereign that he could not alter their "essential power" without "exposing himself to a prompt revolution."[99] Like Montesquieu, he also defended seigneurial justice, which he described as a natural outgrowth of the "territorial superiority" of the fief. It was to this institution that "monarchies owe their longevity, their solidity."[100]

Quesnay was having none of this. In a series of critical notes, he demolished Mirabeau's manuscript and, aiming at bigger game, launched a full-blown attack on Montesquieu. Quesnay began by responding to Mirabeau's pervasive confusion of property and power by reminding him that "sovereignty and the vineyard of Nabboth both have guaranteed rights."[101] He then assailed Mirabeau's rosy view of feudalism. Far from serving the common good, feudal lords had weasled out of their military obligations, "borne arms against the sovereign," and "reduced the nation to slavery." Worse, they had "appropriated regalian rights," a development whose consequences had been disastrous. "From that arose [their] parity with the monarch, [and] from that the end of monarchy." Feudalism, in short, was "a plague, a cancer in the monarchy."[102] As for a constitution built on intermediate corps, Quesnay denounced it as pure "chaos." In his view, it was a mask for "feudal despotism," a system in which the grandees "oppose their force to the sovereign power" and place "the monarch and nation under their dependence."[103] Quesnay accompanied his criticisms with a personal appeal to the *marquis*: "You are frank, pure, and vigorous about the other [social] estates; why do you show self-interest and weakness when it comes to the nobility?"[104] The appeal seems to have worked. Mirabeau made numerous changes to the work and, after a famous "conversion," became a disciple of the doctor.[105]

Quesnay was no Montesquieuian; he opposed feudalism and seigneurialism, rejected the constitutional necessity of intermediate bodies, and advocated instead undivided royal sovereignty. Although he never wrote a general statement of his views, some of his associates did. The most comprehensive of these was Pierre-Paul Le Mercier de la Rivière's *L'Ordre naturel et éssentiel des sociétés politiques* (1767).[106] He began his analysis of the proper ordering of "political societies" with the core physiocratic belief that the purpose of society was to establish and maintain the right of property. This was because property itself emerged as a physical necessity from a fact of nature: human beings had to engage in farming in order to survive. This engendered the need to divide the land between the cultivators, thus giving rise to the "institution of landed property" (23). In the physiocratic view, property was not a legal or historical construction, but rather "the essence of the natural and essential order of society . . . a branch of the physical order" (37).

In a perfect society, "landed property" would be the institution "to which all other institutions are subordinated," and the interests of the "landed proprietor" the ultimate good (23). To guarantee the right of property, a right identical to that of "social liberty" itself, it was necessary to establish a "tutelary authority" (32 and 20). But this raised a critical problem. If this authority were too powerful and unrestrained, it could threaten the proprietors and their properties. But if too weak, it would not be able to defend their interests effectively. The problem in short was to unleash the full power of the sovereign while at the same time guaranteeing its morality.[107] The physiocratic solution was ingenious, but less original than first appears. It was to make the King himself a proprietor, albeit a proprietor of a unique kind. By recognizing him as "co-proprietor" of the surplus wealth produced by the lands in his kingdom, his interests could be automatically and indissolubly harmonized with those of the proprietors. Like them, he would have the "greatest personal interest" in increasing the productivity of the land, for only through a growth in agricultural profits would his co-property rise through increasing tax revenues (41-42). Because of this co-property—the right of taxation which was the "right of sovereignty itself"—"all the interests and all the forces of the nation would come together in the sovereign" (47 and 42). His will, absolute because unchecked, would of necessity be identical to that of every single proprietor.

This perfect concordance of interests, however, would occur only if the sovereign were a hereditary one. Often ignored by historians more interested in the forward-looking elements of physiocratic thought, this condition echoed the first two articles of the Edict of Moulins, establishing the Salic Succession and the inalienability of royal property right. According to Le Mercier, heredity was necessary to make it impossible for the sovereign to "govern badly. . . . To the contrary, it would force [him] to have no other interest than good governance." Instead of seeing his co-property interest as personal and fleeting, he would view it as eternal, because of his desire to pass it on intact to his successor. Indeed, in the absence of the hereditary principle, the sovereign could have no true interest in the common good. Other forms of rule, even if absolutely sovereign, would not achieve the same result without a hereditary character. An elected sovereign had nothing but "usufruct." A magistrate "would take great riches for himself at the expense of his fellow citizens" (143 and 148). Both "had nothing in common with the fortunes" of the proprietors because they "could enrich themselves by impoverishing" their productive subjects (148). If a hereditary sovereign strove for personal enrichment, however, he would impoverish his descendants. Instead, a hereditary monarch would find it in his dynastic interest to enact laws favorable to the growth of productivity, for only by doing so could he increase the surplus wealth which would constitute his descendants' co-property. It was thus the condition of heredity that ensured the mutual, beneficial dependence of the sovereign and society. Under the physiocratic system, Le Mercier concluded, "sovereignty . . . takes all its force from the nation" while at the same time being necessary to maintain "the social body" (201-2). Le Mercier thus demarcates between state and society in order to identify a means of ensuring that "the veritable interests of the one are inseparable from those of the other" (202).

Le Mercier and others who attempted general statements of the physiocratic position wrote in abstract terms.[108] Theirs is a world of "proprietors" and "property," a world far removed from that of the fief, *seigneurie*, and venal office they actually inhabited. Their abstraction makes it difficult to relate their thought to the long-running debate over property and power. The physiocrats seem to have deliberately turned their back on it and refused to engage with—let alone acknowledge—the complex laws and institutions France's long history had created. Their abstraction obscures their position on the problematic types of property that had so exercised the jurists.

There was, however, one physiocrat who explained what the "sect's" abstract doctrines might mean if applied to these controversial forms of property. This was the jurist Guillaume-François Le Trosne. His *De l'Administration provinciale et la réforme de l'impôt* (1779) offered a comprehensive view of how the physiocrats might have applied their theories to the institutional fabric of Old Regime France.[109] The result looks very much like what could have transpired had the various hints and implications of the humanist jurists and their successors been gathered together, made explicit, and implemented.

Like Bodin, Loyseau, and many others, Le Trosne denounced seigneurial justice and venal office. But unlike them, he dared to call openly for their abolition. In his view, these institutions had "denatured everything" (626). "What abuse among us," he asked rhetorically, "has made it [jurisdiction] a patrimonial property?" In his view, sovereignty's struggle against the private ownership of public power was the key to French history. "For many centuries, our history has truly been about the formation of sovereign authority and the effort to free it from the hindrances of feudal government."[110]

This condemnation of *seigneuries* and venality was straightforward and, except for Le Trosne's bluntness, hardly original. His position on the royal domain and the larger question it raised of the proprietary nature of the Crown, however, was more surprising. The physiocrats' insistence on the sovereign's co-property suggested that they viewed the monarchy in proprietary terms, that they sought to base its power in property right and harness its force through proprietary interest.[111] But by reading Le Trosne in conjunction with Le Mercier, it becomes clear that the co-property so central to physiocratic doctrine was of an entirely different nature than the property right of the royal domain. Le Mercier defined the sovereign's co-property as the "right of sovereignty" (Le Mercier, 147). Le Trosne, in turn, defined the "right of sovereignty" as "the land tax" (Le Trosne, 567). Combining the two definitions, we can thus see that by co-property the physiocrats meant the sovereign's right to tax the surplus production of the land. In no way did it give the sovereign a share in its actual ownership. By the standards of Bodin, Loyseau, and the like, the proprietary character the physiocrats attributed to the sovereign was not proprietary at all, but rather (since it consisted only in the right of taxation) purely sovereign. Le Trosne's attitude toward the royal domain confirms this. In his view, "landed properties are not at all suitable for a sovereign" (563). Consequently, he rejected the legitimacy of the royal universal *directe* and reiterated the allodialists' warnings about the degrading effect of royal property right. The King's dignity, he wrote, "cannot receive any *éclat* nor growth through the fictitious prerogatives of feudalism. . . . That is the institution which led to the dismemberment of the kingdom and the nearly total annihilation of royal power" (570). A king concerned with manipulating his domain was nothing but "a big proprietor who ruins himself [by] selling his property bit by bit" (630). In consequence of this, Le Trosne called for an end to the principle of domanial inalienability and urged the King to disassociate the Crown from property altogether by selling off the royal domain (563). Although the physiocrats' insistence on co-property appeared to foster confusion between sovereignty and property, Le Trosne's work makes it clear that they actually envisioned a sovereign empowered to tax, but otherwise stripped of all domanial lands and feudal/tenurial rights over the property of his subjects.

From Le Trosne's rejection of the Crown's feudal supremacy followed his most radical prescription: to abolish the hierarchical division of property right and replace it with a fundamentally different order of property, based on full, undivided ownership. "May lands be as free as men [and] property be complete." To accomplish this, it was necessary to eliminate the "bizarre distinctions of fief and *censive*," for they created a fragmentation of property right "most damaging, most contrary to the fullness of property" (617). Their negative effects were felt in two ways. First, they created a kind of "landed servitude" which, although preferable to the "personal servitude" of medieval times, was "nonetheless a servitude [and] an obstacle to property" (625). Second, the division of property right between several owners was economically unproductive, for only proprietors who owned their lands absolutely would fully invest in their cultivation (633).[112] In a rare physiocratic foray into the realm of history, a highly orthodox survey of the origins of the fief, Le Trosne grudgingly admitted that the "heredity of the fief" was the "Great Revolution" which had "formed the constitution of the State" (621). But Le Trosne did not care. "Should this title make us respect it? This constitution that it founded, does it deserve our regrets? Has it procured power for the State and happiness for the subjects?" His answer, of course, was no: it had only produced "disorder and anarchy" (623-24). Thus, despite its historical legitimacy, Le Trosne believed that France's feudal order should be abolished forthwith by the "common vow of the King and the Nation" (641).

The physiocrats saw themselves primarily as economists, and scholars have generally approached them as such. But there was also a constitutional element to their thought that can be situated in the context of the debate over property and power. The keystone of the physiocrats' constitutional prescription was an absolute monarch with a trans-generational interest in increasing national wealth. Their method for achieving this—hereditary succession—resembled the fundamental law of the monarchy, the Edict of Moulins of 1566. Two centuries before the physiocrats, the makers of the Edict had enshrined a combination of hereditary succession (through the Salic Law) and a fixed proprietary interest (the inalienability of the domain) as the twin pillars of the monarchical order. Like the physiocrats, they believed that the conjunction of these two principles would ensure a permanent identity of interest between the ruler and the ruled. With the exception of the physiocrats' replacement of the inalienable royal domain with the sovereign co-property of the kingdom's surplus wealth, their recipe for good government was a defeudalized restatement of the Edict of Moulins.

The physiocrats' real importance for the debate over the relationship between property and power lies elsewhere. It is found in their persistent abstraction which is, superficially, the most frustrating quality of their work. But their ahistoricism, unconcern with law, and deliberate inattention to actual institutions were novel discursive tactics to bypass the morass of precedent and attain open terrain where fundamental change could be envisioned. This explicit readiness to jettison tradition, even the existing constitution, if it no longer made sense, is one of the physiocrats' real innovations. It clearly fed into the revolutionary sensibilities of 1789. But the abstraction of their discourse of "land," "proprietors," and the "physical order" had an even greater influence on revolutionary attitudes toward the relationship between property and power. Elizabeth Fox-Genovese was the first scholar to focus on the abstractness of their language. But her argument—that the physiocrats deliberately used vague terms to mask feudal class interests—is based on faulty evidence and has been roundly rejected.[113] Nonetheless, Fox-Genovese was on to something when she suspected that the physiocrats' abstract terminology was significant. Their stripped-down language tended to recast property as something whole, tangible, and immutable. By speaking so obsessively of "land" in the abstract, the physiocrats made property seem natural, and thus reduced it to a physical thing. Redefined in this way, the concept of property could no longer encompass power. Nor could it contain the former incorporeal elements (feudal dues and perpetual ground rents) that signified the hierarchical division of property right. Physiocratic abstraction discursively erased the division of property into a *seigneurie directe* and *seigneurie utile*.

It also wrote *seigneurie publique* (seigneurial jurisdiction, venal public office, and privilege) out of the realm of property. The physiocrats thus entirely abandoned the concept of *seigneurie* as a way of understanding property. Their new understanding of property as a natural, purely material thing—in short, as land— thus had enormous implications not just for the idea of property itself, but for pre-revolutionary understanding of the polity as a whole. By writing tenurial hierarchy and formal public power out of property, the physiocrats cut the ties between the political and proprietary realms. This further sharpened the conceptual demarcation between state and society.

Conclusion

The long debate over the origin of fiefs thus raised a central constitutional question, the relationship between property and power. One side in the debate had wanted to separate power from property, unify power itself in the form of indivisible sovereignty, and recompose the hierarchical fragmentation of tenurial holding into full, undivided property right. Loyseau articulated this view more systematically than anyone else. The other side sought to maintain the historical linkage between property and power and distribute sovereignty among different bodies. Montesquieu expressed this stance more persuasively than anyone else. Neither position triumphed, neither argument was conclusive. It would take 1789 to resolve the debate. But these centuries of discussion were not a waste of time, for they set out the basic problem, that of property and power, the revolutionaries would confront.

The gulf between the world of the Old Regime and the one birthed by the Revolution's separation of property and power would be deep. The Great Demarcation of 1789 was so decisive that the constitutional significance of Montesquieu's historical musings on the origin of fiefs was entirely lost. One commentator who should have known better—for he had been a noble, fief-holding *seigneur* who had lived out the first thirty-five years of his life in the Old Regime—was Antoine-Louis-Claude Destutt de Tracy. Writing in the early nineteenth century, from the vantage point of the new world created by the Demarcation, Destutt found Montesquieu's historical chapters so incomprehensible that he dismissed them out of hand. About Books 27 ("On the Origin and Revolutions of the Roman Laws on Inheritance") and 28 ("On the Origin and Revolutions of the Civil Laws of the Franks") he wrote that "as [they] are entirely historical . . . nothing can be drawn from them for a theory of the formation and distribution of power, nor the formation and distribution of wealth." This is astounding, for these very books are the ones that analyze the effect of the Frankish conquest of Gaul on the distribution of property. As for Book 30

("Theory of Frankish Feudal Laws and Their Relation to the Establishment of the Monarchy"), Destutt merely noted that "the reasons which induced me to pass over the twenty-seventh and twenty-eight books, lead me to act in the same manner with this." Its historical musings have "a very remote connexion [*sic*] with the subject which occupies me."[114] Given that his subject was "the distribution of power and "the formation and distribution of wealth," this is nothing less than jaw-dropping.

Destutt's incomprehension of these crucial chapters reveals the chasm the Revolution had opened between the Old Regime and the New. It had done so by resolving the question that had been at the heart of early modern constitutional debate, the proper relationship between property and power. Once that question had been decided in favor of their separation into distinct spheres, Montesquieu's historical chapters on the rise of "feudal government" appear as so much trivia, their former constitutional implications lost to a world that had opted for the Great Demarcation. But in resolving to end the confusion of property and power, the Revolution had set itself a monumental task: to disentangle the two phenomena in law, institutions, and practice. How the Revolution struggled with this challenge is the subject of the remainder of this book.

Loyseau's Legacy

The Night of August 4th and the First Abolition of Feudalism

> The victory of the owner's mastery of the land over the land's mastery of its owner.
>
> —Karl Marx

On the Night of August 4th, 1789, the National Assembly transformed France by destroying the feudal order. The opening words of its decree could not have made this clearer: "the feudal regime is abolished in its entirety." With this, observed François Furet, "the Revolution was complete."[1] The deputies terminated the Old Regime by abolishing the Old Regime of property. They eliminated the principal forms of privately held public power, seigneurial justice and venal office. They also dismantled the tenurial system of landholding by abolishing not only feudal dues and associated lordly prerogatives, such as hunting rights, but also the non-feudal forms of hierarchical tenure. The August 4th attack on "the feudal regime" took the form of an assault on the existing system of property because that regime depended on privatized public power and hierarchical real estate. Such a sweeping revolution in property necessarily had profound economic and social consequences. But these were the byproduct, not the primary purpose, of the revolutionaries' action. The Night of August 4th was a constitutional revolution with social and political consequences.[2]

The Night of August 4th and the Decree of August 11th

In the words of Michael Fitzsimmons, the Night of August 4th, 1789, was the "night the Old Regime ended."[3] Its immediate precipitant was the peasant violence that shook rural France in the latter half of July 1789. At the time, the National Assembly was weighing various constitutional proposals and plans for a declaration of rights, but news of the upheaval interrupted its deliberations. The deputies broke off their debate to deal with the crisis. Many regarded the peasant revolt as a frightening distraction, but others saw it as an opportunity to push through decisive change. Those most determined to seize this chance were members of the Breton Club, a group of deputies who had recently begun meeting outside of the Assembly to concert their parliamentary action. On August 3rd the Club hatched a plan to abolish feudal dues. The following night, one of their members, the wealthy *duc* d'Aiguillon was to step forward and relinquish his. In the event, his colleague, the *vicomte* de Noailles preempted him. This opened the floodgate. Deputies crowded the rostrum, sacrificing privileges, prerogatives, and properties of all kinds. Although some deputies may have maliciously offered up things they themselves did not possess, most observers were struck by the spirit of patriotic generosity that seemed to have gripped the Assembly. When the session finally ended at 2 a.m., the secretaries had compiled an extensive list of abolitions. For the next seven days, the Assembly considered and voted on the list article by article. They approved some, such as those eliminating seigneurial justice and venal office, with no recorded dissent. Others, notably the article on the tithe, provoked sharp debate. On August 11th the Assembly finally approved a definitive decree consolidating and formalizing the renunciations of the 4th. The Old Regime was no more.

Since the collapse of the Marxist interpretation, which viewed August 4th as the critical act in the "bourgeois revolution" that ensured the "transition from feudalism to capitalism," a new orthodoxy has emerged.[4] This holds that the sacrifices of August 4th were a desperate attempt by the panicked deputies of the National Assembly to calm the wave of peasant rioting (subsequently known as the Great Fear) then sweeping across rural France.[5] According to this interpretation, the radical measures adopted by the Assembly were an emergency response to a specific crisis. In the words of Silvia Marzagalli, who has recently stated this position with particular clarity, the Night of August 4th "was not the result of a conscious political programme, but the product of a specific political and economic conjuncture in a socially explosive context."[6]

This interpretation engages only with the most superficial aspect of the Night of August 4th and does little to illuminate its larger purpose. The deputies were certainly responding to an emergency situation, but they necessarily did so by drawing on ideas and assumptions available to them. Why did the deputies respond to the Great Fear in the precise way they did? What do the details of their response reveal about their intentions? By assuming that their only motivation was to pacify the peasantry and treating the steps they took to do so a self-evident, natural reaction to the unrest, the new orthodoxy ignores the intellectual content and context of the deputies' action. This is problematic because even a cursory examination of the renunciations of August 4th and the decree of the 11th shows that their fundamental purpose was much broader than to pacify the countryside.

The peasants' grievances mainly concerned feudal exactions. Yet the decree required tenants to continue paying the hated dues until they redeemed them from their lords. Subsequent legislation set the redemption rate at twenty to twenty-five times the dues' annual value. Some have suggested that these conditions, which put feudal abolition out of the reach of most peasants, were the work of conservative deputies in 1790 who wanted to roll back the generous sacrifices of August 4th.[7] But at no time on that Night or in the debate that followed did anyone ever suggest anything other than gradual, well-compensated abolition. If defusing peasant anger had been the Assembly's sole aim, the means it adopted were singularly inadequate.

In contrast, the decree's other articles were truly radical. But they had nothing to do with feudalism, rural France, or the peasantry. Among these measures were the abolition of venal office, personal and provincial privilege, and unmerited court pensions. The decree also made changes to the structure of the Church and opened professional careers—which few peasants dreamed of entering—to talent. None of this had anything to do with quelling rural unrest. Some of the proposals made on the Night of August 4th, but omitted from the definitive decree, were even less relevant. What did these, notably the abolition of urban trade guilds and colonial slavery, have to do with the troubles of the French countryside? The long list of abolitions proposed on the 4th and the shorter one adopted on the 11th were clearly intended to do more than appease the peasantry. What logic held them together? What did they aim to do? By viewing the abolitions of August 4th as a self-evident reaction to rural crisis, the now-dominant interpretation cannot answer, let alone pose, these questions. It has left in the shadows the very thing that made the French Revolution once seem central to the broader course of history—the deliberate, programmatic nature of the transformations the National Assembly effected on the Night of August 4th.

By failing to examine the ideational content of the decree, the new orthodoxy overlooks its debt to established strands of thought. The provisions of the August 4th legislation were not the "immaculate conceptualizations" implied by the orthodoxy's disinterest in the deputies' ideas.[8] Even though terrified by the peasant revolt and intoxicated by the sublimity of the sacrifices they were making, the deputies did not conjure up their list of abolitions *ab ex nihilo*. A major source informing their thinking was the early modern debate over the proper constitutional relationship between property and power. On the Night of August 4th, the revolutionaries decisively resolved this debate by eliminating the institutions that sustained the confusion of these two concepts. This demarcated the polity along the lines suggested by the jurists, defenders of allodiality, and physiocrats. By abolishing seigneurial justice and venal office, the principal ways that public function had been privately owned, the Assembly excised sovereignty from the sphere of property. By setting up a system of redemption by which tenants could free themselves of feudal and non-feudal lordship, it cut the hierarchical ties of tenure and eliminated the gradients of power they had generated. The purpose of these measures was to pry apart property and power.

There are hints from early 1789 that this momentous change was already in the air. There is evidence for it in the *cahiers de doléances*, the statements of grievances and aspirations drafted in spring 1789 by the French electorate. Although their contents varied, condemnations of patrimonialized public power (especially venal office), divided property right (principally feudal dues), and royal domaniality were frequent.[9] Most of these complaints were laconic. But some took a more developed, literary form that discloses the influence of the early modern constitutional debate. The *cahier* of the Breton town of Saint-Lô provides one example. In terms similar to Loyseau's, it condemned seigneurial justice as the usurpation of "a prerogative inseparable from the Crown" and demanded that "His Majesty be reintegrated into the fullness of this right."[10] The *cahier* of Saint-Sauveur-le-Vicomte (another Breton town) reminded that "the King is only the head, not the proprietor" of the kingdom.[11]

These denunciations of the private ownership of public power, on the one hand, and royal proprietary pretentions, on the other, found their most articulate expression in the *cahier* from the Basque town of Bayonne. Written in the style of a Mably or Polverel, it began with an analysis of the origins of property and concluded by identifying its confusion with power as the central constitutional problem facing the Estates-General. Only a lengthy quote can do justice to the document's intellectual filiation.

> As for property, time confused the lifetime grants with *allods*; over time, feudal lands acquired the right of individual property; but the right of rendering justice, that the weakness of our ancient monarchs abandoned along with the inalienability of the feudal lands, is imprescriptible. By its nature, this right cannot be hereditary in the officers charged with exercising it. . . . This right is and ought to be in the King's hands; it is indivisible and inalienable. . . .
>
> But we must not conclude that the feudal lands, having once been part of the inalienable public domain, should return to that domain; first of all, the property of them has been acquired by prescription over the course of several centuries; but an observation which further guarantees their property in an even more unassailable way is that, by an agreement which is one of the most extraordinary phenomena ever encountered in the abuses of the social order, the *allods* or free properties were converted into fiefs in such great quantity that it would be

impossible to distinguish from among the mass of existing fiefs . . . the *allods* which acquired the privileges of fiefs.

It is by this singular accord that the kings, having abandoned their rights of sovereignty, and the subjects, having abandoned their rights of property [by acquiescing in the conversion of their *allods* into fiefs], exchanged their rights, resulting in the King being seen as the universal owner of the land and the subjects as owners of the rights of sovereignty.[12]

According to the anonymous author of this *cahier*, French history had not only confused property and power, but had actually caused them to switch places in the constitutional order. If the more laconic *cahiers* share a common intellectual pedigree with this more literary one, then we can conclude that the early modern debate over property and power still exerted influence as the meeting of the Estates-General approached.

The *cahiers* themselves were certainly on the deputies' minds during the second half of July 1789 as they considered draft constitutions and declarations of rights. The Committee of the Constitution believed that it was bound by them; one of its first reports to the Assembly was a summary of their contents.[13] This was followed over the next two weeks by discussion of different drafts of a declaration of rights. Although the rural violence increasingly intruded on its deliberations, the Assembly continued for some time to focus on constitutional issues. In light of the dramatic events which followed, most historians have dismissed these discussions.[14] The draft declarations, however, contained principles which struck at the heart of the old order and foreshadowed the program of demarcation outlined on August 4th. Article 30 of the *abbé* Emmanuel-Joseph Sieyès's proposal demanded an end to property in public *seigneurie*. It bluntly stated that "public function can never become property."[15] In article 2 of his draft, Jean-Joseph Mounier made explicit the link between the abolition of privately owned public power and the creation of undivided national sovereignty. "No public function can be considered property," it read. "The principle of all sovereignty resides in the nation, and no corps, no individual can have an authority which does not emanate expressly from it."[16] And Guy-Jean-Baptiste Target contributed a variation on this theme. "The right of property," announced his article 18, "can only exist over things. All power that a man exercises over other men . . . cannot be a property."[17] In the weeks before August 4th, the leading revolutionary figures had already put the imbrication of property and power on the Assembly's constitutional agenda.

The fundamental purpose of the decree of August 11th was to translate the conceptual distinction between property and power into institutional reality. Although its 15 substantive articles worked in concert to effect this overarching goal, they may be divided into three (relatively) distinct categories: those abolishing privilege, those curtailing the Church's independence, and those directly separating property and power. This last group of articles, the most numerous and most prominent in the text, approached the relationship between property and power through the institutions on which the early modern jurists had focused—*seigneuries*, venal office, and divided domain. The other two sets of articles, those concerned with privilege and the Church, went further than the jurists had dared to go.

Privileges conveyed a bewildering variety of capacities, powers, rights, prerogatives, exemptions, and functions. Because of this, they operated like the private property in public power associated with *seigneuries* and venal office. But since they usually adhered to individuals, privileges could not be sold, inherited, or used as collateral for loans like real estate. In a sense, they were personal property in public power. By abolishing them, the revolutionaries were removing public power from the most personal property of all—the individual self. Even though it is not technically correct to consider privilege as a form of property, it resembled privately held public power very closely. Like *seigneuries* and venal office, privilege tended to dilute sovereignty by fragmenting political authority and administrative functions. The abolition of privilege was thus necessary to create a distinct realm of public power and reconstitute the unity of sovereignty.

Four of the most important articles of the decree of August 11th concerned what contemporaries understood as privilege. These were the 10th (provincial privilege), the 11th (birth-based personal privilege), the 15th (unmerited Court pensions), and the 9th (tax exemptions). This last also had significant implications for the legal status of property because it abolished nobility of land, which depended on lordly tenure. Noble property, in short, was the same thing as feudal property. Thus, article 9 was just as much about abolishing fiefs and instituting proprietary equality as about instituting fiscal uniformity. Although the least numerous of the three categories of article, those on privilege were of the utmost importance since they proclaimed the principle of individual equality and heralded the advent of the citizen. But had they stood on their own, their practical effects would have been limited. For if corporate bodies like the Church had retained political power and if individuals had continued to own public function and legal jurisdiction as private property, the promise of equality would have been empty.

A second set of articles—the 5th, 8th, 12th, 13th, and 14th—began the transformation of the Church from a property-owning corps into a salaried branch of the state. As everybody understood at the time, these articles presaged the expropriation of ecclesiastical property and its application to the national debt. But more than fiscal pressure impelled the revolutionaries to move on the Church. In 1789, the Church was not an exclusively spiritual body. It also

possessed extensive political rights and exercised public functions, such as education, social welfare, and controlling civil status. As an independent political
body, a state-within-a-state, it was yet another manifestation of the fragmentation of sovereignty. For those who dreamed of unitary national sovereignty, the
Church's continued existence as an independent, proprietarily endowed *corps
politique* (political body) was just as intolerable as that of *seigneuries* and venal
office.[18] This would be made explicit in the debate over the formal takeover of
the Church's property.

To end the Church's political independence, it was necessary to end its financial autonomy—an autonomy guaranteed by its properties and revenues, its
credits and its debts. The decree of August 11th did not do this entirely, for it
refrained from stripping the Church of its lands. This would occur two months
later. But the decree dealt a fatal blow to ecclesiastical independence by abolishing its principal sources of income and expenditure—not only seigneurial rights,
feudal dues, and ground rents, but also fees charged for religious ceremonies
(article 8), annates (article 12), dues collected by the clergy (article 13), and,
above all, the tithe (article 5). As the tithe was the Church's main source of revenue, its suppression alone meant a salaried clergy. In addition to paving the way
for the eventual nationalization of ecclesiastical holdings, the elimination of the
tithe was necessary to unify sovereignty, on the one hand, and to free property,
on the other. The tithe was not a rent on a specific parcel of land that had once
belonged to the Church. Rather, it was a universal imposition, for it struck all
properties, not just those held under ecclesiastical lordship. Unlike feudal dues
which were levied only on lands originally dismembered from specific fiefs,
explained one deputy, "the lands subject to the tithe had not been conceded by
the clergy." Consequently, it was not a "landed right," but a "tax."[19] As such, it was
an exclusive attribute of sovereignty. But having been usurped as a property by
the Church, it had become yet another instance of power-as-property and had
to be abolished. At the same time, it also functioned like a feudal due or ground
rent by impinging on private properties and making their owners dependent on
the Church. It thus represented an obstacle to the formation of free and equal
property. The abolition of the tithe, therefore, was just as much about creating
undivided national sovereignty and emancipating property as it was about ending the Church's existence as an independent political body.

The last of the Church articles, article 14, abolished the holding of multiple
benefices. Like article 9 abolishing tax exemptions, it served more than one
purpose. By rationalizing the hierarchy of the Church, it ended noble privilege
within it. It thus reiterated the prohibition of birth-based professional privilege
pronounced by article 11.

To sum up the analysis so far, three articles (10, 11, and 15) concerned the
abolition of privilege alone and two others (articles 9 and 14) dealt with it

partially. An additional three (8, 12, and 13) were exclusively concerned with ending ecclesiastical independence. Two others, articles 5 and 14, dealt with it partially. Together the articles on privilege and the Church defined that "remarkably abstract" personage—the citizen—who would become the principal political actor of the New Regime.[20] Thanks to the abolition of privilege, he would possess the same legal capacities, obligations, and aptitude for public power as his fellows.[21] Thanks to the abolition of corps (implicit in the articles on the Church), he would be an individual person rather than a collective entity.[22] These changes were fundamental. But they left much unsaid about the contours of the new polity the citizen would inhabit. That was the aim of the remaining articles, those which sought to distinguish private property from public power.

Placed at the head of the decree, these articles defined the structure of the New Regime. They did so in three steps: first, by unifying the *seigneurie directe* to the *seigneurie utile* to form full property; second, by excluding public power from that refashioned concept of property; and, third, by consolidating the scattered parcels of privatized public power into a single sovereignty. These three actions laid the foundation of the new order.

Two-and-a-half articles abolished property in power. The most important were article 4, abolishing seigneurial justice, and article 7, abolishing venal office. These articles were approved with almost no comment. It is a testimony to the importance the deputies attached to the abolition of these institutions that they were determined to do so despite the sweeping administrative reorganization and heavy financial outlay it would require. Since the thousands of seigneurial courts formed the lowest level in the kingdom's judicial hierarchy, their abolition meant nationwide restructuring. And since the superior tribunals were staffed by magistrates who had purchased their offices, the end of venality meant rebuilding those levels as well. In short, the abolition of seigneurial justice and venality of office meant dismantling the entire justice system.

Many other public functions also depended on venal office. Those functions would have to be reorganized as well. But as daunting as the challenge of remaking the institutional framework of France must have seemed to the deputies, the financial implications loomed even larger. This is because vast sums were invested in venal office. These sums would have to be reimbursed—which is to say, added to the national debt. After many long and contentious years, the debt represented by the offices would finally be paid off—at a cost of 800 million *livres*.[23] The men of 1789 were willing to pay any price to eliminate privately owned public power.

The complement to articles 4 and 7 was article 5, abolishing the tithe. The National Assembly could have taken it over and used it to pay down the debt. But it did not, for the deputies considered the tithe as the usurpation of the sovereign power of taxation. Once again, constitutional imperatives trumped fiscal expediency. Together, the articles on seigneurialism, venal office, and the tithe reconstituted the unity of Loyseau's *seigneurie publique* in the only form he had considered truly legitimate—sovereignty.

Four-and-a-half other articles were intended to reunify the hierarchically divided domains of tenure into independent property. These were articles 1, 2, 3, 6, and, in part, 9. The decree's first article famously abolished the feudal regime. This article is often misunderstood. Historians tend to treat it as an attack on a specific social group—the nobility. This, however, is inexact since many *roturiers* (non-nobles), as well as non-noble corps, owned fiefs. In fact, the largest single fief-holder in France in 1789 was not a great titled aristocrat, but rather the Church. Instead of treating feudalism as a special form of property-holding particular to the nobility, we must rethink it as *the system* of real estate itself. As we have seen, its essence was to produce a quasi-universal hierarchy of tenurial claims, the system of divided domain.

Many divided-domain relationships were not feudal, but rather stemmed from the alienation of non-noble properties in exchange for perpetual ground rents. The division of property right this produced mirrored that created by fiefs. The National Assembly was just as committed to abolishing these non-feudal hierarchies as it was to abolishing the feudal ones. That was the point of article 6, which abolished perpetual, non-feudal ground rents. This article is the key to understanding the better-known article 1, for it makes clear that the decree sought to abolish tenurial hierarchy in all of its forms, both *roturier* (non-noble) and feudal. If we recognize that the abolition of fiefs and ground rents were of a piece, then it becomes clear that the decree of August 11th was actually seeking to create full property by unifying the direct to the useful domain. The result was to be a new order of undivided, independent, and equal ownership—what Loyseau had called *sieurie*.

Seen in this light, the significance of the seemingly minor articles 2 and 3, on lordly hunting and pigeon-breeding, becomes clear. Historians have tended to treat them solely as concessions to pacify the peasantry. But they were more than this. They were intended to end the distinction between lordly property (or, in Loyseau's terms, *seigneurie directe*) and tenant property (*seigneurie utile*). Like articles 1 and 6, they sought to free and equalize property by liberating the useful domain from lordly rights and impositions. Article 9, abolishing nobility of land, did exactly the same thing.

In sum, articles 4, 7, and (in part) 5 unified the realm of public power by ending its private ownership. This cleared the way for undivided national sovereignty. And at the same time it individualized, equalized, and privatized the realm of property by excluding from it all trace of formal hierarchy. Articles 1, 2, 3, 6, and 9 (in part) unified this new, purified realm of property by abolishing tenurial relations, feudal and non-feudal alike. This created a new order of absolute ownership.

Taken together, these articles accomplished the jurists' dream of eliminating privately held public power and reuniting direct to useful *seigneurie*. This created a realm of unified sovereignty conceptually distinct from property, on the one hand, and transformed the now-distinct sphere of property by replacing tenure with ownership. This was the blueprint for a truly Great Demarcation. How the sucessive legislators used it as the basis for a new regime is the constitutional history of the French Revolution.

Social Consequences

The social consequences of the decree of August 11th were complex. This is largely because they transected the three estates (clergy, nobility, and commoners) and also divided social classes (aristocracy, bourgeoisie, and working class). For example, the uncompensated abolition of seigneurial justice was a blow to the nobles, non-nobles, and ecclesiastics who had possessed it. But it was a boon to all other members of those same groups. Similarly, the abolition of venal office, although indemnified, struck aristocratic, bourgeois, and working-class officers, but had no direct effect on the other members of the same classes. In examining the impact of the decree, the conventional categories of estate and class are unhelpful units of analysis. Rather, the decree's provisions drew new lines of division—for example, between *seigneurs* and non-*seigneurs*, between people who held venal office and those who did not—and acted upon those groups.

A word of caution is in order before proceeding further. Many individuals belonged to several of these groups simultaneously. Because of this, they were affected by multiple provisions of the decree, some of which were beneficial while others were harmful. One such person has already appeared in the introduction to this book: the Provençal aristocrat Esprit-Hiacinthe-Bernard d'Albert. As *seigneur haut-justicier* of Bormes and president of the *cour des comptes* of Aix, he found himself stripped of the prestigious public powers he had once owned through his *seigneurie* and venal office (although he was reimbursed for its suppression). Overall, the loss of prestige d'Albert suffered from these abolitions was great, but there is no easy way of knowing how he—or anyone else similarly affected by the decree—felt about the change in social status. It is equally difficult to determine the financial impact it had on him. As feudal lord of Bormes, d'Albert had to relinquish his feudal dues—but only if his tenants indemnified him at a generous rate. But he was also a feudal tenant, holding both his rural fief and urban townhouse from lords above him—the King and the Archbishop of Aix, respectively. The decree thus gave him the right to emancipate his landholdings through the same system of *rachat* that his tenants could use against him.

Because d'Albert was simultaneously the target and beneficiary of *rachat*, it is difficult to determine how much feudal abolition cost him—or if it cost anything at all. In all likelihood, he himself could not accurately foresee its financial consequences. Given the multivalent and sometimes contradictory effects of the decree on single individuals, it is difficult to identify collective winners and losers.

Insofar as it concerned real estate, the purpose of the decree of August 11th was to unify the *seigneurie directe* to the *seigneurie utile* in order to form full property. As the example of d'Albert demonstrates, the mechanisms for accomplishing this, the system of *rachat*, had different, even contradictory, effects on property-holders at the different levels of the tenurial system. Since he sat atop the hierarchy, the King gained nothing, but instead had to accept that all of his *directes* were vulnerable to *rachat*. In contrast, at the base of the proprietary hierarchy, the holders of *censives* (some of whom were ecclesiastics and nobles) lost nothing, but instead gained the right to liberate their dependent properties through *rachat*. In practice, hardly any peasants had the funds to do this. However, a significant number of city-dwellers, ranging from aristocrats like d'Albert to artisans like a certain silk worker in Lyon named Bruyère, were able and eager to do so.[24] For those at the bottom of the tenurial hierarchy, the decree of August 11th was beneficial—at least potentially.

Like d'Albert, property-holders from each of the three estates found themselves simultaneously the subject and object of *rachat*. All feudal lords, whether noble or not, were in this position. Their *censive*-holding tenants and feudal vassals could now buy out their *directes*. And at that same time, these lords acquired the possibility of liberating their own fiefs from the *directes* of the feudal superiors (including the Crown) on whom they depended. The same applied to people who had conceded all or part of their *censives* in exchange for perpetual ground rents. On the one hand, they could now liberate their own *censives* through *rachat*, but their tenants could do the same to them. Given the extent of fief-holding and *censive* in France, the impact of the decree of August 11th on the propertied was highly ambiguous. Almost all property-holders simultaneously gained and lost from it. Only a case-by-case study of the composition of an affected individual's holdings can conclusively determine the true financial impact the measure ultimately had.

The decree's effects on the holders of *allods* needs to be considered separately because those rare properties stood outside of the tenurial hierarchy. There were two kinds of *allod*, designated non-noble and noble (although both types were owned by members of the nobility and Third Estate). The abolition of seigneurial justice, feudal dues, and ground rents affected each type differently. The abolition of *seigneuries*, feudal tenure, and perpetual ground rents had no impact on non-noble *allods* because they had neither jurisdiction nor dependent tenants.

And since they also had no seigneurial or feudal superior over them, the owners of non-noble *allods* benefited from none of these abolitions. The situation was quite different for noble *allods*. Since these possessed either the right of justice, dependent tenants, or both, they suffered from the decree in the same way as *seigneuries* and fiefs. Indeed, the holders of noble *allods* probably suffered more because, as they held their properties from no superiors, they could not take advantage of the possibility of *rachat* as feudal lords could.

So far, the analysis has only considered the decree's impact on different types of real estate. This is because it had no direct effect on moveable property like cash, work tools, and books. Nor did the decree say anything explicit about the propertyless in both towns and the countryside. The poor derived no benefit from the measures abolishing feudal dues and ground rents, since they had no land. But it was understood that the propertyless all across France would gain from the abolition of the prerogatives derived from seigneurial justice, such as bread-baking monopolies, which weighed on every individual living under a given lordly jurisdiction. In provinces where serfdom and obligatory labor service still survived, the benefits to the poor were even greater. The only possible harm the propertyless suffered from the decree was through its ban on the creation of perpetual ground rents. To believe contemporary critics like Sieyes, this may have made the hope of eventual property-ownership even more remote.

The decree's social consequences were thus complex, variable from individual to individual, and often ambiguous or contradictory. The abolitions also interacted with other factors—national taxes, agricultural productivity, the collapse of colonial trade, hyperinflation, and the sale of nationalized properties—to define winners and losers after 1789.[25] It might be possible to account for all these factors and produce a multidimensional, *longue durée* study of the decree's social consequences. But even if such an ambitious study were brought to fruition, it would reveal little about the revolutionaries' intentions. The best method for assessing what they meant to achieve would still be examination of what the deputies said and, above all, the text of the decree of August 11th, arguably the greatest speech act of the Revolution.

This legal-textual approach has the additional advantage of casting some new light on the old question of the Revolution's impact on the French economy. Most scholars have approached this question from a quantitative perspective. Although some have found evidence that the Revolution produced gains in agricultural productivity and laid the foundation for capitalist take-off in the nineteenth century, the majority have reached a different conclusion.[26] Composed of both Marxist and non-Marxist scholars, these researchers have argued that the Revolution retarded French economic growth.[27] A variable neither camp has taken into account is the impact of the abolition of the incorporeal economy on August 11th, 1789. The 70,000 *seigneuries* of France, whose collective worth has never been calculated, disappeared along with their lucrative rights and privileges. The tithe, which produced 100 to 110 million *livres* annually for the Church, was also suppressed outright.[28] Venal offices were likewise abolished, albeit with compensation. But the sum eventually paid to the former officers, 800 million *livres*, was far below the offices' estimated market value of 1.5 billion *livres*.[29] Finally, the entire mass of *seigneurie directe* property, consisting in all kinds of feudal dues and non-feudal perpetual rents, was opened to *rachat* in 1790. By rendering this category of property precarious, this probably reduced its value. In 1793 it was done away with all together, dramatically reducing the total mass of property in France. Far from liberating the incorporeal economy, the Revolution legislated it out of existence. The materialist assumptions of economic history, themselves a byproduct of the Great Demarcation, have blinded that discipline to this mass of circulating, intangible wealth and its abrupt disappearance. By sharply reducing the volume and variety of goods in circulation, its abolition must have had a devastating economic impact. But for the revolutionaries, this was a small price to pay for bringing the New Regime into existence. The brutal simplification of the realm of property this entailed underlines just how utopian the revolutionary project really was.

The Tenurial System and the Divided Domain of Property

The revolutionaries abolished private ownership of public power in mere moments, without second thoughts, and, in the case of seigneurial justice, without compensation. It was simply absurd, exclaimed Philipe-Antoine Merlin de Douai, that "an individual should count as part of his property, just like a vineyard or farm, judiciary power which can only belong to the nation."[30] The tenurial system of landholding was a more difficult issue. Although the deputies believed *seigneurie directe* to be incompatible with the New Regime of liberty and equality, they recognized it as a legitimate form of property. Since it arose from concessions of land and represented the original ownership of the conceded parcel, they believed it had to be respected. To do otherwise would leave the original landlord with neither the original parcel of land nor the dues and rents for which it had been relinquished. Therefore, the revolutionaries never considered abolishing *seigneurie directe* without compensation. Rather, they sought a more gradual, consensual reunification of the divided domains of property. Properly speaking, the revolutionaries did not abolish direct domain property at all, but rather established means by which tenants could buy the *directes* over their holdings. Through this system of *rachat* (repurchase) the holder of the useful domain of a piece of land could unite to his holding the *directe* that hung over it. This conjoining of the direct to the useful domain would end the system of divided domain and replace it with full property. Tenurial holding would become property-ownership.

This process is often described as the "abolition of feudalism" or the "*rachat* of feudal dues." Neither term is strictly accurate because the system applied to non-feudal tenurial relations as well as feudal ones. The specifically "feudal" character of property only became relevant in mid-1792, when the Legislative Assembly began to single out property of that type for special treatment. In 1789, the National Assembly was aiming at something bigger—to replace the hierarchy of tenurial holding in all its forms with "absolute" property.

The deputies of the National Assembly found the hierarchical division of property right intolerable because it bound properties to one another perpetually and unequally in what one lawyer described as "a chain of servitude."[31] To an extent these hierarchies were expressed through rituals which appeared archaic even at the time. But that was not all. More concrete manifestations of hierarchy were the perpetual payments owed by subordinate properties to dominant ones, feudal and non-feudal alike. Until the hierarchies of divided domain were replaced by a system of independent, equal property-ownership, there could be neither liberty nor equality. "Let us follow the example of English America," urged one obscure deputy on the Night of August 4th, and become a nation "uniquely composed of property-owners who know no trace of feudalism."[32] The Assembly incorporated his idea in its initial preamble to the abolition decree: "in a free state, properties must be as free as persons."[33] Although this statement was omitted from the definitive decree of August 11th, it reappeared as the first article of the Constituent Assembly's rural code. "In its entire extent," the article read, "the territory of France is as free as the persons who inhabit it."[34] The revolutionaries thus remained committed to the idea that the emancipation of the citizen could only be achieved through the emancipation of his property. "Legitimate property guarantees independence," wrote Sieyès in a pamphlet on feudal abolition. "Those who depend on the property of others are slaves."[35] Unless rooted in a new regime of independent ownership, liberty would degenerate into servitude, equality would give way to hierarchy, and tyranny would extinguish political freedom. Together with the nation's recovery of usurped sovereignty, the dismantling of the hierarchical model of divided property right was the necessary precondition for the remaking of the polity. Together, they provided a conceptual foundation for the new ideal of civic equality. But to build this new system of property while simultaneously clearing away the debris of the tenurial hierarchy would not be a simple task.

Among the challenges the revolutionaries faced in reunifying the divided domains of property, three related issues stand out. The first was that property right was never "perfect," "full," or "complete," but was always split hierarchically between several people or institutions. The second was that many properties were not physical things, but rather dues and rents representative of the hierarchy of divided domain. The third was that these dues and rents were themselves divisible and commercialized.

The key feature of the real estate system before 1789 was that rights to a single thing were shared by multiple owners who stood in hierarchical relationships to one another. Although the technical term for this system of property was divided domain, many people before and after 1789 referred to it by the shorthand "feudalism." According to it, property right came in two distinct forms: a "right of superiority,"[36] known as the direct domain or *seigneurie directe*, and actual possession, use, and profit, the useful domain or *seigneurie utile*. Before the divided-domain system first appeared in the twelfth century, lords alone had property rights. Their tenants' tenures were entirely dependent on their lords' good will. The introduction of divided domain ameliorated the tenants' condition by inventing for them a legal right, the useful domain, to the land they cultivated.[37]

For several centuries the useful domain was considered subordinate to the direct. But during the course of the seventeenth century, this began to change. The shift took place more rapidly in the southern provinces, which were more exposed to Roman-law influences. By the mid-seventeenth century, Provençal jurists already regarded the owner of the useful domain as "veritable master and proprietor."[38] This shift in the preponderance of property right spread throughout France. The jurist Robert-Joseph Pothier, eighteenth-century France's greatest authority on property law, confirmed this in his influential *Traité du domaine de droit de propriété* (1772). The direct domain, he wrote, was not a true "domain of property," but merely a kind of "superiority." It was "nothing more than the right of *seigneurs* to be acknowledged as such by their tenants and to demand certain dues and payments in recognition of their lordship." The veritable domain of property was the useful domain whose owner, "the useful *seigneur*" (*seigneur utile*) was "the true owner."[39] By 1789 the shifting balance of property rights may have already made the direct domain seem vestigial.[40] But in the first years of the Revolution, no one ever suggested that it was illegitimate.

The classic way a divided-domain property relationship could arise was through a lord's alienation of the useful domain of a parcel of land to a tenant in exchange for recognition of the lord's retention of the direct domain of that property. This recognition was effected through a variety of honorific practices, as well as the payment of certain dues. Although these varied from place to place (and, indeed, from contract to contract), the most onerous were generally the *champarts, terrages, agriers*, and *tasques* (all annual dues in kind) and the *lods et ventes* (mutation fees owed to the lord upon the sale of a property under his *directe*). From both a legal and symbolic perspective, however, the crucial due was the *cens*. Typically no more than a small coin or some other token, payment of the *cens* nonetheless signified the relationship of domination and dependence at the heart of the divided-domain property arrangement. Any property which paid a *cens* "contracted the vice of commonness (*roture*)" and had to pay the basic land tax, the *taille*.[41] Thus, while payment of the *cens* was usually not onerous, it indirectly entailed a significant financial burden.

The hierarchical relationship signified by the *cens* was reinforced by the jurists' tendency to analyze it in terms of debt and credit.[42] From their perspective, the *cens* was analogous to a perpetual interest payment on a perpetual loan of capital. In this case, however, the capital had a material form—the parcel of former fief land that had been granted to the tenant. Jurists thus referred to tenants as "debtors" of a *cens* and to lords as their "creditors." The phrase used to denote the act of paying a feudal *cens* or a non-feudal ground rent—*servir une rente* (to serve a rent)—underlined the hierarchical relationship it created. Nonetheless, the possibility of assimilating feudal dues to interest payments would provide the revolutionaries with the means they ultimately adopted for unifying the domains of property. The metaphor of credit through which tenurial property holding was understood in the Old Regime decisively shaped the concrete *rachat* system the men of 1789 adopted to unify the divided domains of property.

Even though the *cens*, other feudal dues, and even non-feudal ground rents were not physical, they had the legal status of real estate. This is because they were seen as filling the gap left by the alienation of an actual piece of land to a tenant. Construed as replacements of alienated lands, they took on the legal nature of the properties they represented. This had several consequences. One was the emergence over time of "fiefs in the air." These were fiefs from which all physical property had been alienated and which consisted exclusively of dues.[43] Another consequence was that incorporeal feudal property could be disposed of in the same manner as land. It could be bought and sold, divided, leased out, inherited, formed into dowries, and used as collateral for loans. Indeed, such intangible holdings were even more flexible than material ones because their lack of physical existence made them susceptible of almost endless permutations. Incorporeal by essence, direct domain property was eminently commercializable and, indeed, circulated widely and rapidly.

Non-nobles and non-lords frequently acquired such property. Here is a typical example. In 1696 the lord of Paix-la-Quertier in Normandy alienated a parcel of land in exchange for an annual payment of 500 *livres*. This annuity was designated in the contract as a "seigneurial ground rent." In 1725 the commoner Pierre Le Bienvenu bought 400 *livres* of it from the lord. In 1746 Le Bienvenu sold 50 *livres* of his rent to a man named Heurtevent. Five years later Heurtevent sold it to a man named Vautier, and three years after that Vautier sold it back to Le Bienvenu. In 1782 Le Bienvenu's son sold the now-reunited 400-*livre* rent to the father of Charles-François-Michel Préfosse, a lawyer from Cherbourg.

Unaware of its origin, which had been obscured by its passage through so many hands, Préfosse felt victimized when the Revolution abolished it as feudal.[44] The point is not so much that feudal abolition struck people who did not even know that they owned tainted property, but rather that there had been a vibrant market in incorporeal real estate during the Old Regime. The disembodied nature of these goods may have made them especially vulnerable to abolition by the revolutionaries. But at the same time, their massive commercialization complicated the task of abolition by confusing them with non-feudal incorporeal property,— such as rents, annuities, and other credit instruments.

What was true of the hierarchical relationship between fiefs and *censives* was also true of that between dominant and dependent lordships. All fiefs depended upon a superior fief or, if held immediately from the King, the royal domain. The material of which they were composed—the land held directly by the lord and the feudal dues which represented alienated parcels of the original fief— was construed as a useful domain falling under a superior feudal or royal *directe*. As with *censives*, the lords of dependent fiefs had to pay their overlords various dues—for example, mutation fees when bought, sold, or subdivided. The main difference between fiefs and *censives* was that the latter had to pay the demeaning *cens* as a sign of dependence—and, consequently, to pay the *taille*—while the former owed the honorable (and largely theoretical) obligations of homage and military service.

What has been sketched out above applied to 95 percent of all real estate in France. The rest claimed to be allodial.[45] Allodial property was the only kind that recognized neither *directe* nor lord. To put it another way, *allods* were the only properties whose useful and direct domains were united and owned by a single person.

For this reason, it is tempting to regard allodial land as the only modern form of property in Old Regime France, to view it as the model for the non-hierarchical property the revolutionaries wanted to institute. It is certainly true that the terms "liberty" and "independence" had frequently cropped up in relation to *allods* in the debates between allodialists and advocates of the royal universal *directe*. This rhetoric, however, obscures a somewhat different reality: that the divided-domain concept governed *allods* no less than fiefs. This is because *allods* could be divided hierarchically just like any other property. Although they themselves recognized no overlordship, they could be dismembered into subordinate tenures in exactly the same way as a fief. The owner of an *allod* could alienate a portion of his land to a tenant as either a fief or a *censive*. In the latter case, the tenant had to recognize the conceding *allod's seigneurie directe* by paying a *cens*, ground rent, mutation fees, and possibly other dues. And like *seigneuries*, *allods* could have legal jurisdiction over the inhabitants of a given district. Such *allods*—those with dependent fiefs, subordinate *censives*, or jurisdiction—were called noble *allods* and had the same legal status as fiefs and *seigneuries*. They were governed by noble inheritance laws and were subject to the indemnity imposed on non-noble fief-holders, the *droit de franc-fief*. In fact, *allods* were even more privileged than fiefs because, unlike even the greatest feudal domains, they recognized no territorial overlord whatsoever.[46] Ownership of an *allod* meant domination without dependence.

That divided domaniality characterized both feudal property and its supposed antithesis, the *allod*, illustrates the universality of this conception of property right. It could even apply to non-noble properties held in *censive* under a feudal or allodial *directe*. The notarial registers of Aix-en-Provence furnish an example. In 1779 *bourgeois* Jean-Baptiste Bonnet sold a house to sculptor Pierre Julien. The sales contract required Julien to "recognize" Bonnet's "*seigneurie directe*" over the property. He also had to acquit "all seigneurial dues and obligations," as well as serve an "annual and perpetual *cens* of six livres" and pay *lods et vente* should he sell the house. Bonnet imposed these feudal conditions as if he were a lord and the property he was conceding part of his original fief. The reality was quite different, for Bonnet held the property he was selling as a *censive* under the *directe* of the Order of Saint-Jean of Malta.[47] According to the maxim *cens sur cens ne vaut* (a *cens* imposed on a *cens* is invalid), Bonnet had no legal right to impose feudal conditions on it. But like thousands of non-noble proprietors of similarly dependent properties, he did so anyway. This widespread use of feudal terminology by individuals seeking to usurp lordly status or simply retain a degree of control over their alienated properties magnified the effects of divided domain and posed a major challenge to the revolutionaries as they sought to dismantle that system. Decades after 1789, they were still trying to sort out the ambiguities created by *roturier* non-lords who had illegally arrogated feudal prerogatives.

Non-feudal, perpetual ground rents so closely resembled the feudal *cens* in their legal denominations and practical effects that one pamphleteer considered their destruction a "necessary consequence" of the abolition of the feudal system.[48] Like the *cens*, the perpetual ground rent was seen as an interest payment on a loan of real estate.[49] "Represent[ing] interest on the capital of a land,"[50] it functioned very much like a no-money down, low-interest, perpetual mortgage. And like similar mortgages in recent times, the ground rent (and feudal *cens* as well) was praised for democratizing property ownership. No less a revolutionary figure than Sieyès proclaimed that it "has made the People a property-owner" and complained that the ban on the creation of new ground rents (by article 6 of the decree of August 11th) would restrict ownership and harm agriculture.[51] Many shared his opinion.[52] Yet, even though it was generally recognized that the abolition of *cens* and ground rents would place property-acquisition out of the reach of many French citizens, the revolutionaries were willing to pay this price in order to end the reign of divided domaniality and its hierarchies. For like the *cens*, perpetual ground rents (especially those stipulated by emphyteutic leases) created a distinction between the dominant direct and dependent useful domain.[53]

Divided domaniality was thus the rule across the entire spectrum of property—from the royal domain and the great fiefs of the kingdom to the proud *allods* and humble non-noble properties. It was the legal structure of property-holding in Old Regime France.

How to Unify the Domains of Property?

In 1789 there was never any question of abolishing the divided-domain system of property-holding without compensation for the dispossessed owners of *directes*. Whether lords or lawyers, the deputies of the National Assembly all recognized the direct domain of property, the *seigneurie directe*, as legitimate. In addition to their legal scruples, they were also very aware of the example of Savoy, which had guaranteed indemnification when it declared the abolition of feudalism in 1771.[54] In their fateful interventions on the Night of August 4th, both the *vicomte* de Noailles and the *duc* d'Aiguillon proposed requiring tenants seeking liberation to purchase the *directe* over their lands and thereby join it to the useful domain they already held. This buying-out procedure came to be called *rachat*.[55] The categorical language of the first article of the August 11th decree "abolishing in its entirety the feudal regime" was thus misleading. Merlin de Douai, the Revolution's foremost authority on feudal matters, made this explicit for his colleagues. "By destroying the feudal regime," he told them, "you did not intend to destroy properties, but rather to change their nature."[56] The mechanism of *rachat* would ensure this transformation.

To design the *rachat* system, the Assembly formed a Committee on Feudal Rights. It was dominated by two prominent jurists, Merlin and François-Denis Tronchet.[57] The first was charged with distinguishing between feudal rights subject to *rachat* and those to be abolished without compensation. The second was to design the system of *rachat*.

Within days of its formation, the Committee announced that it would not restrict its attention to purely feudal property. This kind of property, it noted, had already ceased to exist as such with the passage of the decree of August 11th. The decree had assimilated the feudal dues representative of feudal *directes* into the mass of non-feudal ground rents. All of these, whether originally feudal, allodial, or non-noble, would be liquidated by a single, comprehensive *rachat* regime that would "reunite [all] direct to useful property."[58] Generalized throughout the kingdom, *rachat* would phase out divided domaniality without violating existing property rights, and a new regime of free and equal ownership would painlessly take shape across the land. But the transformation would not occur overnight. Tronchet expected that it would proceed only at the pace of the real estate market because only the desire to avoid payment of the onerous property mutation fee, the *lods*, would offer a financial incentive strong enough to induce proprietors to liberate their properties. Until the moment of a transaction, proprietors would continue paying their moderate *cens* and ground rents. *Rachat* would be slow, everyone understood, but it alone could unify the domains of property without expropriation.

While the Feudal Committee crafted its *rachat* legislation, it received petitions from all over the country. As Tronchet had foreseen, many of the petitioners were buyers and sellers eager to effect a *rachat* to avoid payment of the *lods*. The Breton merchant Villet Deslandes, for example, wanted to buy a house, but was waiting for the Assembly to establish a *rachat* system so that he could conclude his purchase without paying mutation fees. Others, who had acquired real estate and paid the mutation fee shortly before August 4th, pleaded that the option of *rachat* be made retroactive. One of these was a Monsieur Le Gorlier, who begged the Assembly to revoke the *lods* he had paid in May to the Archbishop of Reims upon purchasing a piece of rural property under that ecclesiastical lord's *directe*.[59] Clearly the lack of a *rachat* system was having an unsettling effect on the real estate market. But so too was the promise of August 4th, which filled those who had concluded real estate transactions earlier in the year with a sense of injustice. As several petitioners pointed out, the conjunction of stirring declarations of principle with uncertain means of execution meant that "commerce in real estate will be extremely inconvenienced."[60]

Pamphlets soon began to appear on the subject of *rachat*. Writers from across the political spectrum condemned it. Critics on the right attacked it as a violation of property rights which would nullify "free contracts between individuals" and leave everything in the hands of the rich by eliminating the advantageous feudal leases which extended property ownership to the poor.[61] Those on the left assailed *rachat* as a cruel illusion, on the grounds that peasants would never be able to raise the sums required to liberate their lands.[62] The Assembly, however, remained committed to *rachat* and never acknowledged these criticisms.

Most of the pamphlets offered suggestions about what kind of *rachat* system to adopt. One bone of contention was whether to restrict the right of *rachat* to individuals or to permit it to be exercised collectively, by groups of tenants or even whole villages. Many *cahiers* had taken this latter position. The principal argument in its favor was that collectivities were more capable than individuals of raising the money necessary to indemnify the lords. Acting collectively, peasants would be able to liberate their properties swiftly, and lords would receive the sums they were owed without contestation or delay.[63] In addition, advocates of collective *rachat* pointed out, some dues had originally been imposed on entire villages rather than individual tenants and thus required a collective approach.[64]

Their opponents contended that collective *rachat* would violate property rights and thwart the ultimate goal of the operation, the absorption of the *directe* by the useful domain of property. *Directes* acquired through collective *rachat* would continue to exist as a communally-owned block of incorporeal property, rather than merge with the specific parcels of land on which they had been imposed. This would prevent their conversion into absolute, individual property. If "a community conducted a collective *rachat* of all the rights of a fief-holder, it would only be substituting itself for their former owner."[65] The Committee agreed with this analysis. It ruled that collective *rachat* would undermine the institution of the purely individual regime of rights necessary to make property both absolute and undivided. After 1789, collective and communal models of property faced a difficult future.[66]

A number of pamphleteers suggested a third approach to *rachat*, one that was neither communal nor individual, but rather domanial. Starting from the premise (established by more than two centuries of jurisprudence and polemics) that all fiefs had originated as grants from the royal domain, they argued that feudal abolition should begin with the King's voluntary renunciation of his domanial *directe*. This would free the highest strata of fiefs, those immediately dependent upon the Crown, from the dues to which they were subject. Compensated in this way, those lords could be compelled in their turn to relinquish their *directes*. Repeated all the way down the feudal hierarchy until it freed the mass of *censives* at its base, it would abolish divided domain without any money changing hands. Most proprietors would either come out ahead or at least break even under this system. The only clear loser would be the royal domain.

The idea of a top-down, royally initiated unraveling of feudalism had a respectable pedigree. No less an authority than Pierre-François Boncerf, whose 1776 pamphlet on the *Inconveniens des droits féodaux* had been publicly burned by the *parlement* of Paris, supported a variant of this method.[67] Le Trosne, the practical physiocrat, had advocated it as well.[68] Now, in the revolutionary context, this scheme still seemed attractive to many. However desirable individual *rachat* might be in principle, they warned, it would never work. Since most peasants could not afford the cost of *rachat*, it would only serve as "a new chain, infinitely more vexatious than the old one."[69] The time for half measures was over. Circumstances urgently demanded "the general emancipation" of property. The only way to achieve this was through a cascade of renunciations initiated by the Crown.[70]

These appeals must have struck a nerve, for they prompted the Feudal Committee to emerge from its closed deliberations and issue a public response. On 12 September 1789, Tronchet took the floor of the Assembly to denounce the idea of domanial abolition.[71] It was unacceptable, he argued, because it would "unnecessarily squander the resources and funds of the nation." According to the most recent estimates available to him, the annual revenue from the royal *directe's* feudal dues and non-feudal ground rents amounted to 3 million *livres,* a small, but non-negligible source of income for the depleted treasury. More importantly, Tronchet observed, this represented a potential capital of about 60 million *livres.* If the owners of fiefs immediately under the royal *directe* availed themselves of *rachat,* paying their money directly to the Treasury, this sum could be used for "the reimbursement of the State's debts." To abandon this resource at a time of such pressing fiscal need was sheer folly.

On several previous occasions, the National Assembly had favored the pursuit of principle over debt reduction. Its negative response to the proposal for domanial feudal abolition is an example of how fiscal expediency sometimes trumped the revolutionaries' commitment to principle. Tronchet warned that a cascade of renunciations initiated by the Crown would perversely favor certain categories of property-holder at the expense of others. Only those whose properties were part of "the feudal chain" would reap any benefit. All others, especially the owners of *allods* and the propertyless, would gain nothing. Worse, they would ultimately have to share in the cost of the operation since the resulting diminution in domanial revenues would have to be made good by tax increases. Rather than cleanly and painlessly unraveling the feudal thread, the renunciation of the royal *directe* would impose on the nation "a very important sacrifice in the sole interest of enriching a certain number of persons." With that, the Feudal Committee resumed its work.

On 8 February 1790, the Committee returned with a report by Merlin on the rationale for distinguishing feudal dues susceptible of *rachat* from those to be suppressed without compensation.[72] The basic distinction to be made, he explained, was between dues which "violated the natural liberty of men" (to be suppressed without indemnity) and those created as "the price and condition of a concession of a parcel of land." The first type of due emanated from seigneurial power—in Loyseau's terms, *seigneurie publique*—and had been imposed solely as a consequence of that power, "independently of all ownership of property." Consequently, such dues were a form of "personal servitude," a sign of "inferiority," and a manifestation of "power and superiority." Since they were "contrary to liberty," they had to be eliminated forthwith. In contrast, the second type of due, those created in exchange for the concession of real estate, fell within the realm of property—*seigneurie privée.* These dues represented the *seigneurie directe,* a legitimate domain of property, reserved by the grantor of a property's *seigneurie utile.* Merlin argued that such dues were legitimate because they were the "condition of a concession" and the product of a "free convention" or "mutually-binding contract." Whereas the first type of due was a violation of the "liberty natural to all men," the second was its very essence. They were thus to be maintained until joined to the useful domain by *rachat*.

In most cases the distinction between the two types of dues would be clear, but Merlin warned that appearances could sometimes be deceptive. To identify the true character of a rent or due, it was necessary to look beyond its nomenclature. It had to be contextualized to discover how it had arisen, how it operated, and to assess its legitimacy. To illustrate why a "thick" approach was required, Merlin pointed to the example of a due that, on the face of it, was a personal, seigneurially derived servitude: the *banalité* (a milling, baking, or pressing monopoly). In many provinces, *banalités* were inherent prerogatives of the *seigneurie*. As an attribute of seigneurial power, they affected all individuals within a lord's jurisdiction simply by virtue of their residence within it, not because of a contractual arrangement or in payment for a concession of land. They were thus one of the many forms of "personal servitude" engendered by seigneurialism—and therefore marked out for uncompensated abolition.

But, Merlin continued, there were some provinces where *banalités* were not inherent to *seigneuries*, but had been stipulated in contracts between lords and their communities. Such *banalités* had generally originated in the lord's concession to the community of land on which to build its mill, oven, or press. In other cases, communities had imposed *banalités* on themselves as a means of raising municipal revenue. Such *banalités* were not personal servitudes imposed by lordly power. Rather, they were the result of free contracts, "sacred to the legislator." To abolish these *banalités* would constitute "an attack on natural law" and the right of property itself. It was thus impossible to decide on the legitimacy of a *banalité* or any other due simply because its name evoked seigneurial oppression.

Merlin drew a crucial conclusion from this. To distinguish legitimate from illegitimate dues, what mattered "was neither the substance of the thing that must be paid, nor the charge that is borne, nor even the person who makes the payment or on whom the charge falls." Rather, the only factor to be considered was "the cause for which the charge or due has been established." Any due which, upon careful investigation, was found to have been created contractually as payment for a piece of real estate was to be upheld and declared subject to *rachat*. This was the essential logic of the *rachat* decree, which declared that all dues "which are the price and condition of an original concession of land" will be "subject to *rachat*," but would "continue to be paid until the *rachat* has been effected." Merlin's notion of a contractual feudalism was the logical culmination of Dumoulin's original insistence on the purely proprietary nature of the feudal relationship.

Merlin's fundamental premise—that substantial aspects of the feudal property regime were contractual, legitimate, and subject to *rachat*—raised a new question: Which dues were contractual and how, in case of a dispute, was contractuality to be determined? On Merlin's recommendation, the Assembly approved a long list of dues to be presumed contractual in origin—the *cens, sur-cens, rente féodale, rente seigneuriale, rente emphytéotique, champart, terrage, tasque, agrier* and many more—unless proven otherwise. These were to be paid until *rachat*. As for dues not on the list, ex-lords could try to prove the legitimacy. The local legal customs of the Old Regime would determine what types of proof would be acceptable. In many provinces, this meant that ex-lords could invoke presumption, expressed by the maxim *nulle terre sans seigneur* (no lands without lords), to support their claims. Tenants would be allowed to combat these claims by producing contradictory titles or, in allodial provinces, by invoking the opposing maxim, *nul seigneur sans titre* (no lord without title).

The law included special provisions to help ex-lords whose titles had been destroyed in the recent rural violence. One article allowed them to use oral testimony. Another gave those who had been coerced into relinquishing their feudal rights ten years to revoke their forced renunciations. Historians have criticized these provisions for being overly legalistic or, worse, for deliberately favoring ex-lords over peasants. This may have been their effect, but this is not surprising, for it had never been the intention of the Feudal Committee to ease the burden on tenants any more than it had been to attack lords. Rather, their principal goal had always been to create a new order of property while respecting prior rights to the greatest extent compatible with the new principles. Merlin and Tronchet may well have lacked political sense. But the feudal legislation they co-authored shows their dogged determination to realize in practice a certain ideal of property, one with deep roots in the legal culture of which they were part.

Merlin's proposals passed into law in March 1790 with only minor amendments. It took another month for the Feudal Committee, represented this time by Tronchet, to present its recommendations for the *rachat* system. Speaking on 28 March 1790, Tronchet delivered his report in two parts. The first concerned the mechanisms of *rachat*. Reiterating the arguments he had made in September 1789 against collective *rachat*, he insisted that *rachat* be both individual and optional. To force someone to initiate a *rachat*, which might be unaffordable or disadvantageous, would violate their liberty and property. From this insistence on the individual and voluntary character of *rachat* flowed secondary recommendations. Owners of multiple parcels of land in a single fief should be free to buy back the ex-feudal rights over selected properties separately. Tronchet also urged that tenants be prohibited from demanding the *rachat* of some ex-feudal dues, such as the *lods*, while leaving others, such as the *cens*, in the hands of the ex-lord. This was unacceptable, Tronchet argued, because the entire package of dues formed the "indivisible . . . price of the concession." Together, they formed the *directe*, a property "all the more sacred for having preceded that of the tenant."[73] Only individuals seeking to liberate their useful domain from the entire bundle of dues would be permitted to effect a *rachat*.

The second part of Tronchet's report established the official rate at which dues could be redeemed. These rates, however, would only apply if tenants and ex-lords could not reach extra-judicial agreement on the conditions of *rachat*. Tronchet hoped that most *rachats* would be conducted amiably, through private transactions setting lower rates than the official ones. He believed that this would happen frequently because it was in the ex-lords' interest to convert their *lods* (potentially their greatest source of revenue, but dependent on their tenants' willingness to sell their properties) into a "mass of funds" which, if wisely invested, would produce a "guaranteed revenue."[74] To capitalize their *lods*, Tronchet predicted, ex-lords would agree to *rachat* on generous terms. Extra-judicial *rachats*, arranged contractually between the concerned parties, were, Tronchet promised the Assembly, "the most efficient means of accelerating the revolution you desire."[75] Recourse to the law, he hoped, would be a last resort.

If compromise failed, tenants would be able to force their ex-lords to submit to *rachat* at rates set by the Assembly. How should these rates be determined? To answer this question, Tronchet turned to the jurisprudence on perpetual ground rents. All feudal dues, he reminded the Assembly, had been transformed into rents of this sort by the abolition of feudalism. And since ground rents had the legal status of interest payments on a capital consisting of land, it would be possible to work backward from that interest payment to calculate the capital value of a given ground rent. Since the standard rate of interest on ground rents was 5 percent, it was reasonable to assume that the *cens* and other fixed, annual, and perpetual dues represented 5 percent interest payments on the capital of the land to which they were attached. It followed that the *rachat* of this landed capital could be effected by paying twenty times its value. However, the *rachat* rate for annual dues in kind, whose value was greater because they were sheltered from inflation, should be set higher, at twenty-five times their annual amount. The Assembly accepted these rates without objection.

As they were based on the established jurisprudence of ground rents, the provisions for the *rachat* of fixed, annual dues posed no problem. But dues which were neither annual nor fixed, especially the potentially heavy *lods* and other property mutation fees, were another matter. In its closed-door sessions, the Feudal Committee had tied itself in knots trying to find a method to convert these variable and irregular payments into a capital equivalent. Not only were there sharp regional variations in the pace of sales and the weight of the *lods* (which ranged from one-half to one-twelfth the sale price), but this rate itself influenced the frequency of property transactions. In areas where the *lods* was heavy, property transactions were less frequent and, consequently, despite their greater weight, generated less revenue over time than a lighter *lods*. Thus, to assign a reasonable capital value to the *lods*, the Feudal Committee had to correlate two mutually influencing variables—the frequency of property sales and the weight of the *lods*. Although Tronchet spent a great deal of time explaining the mathematical formulae the Committee had used to do this, only his final recommendation need concern us here. This was to establish a seven-tier scale of *rachat* for the *lods*, ranging from five-sixths to one-third of the most recent sale's price of the land in question. Tronchet's recommendations, like Merlin's earlier, were adopted with little comment. Perhaps the Assembly was simply satisfied with the Feudal Committee's work. But it may also have been the case that its lengthy reports, heavily laced with jurisprudential erudition, mind-numbing detail, and complicated mathematical calculations went over the heads of most deputies.[76] Perhaps they were relieved to defer to the judgment of such eminent jurists as Merlin and Tronchet so that they could focus on the Assembly's more comprehensible business.

Rachat in Practice

The *rachat* system went into effect in June 1790. Within three years it had been abandoned and feudal dues were abolished without compensation. Given its brief lifespan and inglorious end, it is little wonder that historians of all political and methodological tendencies have agreed that it was a failure. It is hard to argue with this conclusion. Yet, there is reason not to accept it uncritically. There is little empirical basis for it since there have been few local studies of the actual operations of *rachat*. Instead, scholars who have pronounced *rachat* a failure have based their claims on complaints about the system addressed to the Feudal Committee and subsequently published in 1907.[77] To rely exclusively on this source is problematic, since only those with grievances bothered to put pen to paper. Those satisfied with the system did not write to the Committee. In fact, the Committee's archives only contain one or two thousand letters, not a very impressive number if one considers that the abolition of feudal dues and ground rents concerned every piece of real estate in France. One might even take these documents as evidence that those unhappy with the *rachat* system took it seriously, believed that it could be improved, and hoped (once changes had been made) to avail themselves of it. The letters in the Committee's archive are a valuable source, but must be used with caution.

The letters do not speak with one voice, but rather express a range of views on a variety of subjects. They certainly indicate a high degree of discontent with the *rachat* system—as one would expect from such a sweeping reform. But not all the petitions were complaints. Nor were they all from aggrieved peasants who felt that the Assembly's reforms did not go far enough. Some writers were ex-lords who complained that feudal abolition violated their property rights and encouraged "anarchy and license."[78] More commonly, however, petitioners took the Committee to task for its conservatism. Typically, they singled out specific aspects of the *rachat* laws for criticism. The requirement that the entire package of dues be redeemed *en bloc* was widely condemned. So was the prohibition on collective rachat.[79] Many of the complaints also concerned the rates at which *rachat* had been set—rates so high that they relegated feudal abolition to "the realm of fables."[80]

Many of the complaints raised specific regional issues. Writers from Dauphiné complained that the National Assembly had set the *rachat* rate for ground rents higher than the rate that had been set before 1789 (because of the legal victory won by the provincial Third Estate against the province's nobility in a trial that had lasted from 1624 to 1708).[81] For their part, the Provençaux, who had long benefited from laws allowing them to extinguish both ground rents and *banalités* simply by reimbursing the original capital for which they had been created, were even more forceful in denouncing the *rachat* legislation as a step backward. At the same time, they also pressed for collective *rachat*, a facility that they had enjoyed since the sixteenth century.[82] The Dauphinois and Provençal examples illustrate how the historical context of specific provinces could determine local reception of the *rachat* laws.

The strongest evidence for the failure of the *rachat* system is the massive non-payment of feudal dues by the French peasantry.[83] The Committee regularly received reports that the peasants had stopped paying their dues, particularly the heavy payments in kind. Their resistance generally took the form of silent, massive refusal, but at times could rise to the level of threats, violence, and, in a handful of departments (notably the Lot and the Dordogne) actual insurrection.[84] On occasion, local authorities mobilized national guards and even regular army troops, but more often they looked on helplessly, passively, or even complicitly. Officialdom was even known to lead resistance, as in May 1790 when the municipal councils of four villages in the Yonne joined forces to demand that their lords surrender the titles upon which their rights to collect the *champart* were founded.[85] Was such behavior at all surprising, gloated the conservative deputy, the *abbé* Jean-Siffrein Maury, when authority had been abandoned to elected officials "fearful of displeasing the people" who had voted for them.[86]

Repeated attempts were made to restore order in the countryside and get the peasants to pay their dues. Departmental, district, and municipal officials of the New Regime all appealed for compliance. To cite one example, the departmental administration of the Lot published a proclamation on 30 August 1790 calling on the people to "respect individual properties as well as national ones" by paying "rents, *censives*, and other dues which have not been abolished but rather declared subject to *rachat*."[87] Village officials joined the effort. The mayor of Brueyleroi (Loiret) boasted to the Assembly of his tireless efforts—mainly harangues after Sunday mass—to persuade the inhabitants of the need to continue paying their feudal dues until *rachat*. His exhortations, however, were futile, he explained, because three or four troublemakers in the village were constantly fomenting rebellion.[88] The clergy was also enlisted in the struggle to obtain compliance.[89] Even royal authority was brought to bear, notably in July 1790 when the National Assembly asked the royal council to quash the anti-feudal deliberation of the four village councils in the Yonne.[90] That the National Assembly invited the King to strike down a resolution taken by elected, municipal officials shows just how worried the deputies had become about the situation in the countryside.

The Constituent Assembly itself issued address after address, urging compliance with the laws on *rachat* and the abolition of feudalism. The last of these, described by one historian as the Feudal Committee's "political testament,"[91] was Merlin's *Instruction* of 15 June 1791.[92] Reiterating the sacrality and inviolability of property, it attributed the troubles in the countryside to the ignorance of the peasantry and weakness of local authorities. If the disorders did not cease, it warned, the Constitution "would die in its cradle." Even property-holders who owned no ex-feudal dues should be concerned because, unless the peasants were forced to honor their obligations, the "attack against the property of incorporeal domains might one day strike those of landed ones." It was necessary to treat the dues-evaders as "rebels against the law, as usurpers of others' property, and use armed force against them without flinching." It is impossible to know what would have happened had this tough talk been put into action. The King's Flight less than one week later ended whatever hopes Merlin and his colleagues had of obtaining rural compliance through coercion.[93]

There are isolated examples of peasants availing themselves of the laws on *rachat*. For example, on 22 June 1792, ten peasants of the Gascon village of Cadillac repurchased the feudal harvesting dues-in-kind they owed, undoubtedly in anticipation of the approaching harvest.[94] But the bulk of the available evidence tells a different story. From peasant resistance to the desperation of the National Assembly, all signs point to the failure of the *rachat* system in the countryside. Historians have thus condemned the Assembly's feudal policy as a serious political miscalculation or, worse, a "disengenous" attempt to preserve the substance of feudalism in a different guise.[95] But none of them have reckoned with the urban dimensions of feudal property-holding and divided domaniality. *Rachat* was not just a rural phenomenon and did not concern only lords and peasants. The laws on *rachat* also applied in towns and cities, a fact overlooked in the historiography. This is a significant oversight since many of the principal owners of land, both urban and rural, lived in cities and concluded their *rachat* arrangements before municipal officers and notaries. Reevaluated from an urban perspective, the policy of *rachat* appears to have done what the revolutionaries had designed it to do.

Rachat operations began in the cities in the middle of 1790 and continued steadily until word of the National Convention's abolition of feudal dues without compensation (decreed on 17 July 1793) reached them—sometimes weeks later. In Aix-en-Provence, 407 *rachats* were conducted at a total cost of 270,000 *livres*.[96] Nearby Marseille counted 744, totaling over 950,000 *livres*.[97] Although its records for the period after 8 June 1792 seem to have been lost, Lyon had up to that point 247 *rachats* valued at a little less than 600,000 *livres*.[98] The records for Paris are also incomplete. Registers survive for only the first, second, and third arrondissements (about one-third of the city), and these only concern *rachats* carried out between 17 November 1791 and 8 October 1793. Nonetheless, they contain 139 *rachats* for a total of about 550,000 *livres*.[99] Finally, the western city of Tours, whose records cover the entire period, but do not indicate the sums of money involved, had 307 *rachats*.[100] *Rachat* worked well in urban spaces.

The registers on which these figures are based only note *rachats* concluded before public officials. An unknown number of additional *rachats* were conducted privately, just as the Constituent Assembly had expected. These private arrangements were sometimes notarized. For example, a random sample of three notaries from Bordeaux and three others from villages in the department of the Gironde contains 175 *rachats*, most of which are embedded in property-sales contracts.[101] Private *rachats* can be found in other regions as well. Not all were notarized. In the departmental archives of the Isère, for example, the private papers of the Domaine du Percy contain the acknowledgement of a non-notarized *rachat* concluded amicably between an ex-lord and his tenant. In it, a particular lord (Monsieur de Bally) recognized on 31 March 1791 that he had received 48 *livres* from a mason in the village of Chelles to free a house he was purchasing from the lord's *directe*.[102] The large number of such private agreements, whether notarized or not, found in urban settings suggest that, in those areas at least, *rachat* was both more frequent, and more consensual than generally assumed.

Rachat seems to have been easily accepted as part of the routine business of property management in urban milieux. Some urban-based landowners so readily embraced it that they granted powers-of-attorney to their agents to negotiate *rachats* on their behalf. The list of eminent Bordelais who made such arrangements include the wealthy banker Charles Peixoto, the *duc* de Duras, and other ex-lords.[103] The practice was common in other regions as well. In Dauphiné, for example, a president of the *parlement* of Grenoble, de Fayac, gave his estate agent such authorization, as did another Dauphinois grandee, Barthélemy-Artus de la Croix de Sayre d'Ornacieux.[104] The appointment of proxies suggests acceptance of *rachat*—at least by urban elites—and implies that they expected it to endure.

The market in real estate dictated the pace of the *rachat* operations. The principal users of the *rachat* system were buyers and sellers who wanted to avoid payment of the onerous feudal property-mutation fees known in most parts of France as the *lods*. The notarial sample from the Gironde makes this clear: 55 percent of *rachats* were followed shortly by a sale.[105] Evidence from other regions also confirms that the trigger for *rachat* was a property transaction that would have otherwise required payment of mutation fees. Of the 307 *rachats* recorded in Tours, about two-thirds (197) consisted in the *rachat* of the property-mutation fee, the *lods*, alone.[106] The link between *rachat* and property sales was recognized at the time. The Feudal Committee had always assumed that the real estate market would set the pace of *rachat* as buyers and sellers availed themselves of this faculty to avoid payment of the *lods*. Tronchet had made this explicit in his September 1789 speech to the Assembly.

> We can foresee that the *rachat* of feudal and *censuel* rights will not proceed rapidly; few property owners will want to diminish their resources by a *rachat* to free their holdings from a charge [the *lods*] that will not bear on them as long as they retain their property. It will be the instant of alienation that will provoke a *rachat*. The buyer will only want to buy on the condition that the seller delivers him the property free [of all feudal dues]. The seller will feel the full weight of the current transfer fee . . . he will want to avoid the effect of his past indifference at the moment he wants to sell.[107]

The Assembly thus always saw the real estate market as the engine of the *rachat* process. The pace of *rachat* would depend upon the pace of real estate sales, and this was expected to be slow. In March 1790 Tronchet had explicitly notified the Assembly of this, informing them that the average interval between two sales of any given piece of property varied from fifty to eighty years depending upon the province.[108] It is thus clear that neither the Feudal Committee nor the Assembly ever expected the "prompt abolition of the feudal regime," as some historians have asserted.[109]

The key to the whole system, therefore, was the *lods*. People on the verge of a property transaction understood this and sought to avoid payment of this heavy fee by a preliminary *rachat*. But according to the initial *rachat* legislation, they could not liberate themselves from the *lods* alone, but would have to buy back the entire package of dues weighing on the property in question. Many proprietors did not want to do this, or could not afford to do so. Public pressure began to build on the Assembly to relax the law, to allow people to free themselves of the onerous *lods* alone. The Assembly bowed to this pressure. In November 1790 it passed a law allowing the separate *rachat* of the mutation fees of properties under the national *directe* (essentially those which had formerly belonged to the Church or royal domain).[110] This facility may explain why a large number of *rachats* concerned the national *directe*.

Because it has uncritically assumed that "feudalism" was a purely rural phenomenon that concerned only lords and peasants, the literature on feudal abolition has overlooked the fact that the majority of *rachats* were directed against the national domain. Most of these concerned urban ecclesiastical fiefs that had been placed "at the disposition of the nation" by the National Assembly in November 1789. Others concerned feudal dues derived from the former royal domain, which was also "nationalized" by the revolutionaries. There may be a simple explanation for why national *rachats* were so prevalent. Before the Revolution, almost all urban *directes* had been held by ecclesiastical institutions and the Crown. After 1789, they were absorbed into the national domain. Since so many *rachats* concerned urban property (55 percent in the Bordeaux notarial sample), these necessarily targeted nationalized ecclesiastical and domanial *directes*.[111] The relaxation of the *rachat* laws that permitted the separate *rachat* of the *lods* on properties under the national *directe* must have encouraged this tendency. Whatever the reasons for it, the prevalence of *rachats* from the national domain has been virtually ignored. As a result, historians of feudal abolition have overlooked the most vital area of *rachat* activity—in cities, where the well-off, but also the more modest, were freeing their properties from the national *directe* at a respectable pace.

The phenomenon of urban *rachat* raises questions about the social standing of those who availed themselves of the *rachat* system. The prevailing view holds that rates were set so high that all but the very rich were excluded from its benefits. Georges Lefebvre, the father of French Revolutionary peasant studies, claimed that only "nobles and *bourgeois*" were wealthy enough to take part, and, even then, only in limited numbers.[112] One local monograph, on the rural department of the Haute-Vienne, found that fully 40 percent of the rare *rachats* in that region were conducted by feudal lords.[113] These conclusions seem plausible for the countryside, but do not hold up against the urban evidence. While wealthy elites were certainly well-represented, members of more humble social strata also took advantage of the *rachat* laws. In his study of the social characteristics of those who effected *rachats* in Bordeaux, André Ferradou found that people ranging from deputies, venal office holders, lords, and rich merchants, on the one hand, to stevedores, day laborers, and artisans, on the other, effected *rachats*.[114] Ferradou's findings are very suggestive, but he was unable to offer any conclusion about the relative weight of these different social categories within the overall group of those engaged in *rachat*. This is because in Bordeaux, as in most French towns and cities, the registers in which *rachats* were supposed to have been recorded were burned in 1793 for containing feudal terms.

Fortunately, the registers of Aix-en-Provence survived.[115] Although Aix was smaller and less commercial than Bordeaux, the range of social groups which took advantage of *rachat* there was very similar to what Ferradou found for the great Atlantic port. Approximately half (194 of 407) of the *rachats* recorded in the registers include some indication of social status.

Table 2.1 indicates the relatively broad social participation in urban *rachat* operations. While the truly elite categories (deputy, magistrate, and *seigneur*) together represent about 7 percent of the total and those of the wealthy (*bourgeois*, proprietor, merchant) an additional 31 percent, middling and even modest social categories account for over half of the total number of *rachats*. At least for the urban population, *rachat* was more accessible than the historiography suggests.

It would be incorrect to replace the excessively gloomy traditional assessment of the abolition of feudalism with an overly bright one. The system designed by Merlin and Tronchet was politically unwise, in that it did not make sufficient allowance for the actual financial situation of the great majority of the peasantry. And it exhibited a degree of juridical rigor—even hairsplitting—that was imprudent given the combustible political context of the time. Fear, distrust,

Table 2.1 **Social composition of *rachats* in Aix-en-Provence**[116]

Social Category	Number	Percentage of total
Deputy of the 2nd Estate	1	0.5
Magistrate of Sovereign Court	7	3.5
Seigneur	6	3.1
Bourgeois or *Proprietaire*	14	7.2
Négociant or *Marchand*	46	23.5
Lawyer or Notary	18	9.2
Doctor	6	3.1
Local municipal or judicial officer	11	5.6
Military officer	3	1.5
Guild master	13	6.7
Artist or architect	4	2.1
Priest	4	2.1
Artisan or laborer	41	21.0
Agricultural (from landed peasant to urban gardener)	21	10.7
Total	194	100.0

and instability clearly hindered the *rachat* operations, particularly in the countryside. Many feared that counterrevolution might prevail and restore feudalism
in its wake, thus rendering *rachat* a pointless waste of money. Others dreaded
that peasant resistance would scuttle the *rachat* system, either by overthrowing
it directly or by causing so much trouble that the Assembly would be forced to
make drastic revisions to it. In fact, the laws on *rachat* were constantly changing,
injecting an element of unpredictability into the mix that discouraged specula-
tions of all sorts. Nonetheless, in spite of all this, more people participated in
the *rachat* system than the historiography has recognized. These people tended
to be city-dwellers of the middle and upper classes. Their participation in *rachat*
constituted a vote of confidence in the Revolution in much the same way as
buying a national property.[117] Like such purchases, *rachats* were investments
in the Revolution. Both the sums and the people involved could be quite substantial. When someone like the sieur Clappier-Vauvenargues, from a leading
family of the Provençal nobility, paid nearly 13,000 *livres* to free his "former fief
of Vauvenargues" from the ex-royal, now national, *directe*, he was gambling that
neither counterrevolution, nor radicalization, nor jacquerie would render his
investment vain.[118] He was expressing in a very material way his faith that the
National Assembly would not retreat from the commitment it had made in 1789
to abolish feudalism with compensation.

Conclusion

From Monarchiens to Montagnards, the men of the French Revolution all
wanted to end private ownership of public authority and replace the Old Regime
of fragmented, hierarchical property rights with full property. Following Merlin's
and Tronchet's recommendations, they initially sought to do this by allowing
the useful to absorb the direct domain of property by means of *rachat*. Through
this process, all those whose material holdings depended on tenurial superiors
would become independent property owners. The National Assembly knew
that this would take a long time, but believed that it was the only way to bring
about the New Regime of property without violating legitimate rights acquired
in good faith before 1789. Most peasants seemed to have opposed the *rachat* system from the start. By the end of 1791, objections to it began to be voiced within
the political class as well. These would grow in strength throughout 1792, fueled
by rising factionalism, domestic disorder, and a deteriorating international situation. The Legislative Assembly responded by progressively modifying the *rachat*
system, eventually tipping the balance decisively in the tenants' favor. The following year the National Convention abandoned the system altogether and abolished feudal dues without compensation. Whereas the Constituent had sought

to create perfect property by gradually unifying the direct to the useful domain, the Convention pursued the same goal through different means: by abolishing the *directe* outright. This radical measure would have important consequences, many unforeseen, in the years to come. This new departure in the revolutionary remaking of property is the subject of the following chapter.

3

The Death and Rebirth
of the Direct Domain

The Second Feudal Abolition

The Revolution that suppressed feudal dues was a kind of jubilee.
—Napoleon Bonaparte, 19 July 1805

Impelled by persistent peasant unrest, the outbreak of war, and political radical-ization, the revolutionaries began to adopt new methods for bringing about the new order of property in spring 1792. The Constituent Assembly had based its approach on *rachat*, because it believed feudal dues to be payments for pieces of real estate that had been granted by lords to tenants. It followed from this that the *seigneurie directe* was a legitimate form of property because it originated in a free exchange. Although it produced a hierarchical division of property rights and thus had to be eliminated, the *directe* had to be compensated. Hence, the Constituent Assembly's emphasis on *rachat*.

In the course of 1792-93, the Legislative Assembly and National Convention embarked on a very different course. The first body initiated this change of direction by requiring lords to provide documentary evidence of the contrac-tual character of their feudal dues. Shifting the burden of proof from tenants to lords, this reversed the earlier presumption of contractuality. The Convention went even further. In July 1793 it invalidated all feudally tainted contracts on the grounds that feudalism was a form of domination inherently incompatible with the condition of equality required to make contracts truly free. With this, the question ceased to be whether a given due was contractual or not, but rather if a contract was feudal or not. Answering this question proved more difficult in practice than first appears because feudal and non-feudal tenures shared a common vocabulary. In the years after 1793, it became clear that not everyone agreed that a contract was necessarily feudal even if it contained words like *sei-gneurie, cens, directe, lods,* and even *fief.*

Thus, the Convention's law of 1793 did not settle the matter of feudal abolition. Rather, its novel rationale opened a new chapter in the still-ongoing process of converting tenurial holding into full property. In 1793 no less than in 1789, this still remained the revolutionaries' overall aim.[1] But now it was to be achieved by a new means, the uncompensated abolition of the feudal *directe* instead of its reunification to the *domaine utile* through *rachat*. Not everyone was happy with this change. Defenders of the Constituent Assembly's approach—magistrates, lawyers, personnel of the financial administration, and, of course, the proprietors of *directes*—all militated for a return to the old system. Their efforts drew strength from the state's continuing fiscal woes which, they claimed, could be eased by reviving the mass of nationalized direct domain property abolished in 1793. The post-1799 annexations of foreign lands, which contained appetizing quantities of feudal and non-feudal *directes* that had as yet been untouched by revolution, was further grist for their mill. The debate over feudalism thus continued during the Directory, Consulate, and Empire. Most histories of feudal abolition, however, come to a close with the passage of the 1793 law.[2] This chapter explores the long-term consequences of the Convention's policy shift. Rather than take 1793 as the end of the story, as the culmination of the reforms begun in 1789, it treats it as a second abolition of feudalism founded on a new set of assumptions. Those assumptions were at odds with those outlined four years before by Merlin and Tronchet. The result was to initiate a struggle between the two approaches to feudal abolition that continued well into the nineteenth century.

Reversing the Burden of Proof: From Contractual to Coercive Feudalism

On 30 September 1791, the Constituent Assembly met for the last time. It was succeeded by the Legislative Assembly, many of whose members had experienced local revolutionary politics, including the troubled situation in the countryside. Those who had not, soon learned of it, as a surge of angry rural petitions greeted the new deputies. This put pressure on the Assembly to adopt new measures in favor of tenants. At the same time, pamphlets began to appear attacking the notion of contractual or concession-based feudalism which underlay the Merlin/Tronchet laws. The deputies of the Legislative Assembly drew from these writings powerful arguments for modification of the *rachat* system. Finally, the eroding international situation, culminating in the outbreak of war, gave them strong political reasons to do so.

The most common complaints the Legislative Assembly received centered on the heaviness of the *champart*, an annual payment in kind, and on the difficulty of buying-back the onerous *lods*. The high rate at which the existing laws set the rate of *rachat*, they protested, made it impossible for peasants to free themselves from these crippling dues. Petitioners from the village of Heckling in the Moselle went so far as to blame the Constituents for having "rendered the decree of August 1789 useless" by imposing an impossible system of *rachat*. Rather than offering liberation, they argued, its prohibitive rates reinforced "the yoke . . . of tyranny, despotism, and domination."[3] The people were on the point of using "force," warned a petition from a village in the Lot-et-Garonne. If the laws on *rachat* were not radically reformed, there would be "civil war."[4]

In spring 1792 the outbreak of a "great wave of antiseigneurial revolt" reinforced the message and pushed the legislators toward a "more radical approach" to the feudal question.[5] What was that approach to be? On what foundation could it be built? Two of the country's leading legal scholars, Merlin and Tronchet, had classified many of the most hated dues as legitimate property, to be paid until *rachat*. To modify their system meant challenging their authority along with several centuries of distinguished jurisprudence. At the end of 1791 a former *feudiste* named C. Michallet stepped forward to do this. His work, *Le Mystère des droits féodaux dévoilé*, furnished the theoretical basis for the Legislative Assembly's attack on the Merlin/Tronchet laws.

Although his aims were radical, Michallet framed his argument in the most traditional manner, as an erudite, historical analysis of the origin of fiefs. Heavily laced with feudal jurisprudence (Dumoulin, Ducange, Domat, and Hervé) and historical references (Caesar, Tacitus, Montesquieu, and Mably), his tract claimed that feudal dues had arisen through lordly violence.[6] Since they derived from the "superiority and power" of fiefs rather than voluntary, contractual arrangements, Merlin's presumption of their legitimacy was incorrect. Instead, that presumption should be reversed. All feudal dues should be abolished without compensation, urged Michallet, unless their contractual origins were proven.

Although his argument was radical, Michallet made his case in the traditional way, through a "profound discussion of the origin of fiefs" (1). He reexamined and rejected two pillars of the historical argument for the universality and legitimacy of fiefs: the notion that the Germanic invaders had taken the Gallo-Roman lands and that their king had redistributed them to his followers as fiefs. As for the first notion, Michallet dismissed the idea of a mass expropriation. The invaders, he argued, "did not take everything," but instead "left the [Gallo-] Romans the possessions they owned" (22). These lands retained their original, allodial status "as full property in the hands of their ancient possessors." They were never "subjected to the feudal regime" (28). The invaders took only a "very small quantity" of land for themselves and held it only as a temporary, precarious possession rather than true property (26). Thus, not only was there no mass expropriation, but the only real property-owners after the conquest were the Gallo-Romans, who possessed most of the surface area of France as *allods*. The original property regime of France, therefore, was not feudal, but allodial. What investigation of the historical "origin of the monarchy" revealed was not a legitimate origin of feudal dues, but instead "proof of the constitutional liberty of its citizens and properties" (xi).

Since the Franks had not taken the properties of the original inhabitants, it followed that they had little land to redistribute. Consequently, royal grants could not have been the source of fiefs. Moreover, Frankish kings had never even enjoyed the status of proprietor, but only that of magistrate. Thus, with a magistrate-king supervising the distribution of just a few conditional holdings to his closest followers, Michallet concluded, it could hardly be said that the Franks had much at all to do with the origins of property at all. Instead, like other Germanic tribes, the Franks saw property as a collective, temporary holding, redistributed yearly according to changing needs. As warriors and hunters, they did not regard land in the same way as the industrious Gallo-Roman cultivators. To their credit, Michallet pointed out, the Franks recognized this fundamental difference and wisely left the original inhabitants in possession of their lands. The notion that the Frankish king had taken all the land of Gaul and redistributed it as fiefs to his followers thus had no basis in historical fact. The only reason why so many jurists and historians had believed this was that "under the Old Regime," they were "accustomed to see in the person of the King an absolute master . . . and a veritable proprietor" (29).

There was thus neither expropriation, nor royal concession, nor fiefs. Instead, the conquest had left the allodial property regime of Roman Gaul unchanged. So how had the feudal order taken root and proliferated? Perhaps some evidence for Merlin's notion of contractual feudalism could be found in the historical process that had led to the emergence and generalization of fiefs? Again, Michallet turned his traditional methodology to this question and found that feudalism had not spread through freely contracted property concessions.

Michallet argued that the feudal system had spread through usurpation and violence. This argument was hardly novel. Even its staunchest defenders admitted this to have been so. Michallet drew upon these standard historical depictions to show that usurpation had made fiefs hereditary and that violence had reduced the Gallo-Roman *allods* to servitude (32-55). At no point in this evolution had contracts, lordly grants, or other voluntary arrangements played a role. Instead, the driving force behind these "revolutions" was "the violence of the lords" (53).

Feudal dues, Michallet concluded, were neither the product of a contractual understanding, nor the price paid in exchange for pieces of real estate, but signified instead a pure "relationship of subjection" (102). Merlin's presumption of contractuality therefore had no historical or legal foundation and, in the name of justice, had to be reversed. "The owners of these rights should be required to establish clearly that [they] have a legitimate origin," Michallet argued. "Failing that, they should be stripped of them" (183). This was Michallet's fundamental argument: that the burden of proving the legitimacy of a given feudal due should be shifted from the tenant to the lord. This represented a major modification of the Merlin/Tronchet legislation and, as Michallet was well aware, would have led to the invalidation of most ex-feudal dues. Yet, despite his hostility to Merlin's rationale, Michallet shared with him a fundamental assumption: that a legitimate, contractual feudalism, however unlikely, was conceivable. Thus, ex-lords had to be given the opportunity to prove the legitimacy of their feudal dues and, in the rare cases where they could do so, those dues had to be respected until *rachat*. Michallet's work thus provided a theoretical basis for transferring the burden of proof to lords, but it did not completely break with the Constituent Assembly's approach.

By the spring of 1792, swathes of the countryside were aflame, discontent with the *rachat* system had grown, and Michallet had provided an argument for modifying it in the tenants' favor. Anti-noble sentiment had grown too, exposing to new dangers the feudal dues with which the nobility was culturally and historically linked. This combustible mixture was set alight by the internal and external political situation of France. Counterrevolution, emigration, popular uprisings, and tension with foreign powers, converged to pose what many saw as an existential threat to the Revolution.

It was in this supercharged climate, on 29 February 1792, that deputy Georges Couthon, future member of the Committee of Public Safety, set the process of feudal abolition on a new course.[7] Peppering his speech with anti-noble rhetoric, Couthon told the Assembly that France was facing a war that would end either in the triumph of liberty or the reduction of the homeland to "deserts and cinders." The nation's entire strength, especially "the moral force of the people," had to be harnessed to the war effort.[8] Currently, the people were wavering in their attachment to the Revolution because the promises of August 4th had been but "a disappointing illusion." By treating the "ex-lords with unjust generosity" while leaving the people "in chains," the Constituent Assembly had betrayed the nation's trust. To regain it and convert its "deadly indifference" into martial determination, "popular laws" were needed. Couthon proposed abolishing the *lods* without indemnity unless titles proved it had been established as payment for land. The Assembly adopted his motion and charged its Feudal Committee to prepare a law to that effect. It also directed the Committee to "re-examine all the Constituent Assembly's *rachat* decrees."[9]

Couthon's intervention reopened the feudal question. Debate began in earnest on 11 April 1792 with a report by Gaspard-Séverin Latour-Duchâtel presenting the Feudal Committee's draft law. It suppressed the *lods*, except when proven by contract to have been established as payment for a piece of real estate. The change was necessary, Latour explained, because the high rate at which the *rachat* of the *lods* had been set meant that "feudalism had not been abolished" in practice. Since *rachat* was out of most tenants' reach, the ex-lords "retained a veritable *directe* over their property." To "free the nation," it was necessary to remove the obstacle of the *lods*. Scoffing at the notion of contractual feudalism, Latour argued that, except in rare instances, the *lods* did not stem from a "primitive concession of property," but rather resulted from aristocratic "tyranny." It was thus right and proper to make ex-lords prove the contrary if they wanted to keep it.

Having accepted Michallet's analysis, Latour proposed adopting his remedy: to shift the burden of proof from tenants to ex-lords. The threat this would pose to feudal dues which had previously been presumed contractual was not lost on their owners. A number wrote to the Assembly, denouncing the proposal which, they charged, would effectively suppress the *lods* without compensation.[10] In the Assembly, too, conservative deputies protested against the imposition of a standard of proof so "morally impossible" to satisfy that it amounted to expropriation.[11] To win over the support of moderates, they raised the specter of the general assault on property that would inevitably follow passage of the measure. Jean-Marie-Claude Goujoun warned that the new presumption of illegitimacy would be applied to non-feudal ground rents, including those owned by the nation.[12] François-Joseph-Sixte Deusy claimed that it would threaten all real estate and render property an "illusion."[13] Although no longer a deputy, Merlin himself intervened in the debate. In a pamphlet sharply critical of Latour's report, he argued that the burden of proof it placed on ex-lords was unjust, both in its rigor and application to a particular social group. If that standard of proof were extended to all property-owners, no one would be able to produce the required, original titles and "there would be no more proprietors."[14]

Far from redressing ancient wrongs, argued the plan's opponents, it would harm innocent families. Even if the *lods* was a product of usurpation, Deusy claimed, it could not be suppressed without injustice. So many "sales and transfers have been made in good faith, under the authority of the laws" that the *lods*, whatever its origin, had by now become legitimate.[15] Developing this idea, Bernard Journu-Auber enumerated categories of people other than ex-lords who would suffer. Those who had purchased a *lods* as a *bien national* would lose their investment—an investment in the Revolution itself. So too would those had placed their faith in "the stability of the new laws" and already effected a *rachat*.[16]

Finally, the proposal's opponents challenged the notion that relaxing the laws on *rachat* would help the war effort. Journu-Auber pointed out that "you can't make war without money, lots of money." The mass of ex-domanial and ex-ecclesiastic *lods* now possessed by the nation was a necessary resource.[17] Goujon estimated its capital value to be 400-500 million *livres*, a sum which offered a "precious gage" to "the state's creditors."[18] Deusy claimed that it would be unjust to suppress this resource, since the lost revenue would have to be made up by tax increases. Some citizens (those formerly subject to the national *lods*) would benefit at the expense of all the others, who would have to pay more in taxes.[19] Far from aiding the war effort, abolishing the *lods* would deprive the nation of revenue and undermine the right of property.

Debate came to a head in mid-June 1792. It focused on the question of the types of proof that would be accepted as justification for preserving a contested *lods*. On June 13th, the left-wing deputy Jean-Baptiste Lagrévol moved that only "primitive" titles of concession (which in most cases dated back to the creation of the fief centuries in the past) be admitted as proof. The right-wing deputy Joseph-Vincent Dumolard countered that three documents, even of recent vintage, were sufficient.[20] The following day, the Assembly voted on which motion to consider first. Dumolard's won in a narrow vote, a victory for the Right. But then, in a major miscalculation, about 150 conservative deputies abruptly left the chamber, probably in the hope of breaking the quorum, paralyzing the Assembly, and thus leaving the existing feudal legislation intact.[21] This strategy proved disastrous in the context of the dramatic political events that soon followed. On June 16th the King announced that he had dismissed the Girondin ministry three days earlier, and on the 18th General Lafayette's letter threatening the Jacobins reached the legislature. The effect of these explosive interventions was to tip the balance in the Assembly in favor of the Left. Latour's original decree, bolstered by Lagrévol's rigorous amendment, was approved on 18 June 1792.

The collapse of right-wing opposition opened the way for a general intensification of the laws on feudal abolition. This idea was already in the air. Earlier in the debate, one of the left-wing deputies, Jean-Baptiste Mailhe, had called for a formal repudiation of the theory of contractuality—and not just for the *lods*, but for all feudal dues.[22] Criticizing Latour's proposal for not going far enough, he had proposed declaring "all land free and quit of all feudal dues, unless established by authentic titles." Mailhe borrowed from Michallet to deny "the existence of a feudalism resulting from the original concession of lands." Since most French land had remained in the hands of the Gallo-Romans after the Frankish conquest and thus kept its original allodial character, there could be no such thing as "legitimate feudalism." There was nothing but "usurpation." The missing "cornerstone of the Constitution," Mailhe concluded, was therefore "the destruction of all dues without indemnity." The fate of the Revolution depended upon it. "Only when the nation did justice to its members would they hasten to do what the interest of the *patrie* demands."

Through July and into August 1792, the Feudal Committee worked on a comprehensive revision of the legislation on feudal abolition. The effort produced two proposals. The first, presented by Mailhe, overturned Merlin's notion of contractual feudalism by declaring all feudal dues illegitimate unless proven otherwise by original titles. The second, reported by Joseph-François Lemaillaud, permitted the separate *rachat* of the rare dues that could survive this test. Significantly, however, it maintained the Constituent's individualistic notion of property rights by upholding the prohibition on collective *rachat*. These proposals were still pending on August 10th, when the monarchy was overthrown. But this had had no impact on the legislation's progress. During the period August 20-25, the Assembly approved both proposals.

Although there has been no empirical study of the effects of the August 1792 laws, they must have tipped the balance of power decisively in favor of tenants and probably condemned most feudal dues to uncompensated abolition. That was certainly the intention. But from a theoretical perspective, these laws represented less of a break with the Merlin/Tronchet approach to feudal abolition than at first appears, for they gave legal countenance to the possibility (remote though it was) that a contractual feudalism could exist. The men of the Convention would cut even this slender link to the original anti-feudal legislation.

Abolishing Feudalism or Abolishing the *Directe*?

The legislation of August 1792 had an immediate—albeit entirely unanticipated—impact: it gave new impetus to the *rachat* operations. Since the new laws abolished dues lacking original, contractual titles, initiating a *rachat* became a way for tenants to liberate their properties at no cost. Most lords did not have such titles, a fact of which everyone was aware. Tenants, both urban and rural, recognized their opportunity and seized it. They began to use *rachat* demands to force their ex-lords to admit that they had no documentary evidence for the contractual origin of their dues. Thus recast as a tool for empowering tenants, the *rachat* system began to operate at an accelerated rhythm. The pace held steady right up until the law of 17 July 1793 and even a bit beyond.

Although based on the assumption that most feudal dues were usurped, the 1792 laws nonetheless admitted the possibility that some had arisen contractually. This changed radically on 17 July 1793 when the National Convention suppressed without compensation all formerly feudal dues, even those which were indisputably contractual. Little is known about the genesis of this decree.[23] It apparently grew out of a motion made by Jacques Isoré on 15 July 1793 to burn all feudal titles in a national festival to be held on August 10th. This was reported to have sparked a lengthy floor debate, but there is no record of what was said. Two days later Louis-Joseph Charlier presented a draft decree on the "suppression without indemnity of feudal dues." It was approved with no debate and just one amendment—an additional article requiring that the law be promulgated through the municipalities rather than the departmental administrations, then suspected of Girondin sympathies and Federalist ambitions.

The purpose of the decree was to abolish all feudal dues without compensation.[24] It eliminated the possibility of contractual feudalism and with it, the potential legitimacy of the feudal *directe*. It did not, however, condemn all direct domain property. Its second article exempted non-feudal, perpetual ground rents, representative of non-feudal *directes*, from uncompensated abolition. These ground rents would remain subject to the original *rachat* system. The purpose of the law, therefore, was to eradicate all trace of specifically feudal property from the face of France. Secondary articles of the decree mandating the burning of documents containing feudal expressions and dismissing lawsuits over feudal property were to ensure that no vestige would survive.

The decree of 17 July 1793 marked a major break with the Constituent Assembly's approach to feudal abolition. In the legislation that the Assembly had adopted, the technical legal distinction between feudal and non-feudal dues did not matter. The former had been assimilated to the latter and subjected to the same *rachat* procedure. With the passage of the 1793 law, however, this distinction became the sole measure of a given due's legitimacy. Subsequently described by Merlin, then a deputy in the Convention and member of the committee which had drafted the measure (in his absence), as "a law of anger," it redefined feudal property relations as inherently coercive and foreclosed the possibility of a legitimate, contractual feudalism.[25] Its practical effects were profound. Although the law theoretically spared non-feudal, perpetual ground rents, its uncompromising tenor encouraged massive non-payment.[26] It also sowed confusion in the courts and spread insecurity about the fate of property in general. This is because the law's requirement that documents containing feudal terminology be burned invited destruction of the very titles on which all property was based. This provision proved so disruptive to the fabric of social life that it was soon revoked.

It took some time for the people of France to grasp the law's magnitude. The notarial archives of Bordeaux and its hinterland provide numerous examples. News of the July decree did not reach the city immediately, and it was some time before it was integrated into local practices.[27] Until the end of 1793, notaries continued to draft sales contracts which referred in various ways to feudal dues. Certain clauses in these contracts suggest that not all were confident that the categorical abolition of feudalism was permanent. A telling example is found in a contract registered on 2 November 1793 by Jean-Baptiste Dauche, notary of

Cadillac. Selling her house and vineyard to the winegrower Jean Faye, the widow Medard of Bordeaux had Dauche insert the proviso that, although she "expressly guaranteed that [the properties] were free of all *cens*, rents, and other feudal dues and obligations through the present day," Faye would have "to pay any future dues to whomever they may be due."[28] In Bordeaux itself, similar clauses can be found in sales contracts through September 1793, but disappear thereafter.[29] As for *rachats*, they continued to be made at a good pace until the final days of August. One of the last pertained to the sale of a house in the city which, by the same contract, was freed of its "*censive*, ground, direct, and annual rent" as well as the "*lods et ventes*" it owed to the nation (representing the Church of Saint-Michel). The act is dated 22 August 1793.[30]

The delayed reaction of the Bordelais to the July 1793 decree corresponds to that of the Aixois. There, the last feudal *rachat* to be carried out was concluded on 26 August 1793. As in Bordeaux, it concerned the sale of an urban house depending upon a nationalized ex-ecclesiastical *directe*.[31] The healthy pace of *rachat* right up to (and beyond) the law of 17 July 1793 suggests that urban-dwelling property-holders did not anticipate the change in feudal policy. Had they foreseen the uncompensated abolition of feudal dues, they would not have paid good money to liberate their properties. The fact that they continued to do so through mid-1793 shows that they had confidence in the *rachat* system and were taken by surprise by its abrupt termination.

The July 1793 decree caused widespread consternation. Local judicial and administrative authorities were among the first to speak out against it because it threatened the documentary basis of both property and civil status. If all documents containing feudal terms were burned, they warned, social institutions would be jeopardized. The notaries of Gap were particularly emphatic. The ancient notarial regulations of their province (Dauphiné) required them to leave no space between the acts they inscribed in their registers. Consequently, the feudal titles the Convention had ordered them to burn generally occupied the same page as marriage contracts, wills, municipal regulations, and the like. "The destruction of the one," they cautioned, "would necessarily entail the destruction of the other."[32] Pointing to a similar problem, the chief magistrate of the department of the Allier asked how he could consign to the flames feudal expressions "inscribed on the tribunals' registers alongside a multitude of judgments that interest the property and sometimes even the civil status of citizens?"[33] Others noted that the destruction of feudally tinged titles threatened the properties of two key figures of the revolutionary imaginary: the purchasers of *biens nationaux* and the peasantry.[34] On 23 Pluviôse II the Convention finally halted the burning, but much had already been lost.

The second type of complaint focused on the first article of the July 1793 law, abolishing all feudal dues without compensation, even if established contractually or in exchange for a piece of land. Some people simply could not grasp that the Convention had really intended to suppress such dues and assumed (or hoped or pretended) that a mistake had been made in the law's wording. Le Dauphin, a legal official in the department of Mayenne, was one of these. Taking as given that "dues qualified as seigneurial are the price of grants of land," he asked with disbelief if these dues had actually been suppressed. "Shouldn't they rather be regarded as pure ground rents . . . according to article two of the law of 17 July?" In exasperation, one of the members of the Legislation Committee dashed off a response to Le Dauphin's petition. "The rent is not a pure ground rent because it was stipulated by an ex-lord; it is suppressed without indemnity by the first article of the law."[35] Le Dauphin had either misunderstood the article or had feigned incomprehension to delay implementing it.

Others admitted that they understood the law, but sought exemption because of their particular circumstances. One of these was a certain citizen Pinon, probably a well-to-do non-noble.[36] In a carefully detailed exposé printed at his own expense, Pinon explained his situation. In 1772 the *duc* d'Orléans had alienated a farm in the Tardenois to a certain Butaille in exchange for a large *cens*. Annual, perpetual, and, of course, feudal, this *cens* was the sole price of the concession. At some point, Orléans sold this *cens* to another citizen, Blaswai. Blaswai in turn sold it for 40,000 livres on 8 April 1793 to the petitioner Pinon. Pinon explained that he had been willing to invest so heavily in this ex-feudal due because there was clear documentary proof that it had been established in 1772 for a concession of land and was thus guaranteed by the laws of August 1792. Acting in good faith under the promise of those republican laws, Pinon had purchased the due—only to see it suppressed without compensation three months later! Pinon demanded redress for people like himself, who had purchased demonstrably contractual dues in the interval between August 1792 and July 1793. Given the vigorous market in incorporeal goods—feudal and non-feudal alike—there were likely others who found themselves in Pinon's position as a result of the law of 17 July 1793.

Most appeals, however, did not concern individual cases, but instead called for a revision of the law itself. The great majority of these focused on the fact that, since most titles to land contained both feudal and non-feudal stipulations, the destruction of the ones would necessarily entail the destruction of the others. This would lead to the suppression of non-feudal ground rents that had been explicitly preserved by the law's second article. "If each title was in its entirety either a title of former feudal dues . . . or a title of pure ground rents," wrote an anonymous commentator, "it would be easy to satisfy the decree.[37] But most were mixed titles, containing both feudal and non-feudal rents. Given this fact, how could the July 1793 law's first and second articles both be respected? The only way to do so, he concluded, was to examine each title stipulation by stipulation, abolishing those which were feudal, but retaining those which were not. Only careful dissection could separate the feudal dues from the non-feudal ground rents in mixed contracts.

Petitions along these lines soon reached the Convention's Legislation Committee. They arrived at the same moment when the Convention was cracking down on popular activism in Paris. These circumstances encouraged the Committee to act on the petitions. On 7 September 1793, only two days after "Terror" was made the "order of the day," the Committee met for this purpose. Also in attendance were members of the Domanial Committee, concerned because the July law had eliminated quantities of national incorporeal properties. Accompanying them were representatives of the *Régie de l'Enregistrement*, the agency charged with administering these properties.[38] The meeting produced a sweeping critique of the July 1793 law, a critique that was probably the handiwork of the Committee's most eminent member, Merlin, and his colleague (also a former Old Regime legal authority), Jean-Jacques-Régis Cambacérès.[39] The fundamental flaw of the law, the critique began, was that it violated "equality of rights" by establishing different standards for ex-seigneurs and other citizens. Whereas the law abolished the "rents representative of the sales' price" of lands conceded by lords, it preserved exactly the same sort of rents when stipulated by non-lords. This double standard not only affected the owners of rents; it also concerned those subject to them. Was it fair to liberate the tenants of lords from their rents while requiring the tenants of non-lords to continue paying theirs? In either case, the report concluded, rents should be conserved "regardless of the expressions accompanying their creation" if their origin was legitimate. What made a rent legitimate? The "transmission of a property from the hands of its original owner into those of the tenant." Any rent stemming from such a concession was a veritable property and thus guaranteed by the Declaration of Rights.

The representatives of the Domanial Committee and *Régie de l'Enregistrement* reinforced this position with financial considerations. To abolish non-feudal ground rents stipulated in contracts with feudal provisions would deprive the nation of a source of revenue whose annual product they estimated to be 40 million *livres*. Abandoning this "indispensable national resource" in the face of the ongoing fiscal crisis was madness. Bolstered by these considerations of state finance, the Committee drafted a proposal to extract non-feudal ground rents from titles tainted by feudal stipulations and reissue them stripped of the offending provisions.

On 2 October 1793 the Committee presented its proposal to the full Convention. It urged that the modifications it contained were necessary to save legitimate, non-feudal ground rents from unwarranted abolition. The law of 17 July 1793, it argued, "did not intend to prejudice the property of ground rents and dues established by original titles in favor of French citizens who were

formerly *seigneurs*."[40] While the first article of the July law was intended to suppress feudal dues, its second explicitly maintained all non-feudal ground rents.
The coexistence of these two articles proved that the Convention had always
intended to make a distinction between these two types of property. After
heated debate, however, in which "many members allegedly sacrificed justice
and propriety to false popularity," the Convention rejected the Committee's proposal.[41] Moreover, to reaffirm its commitment to its more radical interpretation
of the law of 17 July 1793, it issued a decree explicitly rejecting the proposal to
distinguish between rents which were "purely landed" from those which, "under
the name of *cens* and [*lods*] recalled the tyrannical regime abolished by the law
of 4 August 1789." All "mixed feudal titles"—that is, those stipulating both feudal dues and non-feudal ground rents—were to be destroyed.[42] Henceforth, the
slightest presence of any feudal language in a contract would invalidate all of its
provisions.

Despite this rebuff, the Committee on Legislation was still determined to
press its case. Its timing was not ideal, for its next appeal came as the Convention
was considering the so-called Ventôse Laws, which called for the property of
counterrevolutionaries to be confiscated and distributed to the poor. In this
context, the deputies were unlikely to adopt a measure that would preserve
the property of ex-lords. Predictably, on 7 Ventôse II/25 February 1794, they
rejected the Committee's recommendation to distinguish between feudal and
non-feudal stipulations within mixed contracts. It declared unambiguously that
"all rents or dues tainted with the slightest trace of feudalism, are suppressed
without indemnity."[43] Despite this sharp rebuke, the Committee's resistance was
still not finished. On 30 Prairial II/18 June 1794, it wrote to the Committee of
Public Safety pleading for a relaxation of the law. Citing the "mass of complaints"
it had received, it argued that both the interest of the state and the dictates of
justice demanded revision of the July1793 law.[44] It claimed that three-quarters of
the non-feudal ground rents abolished by the law belonged to the nation. Their
uncompensated abolition would deprive the state of a valuable resource and do
so, moreover, without benefiting the poor. Since only large-scale proprietors
would benefit from the gratuitous abolition, it was a pointless abandonment of a
national resource. It was "prodigality without a legitimate cause," and "ill-placed
generosity."

Of course, the Committee continued, if higher principles required the abolition of the non-feudal, perpetual ground rents, then the pragmatic considerations of state finance should naturally give way. But this was not the case. The
Convention's uncompromising attitude toward the rents was the very opposite
of a principled act of justice. To make this case, the Committee now abandoned
its earlier focus on maintaining equal rights for ex-*seigneurs*—a counterpro-
ductive argument in the prevailing political climate. Instead, it emphasized the

damage done to ordinary citizens by the indiscriminate abolition of ground rents. In the Roman-law provinces of southern France, it had been common for even modest landowners to concede parcels they could not personally cultivate to other peasants "in exchange for a *cens* and *lods*." Middling and even humble city-dwellers had done the same with plots they owned in distant country villages. "Most certainly," the Committee remarked, these arrangements were "exempt from all stains of feudalism." The original proprietors had not meant to give their lands away for nothing. Nor had the grantees ever expected to receive them as a gift. But this was the effect of the July 1793 law and the subsequent interpretive decrees. By declining to distinguish what was feudal in substance from what was feudal in name only, the law unjustly confused "the condition of *sans-culotte*" with that of "*ci-devant seigneur*." Fortunately, the laws had not yet been in effect long enough to do irreparable harm. It was still possible to "limit the damage by rectifying a principle which, while good and just vis-à-vis the beneficiaries of the feudal regime, was, with regard to non-lords, destructive of property." It was not "under the humble roof of these latter that we should seek out and pursue feudalism." Accordingly, the Committee proposed that all ground rents, whoever their owners and in whatever terms they had been created, be recognized as legitimate property. It also urged that all *cens* and *lods* stipulated in contracts issued by non-lords be maintained until *rachat*, according to the laws of the Constituent Assembly.

The Committee of Public Safety met this bold appeal with stony silence. With this, the attempt by the Legislation Committee to distinguish between feudal dues and non-feudal ground rents came to an end. Henceforth, the non-feudal *directe* was in grave danger of being swept up in the uncompensated abolition of its feudal counterpart. Under the Convention's legislation, the attack on feudalism risked metastasizing to engulf the *directe* in all its forms.

Public Outcry

As late as mid-1793, some people (such as Pinon) had thought that the *rachat* system was not doomed. For such people, the law of 17 July 1793 came as a shock. While a windfall for many peasants, some of whom took advantage of it to cease all rent payments, the law was a financial setback for others. The owners of feudal dues, non-feudal perpetual ground rents, and quasi-feudal dues suffered directly. Lords who had rebuffed *rachat* offers made during the preceding three years now regretted their obstinacy. Even bitterer were the feelings of proprietors like Clappiers-Vauvengargues, the former noble and lord from Provence who had invested in the Revolution by effecting a *rachat* of his entire fief from the national *directe*. Such people now found their trust betrayed—often at great expense. Finally, there were others who feared that the gratuitous abolition of government-held dues spelled heavy tax increases and perhaps even debt repudiation in the future. United by their shared opposition to the law of 17 July 1793, people from these groups clamored for legislative change, especially during the Directory. Thus the law of July 1793 did not bring the story of feudal abolition to a close. Instead, it opened a new chapter in the struggle over this contentious issue.

At first, all was calm—the lull before the storm. The owners of even indisputably non-feudal ground rents may have feared that pressing their claims in the prevailing political climate would be unwise.[45] One of these, a certain citizen Dumoustier from Loudon (Vienne), recalled that he had refrained from collecting a large ground rent during this time "because it was the reign of terror and injustice."[46] A more significant cause of hesitation, however, was the depreciation of the Revolution's paper money, the *assignat*. The collapse in its value, particularly after the laws propping it up were lifted, touched almost every aspect of French life.[47] Especially hard-hit were creditors of all sorts, including the owners of perpetual ground rents. In the context of inflation, which began to rise exponentially in 1794, it made little financial sense for them to try to collect their dues. To do so would not only invite payment in declining paper, but also remind tenants that they could free themselves entirely from the rents through *rachat* with the same uncertain currency. Proprietors forced to accept such *rachats* could be ruined. One of these unfortunates was a certain citizen Boudier from Normandy. For several years, he had lived on a 500-*livre* perpetual ground rent he had received in exchange for a parcel of land he had granted to another individual. In 1793 that individual effected a *rachat*, paying Boudier the rent's 11,000-*livre* capital in *assignats*. By Messidor V/June-July 1797, when Boudier demanded help from the legislature, the capital value of his rent had shrunk to just 208 *livres*.[48] Although the *assignats* he had originally received in 1793 had constituted a sizeable (although already depreciating) sum at the time, the subsequent spike in inflation had virtually wiped it out—in the process darkening Boudier's memory of the *rachat* experience.

As owner of a great mass of formerly ecclesiastical and domanial rents, the state had the same financial interest as individual proprietors in keeping a low profile. The administrators of these state rents moved cautiously, sometimes letting years go by without demanding payment. For the most part, those who should have been paying their rents were pleased at the silence of their creditors. Happy that they were not being asked to pay, they perhaps hoped that the seemingly forgotten rents would disappear forever. During the years of rampant inflation, there was a tacit agreement to let rents remain dormant. It proved to be but a short truce in the war between creditors and debtors the Revolution had unleashed.[49]

In Ventôse IV/February-March 1796 the French government began to demonetize the *assignat*. One year later, that process was complete. The end of the experiment with paper money rekindled interest in rents of all kinds, including ground rents. Some charged that unscrupulous owners of such rents who had "made no demands during the existence of paper money" were now reviving their ancient claims and "crushing the unfortunate cultivator." The reactivation of these rents threatened to raise up "a new feudalism on the debris of the old."[50] The proprietors of the rents were indeed keen to recover arrears, which in some cases went back to the beginning of the Revolution. They invariably demanded that these be paid in silver.[51]

At the same time, owners of feudally tinged ground rents which had been suppressed without compensation began to demand redress. Petitions flowed into the legislature calling for the repeal of the Convention's anti-feudal laws. One of their self-described victims, Antoine Jaillant, raged that they had "attacked the right of property and instigated the abolition of all debts." His specific case was typical. Although he was not a lord, he had been stripped of the perpetual ground rent he had established on a mill he had alienated simply because the contract had stipulated a *cens* and *lods*.[52] Other petitions came from magistrates complaining about the ambiguity of the Convention's legislation. One was signed by the entire bench of the civil tribunal of the department of the Tarn. When the "lack of clarity" in the laws had collided with the great diversity of real estate tenures in their region, the judges wrote, the result had been "to excite in court a mass of debates" and place in doubt "the fortune of several thousand families."[53]

The Council of 500 initially responded by forming ad hoc commissions to examine the specific complaints, but ultimately empaneled a permanent commission to re-examine the problem of ground rents in general. It considered petitions from across the country. Mainly from the aggrieved owners of suppressed rents, these documents reveal some of the difficulties which the Convention's approach to feudal abolition had raised. Although most of the petitions assailed the July 1793 law as "forcible expropriation," others warned that any attempt at moderation would end with the revival of feudalism.[54] The battle lines were drawn. Far from bringing the process of feudal abolition to a close, the laws of the Convention had set the stage for a new round of confrontation.

The bitterest petitioners had purchased feudal rents before the Revolution. Although neither nobles nor lords, they had seen their property suppressed without indemnity in 1793 because of its incontrovertible—but often obscure— feudal origin. These petitioners did not argue against the abolition of feudal rents in general, but instead claimed that those which had circulated commercially had been cleansed of their feudal stain. For centuries lords had sold feudal rents to non-lords. Having "entered into the circulation of commerce," they had "no feudal character" and had even been subject to royal taxes from which true feudal property was exempt.[55] The economic benefits of saving these rents from uncompensated suppression would be great. By reviving the rents, "the activity of transactions would increase" because each piece of land would "be doubly in commerce, both in its own right and through the rent that represented it."[56]

As well as making general arguments for the rehabilitation of the commercialized feudal rents, these petitioners pleaded their own specific cases. Préfosse, whose formerly feudal rent was discussed in chapter 2, defended it by claiming that his father had been unaware of its tainted origin when he had purchased it in 1782.[57] Most petitioners, however, admitted that they had known of their rent's character, but that in purchasing it they had acted in good faith under the existing laws. One of these was Guillaume Biré, a captain in the Chasseurs de la Vendée, a revolutionary military formation that had fought against the rebels of western France.[58] Having "lost all his moveable property in the insurrection of the Vendée," he petitioned to recover his only remaining possession: a feudal rent one of his ancestors had bought over a century earlier from a non-lord. "Legally acquired is well acquired," he argued. "A contract made in good faith under the law's sanction is inviolable; the law cannot have a retroactive effect." If this were not enough to sway the legislature, Biré continued, it need only follow to its logical conclusion the Convention's program of feudal suppression to realize its absurdity. Since all property (according to the conventional historico-juridical narrative) had originated in feudal grants, then "there is no domain that cannot be seized." The result would be the "the total subversion of the right of property."[59]

Other complaints came from people whose ground rents had been suppressed because they had been stipulated in contracts containing feudal language. In many parts of France, it was common practice to impose *cens* and *lods* along with perpetual, non-feudal ground rents in land-sale contracts. Local terms for these different sorts of payments increased the potential for confusion. In some regions the word *cens* meant ground rent. In Normandy, an "enfeoffed rent" (*rente fieffée*) had nothing to do with fiefs or feudalism, but rather indicated a rent imposed on a property that had been temporarily alienated from the royal domain. Finally, across great stretches of southern France much land was held in emphyteutic tenure.[60] Although non-feudal, emphyteusis produced a division of the domain and often featured a *cens* and *lods* alongside the basic ground rent. The Convention's legislation had made no concessions to contracts of this sort.

Owners of these kinds of ground rents petitioned the legislature in great numbers, demanding that their property be restored. One of these was Campoin, a Burgundian whose rents had been abolished without compensation in 1793. He noted that far from "possessing his properties as fiefs, *seigneuries*, or even *allods*," he was a simple tenant whose *censives* had all been subject to feudal dues.

Over the years he had sub-conceded these properties in exchange for ground rents to which he attached a modest *cens* and a *lods*. Far from revealing aristocratic pretentions on his part, these provisions reflected the ordinary "custom of the former province of Burgundy."[61] A similar case comes from the village of Saint-Jean du Breuil in the Aveyron, where Paul Julien found himself deprived of various emphyteutic charges by the July 1793 law. His ancestors had imposed a *cens*, *lods*, and *champart* on various alienated farmlands. After 1793, however, his tenants seized upon the term *cens* in their contracts to stop paying. In the Aveyron, Julien argued, the term *cens* was nothing more than the local word for a perpetual ground rent and had no feudal characteristics whatsoever. As for the *lods*, he offered to relinquish it "if you think it smacks too much of feudalism."[62] In effect, Julien was calling for a return to the approach of the Constituent Assembly, based on the notion that distinctions could be made between legitimate and illegitimate dues even if stipulated in the same contract. Many other owners of non-feudal ground rents stipulated with *cens* and *lods* in conformity with their provinces' "former laws" felt the same way.[63]

If the owners of non-feudal ground rents that had been swept away in July 1793 were understandably embittered, those who had purchased such rents from the nation and then seen them abolished by the Convention felt outrageously betrayed. As they saw it, their faith in the Revolution—expressed by their investment in incorporeal *biens nationaux*—had been rewarded with expropriation. One of these was citizen Dehargne of the town of Vendôme (Loir-et-Cher). In 1792 he purchased from the nation a bundle of ground rents that had formerly belonged to the Abbey of the Virginity in Montoire. Upon passage of the July 1793 law, the debtors of his rents stopped paying on the pretext that the contract contained the word *cens*. Noting that "an infinity of purchasers are in the same situation" as himself, he urged the legislature to pass a new law "distinguishing rents suppressed without indemnity from those whose collection is legitimate."[64]

The final type of petition concerned formerly allodial land. As we have seen, allodial properties had no feudal superior, but could be subdivided and alienated under quasi-feudal rents. Despite the formally non-feudal status of the *allods* of which they formed a constituent part, these rents were swept up by the Convention's anti-feudal laws. One of these belonged to Jeanne Quenedy, veuve Oels. In 1785 she and her husband had jointly purchased an allodial land which they had then alienated in exchange for various rents, a *cens*, and a *lods*. With the law of July 1793, payment of these had ceased. Since then, wrote the enraged Oels, her husband had died and the greedy tenants had "gorged" themselves on the "cadavers of a widow and her orphans." Although they lived next to "the paternal field," her three children were starving because they could not collect the rent that was "the sole price and representation" of that very field! If it was a crime to have been party to a contract drafted "in a form belonging to the feudal regime" and "established by the then-existing usage and laws," it was not her crime alone. Her former tenants, who had also signed the contract, "were equally guilty." The contract should be abolished, she concluded, her tenants should be freed from all obligations, and she should recover the full property of her land. "Long Live the Republic!," she concluded, "together with liberty, justice, and equality."[65]

Aggrieved owners of suppressed rents were not the only ones who raised their voices in protest. The backlash against the Convention's laws also provoked a counter reaction among those who feared that the revival of ground rents would lead to a feudal restoration. One petition signed by about twenty-five "citizen-cultivators" denounced the campaign to rehabilitate the ground rents as a maneuver of the "abominable faction" of moderation. These Machiavellian schemers had applauded the abolition of feudalism "in the hope of gain and of putting themselves in the place of the former privileged" class. But to accomplish this perfidious end, they had to keep silent until the end of the Terror. Emboldened by the current "weakening of public spirit," they now sought to "artfully pass off" feudal dues as "ground rents." If nothing was done to stop them, the French people would end up having accomplished nothing since 1789 except to "change masters."[66] Other, less heated petitions also expressed concern about the "public clamor" surrounding the question of ground rents and warned that their return presaged a general attack on "the principles of liberty and equality."[67] For the authors of such petitions, the prospect of reviving the rents amounted to rolling back the most fundamental gains of the Revolution. It followed from this line of reasoning that those calling for the reestablishment of the rents were counter-revolutionaries. The debate over feudalism thus continued—and continued to inflame the divisions that had plagued the Revolution since its inception.

The Legislature Debates Ground Rents

Faced with a mounting number of petitions, the Council of 500 formed a Commission to "examine the decree of 17 July 1793." But despite its efforts, it failed to find a solution capable of satisfying both the opponents and supporters of the law. Because of this failure, conflict over ground rents was still unresolved when Napoleon took power.

The Directorial legislature came closest to settling the matter in Thermidor V/July-August 1797, at the height of the factional struggle which led to the coup of 18 Fructidor V/4 September 1797. Like all other issues debated in the Council of 500 at that time, the question of ground rents became entangled with partisan political maneuvering. Leading the legislative effort to revive ground rents was Merlin's friend Jean-Baptiste Treilhard.[68] On 18 Ventôse V/8 March

1797 he made a motion to this effect, promising that it would substantially increase national revenue. Discussion of Treilhard's motion began with a report by Commission member, Antoine-Joseph Ozun. Concluding that non-feudal ground rents were legitimate property, Ozun proposed decreeing that the law of 17 July 1793 had never meant to abolish them. He also called for a new, more viable system of *rachat* and amnesty for the unpaid arrears of the past five years.[69] Debate on the proposal began on 15 Thermidor V/2 August 1797, but did not produce a definitive resolution. In part, this was because the impending factional showdown crowded the question of ground rents off of the legislative agenda, in part because some conservative deputies felt that the proposal was too lenient. One deputy, François-Balthazar Darracq, complained that to excuse the past five years of arrears "subverted the sacred right of property."[70] Another, Pierre-François Duchesne was even more critical. He argued that proprietors should be allowed to collect all their dues, even feudal ones, if they had been established in exchange for the concession of real estate.[71] In short, Duchesne wanted to return to the legislation of 1790.

The Commission and its supporters resisted these strident calls. Although they defended the ground rents as legitimate property, they tempered their position with conciliatory words designed to gain moderate support and allay republican fears of the return of feudalism. They carefully avoided denouncing the law of 17 July 1793. Instead, they emphasized that it had upheld and even strengthened the sacred right of property by demarcating between feudal and non-feudal rents. After all, they pointed out, its second article had explicitly preserved non-feudal ground rents from uncompensated abolition. It was only through a misinterpretation, they concluded, that these rents had been swept up by the law. It would be a simple matter to clarify the misunderstanding. This would restore "the social pact which maintains properties." To refuse this necessary clarification would unfairly free debtors from their obligation to pay the perpetual ground rents they owed for the lands they had received. This would be a catastrophe that would "take from some to enrich others."[72]

The Commission and its supporters advanced a second line of argument, emphasizing the fiscal needs of the state. The nationalized ground rents were too valuable to ignore in the face of France's terrible financial problems. Estimating their capital value at 400 million *livres*, Ozun predicted that their *rachat* would bring even more money into the treasury than the sale of physical *biens nationaux*. This would not merely facilitate the day-to-day "service" of the armies, but would shore up the nation's "credit."[73] Everyone knew that something had to be done to save the state's finances, added Pierre-Louis Duprat. Would it not be better to collect the nation's ground rents than to raise taxes? To increase taxes while sparing the debtors of national ground rents would treat the latter as a privileged group within the Republic. While the enemies of ground rents posed as defenders of revolutionary principle, he charged, their rhetoric masked the cynical defense of their own financial interests.[74]

At the end of Thermidor V/July-August 1797, the debate petered out, over-shadowed by the looming showdown between the Directory and the Council of 500 and overwhelmed by a welter of competing proposals—five in all—on the ground rents. After the coup of 18 Fructidor, left-leaning republicans rushed to denounce the stillborn effort to reestablish ground rents as counterrevolution-ary. During the last days of the year V/1796-97, Léonard-Honoré Gay-Vernon even claimed that the initiative had been part of a sinister plot to install a "lim-ited monarchy" based on a "limited feudalism." He urged that a special inves-tigation be launched, to uncover the secret political motives of Ozun and his Commission.[75] This was necessary to forestall the return of feudalism and "main-tain the Constitution."[76]

It is tempting to interpret the attempt to reestablish ground rents in partisan terms. But this would be a simplification. In fact, of all the deputies who spoke in favor of ground rents, only one (Duprat) was expelled from the legislature on 18 Fructidor. Even more telling, the campaign to rehabilitate ground rents continued after the coup, this time at the instigation of the Executive Directory, Finance Ministry, and Finance Commission of the Council of 500. Already in Thermidor V/July-August 1797, the Finance Minister, Dominique-Vincent Ramel-Nogaret, had recommended reestablishing ground rents as a way to raise revenue.[77] The Directory had forwarded his recommendation to the Finance Commission, which incorporated it into its general plan for financial recovery.[78] The Council of 500 again raised objections, so the article on ground rents was withdrawn from the plan. The question of ground rents was then referred to a new commission—the first of several which sat inconclusively during the years VI (1797-98) and VII (1798-99). Not just a partisan issue, therefore, the mat-ter of ground rents was multidimensional. With implications for state finance as well as the revolutionary redefinition of property, it transcended the factional cleavages of the time. It was the complexity of the question, rather than politi-cal division, that explains why successive legislatures after 18 Fructidor proved no less capable than their predecessors of resolving it. The fate of the ground rents was still unresolved in Brumaire VIII/October-November 1799 when Napoleon took power.

The Brumairians Try to Revive Ground Rents

Soon after the coup of 18 Brumaire VIII/9 November 1799 that brought Napoleon to power, the Consular government moved to modify the Convention's anti-feudal legislation.[79] The new government's penury lent urgency to this initiative. In the very first meeting of the new legislature, it won approval for a measure reopening the *rachat*—and even sale!—of non-feudal, perpetual ground rents owned by government.[80] If it could get the legislature to complement this with the revival of feudally tainted ground rents, the potential revenue would be multiplied many times over. This was the purpose of the initiative. The idea seems to have originated in Pluviôse VIII/January-February 1800 with the Minister of Finance, Martin-Michel-Charles Gaudin, who promised that it would raise an additional 200 million *livres*.[81] Adopted by the government's Finance Council on 13 Ventôse VIII/3 March 1800, the proposal for reviving these controversial ground rents was presented to the legislature on 18 Ventôse VIII/8 March 1800.[82]

The government's spokesman, Claude-Ambroise Regnier, admitted that the blend of feudal and contractual elements in leases was an "impure mixture."[83] But this was not sufficient reason to abolish a form of property that had "nothing in common with an execrated regime." Yet the Convention had enfolded innocent ground rents and guilty feudal dues in a "common proscription." Justice demanded a return to the path traced by Merlin de Douai in 1789-90 when he had distinguished between contractual and usurped rents on a case-by-case basis. Non-feudal ground rents deserved this consideration "because they were incontestably the price of the concession of real estate."

The government realized that the issue of ground rents was politically fraught. Regnier took great pains to assure the legislators that the government opposed any reimposition of feudalism. "That regime is irrevocably abolished," he pronounced. "The French people hold feudal and seigneurial rights in horror." Aware of the difficulties likely to attend any attempt to reverse nearly a decade of revolutionary legislation, he cautioned that not all problems could or should be addressed. "All the damage caused by the revolutionary crises cannot be mended; to attempt too much on this point would be more imprudent than just." Consequently, the law would not be retroactive. Finally, Regnier invoked the dire financial situation, which demanded that the government mobilize all resources at its disposal—including the mass of feudally tinged ground rents it had acquired through the nationalization of domanial and ecclesiastical property.

The Tribunate referred the proposal to a special commission. Its reporter, none other than the same Pierre-Francois Duchesne who had advocated for reviving ground rents during the Directorial-era debates, gave its recommendation on 23 Ventôse VIII/13 March 1800.[84] He began with an historical narrative of the Revolution's changing approach to the feudal question. In his view, the Constituent Assembly had done all that was necessary, by dealing "the final blow to the hundred-headed hydra" (376). But caught in the grip of factionalism and radicalization, the Convention had gone too far. Although "destined in appearance to destroy the last vestiges of feudalism," its laws, "attacked property instead" (375).

> We all remember with horror the disastrous epoch that followed the fatal days of 31 May, 1 and 2 June 1793. France was covered with a shroud until 9 Thermidor II: ideas of right and wrong were sometimes confused in confiscatory laws; and your Commission does not hesitate to place in this class the law of 17 July 1793. . . . Only the misfortunes of the time can today excuse such measures: they attacked the legitimate rights of citizens attached to the Revolution, and still more egregiously, the rights of the nation, which owned most of the rents unjustly swept up in the suppression. . . . Thus, Tribunes, the nation has seen itself unjustly deprived of 15 to 20 million annually in legitimate ground rents, and a multitude of proprietors, whose titles and possession were equally worthy of favor, have been utterly ruined. (375–76)

Duchesne allowed that the government's proposal was not perfect. It permitted oral testimony in lawsuits over ground rents, thereby breaking with French legal tradition. And it was too timid because it did not repeal the Convention's laws outright.[85] But none of this was sufficient reason to reject the law. He concluded by urging his fellow legislators to put aside their fears of a radical backlash and approve the law.

Debate began a few days later. Some speakers attacked the proposal on precisely the grounds Duchesne had assumed they would, by claiming that the measure was the prelude to a feudal restoration. Former member of the Convention Jean-Pierre Chazal made this case with particular force.[86] He blamed the Constituent Assembly for having committed the original sin of failing to abolish all feudal and quasi-feudal dues by a single, uncompromising law. "Such is the tie binding all feudal rights, that if they do not all die together, they will rise again as one" (458). The Revolution had had two mutually dependent aims, he intoned, "freeing men and freeing lands." The Constituent Assembly had achieved the first, but only begun the second. The Convention had completed its work with the law of 17 July 1793. By rolling back these accomplishments, the proposal would "undermine the Revolution" (457). Chazal evoked the terrifying results sure to follow the revival of the ground rents.

> France covered once again by black bands of *feudistes*; titles that the law ordered burnt produced in the name of the law; reward for those who had resisted the law by keeping them; punishment for those who had submitted to its writ by surrendering them; ruinous trials in every family; new hatreds added to so many old ones; false witnesses bribed;

the titles of the nation sold and destroyed by corrupt guardians . . . judgments, constraints, seizures, sequestrations, auctions, desolation, despair, fallow, sterility, misery, and the gaping wound of feudalism on the breast of the *patrie*, corroding it and spreading each day. (459)

France would be drenched in "torrents of blood" (459). The nation had not undergone a decade of revolution only to see feudalism return. It would not stand for it.

Most of the proposal's opponents, however, avoided rhetorical fireworks. Instead, they attacked it on the same grounds as Regnier had advocated it: the sanctity of property. Their principal concern was that, despite the government's fine words, the law was tainted by the "vice of retroactivity."[87] Although it forgave arrears for the period 1793–1800, the law would nonetheless have major financial implications for property sales effected during that time. Jean-Claude Gillet noted that lands formerly subject to perpetual ground rents had been sold "free and quit of all payments" and thus fetched "higher prices than they were really worth."[88] "Today, can you impose on the purchasers of these properties rents they thought had been legally abolished?" Reviving the rents might well fill the state's coffers, but only by sacrificing "public trust," "the faith of contracts," and "the principles of the Revolution." Gillet granted that the government's intention was pure, that it only wanted to right past wrongs. But "what kind of system would repair an injustice by creating new ones?" (447)

The law's opponents feared that its retroactivity would harm key categories of French society. Among the likely victims were the purchasers of *biens nationaux*, whose confidence in the Revolution and willingness to stake their fortunes on it deserved special consideration. "Now that we want to right old wrongs, let us not aggravate them . . . by striking the purchasers of national domains," urged former Convention deputy Francois-Simeon Bezard. "Let us not revolutionize in a misguided attempt to prove that the Revolution is over."[89] His colleague Gillet predicted that the revival of suppressed ground rents would disturb inheritance arrangements, both past and future, with disastrous results for familial harmony.[90] "If the law is adopted, almost all family successions will have to be redone," he warned. "The suppression of the rents was taken into account at the time of [these arrangements]." Disgruntled family members would "take legal action against their fellow heirs." Jean-Augustin Pénières-Delors identified another group likely to suffer from the retroactive law: the soldiers of liberty.[91] He offered a reading of history which, by attributing the victories of the Year II/1793-94 to the popular energies unchained by the Convention's suppression of feudalism, cast those seeking to revive the ground rents as ungrateful egoists seeking personal profit at the expense of the citizen-soldiers. If the Tribunate approved the proposal, Pénières concluded, "How could we ever cleanse ourselves of the reproach of ingratitude?"

Others spoke of the legal chaos that the reintroduction of ground rents would entail. Far from bringing financial stability to the state, one cautioned, the measure would produce "general torment and innumerable trials."[92] Incredulous, another wondered how the government could have concocted such a divisive initiative at this politically sensitive juncture—just as it was trying to end the Revolution.

> It is now in the Year VIII [1799-1800] of the Republic, it is at this happy moment when the Government is striving to reunite the French, to make them forget the troubles of a great Revolution; it is at the very moment when it has ended, when we are approaching the conclusion of a durable peace, that *you invent trials between citizens over the question of feudalism* and necessarily reawaken political hatreds?[93]

Other speakers warned of massive legal chaos. "Soon all French citizens will become either plaintiffs or defendants, witnesses, bailiffs, lawyers, arbitrators, or judges, and in this civil struggle, society will resemble a State in dissolution rather than a just Government. Aren't you afraid that, by trying to right a few of the wrongs of the Revolution, you might spark a new one?"[94]

The debate over ground rents during the first months of the Consulate was significant not only because it afforded yet another occasion to revisit the feudal question. It was also noteworthy because it resulted in Napoleon's greatest legislative defeat. The proposal was rejected by a vote of 59 to 29. The rebuke was so sharp that the government not only withdrew the measure, but actually reversed itself and abandoned its efforts to revive the feudally tinged ground rents through legislative action. Although the idea continued to be discussed within the regime's inner circle, it made no headway for a decade.[95] The Tribunate's opposition in Ventôse VIII/February-March 1800 had succeeded in forcing the government to retreat—a rare accomplishment in the undistinguished annals of the Napoleonic legislatures.

Merlin's Legal Campaign to Revive Ground Rents

The Ventôse VIII/February-March 1800 proposal was the last legislative attempt by Napoleon's government to revive the controversial ground rents. But the story was far from over. Like many issues that had inhabited the political realm during the revolutionary decade, that of ground rents migrated to the judicial sphere after 1800. The *Cour de Cassation* (the supreme appeals court) led the way. Under the guidance of its chief prosecutor, the indomitable Merlin de Douai, it elaborated a complete legal doctrine for reviving the rents. The Council of State, however, strongly resisted Merlin's new doctrine. Barraged by negative legal opinions from the Council and strict imperial decrees based upon them, Merlin and the *Cour* were forced to admit defeat in 1809. But at just that moment, the doomed ground rents won a reprieve as unexpected as the quarter from which it came, the Emperor himself. Having just begun a policy of imperial annexation, he became aware of the valuable incorporeal properties, feudal and non-feudal, in the lands he planned to incorporate. These were a resource too tempting to resist. For a legal rationale capable of saving the annexed rents from abolition, Napoleon turned to the country's undisputed expert in the field, Merlin de Douai. Although this project collapsed along with the Empire, it shows that the story of feudal abolition was still far from over in the 1810s.

A little more than a year after the government's legislative defeat, the *Cour de Cassation* began to issue rulings giving the feudally tainted ground rents a new lease on life.[96] The first concerned Pierre Laxaque, a non-noble landowner in La Quinge (Basse-Pyrénnées) who insisted on styling himself lord of the village. In 1774 he granted a mill to some inhabitants through a contract stipulating various feudal payments. In 1793 the inhabitants stopped paying those dues on the grounds that they had been abolished by the law of 17 July 1793. Laxaque sued. The case ultimately found its way to the *Cour*. On 4 Vendémiaire X/26 September 1801, it ruled that the dues were not feudal despite the extravagant titles Laxaque had arrogated. Since he "was not the lord of the commune of La Quinge," it reasoned, "he could create only ground rents. . . . Only lords and owners of fiefs could create feudal rents" (87-88). Several months later the *Cour* ruled in a similar case. This time the issue was not the status of the grantor, but rather that of the lands he had conceded. Under the old maxim *cens sur cens ne vaut*, lands held in *censive* could not themselves be conceded feudally. In this instance, the lands in question had been conceded and sub-conceded under various feudal payments (*cens, lods,* etc.), but were themselves subject to a veritable feudal *directe*. Since 1793, the debtors had refused to pay these dues, claiming they were feudal, but again the *Cour* ruled against them. Noting that the lands had been "held in *censive*," Merlin concluded that the "handful of feudal words" in the contract "could not make their concession feudal" (88-90). This ruling contained the essential idea behind the *Cour*'s emerging (but not unfamiliar) doctrine: that it was not the words of the contract, but rather the reality it represented, that determined the feudal or non-feudal character of a contested rent. Merlin made this explicit in a speech to the *Cour* on 19 Nivôse XII/10 January 1804. "The denominations employed in the act of concession . . . do not determine the nature of the payment" (90). The tyranny of words, which Merlin believed had reigned since July 1793, was to give way to a more complex, layered approach, an approach which not coincidentally allowed great latitude for judicial interpretation.

The Council of State followed this emerging doctrine with concern and soon struck back. Its first riposte, a legal opinion of 30 Pluviôse XI/19 February 1803, condemned all contracts, "whatever their nature may be," if they had been "established by titles constitutive of seigneurial payments and dues suppressed by the decree of 17 July 1793" (94). Although the *Cour de Cassation* brushed this opinion off and proceeded as if it had never been issued, it could not ignore the Council's second blast, the legal opinion of 13 Messidor XIII/2 July 1805. The Council issued this opinion on a case involving lands the commune of Arbois in the Jura had conceded to various individuals in 1709 in exchange for a full palette of feudal dues. In 1793 the debtors stopped payments. The commune sued, claiming that since it had never had seigneurial status, it could not have created true feudal dues. Although described in feudal terms, the dues could only be simple ground rents. The matter was submitted to the Council of State for judgment. Its ruling was categorical. "If a due's title presents no *ambiguity*," (my emphasis) the lessor "cannot be allowed to argue that he had not had *seigneurie*" (94-96). Napoleon personally approved this ruling and confirmed it by imperial decree on 23 April 1807. Whenever dues were "stained with feudalism, by their mixture with the *lods et ventes* and others suppressed by the laws," the decree stated, there was no reason to consider either the status of the parties or lands in question (96-98). As the jurist Henri-Jean-Baptiste Dard observed in 1814, this decree meant that, henceforth, "everything was to be judged by the word alone" (99).

The battle lines were drawn. On the one hand, the imperial government's position was that the courts need look no further than the terms of the contract to determine the nature of the dues it stipulated. On the other, Merlin and the *Cour de Cassation* argued that it was necessary to penetrate the veil of language to perceive the true character of contested dues. To remain fixated on the word was to mistake the superficial for the substantive and descend into absurdity and injustice. In a speech of 2 January 1809, Merlin expressed the *Cour's* horrified reaction to the new jurisprudence.

> How strange! How bizarre! We are now being told that the owner of a rent who could not have had it judged seigneurial to his profit before the Revolution, can today have it judged seigneurial to his detriment. Is it not the height of unreason to say to the owner of such a rent: "You would have lost your lawsuit in 1788 if you had argued that it was seigneurial; and today you will still lose it if you argue that it is not." Is this not to admit two standards for the same object? (99–100)

Merlin believed that the Council of State had even exceeded the law of July 1793. Although that law's first article had destroyed the notion of contractual feudalism, and thus the feudal *directe* itself, its second article had recognized the legitimacy of simple ground rents representative of the non-feudal *directe*. It was naturally necessary to liquidate these non-feudal *directes* and their associated ground rents in order to unify the divided domains of property. But since they were a legitimate form of property which had nothing to do with "relations of power" and "subjection," their owners deserved compensation (107-8). However, by prohibiting examination of the substance of contracts, the Council's legislation made this impossible. Its rulings confused the non-feudal with the feudal *directe* and, by prohibiting contextualized analysis of constitutive titles, foreclosed any possibility of distinguishing between them. In short, the Council had effectively declared the direct domain of property in all its forms, feudal and non-feudal alike, abolished without compensation.

Merlin must have felt that for all the Council's emphasis on language, it was remarkably ignorant of the meaning of words. For, as Merlin repeatedly noted in his legal opinions, the very terms it took as indisputable proof of feudalism were in fact highly ambiguous. Merlin perceived in this an ingenious way of salvaging something (specifically, emphyteutic *directes*) from the wreckage. By demonstrating the *ambiguity* of the words *seigneurie, directe, cens, lods* and others, he could use the Council's opinion of 13 Messidor XIII/2 July 1805 to overturn its entire jurisprudence.

Merlin argued that, although these terms were used to designate feudal property relations, they did more than that. They were the fundamental building blocks of the Old Regime's language of property. They certainly could, and often did, signify feudal superiority. But they could just as well indicate purely proprietary relationships between non-lordly individuals. Many perpetual non-feudal leases employed the words *seigneurie, directe,* and so forth—and especially the emphyteutic leases so common in the Roman-law provinces of the south. Merlin hammered home this point in opinion after opinion. In such contracts, he explained, the word "*directe* only designates the direct domain of Roman emphyteusis" and "had nothing in common with the "seigneurial *directe*" (127-28). Indeed, he pointed out, the situation was even more complicated than this. Just as Roman-law emphyteutic contracts employed feudal language, true feudal contracts in the south employed emphyteutic terms! Thus, feudal tenants were routinely called *emphytéotes,* their *censives emphytéoses,* and their feudal leases *baux emphytéotiques.* The linguistic blurring was nearly total. This alone furnished sufficient "ambiguity" to look beyond the language of contracts to determine their character.

Turning the Council's opinion on its head, Merlin's argumentation was a juristic tour-de-force. But not satisfied at this, he went further. He had already shown that linguistic ambiguity called for close examination of the contested contracts. But even this might not suffice. If the grantor had been a lord, for example, that might indicate a feudal lease—but not necessarily. Lords frequently alienated lands under emphyteutic or other non-feudal contracts. Because of this, the social status of the contracting parties could not be taken as proof of a lease's true nature. Ultimately, Merlin concluded, the character of some contracts would be so obscure that it was necessary to establish a standard of presumption. This had to be based on the provincial custom under which the contract had been written. In the case of provinces such as Dauphiné, Languedoc, Provence, and Roussillon, this was allodiality, expressed by the maxim *nul seigneur sans titre* (no lords without titles). In such provinces, doubtful contracts had to be presumed non-feudal unless proven otherwise by title. In a major opinion on one of the contested contracts from Auvergne, Merlin elaborated the rationale for his doctrine of presumption.

> In allodial customs the words *"seigneurie directe"* do not suppose feudal overlordship, but only signify the direct domain which, according to Roman law, is always retained by the grantor of an emphtyteusis. . . . In the absence of formal proofs from the proprietors that these dues were feudal and seigneurial, they should be considered pure ground rents; and the *seigneurie directe* should be seen as the emphyteutic *directe* retained by the grantor, a *directe* not suppressed by the feudal abolition laws. (130-31)

In its ruling of 24 Vendémiaire XIII/16 October 1804, the Cour enshrined his opinion. "Given that the custom of Auvergne was purely allodial . . . dues on properties under that custom, which observed the maxim *nul seigneur sans titre*, are reputed to be pure ground rents, unless positively contradicted by a valid act" (131). With this, Merlin had not only succeeded in asserting the primacy of substance over word, but had also revived the standard of presumption he had convinced his fellow deputies to adopt back in 1790!

Merlin's victory, however, was short-lived. The Council hit back—hard. With opinions of 7 March 1808 and 17 January 1809, it explicitly rejected Merlin's position and openly declared its hostility to the direct domain in any form. Any perpetual rent which "reserved the *seigneurie directe*" for the grantor, the second opinion stated, was to be abolished without indemnity, "whatever its denomination or whatever the quality of the person in whose favor it had been established" (145). This decision came as a shock. The editor of the published journal of the *Cour's* proceedings expressed disbelief. "Does the Council of State really mean to abolish rents which recognize the *directe*, the *dominium directum*, which, according to Roman law, is always retained by the grantor of an emphyteusis?

We cannot believe it!"[97] Yet, the unthinkable was true, and the *Cour* had to accept defeat. In its ruling of 5 July 1809, it grudgingly acknowledged that "the obvious intention of the legislator was to strike with the same anathema and suppress without indemnity, not only perpetual emphyteutic leases qualified as seigneurial, even though they might not be . . . but even those declared to be ground rents" (152–53). The *domaine directe* in its entirety had been sentenced to uncompensated abolition.

Imperial Annexations and the Resurrection of Perpetual Ground Rents

This could have been the end of the Old Regime of property. But at just this moment, the government abruptly shifted course. Napoleon had begun to annex lands which had formerly been satellite kingdoms under his brothers or nominally independent allies. These lands—Holland, northern Germany, and northern Italy—contained a quantity of incorporeal property that Napoleon coveted. Realizing that the Council of State's uncompromising jurisprudence condemned these rents and dues to uncompensated abolition once these territories were annexed and subjected to French law, he began to reconsider his previous policy. The first sign of change appeared in a measure concerning a type of perpetual ground rent common in Tuscany, the *livelli*. Like the emphyteutic ground rents of southern France, the *livelli* signified the grantor's retention of the *seigneurie directe*. They thus fell into the category of rent condemned by the Council's jurisprudence. On 22 July 1809 the Council had actually ruled that the *livelli* should be abolished. But in a short, second article inserted after the main body of the opinion, it granted a special exception for the Tuscan ground rent. Atypical of most Napoleonic legislation up to this point, this exception to a specific law heralded a more general shift in imperial policy.

Napoleon's reversal on the feudal question was somewhat unexpected. In the early years of his rule, members of Napoleon's inner circle had urged him to relax the extant anti-feudal legislation. But following the legislative rebuke of Ventôse VIII/February-March 1800, Napoleon seems to have abandoned all hope of reviving the controversial ground rents. Indeed, he approved the uncompromising rulings of the Council of State and had even confirmed them by imperial decree as late as 1807. The surviving records of his interventions in the Council's debates provide plenty of evidence that Napoleon was committed to maintaining the laws currently in force, the laws of the Convention. "We must not have two legislations," he proclaimed at a session considering what policy to adopt toward feudal dues in Piedmont. "All the annexed countries must be like France, and even if our annexations stretched from the Columns of Hercules to Kamtchatka,

the laws of France must prevail throughout."[98] Despite this categorical statement, however, it appears that the great wave of annexations undertaken in 1810
changed Napoleon's mind. He sketched out his new position on the feudal question in November of that year in a note to the Minister of Finances.[99] "The result
of the suppression of feudalism in these [annexed] lands would mean both a
considerable loss for the State and the ruin of many particulars, without any reason or advantage." It would "despoil the owners of these obligations." To prevent
this, Napoleon continued, it was necessary to avoid slavishly following the laws
of the Convention which had "declared as feudal properties which were not"
solely to "obey [the demands of] politics." "There was no reason," he concluded,
"to subject the new departments to this."

Napoleon appointed a special commission to elaborate a more moderate
approach to feudal abolition in the annexed territories. Napoleon's choice of
the man to lead it, Merlin de Douai, speaks volumes about the commission's
purpose. Aiding Merlin was his old colleague, Cambacérès, who was now
Archchancellor of the Empire. Like Merlin, Cambacérès had consistently advocated the revival of perpetual ground rents, notably in the debates on the Civil
Code. Together, Merlin and Cambacérès drafted their report and presented it
to the Council of State in 1811.[100] A magisterial document, it went beyond local
specifics to propose major changes to general imperial policy. It began with a
leading question: Should the Council's jurisprudence, "which has given such a
strange extension to the abolition of feudal rights," be applied in the annexed
lands? The answer, of course, was no. As Merlin had long argued, these laws confused Roman-law ground rents with feudal dues. The annexations provided an
opportunity to rectify these errors, give proper laws to at least the new parts of
the Empire, and perhaps even extend them to France itself. Rather than impose
existing French anti-feudal legislation on the new departments, Merlin and
Cambacérès wanted to save them from "the extreme and unjust rigor with which
feudal abolition has been interpreted in Old France." To the greatest extent possible, the laws of 1790 should be enacted instead. This enlightened legislation
would set an example for the rest of the Empire. Under its influence, perhaps,
France would finally free itself from the baleful legacy of 1793. Liberation would
flow from periphery to center.

The report was organized geographically. Each section examined how local
conditions in a given area would affect the implementation of the 1790 legislation. First to be discussed was Holland. Formerly a sister republic and then a
satellite kingdom under Napoleon's brother Louis, Holland had already seen a
great deal of anti-feudal legislation. This included decrees issued by the political
authorities who accompanied invading French troops in 1795, provisions of the
successive Batavian constitutions (1798, 1801, and 1805), a decree of 9 June
1806, and three opinions issued by the Dutch Council of State between April

1809 and May 1810. But despite this, no practical mechanisms of abolition had been instituted. The constitutions pronounced the abolition of feudalism in principle, but said nothing about how it would happen in practice. The Dutch Council's opinions were still being debated when Holland was annexed and never became law. Only the 1806 decree treated some specifics of feudal abolition, but it contained provisions incompatible with the French constitutional order because they preserved manifestation of what Merlin and Cambacérès termed "*puissance publique.*" Among other things, it allowed ex-lords to appoint local officials and parish priests. These and other prerogatives ran directly counter to the "great principle that there can be only one sovereignty in a state." Drawing textually on Loyseau's distinction between public and private *seigneurie*, Merlin and Cambacérès asserted that these powers had "originally been public functions confided in subordinates by the sovereign." It is true that they had been usurped and "abusively made hereditary," but they had not lost their "primitive character" and become legitimate property. They could thus be abolished immediately without compensation, as had been done in France. Once this had been accomplished, Holland would be in the same state as France immediately after the Night of August 4th: with public *seigneurie* and feudalism abolished in principle, but not in practice. It would thus offer an ideal stage for the integral implementation of the laws of 1790.[101]

The Italian departments of Rome and Trasimène, the report continued, were like Holland because no practical steps had been taken there to abolish feudal property relations. The governing Consulta had done nothing but issue a general proclamation (24 July 1809) suppressing "feudalism, feudal dues, prerogatives, privileges, titles, and jurisdictions which derive from it." But there had been no execution. Merlin and Cambacérès proposed two measures. The first was to enact the Constituent Assembly's anti-feudal laws. The second was to issue an interpretative law exempting from abolition not only "ground rents created with a mixture of feudal dues," but even "purely feudal dues which were the price and condition for the transfer of property." An explicit reassertion of the idea of contractual feudalism, this would spare the Roman states the "crying iniquity" France had suffered under the laws of the Convention, laws that had "violated every right of property." "Let us share with the Roman states all that is wise and legitimate in our legislation," the jurists concluded. "But it is neither useful nor necessary to inflict on them our injustices and spoliations."

Whereas Holland, Rome, and Trasimène offered relatively uncluttered legal terrain favorable to implementing the system of 1790, Tuscany's long history of feudal reform made French legislation unnecessary. By 1776 François of Lorraine and the Grand Duke Leopold had already abolished most feudal dues.[102] When Napoleon annexed Tuscany, therefore, little remained of its former feudal order. Several French laws had been approved there, but none had yet been implemented. The most important was the imperial decree of 29 August 1809 on *livelli*. Merlin and Cambacérès proposed expanding it. First, they recommended maintaining not only the emphyteutic *livelli*, but even feudal ground rents established in exchange for property. Second, they considered the possibility of preserving the *lods* (although they admitted that this would cause practical problems) and recommended maintaining the right of return—which allowed the Crown to recover a vassal's fief if he died without a male heir. The suppression of this right in France during the early years of the Revolution had established a dangerous precedent. If extended to the Empire, it would cause the state "incalculable losses." "Today the state represents not only the King of France, on whom depend a large number of fiefs subject to return in Alsace . . . but also many princes [of the annexed lands]. . . . .with the same rights over a multitude of fiefs and emphyteuses under their lordship."[103] Merlin and Cambacérès argued, moreover, that the right of return was not even feudal, but rather contractual and, as such, was guaranteed by article 951 of the Napoleonic Code!

Unlike the other areas examined in the report, Liguria, Parma and Plaisance, and Piedmont had already been subjected to the full complement of French antifeudal laws. The imperial decree of 4 Thermidor XIII/22 July 1805 had placed these departments on the same legal footing as all other French departments.[104] Short of repealing the Convention's laws, there seemed little that could be done to spare these territories from the existing anti-feudal legislation of France. But this is exactly what Merlin and Cambacérès proposed—as the prelude to a repeal in France itself. They focused on Liguria to make their case. As allodial, Roman-law territory, Ligurian farmlands were typically held under perpetual emphyteutic leases identical to those of southern France. The Italian leases contained the same linguistic ambiguity as their French counterparts. This made it impossible to tell whether they were feudal or emphyteutic. To condemn these leases simply because they contained the phrase *dominio diretto* (direct domain) would violate the sanctity of property. To right this particular wrong in Liguria would be "an unparalleled act of great justice." But "this act of justice would be greater still and more worthy of Your Majesty if it were extended to all your Empire."

Culminating with this appeal for general reform, the Merlin-Cambacérès report inaugurated a new imperial approach to the feudal question. It heralded the return to what Merlin called the "true principles of 1790." By applying the 1790 legislation to the annexed territories, Merlin and Cambacérès sought to do more than just spare those lands the excesses of the Convention. They also hoped that changing feudal policy in the outlying lands of the Empire would shift the law in France itself. Had it been adopted, their proposal would have revived throughout the Empire the perpetual ground rents that had inspired such controversy ever since 1793. Seen in this light, the Merlin-Cambacérès report was less about feudalism in the newly annexed departments than the feudal settlement in France itself. Their effort to abolish feudalism abroad after 1810 was intended to relax anti-feudal legislation at home.

Merlin and Cambacérès did not address the situation of the new German departments (Ems-Supérieur, Bouches-du-Weser, and Bouches-de-l'Elbe) which had just been formed from former Westphalian and Hanseatic lands, as well as the Grand Duchy of Berg and the Duchy of Oldenburg. Napoleon had instead charged Councilor-of-State Louis-Joseph Faure with designing a particular system of feudal abolition for these departments. Napoleon's orders, however, directed him to pursue the same moderate aim as Merlin and Cambacérès: "to reconcile legislative principles with respect . . . for all types of property."[105] Faure presented his recommendations on 25 November 1811. His report analyzed the plethora of dues and rights in the new departments to distinguish those which implied "personal servitude" from those which stemmed from "concessions made to vassals."[106] The sheer number of these obligations makes an exhaustive recapitulation impractical. Several examples suffice to illustrate the complexity of Faure's task. At Ritterbüttel, a dependency of Hamburg, tenants owed their lords payments in kind known as *ramhhühner*. Villages in Bremen and Verden were subject to the *meier-recht*, comparable to the French right of return. Lauenberg, formerly possessed by the House of Braunschweig-Luneburg, was rife with all kinds of "fiefs and incorporeal rights." In the former Duchy of Oldenburg, peasants in the districts of Vechte and Cloppenburg were still enserfed. Given the multiplicity and diversity of these feudal obligations, the task of distinguishing those which implied servitude from those which originated in property transfers was daunting indeed.

Faure's task was eased, however, by the fact that feudalism had already been abolished in most parts of the new departments. Nearly two-thirds had been carved from the Kingdom of Westphalia, where feudalism had been abolished by a series of laws between November 1807 and December 1810.[107] The lands which had formerly been part of Berg had also been subject to anti-feudal laws.[108] And with minor exceptions, the Hanseatic cities of Hamburg, Bremen, and Lübeck were allodial."[109] Even in those parts which had once been part of the unambiguously feudal Duchy of Aremberg, a step toward abolition had already been taken by the Duke. His ordinance of 3 October 1809 had instituted a limited system of *rachat*. By building on these foundations and "modifying" the French laws (a euphemism for not applying the legislation of 1793), Faure believed it possible to "end the state of humiliation in which certain lords have kept their vassals" while at the same time preventing "vassals from enriching themselves at their lords' expense." By the closing months of 1811, the Merlin-Cambacérès and Faure reports heralded at least a partial return to the feudal legislation of 1790.

This did not go unchallenged. After a particularly heated exchange over the proposals on 19 February 1813, the Council of State's legislative section was allowed to give its opinion on the matter.[110] Théophile Berlier delivered it on 21 June 1813.[111] He attacked two of the recommendations made by Merlin and Cambacérès. The first concerned Tuscany, the case the two jurists had used to argue that property mutation fees such as the *lods* were not inherently feudal. Berlier did not question their legal reasoning. Rather, he highlighted the practical difficulties that reviving the *lods* would create. He reminded the Council that the Tuscan *lods* had been suppressed by the decree of 29 August 1809. To repeal it, as Merlin and Cambacérès had urged, would retroactively alter contracts signed during the past five years.

> What could we tell someone who said: 'I acquired a property that I thought was free from transfer fees and the right of return; I believed so because the law had pronounced it; it is true that you are not demanding back pay; but by reviving for the future a charge that had been extinguished, are you not changing the terms of my purchase? Will my property have the same value? When I try to sell it, will it fetch the same price?'

Berlier then turned to the case of Liguria, cited by the jurists to demonstrate that emphyteutic leases were not feudal, even if they contained terms redolent of lordship. Again, Berlier did not challenge their legal reasoning. Instead, he evoked the legal chaos it was likely to produce in France. "Given the perfect assimilation of Liguria to the territory of Old France . . . we could not apply to this allodial land a legal exception without it being immediately demanded by the [allodial] parts of Old France; and there were many of these." Merlin's jurisprudence was impeccable, Berlier admitted, but he was overlooking a consideration more decisive than legal rigor. This was the "absolute rule" of "upholding whatever has been implemented," a rule Napoleon himself had laid down in the Council of State's meeting of 30 Messidor XIII/19 July 1805. According to the Emperor at that time,

> whether the laws against feudalism are based on just or unjust principles is not the issue: a revolution is a jubilee which destabilizes private property. Doubtless, such an upheaval is a misfortune which should be prevented; but when it has already occurred, we cannot reverse its effects without causing a new revolution, without making property uncertain and unstable: today we would go back on one thing, tomorrow on another; soon no one could be confident of being able to keep what he possesses.

Presented in the midst of the Empire's ultimate military crisis, Berlier's report proved to be the last statement on feudal policy issued by Napoleon's government. Thus, the conservative principle it enshrined—"maintain what already exists"—remains the last word in the story of the Napoleonic abolition of feudalism in Europe. But there is reason to believe that, had Napoleon managed to weather the military crisis of 1813-14, there would have been some relaxation of the anti-feudal legislation across the Empire.[112]

The Wagnerian collapse of the Napoleonic Empire—and its One-Hundred Day encore—marked a pause in the struggle over the feudal question. As soon as the dust had settled and the Restoration found its footing, the debate resumed. Pamphlets for and against the reestablishment of ground rents appeared. Some tried to whip up popular fears of a feudal restoration, while others denounced revolutionary legislation on the matter (still in vigor) as subversive of the principle of property itself.[113] Much of this was pure polemics, but not all the fuss over feudalism was political posturing. Litigation over the rents proliferated in the courts, much of it initiated by the state financial administration, eager to increase the resources (nationalized ground rents) at its disposal. Some of these cases were appealed to the *Cour de Cassation* which was emboldened to issue rulings (on 13 December 1820, 15 March 1824, 27 March 1833, and 3 June 1835) which chipped away at the extant legislation. But these were only partial measures, applicable only to specific cases.[114] Finally on 16 April 1838, the *Cour* issued a general decision. Judging the feudal character of a litigious ground rent that had been created in 1767 by a bourgeois who had fraudulently assumed the title of *seigneur*, the *Cour* ruled that this usurped appellation was not sufficient to make the rent feudal. Only a veritable *seigneur* could imprint a feudal stamp on a rent. In consequence, it was essential to look beyond the terms of the contract (which in this case included not only "seigneur," but also the phrase "seigneurial duties, usages, and customs of the Lyonnais nobility").[115] This implied that the context and substance of a rent, not the words by which it had been stipulated, would determine whether it was feudal or not. This was the position for which Merlin de Douai had long fought. An old man by now (he was 83 when the *Cour* issued its ruling), Merlin must have felt vindicated. He died six months later.

Conclusion

This and the previous chapter have challenged several assumptions characteristic of the literature on the French Revolution's abolition of feudalism. First, they have shown that the question of feudal abolition was not resolved in 1793 by the National Convention, but continued to be the subject of controversy and litigation well into the nineteenth century. Second, they have demonstrated that feudal abolition did not only affect the rural world, but that it applied to towns and cities as well. Finally, they have revealed that the abolition of feudalism did not concern only individual lords and their tenants, but that it also had implications for national finances and the State's constitutional relationship to property. When it took over the seigneurial and emphyteutic holdings of the royal domain and Church, it acquired a mass of direct domain property. The State thus found itself implicated in the question of feudal abolition. The financial stakes were obviously high, for the feudal and non-feudal rents it had acquired represented a significant annual revenue and an even more significant capital. The constitutional stakes were even higher. As long as it retained this mass of direct domain property, the state would remain a domanial one with proprietary rights over the lands and houses of its citizens. Each nationalized ex-feudal due and perpetual ground rent represented a *directe* over an individual citizen's holding. Because of this, the abolition of feudalism was not just about disentangling the respective properties of lords and tenants to make them full, independent, and equal. It was also about erasing the domanial character of the state and redefining its relationship to society and the individual.

4

The Invention of
the National Domain

One of the most effective acts of regeneration the nation can carry
out ... is to take for itself all properties without real owners and
return them to the patrimony of families.
—Jacques-Guillaume Thouret, 30 October 1789

Demarcating the spheres of property and power involved two complementary
operations. Just as the revolutionaries had to get power out of the realm of property, they also had to remove property from the hands of the State. This was a
gargantuan, politically fraught undertaking because the key political instances
of Old Regime France, the Crown and the Church, had enormous proprietary
endowments. The Church was the richest entity in France and the largest single
landholder. And, although one can easily lose sight of the fact in a secular age,
it was an eminently political body, a *corps politique* that had historically rivaled
the Crown itself as the source of political authority. It was, in short, part of the
State—or, alternatively, a state within the State. The revolutionaries believed that
its vast properties made it independent from the sovereign and gave it particular
interests distinct from those of the nation as a whole. The Crown was similar
in important ways but also presented some unique challenges. It too possessed
a large amount of real estate, as well as an incorporeal endowment of feudal
and non-feudal rents. As we have seen in previous chapters, these non-physical
properties were acutely problematic because they represented the direct domain
claimed by the Crown over the kingdom's fiefs and certain other properties as
well. Thanks to the doctrine of the royal universal *directe*, these claims to royal
feudal overlordship threatened to extend their superiority over all the properties of the kingdom. The revolutionaries believed that the property rights of the
Crown and Church encroached upon national sovereignty and undermined the
independence and incommutability of individual ownership. They acted swiftly
and decisively. By the end of 1790, the revolutionaries had stripped both Crown

and Church of their possessions, taken away their very right to own property, and begun to sell their former holdings as *biens nationaux*.

The scholarship on the *biens nationaux* has approached the expropriation and sale of these properties from a financial, economic, and social perspective.[1] To raise money to pay off the debt, the conventional account goes, the revolutionaries took the domanial and ecclesiastical lands and sold them off. The result was a shift in the distribution of landownership (its magnitude is disputed) which in turn produced a transformation of the social structure (also the subject of debate). This way of approaching the *biens nationaux* is valid, but it neglects the constitutional ramifications of the transfer of property from public, political institutions to individual citizens. This chapter argues that the expropriation and sale of the Church and Crown properties was the necessary complement of the Night of August 4th, for it completed the Great Demarcation between power and property. More than just a response to fiscal crisis, the decision to expropriate and sell the *biens nationaux* was a theoretically informed, programmatic attempt to excise property from sovereignty and return it to society.

For the revolutionaries, this was required to realize in practice two goals: the creation of undivided national sovereignty, on the one hand, and the formation of absolute, individual property, on the other. To achieve the first aim, institutions entrusted with public powers had to be stripped of their properties. This is because those properties lent them interests distinct from those of the nation as a whole, as well as the financial means to pursue those interests in practice. Moreover, to allow political bodies to hold proprietary endowments was tantamount to preserving the corporate order. The existence of corporate endowments required permanent councils within those bodies to manage their holdings and allocate their proceeds. If allowed to retain a proprietary existence, therefore, the *corps* would keep their collective personality. To guarantee against the survival of corporatism in practice, the revolutionaries sought to eliminate the properties of the *corps* and reduce them to collections of salaried public servants. By doing so, they aimed to preserve the unity of sovereignty from the threat posed by distinct public bodies with particularistic agendas.

The realization in practice of the new order of free and equal property also depended upon ending the property rights of political bodies. The spread of absolute, individual property to as many people as possible was the essential basis of political liberty, for property-ownership alone provided the personal independence required for citizenship. But as long as the Church and Crown continued to levy the tithe, collect feudal dues, and retain *directes* over properties they had conceded, no individual holding could be fully free. Economic imperatives reinforced these constitutional considerations. The physiocrats had taught that national prosperity depended on the free circulation of properties and their direct exploitation by individual owners. In their view, the Church and Crown, both of which were legally barred from alienating their holdings, diminished the volume of the commerce in real estate. This prevented France from achieving its economic potential. From both a constitutional and an economic perspective, the concentration of property in the hands of the Church, Crown, and other *corps politiques* was an obstacle to the new order.

The need to expropriate the Crown, Church, and other corporations forced the revolutionaries to articulate a theory of national property rights capable of dispossessing these entities while at the same time safeguarding individual ownership. The result was the invention of the national domain. This new domain was based on principles that made it simultaneously stronger and weaker than the old royal domain. It was stronger because the revolutionaries based it on the principle of alienability. Unlike the domain of the Crown, which was bound by the doctrine of inalienability, the national domain would be free to sell the property it contained. But at the same time it was weaker than the royal domain because it would have no overarching right to individual property (like the royal universal *directe*), nor any right to take back what it had legitimately alienated. Once something had left the national domain, it would be gone from the State's grasp forever. The new principle of alienability combined with the renunciation of the royal domain's expansive claims to properties that had left its hands meant that the new national domain was destined to diminish and disappear. It was to be a machine for converting "political" property (of the Crown, Church, the other *corps*, and, eventually, the émigrés) into "social" property (of individual citizens). Although it would continue to hold things unsuitable for individual ownership, such as waterways and roads, the national domain was purpose-built to alienate all State-held properties capable of becoming individual property. Unlike the royal domain whose doctrine of inalienability tended to draw property toward it and bind it perpetually to the sovereign, the national domain was configured to transform the expropriated holdings of the *corps politiques* into absolute property by returning them to society through sale to private individuals. Through its action, the state would be left with nothing but sovereignty, and all property would be in the hands of the citizens.

The Night of August 4th and the Property of Political Bodies

It came as no surprise to anyone when, on 10 October 1789, the bishop of Autun, Charles-Maurice de Talleyrand-Périgord, proposed that the nation take over the property of the Church. Ever since the revelation of the monarchy's fiscal crisis in 1787, there had been no shortage of pamphleteers urging mobilization of ecclesiastical property against the debt.[2] These calls had been reiterated in the *cahiers de doléances* in spring 1789.[3] Yet, although a recent, magisterial survey has described the nationalization and sale of the properties of the Church as "the most important event of the Revolution," it was less revolutionary than it might at first appear.[4] There were Old Regime precedents for using ecclesiastical property to help the state face emergencies. Kings, wrote Louis XIV, had "the free and entire disposition of all secular and ecclesiastical properties to use for the needs of their State."[5] Historical examples and incidents from recent times demonstrated that Louis XIV's assertion was no empty maxim. In the eighteenth century kings had taken over the property of suppressed religious orders—most famously, the Jesuits in 1762, but even more recently the Antonins and Célestins. These precedents were reinforced by philosophical opinion, which had railed for decades against the "luxury" of the Church, as well as by reformers within the Church itself who called for a more egalitarian institution rededicated to its spiritual mission. All these factors converged in 1789 to make ecclesiastical property a tempting target for the National Assembly as it sought a way out of the fiscal crisis. The revolutionaries' approach, however, would differ sharply from that of kings. In previous centuries, monarchs had tapped the Church's wealth and even expropriated part of its property. But they had never dreamed of attempting what the revolutionaries set out to do: strip the Church permanently of its entire endowment and transform it from a *corps politique* to a group of civil servants.

The Church was the richest entity in Old Regime France, even richer than the Crown. As with most large property-holders, its wealth consisted of physical and non-physical goods. With rural possessions concentrated in the northeastern provinces and substantial urban properties in all French cities, the real estate of the Church partook of the same divided-domain system of property as nonecclesiastical holdings. More ecclesiastical real estate probably consisted in fiefs than in subordinate tenures, although in some provinces (e.g., Normandy), the Church held non-noble lands under the *directes* of lay lords. Because it possessed a significant number of feudal lordships, the Church also owned a mass of feudal dues. In all, its landed property, dues, and rents generated an annual revenue of about 60 million *livres*. Real estate, however, was not the most important component of ecclesiastical income. Rather, the tithe, an annual payment (generally in kind) to which all property-holders were subject, accounted for two-thirds (120 million *livres* annually) of the Church's yearly income.[6]

The question of ecclesiastical property was first placed on the National Assembly's agenda on the Night of August 4th, when a deputy made a motion to abolish the tithe. The Assembly had not even begun to discuss this proposal when, on August 7th, chief minister Jacques Necker (1732-1804) appeared before it with a dire report on the kingdom's finances and an urgent request for an immediate loan to keep the government functioning. For the next three days, the Assembly suspended its discussion of the August 4th renunciations to consider Necker's request. The ensuing discussion quickly came to focus on the Church's endowment. A number of deputies suggested using "the properties of the clergy, which belong to the nation," to guarantee the loan.[7] This was in line with the historical precedents furnished by the Crown's periodic reliance on ecclesiastical assistance to see it through crises. But the debate soon rose from this pragmatic, fiscal level to a higher, constitutional plane. There, it coalesced around several key questions. Did the Church or any other *corps* actually have property rights? If so, on what grounds? And if those rights were not inalienable like those of individuals, but rather depended on the national will, was the maintenance of those rights compatible with the new constitutional order?

Left-leaning deputies argued that it was not and called for expropriation. The *marquis* Benjamin-Eléonor-Louis de Lacoste warned that the nation had to strip the Church of its property in order to "reclaim the fullness of its rights." "Public order" demanded that it cease to exist as a political body and that its former members become functionaries "paid by the State."[8] Lacoste's colleague, Alexandre-Théodore-Victor de Lameth, seconded his motion and went further, outlining a theoretical rationale for expropriation. He based this on arguments from Turgot's *Encyclopédie* article on religious foundations. Cited repeatedly in the full-blown debate over the property of the Church two months later, this essay would provide the "nationalizers" with important justifications for their position. Lameth's key Turgotian move was to assert a fundamental distinction between corporate and individual property rights. "There is," he claimed, "a great difference between the properties of citizens and those of corporations." Whereas the rights of citizens "exist independent of society," those of "political bodies exist only by and for society." The nation had spoken on the Night of August 4th: with the annihilation of the "feudal regime," the clergy had been stripped of the ability to possess either public power or collective property. They had ceased to be members of an order and had become "spiritual magistrates."[9] Although the Assembly declined at this time to act on Lacoste's and Lameth's motions to expropriate the Church and transform it into a collection of functionaries, the episode shocked the leaders of the clergy and shaped their initial interventions in the debate over the tithe.

Discussion of this issue began in earnest on the morning of August 10th. Those calling for the outright suppression of the tithe argued that it had been usurped as a property and was not even worthy of the same consideration as feudal dues. As mentioned in chapter 2, the tithe was not attached contractually to properties that had been conceded by the Church to individuals, but rather, like a tax, it struck all properties regardless of their origins. It was on these grounds that opponents of the tithe demanded its immediate, uncompensated suppression. "Property presupposes domain," one deputy observed, but the tithe implied nothing of the sort. Just because a priest took part of a peasant's crop in payment of the tithe, this did not give the cleric a property right to the peasant's field.[10] The tithe was a tax and thus could neither be held nor defended as property. It was necessary, however, to distinguish ecclesiastical tithes, to be abolished without indemnity, from lay tithes (also known as infeodated tithes) which the Church had sold to individuals. Because these tithes were imbricated in contractual exchanges, some of which involved land, they had acquired "the characteristics of [legitimate] property," circulating in commerce and passing from generation to generation through inheritance.[11] Like feudal dues, they had to be converted into ground rents and subjected to *rachat*.

Some of the most hard-line clerical deputies responded that the tithe was a sacred property of the Church. Others, however, accepted that it was a "national property," but argued on practical grounds that abolishing it would hurt the poor by making it impossible for the Church to fulfill its charitable mission.[12] The bishop of Rodez, Colbert de Seignelay, went even further, arguing that ecclesiastical property belonged to neither the Church nor the nation, but ultimately "to the poor."[13] The *abbé* Sieyes, who subsequently published an expanded version of his argument, took a different approach. He pointed out that abolishing the tithe would give a "free gift of 700 million" to the rich property-holders of France who would no longer have to pay it. Rehearsing an argument he would soon be applying to the property of the Church as a whole, he argued that tithes were legitimate property because pious landowners had established them freely on behalf of the Church. The tithe should therefore be maintained and remain in ecclesiastical hands because it had originated in the free exercise of individual property rights. He admitted, however, that the tithe was socially harmful—an obstacle to the flowering of agriculture—and accepted that it had to be suppressed. As a legitimate, but socially detrimental form of property, it resembled a feudal due and should thus share the same fate—gradual extinction through *rachat*.[14]

Raging all day and long into the night, the debate proved to be the most contentious episode in the process of legislating the promises of August 4th. Having retired late to catch a few winks of sleep, the advocates and opponents of abolition seemed poised to resume their contest the following day. But when the Assembly reconvened on the morning of the 11th, the clergy made a surprising announcement. Speaking for his order, the Archbishop of Paris, Antoine-Eléonor-Léon Leclerc de Juigné, rose to place the tithe "in the hands of a just and generous nation."[15] What had been shaping up a decisive show of strength between the Church and the Assembly had ended with a whimper.

Why did the clergy meekly abandon its defense of the tithe and voluntarily give up what was its single most important source of revenue? It was a strategic withdrawal. They hoped that renunciation of part of their endowment would save the rest—and along with it, their independent corporate existence—from destruction. In this first clash over ecclesiastical property, the Church seems to have taken the advice of the left-leaning deputy François-Nicolas-Léonard Buzot, who counseled that there was "no better option than to save appearances and appear to make voluntarily the sacrifices demanded by imperious circumstances."[16]

In the rush of revolutionary events, the Church's delaying maneuver bought it only a fleeting reprieve. In the second half of September, more discouraging fiscal news again prompted the Assembly to take up the question of ecclesiastical property. On 22 September new reports on the massive non-payment of taxes and the failure of government loans conjured up the specter of imminent bankruptcy.[17] The next day the Ecclesiastical Committee—which had been formed on August 11th to begin the institutional reorganization of the Church made necessary by the sacrifice of the tithe—proposed a comprehensive stock-taking of all ecclesiastical property.[18] Then, the day after that, Necker, whose appearances in the Assembly always boded ill for the Church, informed the deputies that financial affairs had reached "the ultimate degree of embarrassment."[19] In response, the Archbishop of Paris offered to contribute the clergy's silver to the nation, but was sharply rebuffed on the grounds that "it doesn't belong to [you]."[20] A proposal for general expropriation would not be long in coming. At stake was not only the Church's right to property, but ultimately that of the greatest political *corps* of all, the nation.

Who Owns the Property of the Church?

The clash over the tithe brought into the open the question of the Church's property, but the clergy staved off discussion in the Assembly by its voluntary sacrifice on August 11th. The respite it gained was the briefest imaginable. The following day, the pamphleteer Armand-Benoît-Joseph Guffroy rushed into print a piece exposing the clergy's maneuver.[21] By accepting the clergy's "offering to the nation," the Assembly had indirectly confirmed not only the Church's right to the tithe but also ensured its continued existence as a *corps politique*. Other articles of the August 11th decree—those calling for the *rachat* of feudal dues and ground rents—would have the same effect, for the Church held many of these incorporeal properties. Although it had intended to do good, Guffroy concluded, the Assembly had unwittingly confirmed "the existence of this dangerous *corps*" and "made the clergy an integral part of the Constitution." The only way to undo the damage was to declare that "all the properties of the clergy belong to the nation."

Guffroy's tract was the first shot in a pamphlet war over the question of ecclesiastical property. Shortly after its publication a response appeared in print. For many astonished readers, it confirmed Guffroy's warning of the dangers that the persistence of a corporate, clerical interest must necessarily pose. The shock was all the greater because its author, the *abbé* Sieyes, had previously been considered one of the leading revolutionaries. Entitled *Observations sommaires sur les biens ecclésiastiques*, his pamphlet defended the properties of the Church by turning the Turgotian distinction between corporate and individual property rights against the nation itself. Yes, Sieyes admitted, the Church was a *corps* and, unlike individuals whose property rights derived from natural law, it could only possess property if permitted by positive law. But the nation was no different than the Church. As a "moral and political corps" itself, the nation had no natural right to property either. Sieyes's counterattack prompted vigorous rebuttal. The primary interest of these responses is that they evoked for the first time a new concept, "the national domain."[22] The short but sharp controversy initiated by Sieyes had not only tied the question of the Church's property rights to that of the nation's, but also suggested that that these issues were connected to the question of the nature of individual property right as well. The debate over Church property had grown from a philosophical discussion of the right of property into a clash over the fundamental nature of the new polity.

The National Assembly did not return to the question of ecclesiastical property, however, until after the October Days (October 5th-6th), which resulted in the transfer of the royal family (and the Assembly itself) from Versailles to Paris.[23] On October 10th Talleyrand moved that the nation take over the properties of the Church and sell them to pay off the national debt.[24] This was the only way, he argued, that the nation could recover its credit and restore its fiscal health. Anticipating objections that the nationalization of Church property would set a precedent for seizing individual properties, Talleyrand trundled out the now-familiar Turgotian distinction between corporate and individual property. The clergy, he explained, "is not a proprietor like others," because it had been given properties "for the performance of [public] functions." As the nation possessed "a very great empire over all *corps politiques* in its bosom," it certainly had the power to destroy "particular aggregations" that it judged "harmful or simply useless." And, of course, the nation's right of life-or-death over *corps* necessarily entailed "a very broad right over the disposition of their properties." No one need fear that exercising this national right over corporate property would threaten the property of individuals, for their respective rights were fundamentally different. The expropriation of the Church would thus entail no "violation of property."

Talleyrand's proposal sparked one of the most important debates in the history of the National Assembly, as well as a national pamphlet war. Yet, it has unaccountably been downplayed by historians, perhaps because the nationalization of Church property seems in hindsight to have been a foregone conclusion.

But at the time, many deputies, not all of whom were clerics, did not think it was inevitable. Moreover, although framed in terms of the question "Does the Church own its property?" the debate actually raised a much wider range of questions. Did the nationalization and sale of ecclesiastical properties make financial sense? What effect would these operations have on religion and morality? What place should the Church and the Catholic religion occupy in the new order? What was the proper relationship between professions and the State? The issue of Church property was one of the most consequential the Assembly would ever face. As the *comte* de Mirabeau put it, it "simultaneously touched on the inviolable rules of property, public religion, the political structure, and the essential foundations of the social order."[25] There is thus ample reason to devote some attention to this neglected debate—not least because it addressed fundamental questions about the line between political power and property rights in the New Regime.

On one level, the debate was driven by financial considerations. To win their case, the advocates of expropriation had to convince their legislative colleagues of the practical need for such a drastic measure. Talleyrand had justified it on fiscal grounds, and many others did so as well. But the clerical deputies and their supporters in the two other estates vehemently denied that the sale of Church property would solve the nation's financial woes. By putting so many properties on the market at one time (especially in the current, uncertain economic context), the operation would produce but scant returns for the permanent loss of an irreplaceable national resource.[26] They maintained that it made much more sense to preserve the Church's endowment and use it (as before 1789) to guarantee the nation's credit. To this end, the defenders of ecclesiastical property offered to take out unprecedentedly large loans on the nation's behalf. Clerical deputies ultimately offered the nation a 400-million *livre* line of credit.[27] In the face of this strong financial argument, the advocates of expropriation realized that they had to appeal to higher principles than financial pragmatism to carry the day.

They found these higher principles on the constitutional plane. This became the principal terrain on which those calling for expropriation chose to make their main effort, and they soon succeeded in shifting the entire debate onto those grounds. The essence of their argument was that the new order could not tolerate the continued existence of political corps, especially ones whose landed interests made selfish and independent. Anticipating his subsequent intervention against the artisanal *corps*, Isaac-René-Guy Le Chapelier introduced this line of attack.[28] The clergy, he began, had already been destroyed along with all other *corps* on the Night of August 4th. It existed only in memory, "among the superb debris of an immense revolution . . . it is the patrimony of history." It was thus not necessary to pronounce its destruction again. But if the Assembly did not strip it of its properties, if it accepted the clergy's offers of money and credit, the clergy would "rise from the ashes to reconstitute itself as an order." The clergy's "gifts are more dangerous than our distress," he warned. If the Assembly were to accept them, it would confirm the property rights of the Church, "consecrate its independence," and "disorganize the political body." The Night of August 4th—and the Revolution itself—would have been in vain.

One hostile deputy of the nobility, the *comte* de la Gallissonnière (1757-1828), remembered with disgust that Le Chapelier's intervention had been decisive and persuaded "many deputies to change their mind."[29] That may well have been the case, but a speech by the *comte* Honoré-Gabriel Riqueti de Mirabeau developed a fuller theoretical argument for expropriation. Mirabeau systematically explained why the New Regime could not accommodate *corps* of any sort. He posited that "individuals are the only elements of any society whatsoever." Society certainly had the power to create *corps* and had done so in the past. But this had been a terrible mistake because "particular societies placed in the midst of the general society shatter the unity of its principles and equilibrium of its forces." The danger of "large political *corps*" lay in "their collective force" and "the resistance generated by their interests." It was thus imperative not to "establish corps, to regard such aggregations as individuals in society, to grant them civil actions, and to permit them to become proprietors like other citizens." It was on this anti-corporate basis that the advocates of expropriation took their stand.

The necessary consequence of suppressing the Church as a *corps* and taking away its properties was that the ecclesiastical calling would become, in the words of Antoine Barnave "nothing but a profession" and its members salaried functionaries, "officers" of the State "charged with a public service."[30] Not even the most reactionary member of the clergy would have denied that the Church had always existed to serve the body of the faithful (a body which, as many deputies on both sides of the debate assumed, was coterminous with the nation itself). The expropriators, however, seized upon the Church's public mission to expose the absurdity of its claim to property. Defining the right of property as the right to "enjoy for oneself" (*jouir pour soi*), Jean-François-Adrien Duport claimed that the clergy had never been true proprietors, but only "simple administrators" of goods destined exclusively for a public function.[31] Making a distinction that would become a conceptual foundation of the nascent national domain, he asserted that their properties were "public properties" and of a class quite distinct from "particular properties." The *comte* de Mirabeau illustrated the point with a striking contrast. "Never had the *corps* of the navy taken for itself the vessels the people have had built for the defense of the State."[32] The Church had always been a profession, and professions had never had property rights. That the clergy was claiming such rights conflicted with its public function. Expropriation was thus not a radical measure, but rather a necessary operation to set things right within the Church itself. Far from weakening the clergy or religion, it would strengthen both by freeing the Church of its distracting temporal concerns and eliminating the opulence that was the cause of its external discredit and internal divisions.

For both the advocates and opponents of expropriation, the question of Church property was more than a fiscal, religious, or professional matter. It was a test of whether the promises of the Revolution would hold. The *comte* de Mirabeau warned that if the Assembly did not vote for expropriation, "all your decrees on the properties of the nobility, proportional taxation, and the abolition of privileges would be but vain laws."[33] From the other side of the issue, Jean de Dieu-Raymond Boisgelin de Cicé, the Archbishop of Aix voiced a plaint that largely confirmed Mirabeau's fears. The prelate chided the legislature that it seemed as if it "wanted to separate our generation from all those which have preceded it."

> We are overturning all established rights, we no longer recognize time-honored possessions; we seem to want to detach the fleeting moment of our feeble and passing existence from its connections with times which are no more. The past no longer has anything in common with the present.[34]

In the debate over Church property, the fate of France seemed to hang in the balance. It had become a referendum on everything that had happened since the Night of August 4th.

The clerical deputies and their allies mounted a powerful defense. Against the anti-corporate argument formulated by Le Chapelier and Mirabeau, they opposed an equally sacred revolutionary principle, the right of property. To seize the properties of the Church, they warned, would do far more than simply violate the Church's rights. It would set a general precedent for despotic national property rights to which all properties would be vulnerable. To make their point, they drew on concepts and a sensitivity to words introduced by Bodin and Loyseau and subsequently honed over more than a century of conflict over the royal universal *directe*. The *abbé* Jean-François-Ange d'Eymar observed that it was an "error and manifest vice of language" that had led some deputies to "exaggerate the rights of the nation over the persons and property of its members." By asserting a national right to property over the Church's holdings, they had fallen into the old trap of confusing sovereignty with property. To do this, to "attribute to the sovereign the immediate or supreme property of the person or property of its subjects," would lead straight to the "highest degree . . . of despotism." For, "there could be only slaves under emperors, kings, and [even] republics that confuse the rights of sovereignty with those of domain."[35] The *abbé* Jean-Siffrein Maury reinforced Eymar's warning, observing that the nation "possesses all powers . . .

but property has never belonged to it."[36] So did the *comte* de la Galissonniére, who asserted that "a nation is sovereign and not property-owning; the individuals who compose that nation are the only ones capable of ownership."[37] Even members of the lower clergy, who wanted the Assembly to use its authority to redistribute ecclesiastical property equitably within the Church, shared these concerns. The parish priest of Cherigné, Jacques Jallet, was just one of several who wanted the nation to reorganize the Church, but balked at the dangerous confusion of property and power an expropriation seemed to entail. "The sovereign cannot possess properties. . . . Thus, it is not as proprietor, but as sovereign that the nation can dispose of the clergy's goods" and "preside over their use."[38] The lines of the clergy's counterattack had clearly emerged. They would respond to attacks on the Church's endowment by reframing the question as that of the nation's property rights.

Given the clergy's reliance on the juridical distinction between sovereignty and property that had been forged in the sixteenth-century debates over the origin of fiefs, it is not surprising to find that they also used historical arguments to bolster their position. They repeatedly pointed out that the Church had already owned its properties before the Franks appeared in Gaul. Since the French nation was created by the Frankish conquest, ecclesiastical property thus preceded the existence of the nation itself. Because of this, the nation could not possibly have property rights over the Church's possessions.[39] It is true, they acknowledged, that some Church property originated from subsequent royal gifts. But to suggest that having a royal origin was sufficient grounds for nationalization threatened all property in France. If such a doctrine were admitted, they warned, first in line for expropriation would be the fiefs. Since fiefs had originated as "ancient land grants charged with a public service" and had been bestowed by kings "in the name of the nation," argued Boisgelin, it followed that the "nation could seize them like the lands given to the Church."[40] The *abbé* Maury put it succinctly: "if we can take the clergy's properties under this pretext," then "why should we respect fiefs?"[41]

In their transparent efforts to associate the nobility with their cause, Boisgelin and Maury had raised on an issue of truly enormous significance for the definition of property in the New Regime. Centuries of historical and juridical scholarship had shown that all or most properties had a direct or indirect royal origin that could be traced through the tenurial hierarchy of fiefs and *censives*. If this were so and if the nation had in fact come into its own rights and reasserted control of the royal domain, then how and where to distinguish between national and individual property? This turned out to be the fundamental problem the Assembly's new Domanial Committee would have to resolve.

Along with juridical and historical arguments, the defenders of ecclesiastical property invoked the principle of individual property rights on their behalf.

Many of the Church's properties, perhaps the majority, had been given to it by pious donors. To seize these properties and use them to pay off the national debt would violate the intentions, and thus the property rights, of these benefactors. "We have been given our properties," Maury noted. In these donations, "everything had been individual-to-individual between the donor who bequeathed and the specific church that received." If voluntary transfers of property by individuals could be annulled, "what property would be safe in the kingdom?" It was clear, Maury observed, that

> we have become proprietors like you, Messieurs, by gifts, acquisitions, land clearings, and the law has guaranteed our properties as it has yours. You have no other right over our goods than that of territorial enclave [within the boundaries of the nation], and if that were to be accepted as a title to property, then it would despoil all of you as well.

In the final analysis, he warned, "our properties guarantee your own. . . . If we are expropriated, you will be next."[42] Either "no property exists," echoed François de Bonnal, the bishop of Clermont, "or ours is unassailable."[43]

The Church's arguments were sophisticated and powerful. The nightmare vision they evoked of an all-powerful, proprietary State confiscating individual property at will must have resonated with the deputies, who had been sensitized to this threat by the clashes over the royal universal *directe*. To counter it, the advocates of expropriation had to find a way to reassure their wavering colleagues that seizing Church property in the name of the nation would not threaten individual property rights. They had to formulate a theoretical rationale of national property rights capable of justifying the seizure of the Church's endowment while at the same time reaffirming the inviolability of individual holdings. In other words, they had to find a way of distinguishing between the inalienable rights of individuals and the contingent ones of *corps*.

One of the most respected deputies of the time, Jacques-Guillaume Thouret, took up this challenge.[44] He found a solution to it by combining the Lockean idea of natural, individual property rights with the Turgotian notion of the nation's absolute authority over the *corps*.[45] Thouret began by asserting a crucial difference between individuals and *corps*. The former were "real," the latter "moral or fictive." From this existential difference between individuals and *corps* flowed a basic distinction in the source of their respective rights. "Existing independently of and anterior to the law," individuals had inherent "rights resulting from their nature and particular faculties, rights that the law did not create . . . rights that it cannot destroy any more than the individuals themselves." In contrast, *corps* "exist only through law," have no "inherent nature," and "are nothing but a fiction, an abstract conception." In consequence, while the law's authority over individuals was limited to protecting their pre-existing natural rights, it wielded "unlimited authority" over the *corps*. Since they were subject to the "absolute empire of the law," there "would be no injustice or oppression" in taking their properties, properties they enjoyed—like their very existence—only by virtue of the law.

It was now essential, Thouret continued, that the nation not only expropriate the Church but also decree that no *corps* could "possess landed property in the future." Political and economic considerations demanded this measure. To foster individual liberty, to strengthen the attachment of citizens to the public good, it was necessary to "spread as widely as possible the distribution of individual properties." By locking up vast quantities of land in their "dead hand," the proprietary *corps* were "thwarting this primary political goal." By returning corporate property to individuals and families, the Assembly would restore economic health to France. It was necessary to "give lands to real proprietors" who, unlike the *corps* which were happy to live off unproductive rents, could alone infuse the agricultural economy with "that zeal and proprietary attachment for which there is no substitute." Given these considerations, he concluded, it was necessary for the Assembly to go beyond the specific question of Church property to abolish all non-individual property-ownership in France. To that end, he proposed stripping all *corps* of their property rights and placing their properties, along with those of the "Crown domains," at the "disposition of the nation."

Thouret's Lockean/Turgotian theory of property rights was potent, but the defenders of ecclesiastical property had a ready response derived from an equally commanding authority: Rousseau. Relying (as had Eymar and Maury) on concepts and direct citations from *Émile* and the *Social Contract*, Armand-Gaston Camus rebutted the distinction between individual and corporate property rights.[46] Thouret's argument was simply "false," Camus bluntly asserted, because there was no such thing as natural property. "The right of property" was a "civil right, founded on law, maintained by law." To claim that individual property existed prior to and independent of the law was absurd. "The distinction of mine and thine is devoid of meaning and effect if there is no law which allows me to claim what is mine and obliges me to leave to others what is theirs." The property of both individuals and corps thus rested on the very same foundation, the social contract. Both were guaranteed by the same institution, the law. It followed that "*corps* legitimately admitted into the State are capable of being proprietors for the same reason as citizens. . . . Moral as well as physical persons are capable of all rights which derive from the law." Individuals and corporations were thus "in the same class." If the nation could take the property of *corps*, it could "just as well and for the same reasons" take the property of individuals.

The advocates of expropriation had transformed the debate from a fiscal into a constitutional one, and now Camus had turned it into a clash between

Locke and Rousseau. There was reason to doubt that the Englishman's conception of property right would prevail over that of the Genevan philosopher. Who would attempt to refute Camus's powerful argument—and how? It was one of the most effective pro-expropriation speakers—the oratorically gifted *comte* de Mirabeau—who took up the gauntlet. Mirabeau had already intervened earlier in the debate, but he rose again to the rostrum. It was November 2nd, the day which would bring the debate to a (relatively) decisive climax.

Mirabeau's fundamental move was to distinguish between the primordial property rights created by the social pact itself at the moment of its formation, and those created thereafter by the law. In his earlier intervention, Mirabeau had followed Thouret's Lockean/Turgotian line and identified the crucial distinction as that between the natural properties of individuals and the contingent properties of *corps*. "Citizens have sacred rights," he had argued at that time, rights that "exist independently of [society]." In contrast, *corps* "are formed by society and must disappear the instant they cease to be useful."[47] In this, his second intervention, he abandoned this theoretical framework and instead chose to do battle on the Rousseauian terrain staked out by his opponent, Camus. Using Rousseau's conception of property, Mirabeau formulated an entirely new rationale for distinguishing between individual and corporate property rights.

He began by accepting the basic premise of his opponent, that there was no such thing as a natural right to property. For individuals no less than *corps*, property right was something created and acquired only with the formation of society itself. "The faculty of being a proprietor is a civil effect," he admitted, "and that depends on society."[48] But just because the property rights of both individuals and *corps* were "civil effects" did not mean that they were identical, for there were different ways that society could produce those rights. In the case of individuals, it was the social contract itself that was the source of their property rights. It was at this critical moment of emergence, when each individual sacrificed a part of his potential rights in exchange for a collective guarantee of those he retained, that property rights arose. Individual property was thus "co-existent with the establishment of societies" and required "no distinct laws to ensure" it. Individual property right was "part of the social pact" itself. But the property rights of *corps* were different, since they were "established after the formation of society" and could have "no right co-existent with it." Their proprietary capacity could only be the "work of the legislature and the law." Mirabeau thus invented a new distinction between individual property, formed at the moment of the social contract itself, and the legal property of *corps*, formed thereafter by legislative act. Although neither was "natural" and both shared a "social" origin, they were neither identical nor of equal weight.

Having distinguished between individual property rights (the immediate product of the social contract) and corporate ones (created by law), Mirabeau then established a distinction between two types of legally created, corporate property. Not all *corps* were the same, he noted, for some were non-political while others were political in nature. The first type, the non-political *corps*, was exemplified by the *corps des arts et métiers* (the trade guilds). Once they had been empowered by law to become proprietors, the non-political *corps* enjoyed exactly the same "domain" over their possessions as individuals. They could freely alienate and acquire, dispose of their profits, and transmit their properties. Like individuals, they were "absolute masters" over what they owned. Because of this freedom, Mirabeau placed their properties in the same class as those of individuals; they were "*particulière*," a term that is perhaps more accurately translated in this context as "private" rather than "individual."

This was not the case with the political *corps*. Their property rights were sharply restricted by the public functions for which they—both the *corps* and their properties—were destined. They could neither alienate their properties nor freely dispose of their profits. And, quite obviously in the case of the Church, they could not pass down their properties to their descendants. Given these limitations, political *corps* were neither "masters," "the holders of usufruct," nor even "proprietors." They were simple administrators of "a great national resource" intended solely to support "a public function." Their properties stood in lieu of the "taxes" which the nation would otherwise have to levy on itself to pay for their functions. In contrast to the private properties of both individuals and non-political *corps*, the properties of political *corps* were of a fundamentally different nature because they were entrusted with public functions. Granted instead of taxes and destined exclusively for the "public utility," these properties thus belonged to the nation. Through his typology of non-political and political *corps*, Mirabeau had transcended the categories of Turgot, Locke, and Rousseau to trace a distinction between private and public property.

Having established a theory capable of expropriating the Church while respecting the properties of individuals and trade guilds, Mirabeau then turned to specifics. He identified two categories of public property over which the nation should reassert its rights. The first was, of course, the properties of the Church, the second those of the royal domain. They were "entirely similar" and both belonged to the nation. In recommending legislative action, however, Mirabeau pulled back from advocating open nationalization and sale. Rather, he urged that the properties of the Church and Crown remain in their current hands, but that the nation use them in the traditional way—as "security" to win the public's "confidence" and shore up the nation's "credit." The decree he proposed was even more hesitant. Rather than explicitly proclaim that the nation owned the Church and Crown properties, it merely placed "all ecclesiastical properties at the disposition of the nation"—and then only on condition that it "provide for the costs of worship, the upkeep of ministers, and relief to the poor."

Perhaps because of its non-confrontational, somewhat ambiguous language, his proposal was approved by a comfortable margin.[49] But because of this, it marked something more of a truce than the decisive step it is often taken to have been.

The decree of November 2nd was thus not the end of the story. Nor was the decree passed by the Assembly on 19 December 1789, which stated that the properties of the royal domain "will be sold" along with sufficient ecclesiastical properties to raise the sum of 400 million *livres*.[50] In fact, the decree was only a declaration of intent and established neither a time frame nor a procedure for carrying out the sale. However, both decrees alarmed the defenders of ecclesiastical property who seized upon the fuzzy formulation of the first and the indefiniteness of the second to continue pressing their case both within and without the Assembly. Clergymen and their allies rushed dozens of pamphlets into print during the first months of 1790. Many argued that the November decree's hesitant language proved that the Assembly itself realized that it had had no legal justification for what it had done. "It felt that it could attribute to the nation only *the simple disposition of the properties of the Clergy*," observed *abbé* Arthur Dillon, vicar-general of the wealthy dioceses of Narbonne and Langres. It had "not dared take for itself this precious heritage."[51] Others took heart from the fact that the Assembly's decree had only posed a principle (and a rather ambiguous one at that), but not actually taken over the administration of ecclesiastical properties. "What does it matter if the clergy is reputed to be proprietor or not of its holdings provided that it gets to enjoy them."[52] It was only in April 1790, close on the heels of the defeat of Dom Gerle's motion to declare Catholicism the state religion of France, that the Assembly took its first decisive step to take effective control of the Church's properties. On 14 April 1790 the Assembly passed a decree transferring their administration to the municipalities in which they were located. This, one anonymous pamphleteer observed, was "the decree that really despoiled the clergy" and made their properties truly "national."[53]

The National Domain and Individual Property

What it meant to declare the Church's properties "national" was far from clear because the Assembly had not yet resolved the question of the nation's property rights. The existence of some sort of "national domain" was implied by the move on ecclesiastical property for, as Treilhard had observed in the course of the debate, the nation's property "must reside somewhere."[54] But its content, shape, and powers had not been determined, nor had its relationship to the still-subsisting domain of the Crown. It was only in the course of grappling with this royal institution that the revolutionaries formally created the national domain and defined its composition and scope. This was of capital importance, for it was only by defining the national domain that they fixed the boundaries of the realm of individual property. The creation of the national domain was the necessary complement to the decree of August 11th, the final step in giving institutional expression to the Great Demarcation between power and property.

Before 1789, the royal domain (also called the domain of the Crown or simply the domain) comprised an array of properties ranging from sovereign rights, such as taxation, to physical and incorporeal real estate of all kinds. In addition, properties deemed insusceptible of private ownership, such as rivers, were also included within it. This basic description does not even begin to hint at the legal distinctions jurists made between the different types of domanial property.[55] Some things were domanial by nature, such as real estate, while others, such as property mutation fees (*droit d'amortissement, centième denier,* and *franc-fief*), had only acquired their domanial status through long tradition. There was an ancient domain, supposedly dating from the dawn of the monarchy, and a recent domain, comprised of newer acquisitions. There was also a grand domain, of royal castles and large *seigneuries,* and a petty domain of smaller bits of property. A distinction was even made between those domanial rights derived from royal sovereignty, such as the mutation fees mentioned above, and those which derived from the King's ownership of *seigneuries,* such as baking and milling monopolies. And there were still other incorporeal rights, such as the *droit d'insinuation* and *droit de contrôle* (taxes on different kinds of legal acts) that were actually indirect taxes but were considered domanial simply because the King had decided that they were.[56] This brief description does not exhaust the complexities of the royal domain, but it suffices to illustrate a key point: that it was composed of a bewildering variety of real estate, sovereign rights, feudal prerogatives, and even taxes. All of these were considered property, as the term "domain" indicated. For domain, explained a standard legal dictionary of the time, meant "property of a good that belongs to us, a good whose property we have justly acquired."[57]

Although the royal domain had the status of property, it was property of a unique kind. The King's freedom to dispose of it was severely limited by restrictions intended to create a perfect unity of interest between sovereign and state. The monarch's "public character," observed one domanial jurist, required that "all notions, all attributes of a private person be absolutely effaced." The King must have no other interest than that of his kingdom. To achieve this, it was necessary to prohibit him from "having his own property, some particular domain, by which his personal interest might diverge from that of the Crown."[58] Accordingly, three restrictions on the royal domain had gradually emerged and become fundamental laws of the kingdom. The first of these was the principle of *réunion* (reunification) which held that the royal domain absorbed the prince's personal property when he became King. Although it had usually been observed by previous rulers, the principle of réunion only became law in 1607, when Henri IV was forced to accept that he could not retain his realm of Navarre as a distinct sovereign state, but had to unite it to the Crown of France.[59] The second restriction mandated the reversion of princely apanages—grants detached from the royal domain to support the splendor of the junior members of the royal family—to the royal domain upon either the extinction of the princely line or the accession of the *apanagiste* to the Throne.[60] The third and most important principle, that of the perpetual, irrevocable, and imprescriptible inalienability of the royal domain, completed the triptych of domanial legislation.[61] Like the principle of apanage reversion, it had developed gradually in practice before being formally enshrined in the Edict of Moulins (1566). In the centuries that followed, the monarchy's fiscal straights would lead it to embrace innovations—especially the use of perpetually revocable grants of domanial property (*engagements*) to borrow money—that verged on actual alienations. But in principle the doctrine of inalienability remained intact. It would become both a hindrance and an indispensable legal tool for the National Assembly as it struggled with the fiscal crisis.

Such was the royal domain with which the National Assembly had to contend in 1789: an unwieldy assemblage of real properties, incorporeal dues, and sovereign rights, all strait-jacketed by a complicated jurisprudence designed to guarantee its integrity. The process of first reforming and then nationalizing the royal domain proceeded in fits and starts. Beginning in October 1789 and ending over a year later in November 1790, the debate over the domain contrasted sharply with that over the property of the Church. Whereas the nationalization of Church property had an inexorable quality, the debate over how to deal with the domain was at times hesitant and unsure. So rather than offer here a step-by-step, chronological account of the false starts and wrong turns on the path from a royal to a national domain, the following paragraphs summarize the general flow of the discussion before concluding with a synthetic analysis of the National Assembly's definitive domanial reform.

The question of the royal domain originated not as a move on Crown property, but as a decision to investigate domanial abuses, particularly those perpetrated by corrupt ministers on behalf of their courtier cronies. On 2 October 1789 deputies from eastern France petitioned the Assembly to form a committee to examine abusive practices that were eroding the "antique patrimony of the Crown" and to revoke any "illicit alienations" they discovered.[62] The Assembly assented, naming a Domanial Committee to conduct a comprehensive investigation of potentially fraudulent *engagements*, exchanges, concessions, and other alienations conducted during the Old Regime.[63] Although it had thirty-five members, one for each *généralité*, two leaders emerged: Bertrand Barère, a magistrate from Tarbes who would later serve on the Committee of Public Safety, and René-Urbain-Pierre-Charles-Félix Enjubault de la Roche, a judge from Lemans who would be executed for federalism at the height of the Terror.

Enjubault presented the Committee's first report on 13 November 1789, soon after passage of the decree placing ecclesiastical property at the disposition of the nation.[64] Compared to that measure, Enjubault's report, which consisted of a historical account of the origins and "revolutions" of the royal domain, would, he admitted, seem antiquarian. But it was important to begin with a methodical exposition of the "arid" details of history in order to address two points on which the Assembly's projected sale of the national properties depended: the origin of the royal domain and its alienability. On the first point, Enjubault turned to the accounts of domanial origins provided by Mably, whom he frequently cited, and Dubos, whom he did not. According to these authorities, the victorious Franks "took individually a greater or lesser part" of the conquered territories.[65] Their king, whom Enjubault referred to as the "chief of the nation," naturally took the largest share of all, out of consideration for his eminent function and the responsibilities it entailed, not because of a superior status inherent in his person. He was thus the first among equals and had received his portion of the spoils of conquest as part of the same general distribution as all the other Frankish warriors. Although Enjubault did not state it explicitly, his implication was that the royal domain had been created not by royal authority, but by the will of the nation.

Originally, the royal domain had been alienable. Indeed, it had been alienated with a vengeance. The kings of the first two "races," the Merovingians and Carolingians, had given away almost all their properties in vain attempts to win the support of avaricious courtiers and grandees. These great nobles gradually transformed their gifts of land and power, which had initially been made for life, into fully transmissible property—the familiar story of the origin of fiefs. Another result of the dissipation of the royal domain was to weaken the last monarchs of the Carolingian dynasty. Their decline allowed their palace mayors to gain power until one of them, Hugues Capet, finally overthrew his royal master and put himself on the throne. He was rich, and his personal property was incorporated into the royal domain, largely reconstituting it after the prodigalities of the two previous dynasties. Realizing that "power came from wealth," he put an end to the former profligacy and pursued instead a "system of aggrandizement." In the fourteenth century his descendants gave it a legal basis by issuing edicts forbidding the alienation of domanial goods. These edicts were the forerunners of the principle of the inalienability of the royal domain. This principle was finally elevated to the status of constitutional law by the Edict of Moulins in 1566.

Having thus implied the national origins of the royal domain and asserted its primordial alienability, Enjubault summarized the modern history of the domain, particularly its seventeenth-century transformation into a "financial operation."[66] Kings had found ways of squeezing more and more money out of the domain, despite the 1566 prohibition on alienation. One way was by conceding domanial properties as *engagements*, precarious holdings offered in exchange for large lump sums called *finances*. In theory, the King could recover these concessions at will, simply by reimbursing the capital of their *finances*. In practice, however, the fiscally strapped Crown never did this. On the contrary, it became more and more dependent on the system to shore up its credit. By periodically threatening to revoke these *engagements*, Louis XIV discovered, the Crown could induce the *engagistes* (the holders of these domanial properties) to augment the capital of their *finance*. This essentially amounted to a method of disguised borrowing, in which the product of the *engagement* itself furnished the annual interest on the capital of the loan—the *finance*—the *engagistes* had provided.[67] Enjubault deplored all this, but at least, he noted, the practice of conceding *engagements* for a one-time, lump-sum *finance* had given way after Louis XIV's death to a system whereby *engagements* were granted in exchange for annual rents. These were often expressed in feudal language.

Although Enjubault's legal-historical treatment hinted at the national origins of the royal domain, he shied away from making this claim too directly. In keeping with the Committee's original charge, he concerned himself primarily with establishing the illegality of past domanial alienations in order to prepare for their revocation at some point in the future. Not once did Enjubault explicitly assert the nation's right over Crown property. To the contrary, some of the questions he posed—"Will the domain of the Crown . . . always be inalienable?" and "What is the form of alienations from the Crown domain?"—even appeared to presuppose the continued existence of a distinct royal domain.[68]

Following his report, the Committee set to work elaborating a concrete proposal, a task it must not have pursued very energetically, for it was not heard from again for five months. In the meantime, on 4 January 1790, the National Assembly took a major (albeit implicit) step toward stripping the King of his domain when it voted to establish a civil list.[69] When he finally spoke on domanial matters four months later, in April, Bertrand Barère made explicit the consequences of this decision. "The King, chief or agent of the power delegated by the Constitution," he noted, had thereby become "the first public functionary."[70] As a salaried civil servant, Louis XVI would need no proprietary endowment to support his public duties. The Assembly asked him to state the sum he required for his civil list. But Louis dragged his heels, declining to answer the Assembly's request. It was not until June 1790 that Louis finally complied. During the six-month interval, the Domanial Committee was left in doubt as to the fate of the royal domain. Thus, when Barère and Enjubault appeared before the Assembly on April 10th with the Committee's draft law, their report and that document were fraught with ambiguity, even confusion.[71] They had not yet fully nationalized the royal domain in their minds, and this was reflected in their language.[72]

This is not to say that the draft decree and accompanying report were useless. For the first time, they explicitly overturned the principle of inalienability and identified which elements of the royal domain could be sold off. In fact, had it been adopted and enacted, the decree would have emptied the royal domain by selling off all of its properties. Nonetheless, it would have retained this empty shell under the appellation "domain of the Crown." Neither Barère's report nor the draft law presented by Enjubault explained what purpose the preservation of a hollow royal domain would have served. Fostering further confusion were a jumble of references to the "goods of the domain," "goods of the nation," "domain of the state," and "public domain." None of these terms were defined, situated in relation to one another, or related clearly to the residual "domain of the Crown." For good measure, the draft decree contained carelessly worded provisions stipulating that certain types of properties that found themselves without owners would revert to the "Crown" or even "to the King." All of this raised a short but sharp firestorm of criticism when debate finally began one month later. Taking aim at the puzzling survival of a vestigial royal domain and equally strange absence of a formal statement nationalizing it, Pierre-Louis Roederer got straight to the point. Since the "royal domain is the national domain," he urged that it would be "quite constitutional" and much preferable to decree unambiguously that "the Crown will not have domains from now on."[73] He was seconded by Camus, who warned that, as it presently stood, the measure was "useless and dangerous." "We must not say 'to the Crown,' because the nation has what belongs to the nation." Such wording "smacked of the Old Regime."[74] Chastened, Barère and Enjubault withdrew the draft decree and went back to the drawing board.

When they returned six months later, on 8 November 1790, they came with a thoroughly reworked proposal that embraced the radical transformation toward which the Assembly had been groping since first raising the matter of the royal domain in October 1789. Approved with no recorded opposition, their proposal became the Revolution's definitive piece of domanial legislation. In place of royal domains, Crown domains, and monarchs, it spoke only of the "national" or "public" domain and defined those novel creations. In so doing, the decree also delimited for the first time its "private" antithesis—the sphere of individual property.

Before considering the new domanial order, several observations about the tortuous process which produced it are in order. The invention of the national domain was connected to the nationalization and sale of ecclesiastical property. The expropriation of the Church required a national domain to seize ecclesiastical property, and that domain had to have the explicit legal right to alienate those properties through sale to private individuals. In its relations with the Ecclesiastical Committee (responsible for the expropriation of the Church), the Domanial Committee was always playing catch-up. The major pieces of legislation on the nationalization of ecclesiastical property (on 2 November and

19 December 1789, and on 17 April 1790) were always followed several days later by hasty reports from Barère and Enjubault. Why did the Domanial Committee lag behind? Perhaps domanial matters had low priority, perhaps it was slowed down by the need to coordinate with so many other committees (at one point, it was meeting jointly with six others!), perhaps its members were less attuned to the new ways of thinking, perhaps they were simply not as sharp or energetic as their colleagues. All of these are plausible explanations—but they are only partial. The Domanial Committee's task proved to be more conceptually challenging than anyone had anticipated. It was one thing to investigate fraud in the royal domain, the Committee's initial remit, but quite another to dismantle that institution and construct a national one in its stead. To do this demanded not only the creation of a new category of property, public property, but also the drawing of a clear line between it and the new type of property (which could only be called truly "private" with the delimitation of the national domain itself) brought into existence in August 1789. The resulting distinction between public and private, between the realm of the state and that of society, completed the Great Demarcation begun on the Night of August 4th.

The Alienability and Inalienability of the National Domain

The Committee's first concern had been to reaffirm the principle of inalienability, which was necessary to justify the recovery of abusively alienated portions of the royal domain. This was the main goal of Enjubault's report of 13 November 1789, the Committee's first. But mindful of the likelihood that the nation would begin selling off these same properties in the not-too-distant future, he simultaneously had to elaborate a new rationale of alienability to permit the anticipated sale. To do this, Enjubault rejected the traditional understanding of inalienability as a perpetual entailed inheritance passed down through primogeniture in the royal family and advanced a new justification for the doctrine. This was that the domain had originally belonged to the nation, which had given the kings usufruct of it to enable them to perform their sovereign functions. Because of its national origins, it could not be alienated "without the consent of the nation." Kings were like clergymen in that they were nothing but "simple administrators" in the nation's service. As such, they had no authority to "transmit a property that does not belong to them."[75]

Although the implication that the royal domain was actually a national one was unmistakable, Enjubault did not make it explicit at this point. In fact, it was only with the passage of the definitive domanial decree on 8 November 1790 that the domain formally became national. "The public domain in all its integrity," it read, "belongs to the nation." "Any concession, any dismemberment of the public domain is essentially nul or revocable if done without the agreement of the nation." As for domanial properties that had been alienated without national consent before 1789, the decree continued, "the nation retains . . . the same authority and rights as those over properties which remained in its hands." Neither "lapse of time" nor previous legal judgment could hinder the nation's right to recover these unauthorized (i.e., royal) alienations.[76]

But the principle of inalienability could cut two ways. Although it was necessary to recover the nation's rightful patrimony, a patrimony that had been squandered by prodigal kings and avid courtiers, inalienability posed a very real danger that it might sweep up legitimate individual property by mistake. This dangerous potential was inherent in the established feudal narrative of the origin of property in France. Enjubault explained this for those deputies (if there were any, which is unlikely given that they were almost all lawyers and/or proprietors) who did not already sense the problem. "Casting one's eyes on the origin of the monarchy, we recognize that very many private properties were successively dismembered from the public property. These gradual dismemberments go back to the origin of fiefs."[77] If all property originated directly or indirectly from royal grants of fiefs, then all existing individual properties were dismemberments of the domain—and thus perpetually revocable national property. If this problem were not addressed, the revolutionary assertion of the nullity of all pre-1789 alienations risked creating a monster worse than anything the agents of the royal domain had come up with—a universal national property right.

This was obviously something from which the revolutionaries recoiled. They did not want a state which could invoke the inalienability of the national domain to dispossess individual proprietors at will. To the contrary, they believed that legitimate individual property rights had to be consecrated in law and guaranteed against the vexations of the state. To do this, an impermeable barrier had to be raised between public and private property, between that of the national domain and that of the individual citizen. Where should the boundary be placed? Just as Old Regime jurisprudence had caused the problem, with its narrative of the royal origin of property and theory of the universal *directe*, Old Regime jurisprudence would offer the solution.

This would be to draw the line between individual and domanial property in 1566, the year when the Edict of Moulins definitively established the principle of inalienability. Accordingly, the decree of November 1790 ruled that all properties held by individuals before 1566, even infeudations and even if of proven domanial provenance, would henceforth become incommutable property. It was these pre-1566 domanial alienations that would populate the sphere of private property that this chronological boundary would outline. The corollary was that all properties which had been dismembered from the royal domain after

1566 would be legally reclassified as *engagements* and, as such, become perpetually subject to revocation and reunification to the national domain.[78] Finally, the decree summoned all *engagistes* to present themselves and their titles to the local civil authorities within two months or face punishment. A national domanial inquisition was in the offing. How it unfolded will be addressed in the next chapter.

Before turning to the question of how the revolutionaries tried to square the doctrine of inalienability (indispensable for recovering domanial properties that had passed into individual hands) with the need to alienate those very same properties, it should be noted that not everybody welcomed the Assembly's decision to renounce the nation's rights to pre-1566 domanial dismemberments. One critic urged the revolutionaries to assert the nation's full rights.[79] He argued that the principle of inalienability authorized the nation to "reunite to its domain all heritages and fiefs held immediately from the Crown," as well as "all sub-fiefs and lands" dependent upon them. If the 1566 restriction were lifted, all these properties would return to the domain, and the nation "would once again become proprietor of nineteen-twentieths of the kingdom's land"— just as it had been immediately following the Frankish conquest. Only allodial properties would remain in individual hands. It is hard to know what to make of this domanial model of collectivization. The quasi-feudal means it proposed for realizing the proto-communist vision it evoked brings to mind the radical ex-*feudiste* François-Noël Babeuf, but the pamphlet's provocative rhetoric and ultra-absolutist position makes one think of Simon-Nicolas-Henri Linguet.[80] Could either of these men have been the anonymous pamphlet's author?

Although the revolutionaries rejected this extreme recommendation for a national-domanial takeover of virtually all property, they did recognize that the doctrine of inalienability was a powerful, indeed indispensable, instrument for asserting the nation's rights to property the Crown had squandered. But they also understood that it was a formidable obstacle to the sale of those properties, as well as those once held by the Church. The sale of these former royal and ecclesiastical properties, soon to be known collectively as the *biens nationaux*,[81] required that the Assembly also adopt the opposite doctrine, that of alienability, and uphold both simultaneously. It would use the first to recover dismembered properties and the second to sell them to individuals.

While monarchs may have indulged in it, domanial alienability had no foundation in French public law, which had firmly and repeatedly prohibited it. To repeal this long-established constitutional doctrine seemed to demand some legal justification. But the Assembly had never provided this, never having formally decreed that the domain was alienable. When he rose to present the Domanial Committee's initial, ill-fated draft decree on 10 April 1790, Barère's irritation over this omission was palpable. Was it not advisable, he carped, "to

devote a few instants" to discussing the "annihilation" of a "principle consecrated by the wish of more than ten assemblies of the Estates-General?" The
"simple enunciation of the word 'alienation' in the National Assembly's decree"
was hardly "sufficient to decide positively that the domain is alienable."[82] Barère
ultimately had his way. The Assembly's definitive decree declared that "the
power to alienate, an essential attribute of the right of property, resides . . .
in the nation."[83] The same principle—the national origin of and right to the
domain—would justify both the essential inalienability of domanial dismemberments made without the nation's consent and the absolute alienability of
those effected at its behest.

It was not mere lawyerly scruples that led Barère to insist so strongly upon
formal recognition of the principle of domanial alienability. There were practical reasons to do so—and to do so as soon as possible. With the impending sale
of the *biens nationaux*, it was imperative to "fix public confidence," to reassure
potential purchasers that they would be acquiring truly incommutable possessions.[84] Otherwise, echoed Enjubault, people "would be afraid to acquire a type
of property exposed to eternal investigations."[85] The sale of *biens nationaux*, upon
which the National Assembly now counted to extricate France from its fiscal
straights, demanded the formal revocation of the doctrine of inalienability.

By making this long-overdue pronouncement, the nation would be preparing
itself to alienate its way to fiscal health. In everything having to do with *biens
nationaux*, financial considerations always loomed large. But other considerations of a political-economic and constitutional nature were just as decisive for
the Domanial Committee as it urged the Assembly to proceed with the sale of
the properties that had once constituted the royal domain. It was necessary to
rid the domain of these properties in order to regenerate the monarchy, which,
at this point, was still a part of the new constitutional order. A domain was only
good for "tempting the monarch's generosity" and thereby affording "courtiers
the means of usurping the nation's properties." Moreover, the creation of the
civil list made it unnecessary to reserve domanial properties for the King. Most
important, it would be extremely dangerous to mix power and property in this
way. "To what dangers would the nation be exposed," asked Barère rhetorically,
if it left the monarch

> two sorts of empire: empire over the nation and the empire of his prop-
> erties. No, Messieurs, kings cannot be proprietors for themselves, they
> cannot be proprietors for their family; they cannot dispose of inher-
> ited properties like other citizens. A king is a being raised above all the
> other citizens, with . . . no other interest than the nation's. . . . From the
> moment he accedes to the Throne, all his properties, all his domains . . .
> become national domains. The new constitution . . . no longer permits

public services to be supported with anything other than free and voluntary tributes.[86]

In sum, fiscal, economic, political, and constitutional imperatives intersected to demand a formal declaration of alienability. The very regeneration of the polity depended on it.

The decision to alienate the domain called for a ruling on which of its heterogeneous elements could and should be sold off. The royal domain contained attributes of public power and manifestations of sovereignty whose alienation would run counter to everything the Revolution had accomplished to date. It was thus imperative to ensure that they were not inadvertently included in the mass of goods to be sold. To this end, the Domanial Committee proposed extending the demarcation between property and power to the royal domain itself. Many of its constituent parts, Enjubault noted, were not proprietary at all, but rather expressions of "public power." He specified what these were: a mass of "offices with public function," different rights "emanating more or less directly from sovereignty," and "purely fiscal dues that differ in no way from taxes."[87] As none of these were really domanial, they had never belonged in the royal domain in the first place and now had to be excluded from it formally. They were, in Barère's words, "inalienable and imprescriptible," part of the "natural domain of public power."[88]

Once this distinction had been made and these manifestations of sovereignty reclassified as non-domanial, all that remained was what Enjubault termed in his definitive report the "domain in its proper sense" (*le domaine proprement dit*).[89] This domain, the true domain, consisted solely of "lands and real rights."[90] Although eminently susceptible of becoming individual property and circulating in society, they had been improperly "unified and incorporated to the Crown"—that is, to sovereignty itself—by a "fiction," by a "convention" between the nation and its king. Like any convention, this one could be rescinded by a "contrary convention." This is precisely the action the Domanial Committee urged the Assembly to take. Once set free from the Crown and recovered by their true owner, the nation, the ex-domanial properties would become available for sale to individuals as part of the general mass of *biens nationaux*. As for the King's "feudal dues," they would be alienated through *rachat*, an operation expected to furnish "quite considerable resources."[91]

From these components—inalienability (albeit halted at the great barrier of 1566), alienability, and a domain containing nothing but real estate—the revolutionaries had manufactured a machine to sweep up, digest, and disgorge back into society properties defined as *biens nationaux*. As a swelling torrent of decrees soon made clear, the ultimate goal was to sell these properties to individuals, not to constitute a vast national patrimony. As Enjubault noted in his definitive report of November 8th, "your decrees have opened the national domain to commerce; [its former properties] will henceforth be acquired and possessed under perpetual and incommutable title."[92]

The Assembly's determination to alienate all national properties susceptible of individual ownership raises several questions. Once all these properties had been sold off, what would the national domain look like? What would be left for it to hold? Clearly it would no longer contain dismemberments of sovereignty or subordinate public powers. Nor would it contain real estate that had been alienated before 1566, for this would constitute the realm of individual property. Nor would the national domain hold anything alienated after 1566 for these properties, once recovered for the nation, would be sold off as quickly as possible and thereby change from public into private property. Everything having to do with public power would be redefined as non-domanial and reunited with the undivided sovereignty of the nation. Everything capable of individual ownership would be alienated from the domain. Would there be nothing left at all? Would the national domain be as empty as the ill-conceived, self-contradictory royal domain envisioned by the Committee in April 1790?

No. Something would remain, a new category of property which had begun to take shape in the debates over Church property (especially in Mirabeau's critical second speech) and which finally received a precise definition in the Domanial Committee's decisive legislation of November 8th. This was "public property," defined in opposition to individual property by Enjubault as "everything that cannot belong to anybody."[93] This paradoxical property (because lacking what the term "property" seemed to require—an owner) fell into one of two categories. The first, which he defined as all that "is not susceptible of individual property," comprised streets, city walls, ports, and other things "whose usage was common." It also included the royal forests because their wood was needed for the navy—necessary for national security, on which individual property itself depended.[94] Enjubault defined the second type as goods "without a master"— that is, individual properties that found themselves temporarily without owners because of particular circumstances.[95] In practice, this category was restricted to unclaimed inheritances. To reduce their number to the bare minimum (for property, to the revolutionary way of thinking, abhorred a void no less than nature itself), the definitive decree of November 8th included articles suspending the usual rules of inheritance if a succession risked becoming "vacant." In such cases, any relative from any branch of the deceased's family would be authorized to inherit, regardless of legal restrictions. Even the families of foreigners who died intestate and whose holdings had reverted to the Crown before 1789 by virtue of the domanial right known as the *droit d'aubaine* would now be allowed to inherit.[96] The need to assign owners to properties susceptible of individual ownership was an imperative that trumped even the strictures of lineage, gender, and nationality. Individual property was king, individual property was the priority. That was the driving assumption behind the definitive domanial legislation passed on November 8th. All property needed and tended toward individual ownership. Only if absolutely incapable of achieving that status would property default to the national domain. This masterless property alone would constitute the new category of "public property" to fill the equally novel "public domain" of which the law spoke for the first time.[97]

Conclusion

It is perhaps not surprising that the revolutionary concept of public property was constructed in opposition to private property—that the public or national domain served as a reservoir to which everything insusceptible of individual ownership would be relegated. It is important however to take note of the sharp dichotomy built into and expressed through the New Regime of property, for it illustrates just how far the revolutionaries had come in little more than one year. Before the Revolution there had been neither public nor private property, for all "property" had been both simultaneously. We have already discussed many examples of the "private" ownership of "public" power during the Old Regime. But even things the revolutionaries would classify as incapable of being owned by individuals, such as rivers and roads, had been owned "privately" by lords in virtue of their seigneurial justice. At the same time, what the revolutionaries would reclassify as "private" property was "public" as well—witness, the royal domain and, especially its claims to a universal *directe* which sought to tie all individual properties to the Crown. The imbrication was total. With its domanial law of 8 November 1790, the Revolution completed the Great Demarcation begun in August 1789 by extricating property from the state.

Emptying the Domain

The Problem of Engagements

In domanial matters, it is much easier to establish principles than to
guarantee their execution.
— Enjubault de la Roche, 8 November 1790

The alienation of the properties of the national domain, a process usually referred
to by historians as the sale of the *biens nationaux,* was one of the Revolution's most
complex undertakings. It took hundreds of laws and more than seventy years
before (in 1867) the last national property was finally converted by sale into a
private one. Thanks to a still-growing body of literature already consisting of over
800 titles, the story of the *biens nationaux* is well-known.[1] But historians working
on this subject have overlooked one species of national property: the exchanged
and engaged properties of the former royal domain. This is not a minor oversight. *Échanges* and *engagements* constituted the largest category of former royal
domanial property. Their composite public-private nature tested the Revolution's
new order of property in ways much more fundamental than the sale of the *biens
nationaux* ever did. As pieces of the former royal domain in the hands of particulars, they partook of both the domanial and the individual, the public and the private. This challenged the Great Demarcation the revolutionaries were attempting
to make concrete. Until the *échanges* and *engagements* had been dealt with, private
property could not be truly secure, for the government's right to recover these
domanial alienations would subject all property to a perpetual inquisition. How
the revolutionaries and their successors tried to reconcile the public and the private dimensions of these properties is the subject of this chapter.

Echanges and *Engagements*

Perhaps the most problematic types of property the Revolution had to confront were those which belonged to the royal domain, but had been temporarily

conceded to individuals. These concessions were of two basic types, *échanges* and *engagements. Echanges* were domanial properties transferred to individuals (known as *échangistes*) in exchange for equivalent properties transferred to the domain by those individuals. *Engagements* were domanial properties granted to individuals (known as *engagistes*), in return for either a capital sum or an annual rent. Enshrined by the Edict of Moulins (1566), the principle of the inalienability of the royal domain applied to both *échanges* and *engagements*. This permitted the Crown to recover these types of concessions by restoring to the *échangistes* and *engagistes* the property or capital they had originally furnished. Because they were perpetually revocable, neither *échanges* nor *engagements* were considered true alienations conferring full property rights. Rather, they were temporary grants of usufruct. This separation of use from ownership stood in the way of the revolutionaries' ideal of full property. But it would prove very difficult in practice to find a method of handling these hybrid properties that would simultaneously respect the rights of the public (as expressed through the national domain) and those of the individuals who held them. Nonetheless, remaining faithful to fundamental principles established in 1790, the revolutionaries pursued their effort to convert the *échanges* and *engagements* into full, private property well into the nineteenth century.

Of what did *échanges* and *engagements* consist? *Echanges* were generally very substantial grants, often consisting of titled *seigneuries*, made to powerful nobles and courtiers. On occasion, kings even went so far as to carve out sovereign territories from the royal domain and grant them as *échanges* to particular favorites. The most striking example of this was the Principality of Boisbelle and Henrichmont, a "small power absolutely independent of France" enclaved within the former province of Berry. The Crown had granted it to Sully in the early seventeenth century.[2] *Engagements* were more diverse than *échanges*. They involved a wide spectrum of physical and incorporeal properties. Many consisted of fiefs, complete with feudal dues, property mutation fees, ground rents, and the like. This made the *engagement* contract one of the most common ways individuals in Old Regime France could become feudal lords. In the province of Dauphiné alone, over 170 communities fell under the domanial lordship of *engagiste-seigneurs*.[3] Other *engagements* involved grants of public power in the form of free-standing public functions and seigneurial jurisdiction. Among such *engagements* made in what became the department of Loir-et-Cher, were the "high justice and meat butchering monopoly" of the town of Condé, the mutation fees attached to the Viscounty of Landes, and the banal oven of Saint-Dyé.[4] In Normandy, a province more richly endowed than many others in picturesque *engagements*, one could find among its engaged properties the full panoply of minor judicial offices, from *tabellionages, sergenteries, greffes,* and *notariats* (sergeantries, registration offices, and notarial practices) to the modest position of *procureur-vendeur de meubles* (public auctioneer of judicially-seized goods) in the town of Avranches.[5] Other *engagements* consisted of royal *péages* (rights to collect tolls on roads, bridges, and rivers), legal jurisdictions, and even the right to collect beef tongues from municipal slaughterhouses.[6] In short, any part of the royal domain, with the exception of royal sovereignty itself, could be conceded to an individual as an *engagement*. *Engagements* were one of the many ways individuals in Old Regime France could "own" public authority.

While *échanges* were generally the preserve of the great and powerful, *engagements* were often found in the hands of less illustrious families. Their social diversity was increased by the tendency of the larger *engagistes* to sub-alienate bits of their *engagements* to peasants, often under feudal conditions. This social diversity was further reinforced by the frequent sale of *engagements* which, like *seigneuries*, had become objects of commerce by the eighteenth century (if not earlier). In Dauphiné, sixty-four different *engagements*—seigneuries, riverine property, *péages*, rights of justice, cultivated land, meadows, mountains, and more—were advertised for sale at public auction from 1722 through 1779.[7] Because of the commercial circulation of *engagements*, one commentator observed, it was "a false idea" to consider the actual holders of these properties in 1789 as "the original *engagistes*."[8] Any given *engagement* had potentially passed through many hands since its original concession by the royal domain. In such cases, its domanial origin "had faded and been lost to the memory of man," erased by "exchange, sale, donation, and all the acts that legalize, characterize, and transmit property."[9] Just as owners of feudal properties whose primordial origin had been obscured by repeated sale were shocked to learn in 1793 that they had been abolished, so too were unwitting *engagistes* horrified to discover that they did not really hold full property rights over what was, in some cases, the sole source of their livelihood.

Although in principle quite simple, *engagements* had a complicated legal status. From one perspective, an *engagement* was a credit arrangement, used by the state to borrow money. In lieu of interest payments on a loan, the Crown authorized its creditor (the *engagiste*) to exercise usufruct rights over a particular domanial property and pocket the profits. This conception of the *engagement* had been firmly established in domanial jurisprudence long before the Revolution. "What is an *engagement* contract," wrote the Old Regime legal authority, Auguesseau, "if not a convention by which the king abandons the enjoyment of one of his domains instead of interest payments for the money that has been lent to him, until he can return it to his creditor?"[10] Known as *antichrèse*, this type of credit arrangement assigned the lender usufruct of a piece of real property in lieu of an interest payment. An *engagement* offered the creditor an enhanced degree of security, but did not imply a transfer of full property rights. Consequently, the sale of an engaged property did not require payment of the *droit de lods*. Nor did *engagements* possess the legal status of immovable property.[11] As lawyers, the revolutionary legislators were familiar with these characteristics of the *engagement* and, indeed, made it the basis of their laws on the subject. "There is little difference between a state creditor and the *engagiste* of a domanial property," noted one deputy at the height of the decisive debate over *engagements* in the year VI. "The only [difference] I can find is that one, in lending his money, has been satisfied with a parchment, while the other has wanted more solid collateral."[12]

Engagements also resembled venal offices.[13] Both were credit arrangements used by the Crown to borrow money indirectly. Like venal offices, *engagements* often conveyed public functions. Finally, both *engagements* and venal offices could be revoked at any time by the Crown simply by reimbursing the capital invested in them. Because of the perpetual revocability of their holdings, *engagistes* were subject to fiscal manipulations similar to those aimed at officeholders. To wring additional capital from the *engagistes*, the Crown repeatedly threatened to revoke their *engagements* unless they provided additional sums, generally referred to as a *"supplément de finance."*[14] Although this practice predated the reign of Louis XIV, a veritable "fiscal inquisition" was launched in 1651 and continued into the 1780s.[15] In all, the Crown carried out seventeen such operations between 1601 and 1781.[16] Unlike offices, however, many *engagements* consisted in real estate, rather than public function, and thus possessed a corporeality offices lacked. The fact that many of these landed *engagements* had been held by families for centuries, transmitted across the generations, and improved by their successive holders gave them more substance, moral as well as physical, than offices—which were frequently sold once they had done their ennobling work—could ever enjoy.

Whether from ignorance of their primordial domanial quality, from a feeling of entitlement fostered by long possession, or from a sense that the Crown would never really revoke their holdings, many *engagistes* thought of their holdings as their property. After 1789, the revolutionaries would recognize that, despite the formal legal definition of *engagements* as precarious, perpetually revocable concessions of usufruct over domanial goods, there was some justification for the notion that the *engagistes* had quasi-proprietary rights. It was doubtful, one deputy pondered, that the nation could simply expropriate a "family that had possessed for one, even two centuries, a domanial property that it had fertilized by its care and labor and that it was accustomed to consider as its patrimony."[17] Further complicating matters were the facts that many of the engaged (and exchanged) properties were seigneurial and that many of their beneficiaries were nobles, often of the highest rank. The taint of "aristocracy" this lent to these domanial properties added a further, politically charged dimension to the debates over them. Legally a credit arrangement, but resembling in practice a venal office, real estate, a *seigneurie*, and a courtly pension all at once, the *engagement* was one of the most troublesome types of property with which the revolutionaries had to contend.

The Revolution's First Steps

A denunciation of one of the most notoriously corrupt *échanges* first brought the question of domanial alienations to the attention of the National Assembly. On 2 October 1789, the deputies of Blois, Valenciennes, and Bar-le-Duc issued a joint condemnation of the *échange* of the County of Sancerre that had been authorized a few years earlier by the disgraced minister Calonne in favor of the *comte* d'Espagnac. Branding the *échange* "monstrous," the "scandal of France," and the fruit of a "shameful prostitution," the deputies called on the Assembly to investigate not only the specific case of the *échange* de Sancerre but also to take up the question of domanial alienations in general. The Assembly readily agreed, voting to form a committee (the Domanial Committee) to examine "all *engagements, échanges*, concessions, and alienations whatsoever of the goods and domains of the Crown" and "specially [that] of the *comté* de Sancerre."[18] The Committee rapidly adopted an approach to *échanges* that would prove, in comparison to its legislation on *engagements*, markedly uncontroversial. All *échanges* would be investigated. Those found to have been above-board and equitable were to be confirmed as incommutable private property. Those deemed to have involved the exchange of a more valuable domanial property for an individual property of lesser worth would be annulled. This method for dealing with the *échanges* produced a number of high-profile legal cases involving some of the most prominent courtier dynasties of the Old Regime, Béthune-Sully, Polignac, Rohan-Guémenée, and Condé among others.[19] Although much ink was spilled over these lawsuits (and many lawyers undoubtedly reaped rich rewards from them), their resolution ultimately depended on weighing the respective claims of rival property surveyors. From a constitutional perspective, the *échanges* are thus of secondary interest. Such was not the case with the *engagements*. Their dual nature strained the theoretical rationale of the Revolution's new order of property and power to the breaking point.

The formation of the Domanial Committee in September 1789 encouraged a number of concerned citizens to write to the Assembly. They pointed out the vast financial potential of revoking the alienation of domanial lands and either reselling them as full-fledged private properties or using them to back up issues of paper money.[20] The Committee's two principal speakers, Enjubault and Barère, soon addressed the question of whether such an operation would be a good policy. Their answer was a qualified yes. Clearly, Barère noted, there was financial promise in a general revocation and resale of the domanial alienations. This would provide the nation with "immense resources" since most of the domains had been "conceded as *engagements* for next to nothing, given, or alienated under all sorts of titles at a time when favoritism and intrigue surrounded the Throne." Moreover, the sale of recovered domanial goods as true private property would stimulate "agriculture and commerce" and "increase the number of property-holders [and] make them veritable citizens."[21]

Enjubault struck a more cautious note. Although some revocations and resales would be beneficial, to generalize this operation to all domanial alienations would be too costly for the nation at this juncture. "By revoking all *engagements* by a general law, the State would suddenly find itself [obliged to reimburse] all the finances it had received, which would prodigiously increase the national debt." Moreover, a "rigorous" revocation that made no distinction between ancient and recent *engagements* would have a dangerous effect on "the civil order and inflict an infinity of partial wounds on the sum of the general good." If not bounded and strictly limited by a chronological "floor," such an operation would threaten all property rights in France. "If the National Assembly does not fix a chronological limit beyond which we cannot go, all individual properties will be threatened."[22] As discussed in the previous chapter, this consideration led to the establishment of 1566 as the chronological line between public and private property, between what belonged to the national domain and what would forever be beyond its reach.

Up to this point, the only possibility the Committee had considered for dealing with the *engagements* was compensated revocation and then resale as part of the general mass of *biens nationaux*. This was the course charted by the domanial decree of 1 December 1790 which declared all *engagements* revocable upon reimbursement. It did not, however, actually decree revocation. It merely established the principle of revocability, but postponed any decision about how and when to put it into practice. It was only in the waning days of the Constituent Assembly that the deputies first considered a decree of revocation. This was presented on 22 September 1791, shortly before the close of the Assembly's session. Debate began, but the vote was put off, and the measure passed into oblivion.[23] For its part, the Legislative Assembly did nothing until shortly before the convocation of the National Convention. Then, on 3 September 1792, it approved a slightly modified version of the proposal of 22 September 1791.[24] Probably because the law was passed by a rump assembly in the throes of a momentous political transition, its actual execution seems to have been deferred. Five years later, the Council of 500's commission on domanial legislation reported that it could find "no information on the execution of this law" and speculated that since it had been "passed at the end of the Legislative Assembly's session, the agents of the domanial administration waited for a new law from the Convention."[25] The circulars issued by the direction of the *Régie de l'Enregistrement*, the administration entrusted with domanial affairs, show that executing the law was not a high priority and that local agents, sensing the reluctance of their superiors, did not pursue it with vigor. It was not until 30 November 1792, three months after the law's passage, that it was transmitted to the local bureaux of the *Enregistrement* with instructions for its implementation. This tardy notice was followed by further circulars complaining of the agents' inaction (17 March and 23 May 1793), but also raising questions of interpretation that further delayed the law's execution (21 March 1793).[26] Records from departmental archives show that some small attempts were made to carry out the law, but these were insignificant.[27] One contemporary observer believed that the local agents were too overwhelmed by their other responsibilities to devote much time to searching for and revoking *engagements*.[28] Pierre-Joseph Cambon, the member of the Convention who would be charged with proposing more effective legislation on the *engagements*, saw more sinister reasons for the years of inaction. He pointed to the delaying tactics of the *engagistes* who, "patiently waiting for the counter-revolution they desire," had "paralyzed the execution of the decree."[29] Whatever the reasons may have been, nothing was done.

Revocation in Practice: The Law of 10 Frimaire II/30 November 1793

It was not until the Convention had been in power for more than a year that it turned its attention to the issue of *engagements*. Unlike its approach to feudal abolition, which broke sharply with that of the Constituent Assembly, the Convention respected the domanial principles laid out in 1790. In his 1 Frimaire II/21 November 1793 report recommending the revocation of *engagements*, Cambon emphasized that the conceptual approach he and his colleagues had followed amounted to no more than "the confirmation of the decree of the legislative body which had as its basis the domanial principles of the old government."[30] This was true. Like the Constituent Assembly, the Convention only ever considered dealing with the *engagements* through a revocation. However, the rhetoric in which Cambon couched his proposal was significantly more inflammatory than that used by Enjubault and Barère several years earlier, as were several of its ancillary provisions. The *engagistes* were "vampires, calling themselves nobles ... who monopolized the enjoyment of these properties." No means was too drastic "to recover for the nation the goods that the flattery of a courtier had extorted from a tyrant." The measures of execution Cambon proposed were indeed rigorous. All post-1566 *engagements*, as well as those with revocability clauses, would be cancelled, and the *engagistes* immediately dispossessed without preliminary reimbursement. They would have to turn over their titles to the *Enregistrement* within one month or "be declared suspects and arrested." All third parties, including notaries, would face the same penalties if they failed to disclose relevant information in their possession. The seized properties would be sold as *biens nationaux*. Once dispossessed, *engagistes* could claim reimbursement, but only after a lengthy estimation process. Lawyers, feudal experts, and those who had formerly leased the right to collect feudal dues were explicitly excluded from the role of estimator, which was to be entrusted exclusively to peasants, artisans, and "*sans-culottes*." Once designated, the estimators would deduct not only the cost of degradations from the principal sum to be reimbursed, but also suppressed feudal dues which had formed part of the original *engagement* "in order to punish the possessors with the penalty their vanity deserves for having dared to exploit a privilege contrary to the rights of man." If the estimators found that the last ten years' of revenue produced by the engaged property equaled or exceeded the capital originally invested in it, then the reimbursement claim would be denied on the grounds that the *engagiste* had already received sufficient compensation from the exorbitant profits he had reaped. If granted, reimbursement would come in the form of government debt, which is to say modest annual interest payments in *assignats*. After all, Cambon explained, the *engagistes* were nothing more than "creditors of the Republic" and should be treated no differently than others of their ilk. The only concession the proposal made was to holders of very small alienated domains and those worth less than 10,000 *livres*. Even this exemption, designed to "favor the *sans-culottes*," was contingent upon production of certificates of non-emigration and civic virtue.

The Convention approved Cambon's proposal with no debate on 10 Frimaire II/30 November 1793. The direction of the *Enregistrement* wasted no time ordering its local agents to put it into practice. In the year V, the spokesman for the Council of 500's domanial commission reported that the law had received "an execution more or less active, according to the vigilance or knowledge of the diverse agents of the domain, and possibly also the varying degree to which they favored the *engagistes*." Although some areas of France escaped relatively unscathed, he concluded, "a fairly considerable number of [them] were despoiled."[31] Evidence from departmental archives supports this assessment. In the department of the Aude, fifty-five *engagistes* presented themselves to the authorities to declare their domanial property. In the district of Blois alone, there were ninety-six.[32] In other departments, such as Calvados and Vienne, the registers of *engagistes'* declarations do not appear to have survived, but the voluminous correspondence between the agents of the *Enregistrement* and departmental administrators shows that the law was put into execution there as well.[33] All of this activity took place in the space of a few months, and it seems to have been widespread.

The execution of the law of 10 Frimaire II/30 November 1793 encountered problems. Although it required *engagistes* to present their contracts to departmental authorities, many of these documents had been destroyed as a result of the law of 17 July 1793 mandating the burning of all feudal titles. If they lacked these titles, *engagistes* could neither comply fully with the Frimaire law nor prove the amount of the finance for which their *engagements* had been conceded. Two *engagistes* who found themselves caught in this Catch-22 were the Caussat sisters, Margueritte and Jacquette, of Narbonne. They held a rather typical seigneurial *engagement* in the village of Portel consisting of a "former chateau," pigeon coop, ex-banal oven, and a great diversity of "suppressed feudal dues" in money and kind. As good patriots (or seeking to be seen as such) they had acted with such alacrity to observe the law of 17 July 1793 that, when summoned to deliver to the authorities their *engagement* contract as required by the Frimaire law, they had nothing to offer but a verbal estimate of their concession's finance.[34] This was a common problem. So too was the more serious one which occurred when the authorities erroneously initiated revocation proceedings against pre-1566 *engagements*. These, of course, had been confirmed as incommutable private property by the law of 1 December 1790, but elected officials and agents of the *Enregistrement* sometimes made mistakes. This occurred in the Vienne in Germinal II/March-April 1794, when the householder André Fayolle of Poitiers indignantly declared to the authorities that his property had belonged to him "since time immemorial" and (displaying his knowledge of the relevant legislation) well "before 1566." Many other citizens, whose houses were located in the same part of the city, were summoned in error, suggesting that the confusion stemmed from ambiguities in the records at the authorities' disposition.[35]

In other cases, problems arose as a result of excessive zeal on the part of the authorities. The register kept by the department of the Isère (which recorded the declarations of *engagistes* whose concessions not only lay in that department, but also in the two other departments, the Drôme and the Hautes-Alpes, that had formerly been part of the province of Dauphiné) contains some particularly striking instances.[36] This document shows that the departmental officials not only fielded declarations, but, exceeding their authority, actually sold a number of engaged properties as *biens nationaux*. To make matters worse, they made no move to reimburse the concerned *engagistes'* finances. The victims of these practices complained to Paris that the overzealous local officials had failed to "observe the forms prescribed by the law." They had sold the confiscated *engagements* before "the nation had legally taken possession" and done so without any estimation of their value whatsoever.[37] This incident points to a further problem which would develop into a serious political matter during the Directory: conflict between would-be purchasers of *biens nationaux* and *engagistes* over the right to acquire full property of the *engagements*.

Biens Nationaux and Engagements

The coup of 9 Thermidor II (27 July 1794) loosened the lips of aggrieved *engagistes*. Petitions began to flow into the Thermidorean Convention demanding the redress of particular wrongs, as well as a more favorable legislative regime in general. Petitioners like the medical doctor Jean-Olivier Marmion complained that they had willingly complied with the law and been dispossessed, but had never had their finance reimbursed. Others, like a petitioner who identified himself only as citizen Michalet, had never accepted the legitimacy of the law and demanded their *engagements* back. One petitioner, an 87-year-old widow who had held a house on the Pont Michel in Paris as an *engagement*, complained that her tenant was refusing to pay his rent on the grounds that, according to the law of 10 Frimaire II/30 November 1793, she was no longer the owner of the property. And many claimed that they had only complied with the law out of fear. One of these, citizen Duroure of the department of the Maine-et-Loire, recalled that he had only acceded to his dispossession because it was "the time of the greatest terror," that he had actually been incarcerated, and that even if he had been free, he would not have dared to protest because the "only response [at that time] to similar complaints was the guillotine."[38] Reflecting on the execution of the Frimaire law some years later, one publicist remembered it as "a purely military invasion."[39]

Reacting to the "multitude of complaints" it was receiving, the Thermidorean Convention considered ways of modifying the law to stop "the financial avidity of the pursuits." It first heard a proposal from the joint committee of Domains and Finance presented by Charles-François Delacroix. He proposed requiring that the agents of the *Enregistrement* prove the domaniality of the non-noble lands they believed to be *engagements* since it was only just "to presume that the holder, the cultivator of a property, was its owner." In contrast, such a presumption was inapplicable to "lands held in fief" since "originally all fiefs were only emanations of the public domain."[40] Had Delacroix's recommendation been approved, it would have lifted the 1566 domanial limit for formerly feudal property. Since as much as 95 percent of all real property in France could ultimately be traced to a feudal grant, this would have had a profoundly destabilizing effect on individual property rights in general. For this reason and because the legislators were uncomfortable with reviving legal distinctions between noble and non-noble land, the report was sent back to the committee. The law, intoned one critic of Delacroix's proposal, required that "justice be the same and equal for all." A modified proposal was drafted and presented to the Convention, but it too was returned to the committee.[41] The problem of working out an equitable yet effective system for revoking illegitimate *engagements* while at the same time respecting private property rights was proving to be more of a challenge than

anticipated. To prevent further expropriations while the committee was working on an acceptable solution, the Convention voted on 22 Frimaire III/12
December 1794 to suspend the execution of the law on *engagements* it had
passed just a year earlier.

The committee was slow to recommend new legislation.[42] Indeed, one outraged petitioner complained at the end of the year V, it had "shown "no sign
of life" for nearly two years. Its inaction, he continued, "inflicted considerable
injury on a great number of citizens by depriving them of the revenue of their
properties" which had been confiscated under the law of 10 Frimaire II.[43] To
make matters worse, the suspension itself had unanticipated consequences and
raised unforeseen questions. To begin with, local officials interpreted the suspension's meaning differently from department to department. Some understood it as requiring that confiscated *engagements* be returned to their *engagistes*.
Others, however, did not. In many areas, expectant *engagistes* were astonished to
learn that the suspension law, "not having revoked, but merely frozen the execution of that of 10 Frimaire," maintained all confiscations that had already taken
place until further action by the legislature.[44] In departments that followed this
line, the suspension had the perverse effect of maintaining the dispossession of
those *engagistes* who had complied with the law of 10 Frimaire II/30 November
1793 while allowing those who had evaded the obligatory declaration to retain
their *engagements*. Law-abiding *engagistes* did not hesitate to point this out in
fiery petitions to the legislature. "The *engagistes* who had not been dispossessed
are the only ones who have benefited from the suspension," fulminated Nicolas
Vimar, an aggrieved *engagiste* who would be elected by the Seine-Inférieure to
the Council of Elders the following year and there continue his campaign on
behalf of dispossessed *engagistes*.[45] One embittered petitioner who called himself as a "former property-owner" described an even more desperate situation
in which he and other *engagistes* found themselves. He had been stripped of his
land four years earlier by the Frimaire law, but had received neither reimbursement of nor interest payments on the capital he had originally paid for it.[46] This
reveals the second perverse effect of the suspension: as well as maintaining the
dispossessions which had already been effected, it halted the already-glacial
reimbursement process. Given the catastrophic discredit of the Republic's paper
money, perhaps this was a blessing in disguise for the *engagistes*.

The problems created by the suspension were compounded by the law of 28
Ventôse IV/18 March 1796 reactivating the sale of *biens nationaux* (which had
been suspended at the height of hyperinflation). We have already witnessed the
troubles the authorities faced when trying to walk the line (of 1566) between
private property and *engagements*. The re-starting of the sale of *biens nationaux*
unintentionally inflamed a new conflict—between citizens who wanted to purchase *engagements* as *biens nationaux* and *engagistes* who wanted to preserve what

they felt to be their rightful property. Tensions between the purchasers and *engagistes* were not new. Indeed, they had arisen as soon as the first sales of *biens nationaux* had begun in 1791 and occasionally swept up *engagements*, whose fate had not yet been decided by the Assembly, into the palette of properties on offer.[47] But these early troubles had been localized and infrequent. The law of 28 Ventôse IV/18 March 1796 spread these conflicts across France.

Although the law did not authorize the sale of confiscated *engagements* as *biens nationaux*, neither did the law exempt them from sale. Its silence bred ambiguity. Local administrators were left to rely on their own interpretations. Some judged that the suspension protected confiscated *engagements* from sale as *biens nationaux*. In many cases this spared *engagistes* the additional hardship of seeing their confiscated *engagements* sold at auction to third parties. But in some cases, it worked against the *engagistes*. One of these was the long-suffering Vimar who, in his desperation to recover his engaged property had actually welcomed the 28 Ventôse IV law as an opportunity to acquire the full property of it—by buying it as a *bien national*! Although he had begun the purchase process and actually paid for the property, a late-arriving ministerial instruction put a halt to these proceedings. As a result, he wrote in the year V, he now found himself deprived of the finance he had originally paid for his *engagement*, the sum he had paid to buy it as a *bien national*, and the property itself—all of which were now "in the hands of the Republic."[48]

Unlike Vimar, most *engagistes* viewed the law of 28 Ventôse IV/18 March 1796 not as an opportunity to recover their *engagements*, but rather as an invitation to predatory speculators who coveted their properties. In Thermidor IV/July-August 1796 the widow Tingry of Caen wrote that her *engagement* had been confiscated two years ago without any indemnity and, "what is even more unjust" had been put up for auction and "was on the point of being sold."[49] Another warned that the nation's seizure of the engaged properties "exposes them to the cupidity of that multitude of speculators who see [them] as prey."[50] Still another noted that, in the state of "incertitude in which [we] are left by the Convention and Legislative Body," a struggle had developed between the *engagistes* and the buyers of *biens nationaux*, whom he described as "avid speculators." However, he continued, ultimate responsibility for the mess lay with the successive revolutionary legislatures, for the question of *engagements* had "been made litigious by the laws themselves."[51] While the basic principles established by Barère and Enjubault were sound and would stand the test of time, the decrees which attempted to put those principles into action were fatally flawed. And now they had run head-on into the juggernaut of revolutionary domanial policy—the sale of the *biens nationaux*.

The Directorial legislatures found themselves caught between *engagistes* who demanded a specific law allowing them to recover their confiscated properties and would-be-purchasers of *biens nationaux* who wanted to assimilate those same properties to the general mass of national properties on offer. These were the basic positions in a clash between two distinct categories of property-holder who had been set on a collision course by poorly thought out and ambiguously worded laws.

The legislatures considered several initial options for resolving the conflict, but ultimately rejected them all. One of these was described by the Council of 500's commission on domains as "co-property." It would have permitted the sale of a confiscated *engagement* as a *bien national*, but would have left the *engagiste* in possession of the usufruct of that same property. As this would respect the terms of the original *engagement*, the state would not have to reimburse the *engagiste* his finance. This was the idea's principal advantage.[52] But however much money this plan would have saved, it would have generated an unacceptable level of legal confusion and conflict between purchaser, *engagiste*, and the state. And it worked at cross-purposes to the Revolution's aim of replacing the regime of divided property rights with full, independent ownership. It was thus rapidly discarded.

A more promising idea was to assimilate confiscated *engagements* to *biens nationaux* and offer them for public sale, but with a provision giving their former *engagistes* the first chance to purchase them.[53] A draft law to this effect was passed on 20 Frimaire V/10 December 1796 and submitted to the Council of Elders for approval. Almost immediately, outraged petitioners wrote to the Elders, demanding that it refuse "to grant a new privilege" to the *engagistes*, almost all of whom were from "formerly privileged families who had enriched them-selves exclusively from the debris of the public fortune."[54] They need not have worried. After a careful examination, the Elders rejected the measure as highly ambiguous and possibly unconstitutional. If meant to give formal preference to the *engagistes*, it amounted to "a grace, a particular favor," which was "repugnant to the Constitution, according to which the law must be equal for all."[55] If not intended to grant a privilege to the former *engagistes*, then the proposed law was superfluous. The general legislation on the sale of *biens nationaux* would suffice.

Back to the Past? The Law of 14 Ventôse VII/4 March 1799

The rejection of the law by the Elders effectively ended the effort to address the issue of dispossessed *engagistes* through the general legislation on the sale of *biens nationaux*. Debate now shifted to the question of giving the *engagistes* special means of recovering their engagements. Many members of the legisla-ture and the public felt that the creation of distinct laws for the *engagistes* would amount to the resurrection of privilege for a class they already viewed in a very dim light. According to one vehement deputy, the *engagistes* were

> men who, for the most part, regret the *ancien régime* which showered them with favors and riches, who have armed their children against the homeland, who detest your government, for whom equality is a torture, who have always been the leaders of conspiracies against the Republic.[56]

A similar rhetoric of social hatred characterized most of the speeches, petitions, and pamphlets against the *engagistes* and tended to obscure the substantive arguments against giving them preference. These were straightforward. To single out the *engagistes* for special treatment would violate the principle of legal equality, and the cost of treating them favorably would have to be borne by the rest of the population. Such treatment was unwarranted since the *engagistes* had never had true property rights over their holdings. Finally, the suspension of the year III/1794-95 had not nullified the laws on revocability (1 December 1790) and actual revocation (3 September 1792). These remained in force. Far from deserving preference, the *engagistes* were "in the least favorable position of all the creditors of the State."[57]

As we have already seen, the *engagistes* opposed these attacks with counterblasts of their own. They also employed inflammatory social rhetoric. Their denouncers, they claimed, were nothing but "merchants of *biens nationaux*" or "vampires of the public fortune."[58] Innocent victims of these "avid purchasers," the *engagistes* deserved special consideration. It was simply "equitable and wise" to "prefer the current possessors to new purchasers." This would not only be "gentler and more efficient than dispossession and resale at auction" but also offer the government a means of raising badly needed money by offering the *engagistes* "irrevocable property" of their holdings "in return for a *supplément de finance*."[59] This suggestion would have meant abandoning the policy of revocation all revolutionary governments had pursued since 1789 and replacing it with a new approach reminiscent of the fiscal manipulations of the Old Regime. Yet, this is precisely how the vexing question of *engagements* was finally resolved.

What turned out to be the definitive legislative debate over the question of how to convert the *engagements* into incommutable private property began at the end of the year VI/1797-98.[60] Despite the continuing strength of the sentiment against preference for the *engagistes*, a majority emerged in both chambers in favor of passing a particular law on their behalf, to enable them to acquire full property of their engaged holdings. The central question then became how this ought to be done. Most of the deputies agreed that the simplest method for transforming *engagistes* into property-holders was that tried-and-true technique of the monarchy, the *supplément de finance*. In exchange for an additional pay-ment on top of their original finance, the *engagistes* would receive the full prop-erty of their holdings. It was first proposed that the amount of this *supplément de finance* be set at one-fifth of the estimated value of the property in question. This was bitterly opposed by deputies who, having earlier sought unsuccessfully to deal with the issue of the engaged properties through the general legislation on *biens nationaux*, now strove to ensure that the *engagistes* pay as much as pur-chasers of national properties. The law of 28 Ventôse IV/18 March 1796 had required these purchasers to pay one-fourth of the price of their acquisition in metallic currency. It would be an "unheard of privilege" to treat "the current holders [of *engagements*] better than the purchasers [of *biens nationaux*]."[61] This notion prevailed, and it was decided to make the provisions for the *engagistes' supplément de finance* conform as closely as possible to the mode of paying for *biens nationaux*.

After further debate in the Council of Elders, which returned the resolution to the Council of 500 for technical modifications, the proposal was finally adopted by the upper chamber on 14 Ventôse VII/4 March 1799.[62] This law established the definitive framework for liquidating the remnants of the royal domain which still remained in private hands. It remained in force and was executed in fits and starts well into the nineteenth century. What did it say? First, it gave the status of full private property to small, uncultivated holdings which had been alien-ated by the Crown to encourage agriculture. Second, it set aside the question of certain especially problematic domanial issues, such as colonial and riverine property, for distinct legislation.[63] Third, it established a coherent mechanism for *engagistes* to convert their holdings into private property. All *engagistes* (and *échangistes* whose *échanges* had been revoked) were directed to declare their holdings to the *Enregistrement* within one month of the law's publication. Those who failed to do so would face confiscation.[64] Following an estimation, *engagistes* and *échangistes* could acquire full property rights by paying in metallic currency a *supplément de finance* equivalent to one-fourth of the estimated value. When necessary, *engagistes* were authorized to sell part of their holdings to help them raise these sums. If, however, any *engagistes* preferred reimbursement of their original finance, it would be returned to them, but in the form of government obligations, "in the same manner as with other state creditors."[65]

Although the law of 14 Ventôse VII/4 March 1799 would prove durable, it was not beyond reproach. Some critics sneered that it reeked of absolutist fiscal manipulation. It was variously branded "nothing but a *supplément de finance*," a "purely financial idea," and a mere "addition of finance."[66] Far from denying this, its defenders admitted the similarity but also pointed out the fundamental dif-ference between the new law and its absolutist precedents.

It has been said that the measure is too fiscal, that even the kings themselves never dared to demand from the [*engagistes*] one quarter of the
estimated value of their domains. ... Doubtless ... but in subjecting
the *engagistes* to a finance, did the kings ever transfer to them an incommutable property? ... In contrast, by the resolution, the status of the
engagiste is entirely changed. From a simple holder, he becomes a property owner with no further finance, no future revocation to fear. He will
henceforth own a truly patrimonial property.[67]

The measure's defenders were right. The law of 14 Ventôse VII/4 March 1799
certainly promised to squeeze additional money from the current *engagistes* in a
manner similar to the Old Regime's *supplément de finance*. But this was not the
primary purpose of the law. Rather, the supplemental payment was intended to
approximate the legal effect of a sale, thereby transforming the *engagistes'* title
from a revocable domanial holding into one of property.

Execution of the Law of 14 Ventôse VII/4 March 1799

Although the mass of *engagements* was of little value relative to the other categories of *biens nationaux*, their conversion into full property was an essential
element in the demarcation between a sovereign state and a society of independent, property-owning citizens. Implementation of the law began soon after its
passage, but the results fell short of the decisive intentions which produced it.
First, the Brumaire coup temporarily interrupted operations. Then, less than
three months after having come to power, the consular government proposed a
three-month extension to the deadline imposed on the *engagistes* by the law of 14
Ventôse VII/4 March 1799. With evident distaste, but still greater resignation,
Louis Portiez, the tribune charged with presenting a recommendation on the
proposal reluctantly asked his colleagues to approve it. "By some strange fatal-
ity," he sighed, "the citizens least concerned with executing the laws on finances
[the *engagistes*] have been treated most favorably" during the Revolution. He
pointed out that this new extension was merely the latest in a long line of *de
facto* extensions stretching back to the original law of 1 December 1790. The
engagistes had already been given more than a decade's reprieve. It was only out
of consideration for the political and economic turmoil of those years, as well
as the government's desperate need for metallic currency, that the commission
called upon the legislature to approve the proposal.[68] It followed Portiez's recommendation and formally accorded the delay. Although it specified that "once

this delay has expired, those who have not taken advantage of it will be irre-vocably dispossessed," this proved to be yet another idle threat. *Engagistes* who failed to comply retained their properties without being troubled well into the Restoration—and sometimes beyond.[69]

The records of the local agents of the *Enregistrement* reveal an initial burst of activity. In the Loir-et-Cher, for instance, forty-three *engagistes* who had hith-erto escaped scrutiny came forward between Germinal VII/March-April 1799 and Floréal VIII/April-May 1800 to pay their *suppléments de finance* and acquire full title to their *engagements*.[70] But as Napoleon's consulate moved into its sec-ond year and the various delays quietly expired, these efforts dwindled, in part because the *Enregistrement* now began to prioritize a new activity, the quest for previously overlooked "national rents." But the hunt for unresolved *engagements* continued, albeit at a slower pace.

The papers of an Inspector of Domains named Lezourmel offer a rare glimpse into these operations. Although the archives of the Ministry of Finances, includ-ing those of the *Enregistrement,* were consumed by fire during the Paris Commune, Lezourmel's work journal for the period from 1805 through 1811 somehow sur-vived. It contains a running account of Lezourmel's efforts to discover lost *engage-ments* and other national properties in the archives of the Paris region. It provides a concrete illustration of what the government's campaign to root out the *engage-ments* entailed. Here is what Lezourmel recorded in his journal for the first two weeks of April 1807.[71] He began by looking for outstanding debts owed to the princely house of Bourbon-Penthièvre but which had been seized by the nation when the family emigrated. In this endeavor, he combed through twenty-five boxes of papers, but found only a 93-*livre* obligation. He also looked for debts that had been owed to the nationalized Abbey of Saint-Germain des Près, but found nothing in the twenty-one boxes he consulted in its archive. He had more luck searching for *engagements*. In the papers of the domanial council of the dukes of Lorraine, he discovered fourteen post-1566 alienations, most in the department of the Meurthe. He also spent some time in the Imperial (now National) Archives where he found another unresolved *engagement* contract, this one for a formerly banal oven in Sedan. And so it slowly went, week after week, month after month.

To accelerate the execution of the law of 14 Ventôse VII/4 March 1799, the imperial government decided in 1806 to authorize private individuals to join the search for lost titles.[72] They would receive as their reward one-quarter of the value of the properties they brought to the administration's attention. The law also allowed them to take legal action on their own initiative against delinquent *engagistes*. After several years, however, the government began to question the wisdom of this policy. Councilor-of-State Joseph Fiévée believed that its desta-bilizing effect on legitimate property was not worth the small amount of extra revenue it generated.

Who can be certain that his property had not been part of the public domain in the distant past? And even though there are protective laws . . . it is worrying to be exposed perpetually to the baseless schemes of a greedy man?[73]

In 1809 the imperial government acted. Although it continued to permit private individuals to try to identify non-compliant *engagistes* and forgotten *engagements*, it now restricted the scope of their action to informing the Ministry of Finances in exchange for a reward. In 1812 the government further reinforced the restrictions on independent investigators after one particularly ambitious individual, a *sieur* Sevestre, sought to claim that the entire county of Champagne had been granted as an *engagement* with an explicit reversion clause in 1334 to the duchess of Burgundy. Armed with a veritable archive of ancient charters, he demanded the right to one-fourth of the value of approximately 20,000 arpents of land. Ultimately referred to the Council of State, Sevestre's pretention was angrily and decisively struck down as a threat to all private property.[74]

The national domanial administration was naturally hostile to private contractors encroaching on its functions. But it was not much more successful than they were at tracking down lost *engagements*. During the twenty-year period from 1800 to 1820, it collected only 5 million francs from *engagistes* paying their one-fourth *supplément de finance*. Other *engagistes* elected to receive the reimbursement of their capital and relinquish their *engagements*. Their properties were sold by the domanial administration as *biens nationaux*, raising an additional 24 million francs.[75] From a financial perspective, the fiscal benefits of these operations were modest. It is not clear why. Perhaps there had not been very much engaged property left. But there may have been another factor at work. The personnel charged with looking for lost *engagements* were also responsible for administering some of the state's most important indirect taxes, notably the stamp tax and the property-mutation fee (the *droit d'enregistrement*). Together, these and the other taxes for which the domanial personnel were responsible accounted for as much as 40 percent of total national revenues and thus represented a more pressing concern than looking for lost titles to scattered parcels of property.[76] There is abundant evidence that the personnel of the *Enregistrement* were lax in their execution of the law of 14 Ventôse VII/4 March 1799. Some *engagistes* who tried to comply with the law were actually prevented from doing so by the *Enregistrement's* lack of interest or preoccupation with its other business. For example, the *dame* de Pons, holder of the former engaged fief of Tullins, made her declaration a few months after the law's passage and named an expert to estimate its value in conjunction with an expert to be named by the domanial administration. Nearly ten years passed, however, before the administration appointed its expert. An estimate was drawn up, but the *dame* de Pons contested it. The local prefect was supposed to judge contestations of this sort, but he also took his time. For the next two decades, nothing more was heard of the matter. It was only in 1843 or 1844 that the business was finally settled.[77]

The efforts of the domanial administration and its contractors thus had little financial impact. However, the national campaign to discover lost domanial titles was a crucial episode in the history of the formation of modern archives. At the time, it was one of the greatest archival research projects the world had ever seen. It mobilized the efforts of hundreds of researchers, both government functionaries and private contractors. Many of these men had been employed before 1789 in the subaltern ranks of the legal profession, or as feudal or domanial agents, but had been put out of work by the revolutionary reforms. With the nationalization of ecclesiastical property and the royal domain, the sale of *biens nationaux,* and the pursuit of *engagements,* these men soon found themselves back at work, often liquidating the very properties that they had managed during the Old Regime. To dismantle the Old Regime, the Revolution had to rely on the expertise of the very men who had made it work. In their efforts to discover lost *engagements,* they used many of the methods that still characterize modern historical research: reading in the secondary literature, archival digging, consulting colleagues, and oral history. Here is how one lower-level domanial agent described his efforts to discover information on a feudal *engagement* near Narbonne, the Barony of Saint-Sulpice et Villelongue. "I began by combing through collections in public archives, notably the town hall and sub-prefecture, consulted numerous octogenarians, [as well as] M. Lafont, *antiquaire* [an erudite interested in history], possessor of essential notes on the ancient and modern history of Gaulish Narbonne, [and finally] lawyers, notaries, and other men of law." He finished his account by describing the help he received from his colleagues in "Ginestas, Lezignan, and Sigean."[78]

Unlike most archival research today, the search for domanial titles was not a solitary exercise. Rather, it was a collective endeavor that brought into existence networks of correspondence linking France's many peripheries to the center, as well as local investigators laterally to their colleagues in other parts of the country. Perhaps the most important consequence of these connections was to form an overall picture of the French archival landscape from the fragmented repositories and caches left behind after the destruction of the Old Regime. Although the National Archives of France had been established in 1790 (in large part to collect the titles to national properties), its character was markedly Parisian. It was the lattice of communication and community of knowledge spawned by the domanial investigations that really founded a truly national archival regime in France.

An End at Last?: The Great Push of 1828-1829

This, however, was not the chief aim of the French government. Rather, it was to end the doubt and uncertainty that continued to dog the status of the *engagements* many decades after the law of 14 Ventôse VII/4 March 1799 had supposedly settled the matter. To transform these insecure, hybrid holdings into full property, the government proposed that all *engagements* not facing pending action by the *Enregistrement* be declared incommutable properties on 1 January 1821. Introducing the law to the Chamber of Deputies on 4 January 1820, the Minister of Finances, Antoine Roy, explained that its goal was the "complete and definitive liberation" of the *engagistes*. It would free their properties from "all the uncertainties that diminish their value, hinder the business affairs of their owners, and prevent improvements."[79] To preempt charges that the law would grant a special favor to the *engagistes*, Roy explained that its intention was to benefit society as a whole. It would "assure the stability of all properties, the tranquility of society, and that of all families" (166). Not to fix a term to the *Enregistrement's* investigations would leave the state with what one deputy termed "a weapon of constant dispossession" (181). Justice and social stability demanded an end to the *Enregistrement's* inquisition, for many of its victims were small-holders who had not known of the domanial nature of their properties when they had purchased them (25). Nor were there pressing financial reasons to perpetuate the search for engaged properties. After decades of investigation, "the agents of the fisc ... who have a hundred eyes and arms ... are no longer finding gold in the dust of the archives" (181). And given the seventeen revocations and *suppléments de finance* that had taken place since 1600, the *engagistes* had effectively paid for their acquisitions many times over by now (230). In any event, pointed out François Barbé-Marbois in his report on the matter to the Chamber of Peers, "the public revenue generated from mutations [essentially the stamp tax and *droit d'enregistrement*], will more than make up for the feeble debris" of ancient and half-forgotten domanial *engagements* (343). If approved and carried out, the measure would ensure that all that remained after 1820 would be "patrimonial properties governed by uniform laws" (175). This had been the goal all along— to convert the precarious *engagements* into full property without despoiling the public domain.

There was not a single legislator who did not hope for "the moment when all types of properties, equally free from all fears for the future, could circulate with equal confidence" (135). But a number of them had criticisms of the proposal. Several expressed concern that it was unjust, for it effectively gave away "an infinity of properties to their holders" and "rewarded them for having disobeyed the laws" (153). Worse, the proposal actually seemed to encourage malfeasance.

In effect, it seemed to be saying to dishonest *engagistes* "resist the law, hide, receive stolen goods, corrupt [others], and perhaps you will hold out until the moment . . . of liberation" (176). Other critics wondered if the domanial well had truly run dry. A new round of investigations, one deputy claimed, should "bring into the treasury considerable capital that will make up part of the deficit" (153).[80]

The opponents of the proposal did not agree on an alternative to the government's plan. Some, who viewed it as yet another attempt to favor the *engagistes* at the expense of everybody else, wanted to maintain the existing laws and not place a time limit on the domanial investigations. Others, more concerned with making sure that the *Enregistrement* had enough time to finish pursuing the remaining handful of recalcitrant *engagistes*, sought only an extension of the deadline and proposed amendments to that effect. The government accepted a time extension and, thus modified, the measure passed into law on 12 March 1820. Its principal provision was to establish a point in time, specifically thirty years after the law of 14 Ventôse VII/4 March 1799 had gone into effect, as a deadline beyond which the *Enregistrement* could not initiate investigations of suspected *engagements*. After that point, all such holdings not currently the subject of domanial legal proceedings would be declared full-fledged private property. This law promised a definitive end to the ancient principle of domanial inalienability which had hung until then like a "sword of Damocles" over all property in France (177).

Since the law of Ventôse VII had been promulgated in most departments in February 1799, the new measure established a nine-year period in which the *Enregistrement* could launch new investigations. It showed very little sign of activity during most of this time, which one observer described as "eight years of silence and inaction."[81] But in early 1829, shortly before the deadline was to expire, the local bureaux of the *Enregistrement* in over fifty departments burst into activity. They issued summonses (reportedly 50,000) to holders of suspected domanial properties, essentially with the intention of preserving the right to launch future investigations.[82] As the Minister of Finances stated in his circular of 8 December 1828, the fundamental aim of the operation was to "protect entirely the interests of the state before the rapidly approaching expiration of the delay."[83] Domanial agents in the localities followed this instruction to the letter, even to the point of instituting claims to *engagements* that were obviously seigneurial and, as such, had been abolished in the early 1790s.[84] One can only wonder what a puzzled ex-*engagiste* of a *seigneurie*, public office, or privilege must have thought upon receiving such a summons, but there can be no doubt about the intention of the domanial administration: to keep all of its options open.

Targeting every *engagement* that had ever existed and figured in the Enregistrement's records, the 1828-1829 domanial inquisition was sweeping and indiscriminate. In some instances, this prompted cowed *engagistes* to pay up. Not infrequently, however, they attempted to avoid doing so by various means. Many claimed exemption on the grounds that their engaged properties had originally been conceded as small, uncultivated plots.[85] Some argued that the persecution they had faced during the Terror—the sequestration of property, the burning of papers, imprisonment, and forced emigration—made it necessary for them to have an even longer delay.[86] In contrast, others claimed that their earlier compliance with the law of 10 Frimaire II/30 November 1793 excused them from having to comply with that of 14 Ventôse VII/4 March 1799 as well.[87] In at least one case, an *engagiste* who had initially offered to pay the one-fourth *supplément de finance* now sought to retract his offer and receive reimbursement.[88] Others contested the domanial quality of their possessions, leading in one instance to a lawsuit that was not resolved until 1877.[89]

The *engagistes* also resisted the *Enregistrement*'s offensive by appealing to their legislators in Paris. By late May 1829, so many petitions from aggrieved *engagistes* had arrived that the Chamber of Deputies again turned its attention to their plight. The *Enregistrement*'s eleventh-hour offensive, noted the *comte* Pierre-Antoine-Noël-Bruno de Daru, the deputy charged with reporting on the petitions, threatened to submerge the nation in chaos.[90] The veritable "deluge" or "storm"[91] of summonses unleashed by the *Enregistrement* risked provoking a cascade of lawsuits in a horrific chain reaction. The current holders of *engagements* were beginning to pursue legal action against the people from whom they had purchased their properties. These, in turn, were filing countersuits. Moreover, since the properties in question had been divided in inheritance settlements, transmitted by marriage contracts, and used as security for loans, the result was that "a multitude of citizens who have never contracted with the royal domain now found themselves having to defend themselves against its demands." If action were not taken to halt the madness, the result would be "a general conflagration," "a multitude of lawsuits" which would "cast sterility upon a mass of properties," "revoke all past successions," and "make impossible all future inheritance arrangements." Given all this, Daru warned, the 50,000 summonses issued by the *Enregistrement* could easily generate 500,000 lawsuits. The situation was so potentially catastrophic that even local agents of the *Enregistrement* were taking steps of their own to "mitigate" the damage.[92] Clearly legislative intervention was necessary. To put an end to the disorders, Daru proposed asking the King to propose a law declaring null and void all investigations begun by the *Enregistrement* subsequent to the publication of the law of 12 March 1820. This proposal was approved on 25 July 1829 and transmitted to the Chamber of Peers. But the upper house dithered until the Revolution of July 1830 swept it away.

The *Enregistrement* continued sporadically to look for outstanding *engagements* and pressure their possessors to comply with the law of Ventôse VII. One finds in the departmental archives instances of the *Enregistrement* pursuing delinquent *engagistes* through the middle of the nineteenth century—and occasionally beyond.[93] The process of turning domanial into private property was at least as lengthy and complicated as the abolition of the tenurial property regime. And, as will become clear in the following section and the next chapter, the two processes were interconnected.

When the Domanial Met the Feudal

Many *engagements* consisted of feudal material. Others had been conceded by the royal domain under feudal conditions. One might think that the anti-feudal legislation of 1789-93 would have abolished these feudally tinged *engagements* and *engagement* rents. But that was not what happened. In fact, legal rulings would perpetuate feudalism in the *engagements* well into the nineteenth century.

Many *engagements*, particularly those arranged after the end of Louis XIV's reign, had been conceded not for a capital sum, but rather in exchange for payment of a perpetual rent or due. These rents were often characterized as feudal by the *engagement* contracts which established them. A question thus arose: Did *engagistes* have to keep paying these rents to the nation, as the price and condition of the now-national properties they had received, or had these rents been suppressed by the Revolution's laws on feudal abolition? The legal squabbles over this question would ultimately produce one of the most perverse features of the post-1789 attempt to nationalize and alienate the former royal domain—the effective survival of feudal dues.

As long as the status of the *engagements* remained undecided, the revolutionaries had not had to confront the problem of the feudal *engagement* rents. But as the law of 14 Ventôse VII/4 March 1799 began to be executed, conflicts over this issue emerged between *engagistes* whose *engagements* had been conceded for feudal rents and the domanial administration. The *engagistes* argued that, since the National Convention's decree of 17 July 1793 had suppressed all dues stipulated in contracts containing feudal terminology, they owed nothing subsequent to that date. Against this, the domanial administration claimed that the laws on feudal abolition applied only to private property, but not to *engagements* because they were neither private nor property, but rather perpetually revocable dismemberments of the domain. Until the *engagistes* paid their one-quarter *supplément* and acquired the incommutable property of their concession, they had to keep paying their feudal *engagement* rents. This also meant paying accumulated arrears for the 1790s and sometimes earlier. In some cases these arrears were substantial.

The first authority to weigh in was the Minister of Finance, who had overall responsibility for the execution of the Ventôse law. His decision of 15 Nivôse

IX/5 January 1801, which ruled that feudal *engagement* rents had been abolished by the law of 17 July 1793, was a victory for the *engagistes*. But a mere ministerial decision could hardly be expected to settle the matter, and indeed it did not. Numerous cases were heard in provincial courts until, on 10 Brumaire XII/ 2 November 1803, an appeal reached the *Cour de Cassation* from the Appeals Court of Lyon.[94] The case pitted the *Enregistrement* against an *engagiste* with the improbable name of Claude-Philippe Tête-Noire-Lafayette. The litigation concerned the Grand Mill of the town of Saint-Etienne, which had been conceded by the royal domain in March 1789 in exchange for a *cens* and payment of *lods et ventes* if the *engagiste* sold it. The *Enregistrement* claimed the right to collect the *cens*, despite the feudal language of the *engagement* contract, but Tête-Noire-Lafayette refused to pay. He argued successfully before the Appeals Court of Lyon that the rent had been suppressed as feudal by the laws of the Convention. Now the *Cour de Cassation* was being asked to rule on the *Enregistrement's* appeal.

It fell to none other than Merlin, then serving as chief prosecutor, to report on this contestation. Merlin began by noting that the law on feudal abolition "only intended . . . to free property owners from the feudal charges with which they were burdened" and that it effected such charges "only insofar as they represented perpetually alienated properties." The law had not meant "to suppress those charges . . . when they had been stipulated by acts of concession whose effect had not been to transfer the property of the conceded objects." To do so would transform the laws on feudal abolition into laws giving those who had signed temporary leases full rights to the properties they were leasing, something the revolutionary legislatures never intended.[95] Moreover, the *Cour de Cassation* had recently judged that laws on feudal abolition applied only to incommutable property in a ruling on emphyteutic leases of 29 Thermidor X/18 August 1802. The same principle had been consecrated earlier by the Directorial-era legislature shortly after the left-wing coup of 18 Fructidor, when it upheld the legitimacy of *rentes convenancières* (a feudal lease common in Brittany according to which the lord retained both domains of property, the *directe* and *utile*, and could therefore expel tenants at will). Thus, the sole issue to determine in the case of Tête-Noire-Lafayette was whether he had incommutable property of the *engagement* in question. The answer, of course, was no. The Edict of Moulins, confirmed by all subsequent domanial legislation passed by successive revolutionary assemblies, had converted all post-1556 domanial concessions into *engagements*, regardless of the terms employed in the original contract of concession. The *engagiste's* claim to the benefits of the law of 17 July 1793 was thus inadmissible until the moment he acquired full property of it by paying his *supplément de finance*, as stipulated by the Ventôse VII law.

The *Cour de Cassation's* ruling, that the law of 17 July 1793 applied only "in the case of perpetual concessions of property," was upheld by the Council of

State on 22 Fructidor XIII/9 September 1805. It was reaffirmed by the *Cour* on 16 August 1809, when it pronounced explicitly that "the laws suppressing the feudal regime . . . only intended to liberate landed property, encourage and improve agriculture; [and] that they had only been passed in favor of the proprietors of the aforesaid lands."[96] Feudalism, it seems, was not quite dead. It survived in the concessions of the ex-royal, now national domain.

The ramifications of this jurisprudence were potentially vast. It threatened to affect not only direct *engagistes* such as Tête-Noire-Lafayette but also all sub-*engagistes* whose holdings belonged to a larger domanial concession which had been parceled out under feudal conditions by the primary *engagiste*. And many had done so. The case of the Norman *engagiste* Louis-Gaspard Le Coustelier offers a good example.[97] His *engagement* not only sprawled across several communes, but Le Coustelier had massively sub-conceded it. In the year II/ 1793-94, when he made his required declaration to the district of Bayeux, it consisted of 178 distinct parcels, including 11 which he had sub-conceded as fiefs in their own right, as well as 36 freestanding feudal rents. These were of the most astonishing diversity. For example, Pierre Costil, son of Pierre, owed Le Coustelier one pound of pepper annually for his plot, and the widow Le Carpentier had to pay 30 *sous* (shillings) and a capon for hers. Would sub-*engagistes* like Costil and Le Carpentier have to continue paying these feudal dues to Le Coustelier, the direct *engagiste* from whom they held their land? If so, the abolition of feudalism risked becoming an empty slogan for thousands of modest tenants.

A case of this sort was brought before the prefect of the Isère in 1812. In 1772 the Crown had conceded to Louis-François de Vachon a domain, known as the Plaine de Voye, as an *engagement*. The act of concession explicitly permitted Vachon to sub-concede parcels of the property to various tenants. This Vachon did, granting portions of his original *engagement* to tenants under ground rents "mixed with feudal expressions." Having complied with the law of 14 Ventôse VII/4 March 1799 and thus acquired the full property of the Plaine de Voye, legally confirmed in 1812, the Vachon heirs sought to collect these feudal rents on the grounds that the law of 17 July 1793 had only suppressed tainted dues of this sort "in favor of property owners." As neither they nor their tenants had been proprietors, but merely *engagistes* in 1793, feudal suppression had not affected them.[98] The prefect agreed. Citing Merlin's opinion in the Tête-Noire-Lafayette case and the various rulings that confirmed it, he noted that the law of 17 July 1793 was "only applicable to debtors who held their goods as incommutable property and not under a temporary and precarious title."[99] The entanglement of the *engagements* with the tortuous process of feudal abolition, as well as their periodic brushes with the *biens nationaux*, go far toward explaining why their transformation from public into private property took so long.

Conclusion

This chapter has examined how the post-revolutionary state tried to shed its domanial character by converting the engaged holdings of the former royal domain into "absolute" property. This process completed the demarcation of distinct spheres of property and power begun on the Night of August 4th. During that Night, the revolutionaries had abolished private ownership of public power, thus removing power from the sphere of property. But at that time they did not evacuate property from the realm of the State. Only by nationalizing and alienating the properties which had been attached to sovereignty before 1789 was this second aspect of the Great Demarcation accomplished.

The liquidation of the former royal domain required that the revolutionaries simultaneously put into practice two opposite principles, inalienability and alienability. To empty the national domain (that is, to sell or alienate the properties of the Church, Crown, émigrés, etc.), the revolutionaries had to reverse the principle of domanial inalienability, a constitutional maxim enshrined by the 1566 Edict of Moulins. Seen as a revolutionary step at the time, this measure must not be dismissed as a piece of legal trivia. Rather, it was the sine qua non not merely of the sale of all domanial properties (thus, the sale of *biens nationaux*) but also of the existence of incommutable private property in general. For without the abolition of inalienability, the sovereign (whether king or nation) would have retained a powerful claim to all private property in France.

For private property to live, therefore, domanial inalienability had to die. But it could not be allowed to expire completely until all domanial properties in the hands of individuals had been transformed into full, incommutable property. The only way to do this was by invoking inalienability, albeit limiting its applicability to properties conceded by the Crown subsequent to the crucial 1566 cut-off date. Until the last of these post-1566 domanial dismemberments—all redefined as *engagements* by the law of 1 December 1790—had been recovered or converted into incommutable property, the principle of inalienability would have to co-exist alongside that of alienability. Together, the two principles formed a powerful legal mechanism for recovering domanial properties and then converting them into the new-style private property. However, it was not an easy co-existence, and many pointed to the tension inherent in it. During the Restoration, at the height of the domanial administration's great inquisition of 1828-1829, Daru denounced the contradiction as the

> sad result of a vain compromise between long-accredited maxims and a new system.... The Domain, says the legislator, is and remains inalienable; and immediately after adds that these properties can be alienated incommutably and in perpetuity.... This is obviously a contradiction.[100]

The contradiction to which Daru pointed did indeed cause problems. Inalienability threatened private property, while alienability allowed public properties to escape detection and usurp the status of private ones. But for all these drawbacks, the duo of alienability and inalienability was potent. Its one-two punch made it possible to transform domanial property into incommutable private property—an indispensable part of the attempt to create a new polity based on the demarcation between power and property.

6

When the Nation Became a Lord

Feudal Dues as Biens Nationaux

Even if this mine could liberate the state singlehandedly, it still must be proscribed, for it is a remedy more dangerous than the evil itself.
—M. Boudin, *Nouvelles reflexions sur le rachat des droits féodaux* (1790)

The previous chapters have taken stock of the two major operations the revolutionaries undertook to make a new order of property and power. Chapters 2 and 3 explored how the revolutionaries attempted to banish public power and perpetual hierarchical tenure from the realm of property. They did so by abolishing private ownership of public power (in the form of *seigneuries*, venal office, and privilege) and by dismantling the gradations of superiority and subordination generated by the system of divided domain. Chapters 4 and 5 examined the revolutionaries' eviction of property from the realm of public power—that is, from the state and great political *corps*. To do this, they took over the royal domain and ecclesiastical holdings in the name of the nation and began to convert them into private property by selling them to individuals. Both endeavors encountered difficulties. Particularly problematic were the non-feudal, perpetual ground rents, which tested the limits of the new conception of ownership, and domanial *engagements*, which straddled the line between public and private property. This chapter explores an even more difficult type of property that simultaneously engaged both dimensions of the Revolution's Great Demarcation. This property was known by a variety of names: first "feudal dues belonging to the nation," then "incorporeal national dues," and ultimately the deliberately anodyne "national rents." But despite this flight toward a bland nomenclature, this was a type of property that was anything but simple, for it brought into explosive contact the two most sensitive issues involved in the revolutionary demarcation of property and power.

The national rents consisted of a wide range of feudal and non-feudal dues that had belonged to the royal domain and Church before 1789, but had become national property with the Revolution. In taking them over in the name of the nation, the revolutionaries burdened themselves with a form of property that simultaneously embodied the problems of feudalism/divided domain, on the one hand, and domaniality, on the other. The national rents thus brought into contact the two major challenges the revolutionaries faced in creating a new order of power and property. This was complicated enough, but the question of national rents could not be settled on the basis of principle alone. Since these ideologically toxic national properties represented a valuable asset, their fate became entangled with fiscal considerations. Moreover, as the rents had the legal status of *biens nationaux*, they became embroiled in the multiple conflicts their sale spawned. Merging the issues of feudal abolition, the national domain, fiscal crisis, and the *biens nationaux*, the national rents simultaneously raised all the major problems the revolutionaries faced in remaking the order of property and power.

The National Rents

The nation acquired a mass of incorporeal property, both feudal and non-feudal, when it took over the property of Church and Crown. Its extent was very great. Before 1789, the royal domain had successfully claimed a seigneurial *directe* over all immediate fiefs of the Crown and, less successfully, a *directe* over the *allods*. Although its physical holdings were few, essentially palaces and forests, the royal domain's *directes* formed a significant mass of incorporeal property— *cens*, ground rents, *lods*, and other dues. The properties of the Church, however, dwarfed those of the Crown. Before 1789 the Church was the single largest lord in France, blanketing both urban and rural space with its *directe*. Few cities lacked ecclesiastical lordships. In Aix, whose population was only 20,000, the archbishopric and over thirty other religious establishments possessed 1,590 *cens*, ground rents, and other annual dues. Together each year they generated 24,150 *livres* and approximately 16.5 metric tons of grain for the Church.[1] In Marseille, which was much more populous but possessed only a bishopric, over fifty religious institutions owned 1,165 incorporeal properties—mostly ground rents on urban dwellings. Their annual yield was 77,316 *livres* cash and payments in kind of over 12 metric tons of grain, as well as a quantity of oil.[2] In Limoges the bishop claimed lordship over more than 700 urban properties and many rural sub-fiefs. These, in turn, claimed many hundreds of properties under their respective *directes*.[3] Ecclesiastical lordships were so ubiquitous that they were the subject of a manual published just before the Revolution. In addition to its "domains, ground rents, and similar kinds of property," the work explained, the Church also owned "*seigneuries*," "*directes*," and "rights attached to the exercise of public power."[4] All these ecclesiastical possessions became national properties in November 1789.

Ecclesiastical fiefs covered much of rural France as well. When the revolutionaries placed them "at the disposition of the nation," they were transformed into "national fiefs" (*fiefs nationaux*).[5] An example is the small rural fief of Bordeaux (confusingly located in Normandy), owned by the Order of the Bonne Nouvelle of Rouen, which generated about 860 *livres* per year in feudal dues.[6] The Abbey of Fécamp, also in Normandy, owned many fiefs. One of these, called "Le Chateau," was the "dominant fief" over 400 to 500 acres of *censives*. Although the value of the annual "*cens*, rents, and seigneurial dues" the fief collected amounted to little, the mutation fees (called *treziemes* in Normandy) paid by the lands depending on it were substantial.[7] Some religious orders preferred to sub-infeodate their rural fiefs rather than exploit them directly. One of these was the "noble fief of Gennelais," granted by the Abbey of Saint-Georges de Bocherville in 1771 to Jean-Charles le Noble, councilor in the supreme financial court of Normandy. In addition to chateau and demesne lands, Gennelais consisted of the full complex of incorporeal feudal dues and prerogatives.[8] Not all of the Church's feudal property was so impressive. Much of it had been fragmented, separated into its component parts, and distributed at the lower echelons of the ecclesiastical hierarchy. Thus, the vicar of the Chapel of Notre Dame de Lorrette of Saint Peter's church in the town of Dorat in the Limousin owned merely one "noble rent" and four ground rents. The feudal endowment of the *curé* of Saint-Priest le Betoux was even less substantial: "one part of a feudal rent on the hamlet of St. Priest," payable in grain.[9] By the end of 1789, all of this became part of the national domain. Incorporeal ecclesiastical properties constituted the lion's share of what came to be called the "national *directe*."[10]

Although sometimes termed "national ex-feudal dues," these rents were more commonly described as "national incorporeal dues" during the revolutionary decade. Under Napoleon, they would change names again, becoming simply "national rents," a title they retained well into the nineteenth century. In addition to those which had been truly feudal, they also included a great quantity of non-feudal incorporeal goods. In particular, there were many perpetual ground rents. Like those in the hands of individuals, many were enunciated in contracts containing feudal language. In addition, the Church possessed certain types of non-feudal, perpetual rents specific to it. These included obituary rents, established by pious bequests to fund prayers for the souls of the departed, and mass-endowing rents (*rentes de fondation de messe*), created for masses to be sung on certain saints' days. Although the National Assembly snapped these up along with the rest of the Church's endowment, it did not assume responsibility for the religious services they had been established to support. Far from it. The Civil Constitution of the Clergy so decimated the clergy that many parishes no longer had personnel to say endowed prayers and masses. And in some cases, the revolutionaries sold as *biens nationaux* the very chapels to which these rents were attached. Yet, the state continued to demand that the debtors of these pious rents keep paying them. This angered descendants of the original benefactors.[11] But in the eyes of the revolutionaries, a national rent was a national rent, regardless of the purpose for which it had been created.

It is impossible today to know the exact value of the former domanial and ecclesiastical rents. The revolutionaries themselves were not sure. Their initial estimates varied, ranging from as little as 3 million to as much as 22.5 million *livres* in annual revenue.[12] Any supplement to national revenue was not to be scoffed at, but the real fiscal potential of the national rents lay elsewhere. As ex-feudal dues and ground rents, they represented an annual interest payment on the capital value of the properties on which they had been established. If the owners of those properties could be induced to redeem the capital of those dues and rents through the *rachat* system, this could raise a very large sum indeed. Again, estimates varied, ranging from 200 to 500 million *livres*.[13] Whatever the exact figure, it was clear to everybody that the national rents could go a long way toward paying down the debt if converted into a capital sum through *rachat*.

Alienating the National Rents: Sale and Rachat

From the moment the deputies began to concern themselves with "the feudal regime," they never considered renouncing the ex-feudal dues and ground rents the nation had acquired from the royal domain and Church. Their potential value was simply too great. Some outside observers, however, were troubled by the political and social implications of overseeing the collection, *rachat*, and possibly even sale (as *biens nationaux*) of ex-feudal dues in the name of the nation. One of these was none other than Boncerf, who had opened the public debate over feudal dues in 1776 by publishing a pamphlet urging their abolition. For Boncerf, it was essential that the nation engineer a cascading universal renunciation of feudal dues by abandoning its own claims and requiring, in return, that the entire chain of subordinate lords do the same with theirs.[14] A pamphleteer named Boudin also advocated this approach. Although acknowledging the great value of the national rents, he cautioned that it was "a remedy more dangerous than the evil itself."[15] These and other warnings had no apparent effect on the deputies of the National Assembly. If they felt any qualms at putting the nation in the same position as a feudal lord, they kept their doubts to themselves. The hope that the national rents could mitigate the fiscal crisis overwhelmed whatever misgivings they may have had about making the nation a lord.

In its very first report to the Assembly, delivered by Tronchet on 13 September 1789, the Feudal Committee proposed maintaining and exploiting the national feudal dues to extract money from "the nation's ... immediate vassals and *censive*-holders."[16] Many others, both deputies and outside observers, concurred. The first comprehensive plan submitted to the Assembly by its Committee on Finances assumed that the nation would collect the former royal-domanial property transfer fees. Unsolicited proposals from a variety of individuals—the *baron* d'Allarde, the bishop of Limoges, d'Argentré, and the future republican minister, Jean-Marie Roland—also looked to the resources of the soon-to-be ex-royal domain.[17] Nor did they neglect the feudal property of the Church, which, like that of the royal domain, had not yet been formally nationalized. Even before the debate over Church property had begun, Pierre-Samuel Dupont urged his colleagues in the Assembly to turn their attention to the "seigneurial dues" of the Church.[18] He was seconded by Pierre-Toussaint Durand de Maillane, who emphasized the ubiquity of "feudal ecclesiastical *seigneuries*."[19] Even a prominent member of the First Estate's deputation, bishop Lafare of Nancy, was assuming that the Assembly would opt to exploit the feudal dues it had acquired when he offered the nation the Church's feudal rights on the Night of August 4th.[20] Indeed, the belief that it was normal and natural for the nation to take over such properties and exploit them like a lord seems to have been so widespread that individuals outside the Assembly began to prepare for the national administration of feudal dues. For example, the businessman who held the lease on the fiefs of the Chapter of Romartin, the notary Guion, began on his own initiative to issue requests for the payment of feudal dues in the name of the nation. He did this less than two weeks after the passage of the November 2nd decree placing the Church's property at the nation's disposition.[21]

The only thing keeping the Assembly from immediately collecting or demanding the *rachat* of the feudal and non-feudal rents it had taken from the Church was the absence of a legal structure for doing so. The Feudal Committee would not present its final report on the *rachat* system until June 1790. Impatient, the Ecclesiastical Committee pressed its colleagues to hurry up. Since the nationalized ecclesiastical properties consisted heavily in "*cens*, rents, etc., and other dues of that nature," grumbled Treilhard, they could not be sold "until the Feudal Committee presented a mode of *rachat* for feudal dues."[22]

The Assembly soon lost patience with the tardy Committee. Recognizing that the ex-ecclesiastical dues were just as much national property as the Church lands, it included provisions on them in its legislation on the *biens nationaux*. The law of 14 May 1790 initiating the sale of *biens nationaux* authorized municipalities to purchase former ecclesiastical "rents and payments," including "*droits casuels*" (feudal property mutation fees, such as the *droit de lods*).[23] Municipalities could buy these incorporeal properties either separately, as freestanding rents, or as elements of a complete fief-*seigneurie* complex. Many seized this opportunity to acquire the dues and rents to which they were collectively subject. Some actually collected these dues. Among them were Grenoble, which collected ten *lods* in 1789–92, and Bordeaux, which collected sixty-one between August 1789 and December 1791.[24]

However, the main reason why towns and villages purchased national rents was to evade the Assembly's prohibition on collective *rachat* and extinguish the dues to which their inhabitants were jointly subject.[25] For example, the village of Billon purchased a great variety of feudal material: the "rents and dues, as well as the right of *directe*" formerly held over it by the Chapter of Saint-Cerneuf de Billon, the fief of Billon (which had been owned by the bishopric of Clermont), and a number of smaller *directes*, annual dues, and property mutation fees. On the outskirts of the capital, the village of Rungis acquired the *cens*, rents, and *lods* imposed on a portion of its territory by Notre Dame de Paris. The tiny village of Brou made a small acquisition, the feudal property mutation fees which had formerly belonged to the Priory of Brou. At the other end of the spectrum, the city of Orléans purchased an 11-page list of former ecclesiastical ground rents. Their cost exceeded 160,000 *livres*.

These and hundreds of other examples make it clear that municipalities used the legislation of 14 May 1790 to elude the prohibition on the collective *rachat* of feudal dues. Municipal officers understood that the dual nature of the national rents—simultaneously feudal properties and *biens nationaux*—allowed them to invoke one body of legislation or the other, as suited their interests. To a lesser degree, communes also acquired national ex-feudal dues in order to resell them at a profit to individuals, an operation the law also encouraged. Thus, in April 1791, the village of Ruan sold to five of its citizens the ex-ecclesiastical *champarts* that had formerly belonged to the Chapter of Saint-Aignan d'Orléans. The village had itself acquired the *champarts* only two months earlier, with the intention of reselling them. The transaction came to over 180,000 *livres*.[26]

The law of 25-29 June 1790 extended the sale of *biens nationaux* (including incorporeal ones) directly to individuals. Buyers acquired many of these as a matter of course when they purchased national fiefs and large domains. When they bought such properties, they acquired not only the land and buildings they contained but also the dues, both feudal and non-feudal, they were entitled to collect from dependent properties. An example of this type of *bien national*, posted for sale in Grenoble on 3 February 1791, concerned lands formerly belonging to the Sacristy of La Chatte. Although the physical parcels were estimated to be worth only 1,500 *livres*, ownership of them brought with it the *directe* over thirty-one subordinate properties. The annual rents in kind they generated, together with the mutation fees to which they were periodically subject, were expected to produce over 2,200 *livres* per year.[27] Ex-ecclesiastical feudal property was thus advertised and sold like any other type of *bien national*. Although this troubled some observers, such as the three anonymous petitioners who in 1792 or 1793 denounced the practice of "selling *directes*" as "a direct violation of the constitution," neither the purchasers nor the local officials overseeing the sales expressed any sign of discomfort.[28]

National incorporeal dues were also offered for purchase in their own right, unattached to any physical property. On 14 April 1791, for example, a Monsieur Huet of Dieppe acquired from the nation four feudal rents which had formerly belonged to the Abbey of Longueville. The purchase price was nearly 4,400 *livres*.[29] The following month in the town of Limoux, printed posters went up advertising a non-feudal ground rent consisting in a mix of payments in kind, silver, and poultry established on a garden called La Condamine which had previously depended on the former Chapter of Dalet. It was sold a few weeks later for 2,500 *livres*.[30] One purchaser of national incorporeal properties in Limoges was very careful to specify that he wanted to acquire not only the former ecclesiastical "*cens* and rents" on five properties but also the much more lucrative feudal property transfer fees to which they were subject.[31] It is not clear what this particular individual intended to do with these incorporeal dues, but some purchasers made no secret of seeking them out in order to convert them into capital through *rachat*. For example, a Monsieur Delarozière of Roanne purchased the *directe* of the former Benedictine abbey of Charlieux for 93,000 *livres* "solely in order to receive the *rachat* of [his] canton."[32] For this purchaser, the potential capital value of his national incorporeal due, once unleashed by *rachat*, was the most attractive thing about it.

The National Assembly viewed the national incorporeal properties in exactly the same light. Only if it proved impossible to alienate a national incorporeal property, whether through sale or *rachat*, would the National Assembly resign itself to collecting it. Alienation in either form was preferable to the costly business of enforcing the payment of often-negligible annual dues, for it alone could transform the modest rents into capital. But implementation of this policy had to await the Feudal Committee's law on *rachat*. And that was not all. Since the issue of the national rents had so many dimensions—domanial, ecclesiastical, fiscal, and others—it required cumbersome joint meetings of multiple committees to design specific mechanisms for their *rachat*. At one juncture, no fewer than seven committees were meeting together for that purpose.[33]

A complete system for the *rachat* of feudal and non-feudal dues from the national *directe* emerged only piecemeal from this process. In their report of 10 April 1790, Barère and Enjubault had proposed entrusting *rachat* operations to the locally elected departmental authorities.[34] Their recommendation was partly adopted by the comprehensive law on *rachat* passed on 3 May 1790. It mandated that departmental authorities would handle the *rachat* of ex-ecclesiastical dues, but did not state who would receive the *rachat* of those of royal-domanial origin. The doubt was soon lifted, however, by a supplementary law which assigned responsibility for the ex-domanial rights to the *Régie des Domaines*, a consortium of financiers who had leased the right to collect these fees before the Revolution and whose lease had not yet expired.[35] To facilitate the *rachat* of the national incorporeal dues, another law was passed on 14 November 1790 permitting individuals to buy back the dues they owed the nation piece-by-piece—a facility many petitioners had sought unsuccessfully from the Feudal Committee for those ex-feudal dues held by private individuals.[36] Although several changes would be made, the most important being the transfer of authority over the former royal-domanial rights to a newly created administration, the *Régie de l'Enregistrement*, these laws determined how the *rachat* of national feudal dues would proceed.

The *rachat* of national rents and dues, both feudal and non-feudal, was vigorous. As with *rachat* in general, this was especially so in urban settings. In Aix, more than half (283 of 407) of the *rachats* conducted between the beginning of operations in June 1790 and the implementation of the law of 17 July 1793 had as their object the national *directe*.[37] These *rachats* netted the nation 270,000 *livres*. Things happened on a grander scale in Marseille, where 744 *rachats* raised over 950,000 *livres*. All but a handful of these were of national dues, which was not surprising since most property in the city had been held under an ecclesiastical or royal *directe*.[38] *Rachats* appear to have proceeded at a healthy clip in Paris as well, although the loss of the registers in which overall figures were recorded make it impossible to offer comprehensive figures for that city. Excellent records for the Abbey of Sainte-Geneviève, however, survive. They indicate that between December 1790 and February 1792, *rachats* concerning its nationalized *directes* raised over 8,000 *livres* in revenue for the state.[39]

Urban interest in the *rachat* of national rents may have had a spill-over effect into the countryside, since much rural land was held by city-dwellers. The city of Rouen provides a suggestive illustration. Between 11 November 1790 and 27 September 1791, the local authorities received thirty-two requests for the *rachat* of former ecclesiastical rents. Of these, about two-thirds (21) concerned agricultural land, one-third (10) houses and gardens in the city itself, and one was an unspecified rent.[40] At the same time, the "country districts" of Lyon effected 144 *rachats*, netting the state approximately 200,000 *livres*.[41] Even purely rural districts experienced their share of national *rachats*. In the rural district of Jouques in the hinterland of Aix, five of the ten *rachats* effected there between 28 February 1791 and 16 November 1793 were of national dues, raising over 825 *livres*.[42] In the district of Gardanne, the proportion was reversed; between 28 April 1791 and 15 September 1793, only six of nineteen *rachats* concerned the national *directe*.[43] Other parts of France, such as the rural department of the

Haute-Vienne, had very few *rachats* of any kind. Only ten *rachats* are known to have been effected there, most of nationalized ecclesiastical *directes*, but also two of whole fiefs dependent on the ex-royal domain.[44]

Rachats by ex-lords of the former royal *directe* over their fiefs was not uncommon. Doing so allowed them to sell their fiefs without having to pay the onerous transfer fees such transactions generated. These transfer fees were so heavy that the ex-lords were often willing to pay very substantial sums of money to liberate their holdings. One of these was the lord of Vauvenargues, who paid 12,864 *livres* in June 1791 to free his entire fief from the "domanial dues" established upon it.[45] Another was the *marquis* of Allein. In 1791 he sent his representative, Louis Talon, merchant of Allein, to Aix to negotiate a *rachat* with the district receiver of Aix. As his employer was apparently intending to sell the fief, Talon took advantage of the faculty of separate *rachat* open to those intending to free their properties from the national *directe*. A deal was struck on 8 August 1791 by which the marquis agreed to pay the nation 670 *livres* for the property mutation fees that the royal domain could impose on his fief in case of sale.[46]

Another Provençal lord, the *seigneur* of Aurons, found an ingenious way to liberate part of his fief, which owed a heavy annual *cens* to the former Priory of St. Martin de Sonnaillet for lands which his ancestors had purchased from it in the sixteenth century. He realized that the laws on the sale of *biens nationaux* and those on the *rachat* of national ex-feudal dues overlapped. In some circumstances, this rendered the operations of purchase and *rachat* identical in effect—although not in cost. The *seigneur* of Aurons sought to save money by exploiting the confusion. Whereas a *rachat* would have required him to pay the nation twenty times the annual value of the *cens*, purchasing the same due as a *bien national*, he hoped, would generate revenue for himself that would offset the purchase price. Although d'Aurons had to serve the Priory's *cens*, he claimed that he held the feudal *directe* over the physical property on which it was imposed, thus giving him the right to collect a *droit de lods* every time it changed hands. Thus, if the nation sold him the *cens*, he would be able to collect a *droit de lods* from the nation! He therefore proposed an exchange: the nation would give him the *cens*, thus extinguishing it, and he, in turn, would renounce his *lods*. The situation was complicated, however, by the fact that the lords of Aurons and the Priory had been embroiled in lawsuits since the seventeenth century over the question of whether the lord actually possessed (as he claimed) the *directe* over all the lands of the fief. Given that this was far from clear, the departmental authorities rejected the deal, noting that the ex-lord could not claim the *lods* "unless he exhibits the titles constituting his *directe* over the *cens* that he wants to acquire."[47] This example not only illustrates the complexity of the problems faced by the revolutionaries as they liquidated the divided-domain system of tenure but also shows how the intersection of domanial rights, private property, *biens nationaux*, and feudal abolition coalesced around the national incorporeal dues to make these challenges more complex.

Collecting the National Rents

The National Assembly intended and expected that all the national incorporeal dues would eventually exit the national domain through either sale or *rachat*. It was clear, however, that this would not happen immediately. While awaiting alienation or *rachat*, the nation's dues would have to be collected. For the deputies, this was a last resort because it was cumbersome, inexact, and incapable of generating the same level of revenue as the other two methods. The administrative costs of collecting the often-modest rents that had become national property would certainly absorb a great part of the revenue they might generate. Yet, however mediocre they might be, the deputies believed, all national resources had to be mobilized. The question of how best to do so was addressed simultaneously by the Committees on Alienation and Domains. They readily agreed that the still-extant domanial administration of the Old Regime should continue to collect dues pertaining to the former royal *directe*.[48] But they had trouble reaching common ground on the collection of nationalized ecclesiastical dues.

On 6 October 1790, Charles-Antoine Chasset, speaking for the Committee on Alienation, proposed that the elected local administrations farm out the collection of national incorporeal dues to entrepreneurs.[49] At this, Jacques-François-Laurent de Visme, a member of the Committee on Domains, rose to interrupt Chasset's report to urge instead that collection be entrusted to the existing royal-domanial administration.[50] The contours of the "former feudal regime" did not correspond with the "new division of the kingdom." How would local administrations be able to deal with national *directes* that sprawled across departmental boundaries? Rival local officials would fight over such *directes*, and the farming-out leases that ensued would reflect the confusion. In the end, local authorities would be submerged in a deluge of lawsuits which would "consume their precious moments." Even worse, some of the holders of farming-out-leases would be dishonest. Instead of faithfully collecting the nation's dues, they would enter into "clandestine combinations" with those from whom they were supposed to be collecting and overlook legitimate national titles. Over time, these would be forgotten, if not destroyed, and the national domain would be permanently degraded. To avoid this, De Vismes proposed that the collection of all national incorporeal dues be entrusted to a single agency: the ex-royal domanial administration. With its expert personnel, incomparable records, and national reach, the domanial administration would bring efficiency, clarity, and, above all, uniformity to the collection of the national dues. It was true, De Vismes admitted, that it was an Old Regime administration which owed nothing to the Revolution, but its compliance with the new order could be ensured simply by having local authorities supervise its operations. This safeguard did not appear sufficient to the Assembly. After a heated debate, it voted to have local administrations lease out the ex-ecclesiastical dues.[51]

Local administrations complied with the law, and by early 1791 entrepreneurs were collecting the nation's incorporeal dues. The men who bid on and won the leases were almost always the same people who had leased the right to collect the ecclesiastical dues before the Revolution. Thus, the district of Montivilliers in Normandy leased the collection of dues depending on the former Abbey of Fécamp to Pierre-Grégoire Picard, former feudal manager of the same abbey, the feudal rents of the abbeys of Du Vallasse and Longueville to their former *feudiste* Lamaure, and those of some of the Abbey's outlying rural property to their former *feudiste* Vitecoq. The district's nomination of the former military officer, d'Auberville, to collect the dues of the Abbey of Montivilliers was a surprising exception that proves the rule.[52]

An in-depth example, from the small town of Saint-Chamas in Provence, gives a more textured sense of how the leaseholders operated. In January 1787, Germain Henrique signed a lease to collect the dues owed by the inhabitants of Saint-Chamas to their lord, the Archbishop of Arles, through the end of 1793. In 1791 the departmental administration of the Bouches-du-Rhône signed an agreement maintaining Henrique in place as "*fermier* of the nation." The agreement specified that he would pay 1,035 *livres* annually to collect the ex-ecclesiastical *cens* and 375 for the *lods* through the end of 1793.[53] Provence also reveals another common practice, the sub-contracting of collection. Thus, a Monsieur Devolx, who had leased the dues of various fiefs of the order of Montmajor in Marseille and whose lease was maintained by the nation after 1789, sub-farmed his rights to other entrepreneurs. Pierre Brunache and Simon Roux acquired the sub-farm of Pelisanne from Devolx for 3,800 *livres* annually, André Guien obtained that of Jonquières for 5,700, and Pierre Lyon, a Monsieur Niel, and Jean Clerc (son of the former Old Regime leaseholder) received that of Miramas for an undisclosed sum.[54] Because the leasing-out system tended to rely on existing personnel and practices, many tenants of national fiefs continued to pay their dues to the same people as they had before 1789. This continuity is not surprising, since few people were eager to start a new career in the collection of feudal dues in 1790-93. Only the existing personnel had the experience, knowledge, and records necessary to carry out this complicated—and politically sensitive—business.

The decision to farm-out the national feudal dues soon came under heavy criticism.[55] So too did the decision to divide their collection between two distinct administrations, the former royal domanial administration (for the royal *directe*) and the departmental authorities (for that of the Church).[56] In response to these complaints, the seven committees concerned (listed in note 33) met jointly to take another look at the administration of the national incorporeal dues.[57] It determined that the leasing-out system was inefficient and prone to abuse. First, the prices of the contracts were too low. This is because only the Old Regime leaseholders really knew the value of the dues in an ex-ecclesiastical *seigneurie*. As a result, they were the only ones to place bids. In the absence of competitive bidding, prices were excessively low. Second, even if the exact value of the dues in a given national *directe* were known, there would still be no additional bidders. Without expert knowledge and experience, it would be foolhardy to attempt the task of collection, an arduous one since most dues were fragmented and widely scattered, as well as a dangerous one in areas where peasant resistance was strong. To make matters worse, the most solidly established dues were the ones most likely to be extinguished by *rachat*. Because of these obstacles, the former *feudistes* had reacquired their old leases at prices so low that it amounted to theft from the nation. The leaseholders were nothing but "speculators," "cold and greedy men . . . ready to fall upon their prey," in a word "blood-suckers." The time had come to end their exploitation by instituting a new system for administering the national incorporeal dues.

Fortunately, the joint committee concluded, an alternative was available. There was now a new administration borne of the Revolution, worthy of its confidence, and armed with new tools to help it in its collection of the national dues. This was the *Régie de l'Enregistrement*, established in December 1790 to administer the new national property sales tax, the *droit d'enregistrement*, which the Assembly had created to replace the Old Regime's *droit de contrôle*.[58] This made the *Enregistrement* uniquely qualified to collect national incorporeal dues. Since it was supposed to record all property transactions in France, it would be able to levy mutation fees on all sales under the national *directe*. One deputy optimistically predicted that happy buyers and sellers would appreciate the convenience of "paying at the same time and place their *droit d'enregistrement* and incorporeal due."[59] Moreover, noted the joint committee's spokesman, "in such difficult times" as these, "when the collection of former feudal dues suffers so much from unpopularity and resistance," only a "corps acting in the name of the State" could proceed without "fear."[60] Operating under the supervision of elected local government, concluded the report, the *Enregistrement* would be ideally suited to administer all the nation's dues. The committee's recommendation became law on 9 March 1791. The *Enregistrement* actually entered into its new functions in September 1791, taking over responsibility for the national incorporeal dues from both the *Régie des domaines* and local officialdom. To give it time to conduct the archival research and gather the records it needed, the Assembly suspended the prescription of national incorporeal dues through 1794.[61] This was necessary because the former officials of the royal domain dragged their feet in handing over their papers to the new administration.[62] Without those papers, the *Enregistrement's* knowledge of the national domain would be tenuous.

Nonetheless, with the information it had at its disposal, local agents of the *Enregistrement* began to enforce payment of the national rents. They focused on collecting the *droit de lods*, which was much more lucrative than annual rents and *cens*. Like individual ex-lords, they do not seem to have been particularly successful at enforcing this ex-feudal, now national, due. In the district of Alzonne, a thinly populated corner of the mountainous Aude, the local receiver managed to collect the *lods* on the sale of only twelve properties under the national *directe* between 12 September 1791 and 1 April 1792.[63] In the Var, his counterpart in the village of Correns collected only five.[64] Similar efforts in Paris were barely more successful. From 17 November 1791 through 29 September 1792, the receiver of the first, second, and third arrondissements took in only twenty-three *lods* for the nation.[65] From a financial perspective, these operations had a negligible impact. Their real significance lies elsewhere.

The main purpose of the collection of the national incorporeal dues was to flush out their debtors and induce them to make a *rachat*. If carried out on a nationwide scale, this would transform the small annual revenue the dues produced into a substantial capital. This could be used to help pay down the debt. Before 1789 the royal domain had often neglected to collect the smaller dues and rents it was owed; it was simply not worth the effort. But *rachat's* ability to transform those small payments into significant capital changed the financial calculus. This led the revolutionaries to direct the *Enregistrement* to identify and pursue national dues that had long been forgotten or neglected.

Historians once thought that eighteenth-century France had experienced a "feudal reaction," a campaign by French lords to collect lapsed dues. But revisionist research in the 1960s and 1970s showed that there was nothing new about this, that lords had always engaged in periodic attempts to reassert their prerogatives. A case could be made, however, that a real feudal reaction took place after 1789, in the context of the National Assembly's determination to use the national incorporeal dues to pay down the national debt. The potential revenue that could be raised through their *rachat*, sale, and collection led to an unprecedented nationwide search for lost dues and their delinquent debtors. Upon reading the orders from his boss, one overwhelmed receiver confessed his powerlessness. "I have neither registers nor titles in my office that could justify any of these dues, even though most of them depend on the former [royal] domain." These records had never been needed before, he continued, because "I am in a district that has never paid the *lods* nor any other feudal dues."[66] Paradoxically, the drive to convert national feudal dues into capital through *rachat* led to something resembling a revolutionary feudal reaction.

In choosing to exploit the former feudal dues of the royal domain and Church, the nation had effectively made itself a lord. This created strange situations. The city of Aix provides one example. On 25 April 1792, the retired Aixois coachman, Jean-Joseph Boulard, appeared before notary Pierre Boyer to complete the purchase of a small olive grove from *demoiselle* Marie Ricard. Before the Revolution, the property had depended upon the *directe* of the monastery of Saint-Barthélemy of Aix. Had the transaction occurred before 1789, Boulard would have had to recognize the monastery's lordship of the property, promise to pay the annual *cens* attached to it, and then pay the *droit de lods* for his acquisition. But with the abolition of feudalism and the nationalization of ecclesiastical property, this was no longer the case. Instead, three days after his purchase, Boulard presented himself to Gayetan Courren, the local *Enregistrement* receiver at Aix. In terminology redolent of the Old Regime, the attending notary recorded what happened in an "*acte de reconaissance*" (a legal document formally recognizing feudal overlordship) identical to those routinely drawn up before 1789. Boulard recognized that his newly acquired property fell under the "*directe* of the nation," and then handed over 37 *livres* 10 *sols*—the amount of the *droit de lods* he owed to that *directe*. Finally, he swore to serve the "annual and perpetual *cens*," create no "*surcens*" on the property (by alienating it under an emphyteutic sublease), make further "*actes de reconaissance*" whenever required, and respect "all the other clauses, qualities, reserves, and conditions" formerly imposed by the monastery of Saint-Barthélemy.[67] From Boulard's perspective, the nation looked very much like a feudal lord.

By the spring of 1791, there were indications that the National Assembly was becoming uneasy with this. In March, the joint committee urged ending the sale of national feudal dues.[68] Rumors had reached it that they had become "the principal object of speculation" of the large purchasers of *biens nationaux*.[69] It was said that "companies" were preparing to buy the national dues in bulk. If allowed to happen, the "feudal regime . . . would reproduce itself in a more hideous and oppressive form" than before. In the hands of the nation, "feudal dues . . . pose no threat to public liberty." But "once they had left its hands, they would form, under another name, as many new fiefs as there are purchasers." These new, quasi-feudal lords—the "worst sort" of men—would impose "servitude" on those subject to their *directes* and thereby revive "dangerous dependence." "Nothing is more contrary to the spirit of the Constitution," the joint committee concluded, "than the sale of incorporeal dues."[70] It eventually emerged that these fears were unjustified, as the Convention's Committee of Legislation eventually recognized in an internal note dated November 1792.[71] Nonetheless, following its pressing recommendation, the Assembly banned their sale, although it confirmed sales that had already been effected, as well as the farming-out leases that were already in force.[72] The *rachat* and collection of the national dues continued as before. The policy of selling all state-held property, including the ex-feudal dues, to pay off the national debt had collided with the revolutionaries' commitment to abolishing the system of hierarchical, tenurial holding. At this juncture, the revolutionaries chose to subordinate fiscal concerns in order to advance the abolition of the tenurial system of property-holding and avoid the political fallout the sale of ex-feudal dues was generating. But by refusing to relinquish the national dues altogether, the nation remained in the position of a lord. An even more disturbing consequence soon became apparent: the nation had also become a vassal.

The Nation as Vassal

The preceding pages have treated the nation's strange career as a quasi-lord, but lordship was not the only embarrassing situation in which it found itself. Given the complex hierarchies of interlocking *directes* before 1789, it should come as no surprise that many ecclesiastical properties depended upon secular lordships. When the National Assembly took over the Church's properties, the nation became a tenant to those secular lords. The extent of national servitude varied from place to place. It seems to have been especially common in Normandy. Here is an example from that province. As ex-lord of the fief of Orival, Madeleine-Henriette-Celestine-Mélanie Baillard Saniée had the right to feudal dues from a variety of ecclesiastical properties under her *directe*. The parish priest owed her a small feudal rent (two-thirds of a chicken, payable at Christmas), as well as mutation fees for a field depending upon her fief. The Cannonesses of Notre Dame de la Ronde of Rouen owed her another rent (5 *sous*, 4 *deniers*, payable at Michaelmas) and mutation fees for three pieces of farmland totaling 20 acres. Finally, the parish treasury owed her yet another miniscule rent and mutation fees for a small plot it held under her *directe*.[73] When these properties were nationalized, they remained subject to Sanniée's lordship. This was just a small example of a much larger phenomenon. Even more problematic than modest fiefs such as Orival were the huge tracts of ecclesiastical land that depended upon great ducal, baronial, and comtal lordships, such as those of the Montmorencys, Bourbon-Penthièvres, and Colberts.

The National Assembly was aware of the difficulties privately held *directes* over nationalized properties could cause. The most common occurred when local authorities sold *biens nationaux* which depended upon such *directes*. In such cases, the ex-lords were entitled to demand a property mutation fee. To cite just one example, Paul-Charles-Cardin Lebret demanded that the nation pay him the *droit de lods* (or alternatively, effect a *rachat*) when it sold a *bien national*, the former priestly living of Chatillon-sur-Cher, which depended on his fief of

Selles-sur-Cher.[74] If individuals like Lebret could demand such payments, the deputies realized, it would greatly impede the sale of national properties. To address the problem, the National Assembly decided to have the nation itself effect whatever *rachats* were necessary to spare the purchasers of *biens nationaux* that fell under private *directes*.[75] This resulted in a great mass of feudal *rachats* conducted by the nation itself. These national *rachats*, buried in the acts of sale of *biens nationaux*, have been overlooked by existing studies of feudal abolition. If factored into the larger *rachat* picture along with the urban *rachats* discussed in chapter 2, the prevailing consensus about the failure of those operations would have to be revised.

Here are some examples of national *rachats* in the department of the Isère. In the district of Grenoble, Françoise Prunier, wife of a lieutenant general and lord in her own right of Bussière, Bellecombe, Chaparaillan, Barrat, Saint-André, and Auberives, demanded that the local authorities pay her for the *rachat* of dues owed to her by the ex-ecclesiastical properties dependent on her fiefs. Other notable personages—Alexandre-Joseph Falcoz de la Blache, François-Joseph de Meffray, Jean-François de la Croix de Pisançon, General Nicholas-François de Langon, and the wealthy merchant Claude Perrier—all found themselves in a similar position of tenurial superiority vis-à-vis nationalized properties. But not only the great and powerful had such claims on the nation. Other Grenoblois in the same situation included Jean Robert (*bourgeois* of Chatte), Denis Dupré (citizen of Grenoble), and Jacques Mante (mayor of Tullin). Even ecclesiastical establishments that had not yet been suppressed, such as the Tournon military school and the Order of Malta at Saint-Antoine, found themselves asking the nation to reimburse them for *directes* they held over other ecclesiastical establishments that had been placed at the disposition of the nation![76] Similar situations were found across France.[77]

The examples given so far concern the sale of *biens nationaux* under individual *directes*. What happened to national properties still waiting to be sold? Would the nation have to pay the annual feudal dues and rents they owed to secular lords? Until the radical suppression of such charges in July 1793, this is exactly what happened. In Normandy, where a number of great lords held *directes* over Church property, this took place on a massive scale. During the period 1790-92, representatives of the Montmorencys, Bourbon-Penthièvres, and Colberts all presented to the local administrations long lists of dues owed to them by nationalized properties. The title of one of these, "List of dues owed to M. Anne-Léon Montmorency by the General Hospital of Saint John the Baptist of Le Havre, by the College of Rouen or the Nation, and of other dues that he is demanding from the aforesaid nation, because of his domain of Tancarville" (31 May 1792), suffices to evoke the odd dynamic these situations generated. The bills ran into the thousands of *livres*.[78] The spectacle of the nation paying feudal dues to courtiers and princes of the blood is not found in any history of the French Revolution. Nor was it one the revolutionaries wanted to publicize or perpetuate. Yet, it continued right up until the second abolition of feudalism in July 1793. As late as 12 July 1793, the central direction of the *Enregistrement* in Paris was still corresponding with its agents in Rouen about "the dues and rents owed by the nation to particulars."[79]

The National Rents and the Second Feudal Abolition (July 1793)

As the Legislative Assembly and National Convention elaborated their increasingly uncompromising approach to feudal abolition, the response of those charged with administering the national rents ranged from incredulity to resistance to resignation. The laws of 1792 and 1793—abolishing the *lods* without compensation, invalidating dues lacking original titles, and ultimately nullifying titles containing feudal language—materially reduced the quantity of incorporeal goods at the *Enregistrement*'s disposition. This had financial consequences for its personnel. To encourage employees to collect dues diligently and to search for long-forgotten titles in archival depots, bonuses calculated as a percentage of the total amount of revenue each local bureau generated were offered to the staff. The abolition of entire categories of incorporeal property thus threatened their livelihood quite directly. The central direction of the *Enregistrement* in Paris and its local agents in the provinces mobilized to protect their interests.

In response to the laws of 1792 laying down a three-month deadline for the holders of ex-feudal dues to exhibit their original titles, the *Enregistrement* prepared a petition to the Convention. If the three-month requirement were not revoked outright, or at least extended to two years "in favor of the national *directe*," it claimed, the nation would lose 50 million *livres*.[80] It is not clear when, if ever, the petition was sent. In any case, it failed to sway the Convention. Undaunted, the *Enregistrement* did what it could to preserve as many national rents as possible. It mounted a campaign in late 1792 and early 1793 to take stock of the national *directe*. By dint of its efforts, it managed to preserve a mass of national incorporeal dues and even rediscover some lost titles. In Paris alone, it claimed valid titles for about 22,000 rents originating from 75 former ecclesiastical *directes*, as well as from the ex-royal domain.[81] A similar hunt for titles took place in the provinces.

Until the second half of 1792, local *Enregistrement* personnel undertaking these investigations had been able to rely on the presumption of the legitimacy of concession-based feudal dues established by the Constituent Assembly. With the passage of the laws of 20-25 August 1792, which required the owners of ex-feudal dues to back them up with original titles, local *Enregistrement* agents had to search for those documents in archives of the former ecclesiastical establishments. The work was arduous. "You are surely aware," one agent wrote to a colleague, "how difficult and boring this work can be, given the disordered state" of the archives of the former ecclesiastical establishments. "You often have to spend hours before finding a single useful title."[82] As with the search for *engagement* contracts, the hunt for titles to the national rents was a major archival research project—one that contributed to the creation of the present-day archives of France.

The law of 17 July 1793 nullified much of this effort.[83] The heads of local bureaux of the *Enregistrement* from all over France wrote in disbelief to the central direction in Paris. Their national director responded with a circular emphasizing the need to "distinguish carefully between [rents] which are feudal and those which are not" in order to avoid "any error . . . that would be prejudicial to the interest of the nation."[84] This amounted to tacit authorization to extract non-feudal provisions from feudally tinged contracts and define "non-feudal" as broadly as possible.

At the same time, the director petitioned the Convention and testified before its sympathetic Legislation Committee. As discussed in chapter 3, this ultimately provoked that Committee to make repeated attempts to persuade the Convention to revise the July law. When it finally issued its categorical decree of 7 Ventôse II/25 February 1793, however, the director of the *Enregistrement* admitted defeat and directed his local agents to adopt the decree's rigorous definition of "feudal."[85] Even so, they still had some discretion in applying the law. But not much.

The tightening of the legislation on feudal abolition had a marked effect on the administration of the national rents. Pending leases of national dues had to be rewritten or even cancelled, and people who had purchased ex-feudal dues as *biens nationaux* had to be indemnified. The Legislative Assembly had actually begun to make provisions for this as early as mid-1792 when it abolished the *lods*. Purchasers of these mutation fees were given the option of renouncing their acquisitions and getting a full refund.[86] Further laws broadened this facility to those who had acquired suppressed dues of any sort from the nation.[87] For the next several years, local *Enregistrement* agents were kept busy with these demands. The departmental archives of the Vienne hold a complete register of these requests (twenty-three in all), offering examples of reimbursement for all sorts of things—ecclesiastical fiefs, feudal dues, *directes*, ground rents, and mutation fees—that had been sold as *biens nationaux*.[88]

These operations occurred throughout France. At the end of 1792, for example, the Blois notary Jean-François Riffault, petitioned the local *Enregistrement* bureau for a reduction in the purchase price of farmland of the former Priory of Saint-Avertin which he had acquired as a *bien national* in April 1791. Given that his acquisition included a now-suppressed *droit de terrage* (an annual payment in kind, similar to the *champart*) over 800 arpents of agricultural land, he requested—and received—a refund of 18,000 *livres*.[89] In the Isère, a citizen Moussier, who had purchased the right to collect the "*cens*, rents, and feudal dues" of the former Chapel of Saint-Chef, demanded a 36,000-*livre* indemnity for lost income. He was still haggling over the exact amount of his reimbursement one year later.[90] In 1793 in Rouen, the banker Barrois, who had acquired "agricultural land, domains, feudal rents, and *treizièmes*" formerly belonging to the cathedral chapter of the city, demanded a full refund.[91] While most of the requests for reduction and reimbursement had been processed by spring 1794, some difficult cases—such as that of citizen Gentry de la Borderie of Limoges, who had purchased the "rents and mutation fees" of the ex-Priory of Chastaing—dragged on for years.[92]

The abolition in 1792-93 of feudal dues that had been maintained as legitimate in 1790 had a paradoxical result: more rigorous collection of the non-feudal dues which remained. This stemmed from the self-interest of commission-seeking *Enregistrement* agents, as well as vindictiveness inspired by the suppression of the dues from which they had made their living. A circular issued shortly after the law of 25 August 1792, abolishing without indemnity all ex-feudal dues lacking an original title, opened by praising the measure for accomplishing "the entire destruction of feudalism." However, it continued sternly, "the greater the generosity of the nation on this occasion, the greater its right to demand that legitimate dues continue to be paid." It concluded by urging ever greater vigilance not only in their collection but also in the search for titles. In both Limoges and Rouen, the *Enregistrement* abruptly stopped granting reductions in dues' payments to tenants, a traditional practice of ecclesiastical lords that had, until that point, been continued by revolutionary administrations. In lieu of that flexibility and personal touch, the *Enregistrement* began to send out printed notices *en masse* to citizens who owed unpaid dues to the Republic. Before passage of the law of 17 July 1793, the notice read "Citizen, the original title of the due of ___ established on ___ that you possess exists in the national archives. . . . In consequence, you are requested to pay, within a week, the arrears you have accumulated." After that law abolished even those ex-feudal dues backed by original titles, the wording of the form letter was changed to read: "Citizen, this is to inform you that the title of the purely landed rent [*rente purement foncière*] of ___ due to the nation on the property you possess . . . exists in the national archives."[93] If met with passive noncompliance or open refusal, the *Enregistrement* did not hesitate to institute legal proceedings against delinquents. Although it could not reverse the devastating effect of the 1792-93 laws on the mass of ex-feudal national dues, it nonetheless managed to preserve much non-feudal incorporeal property for the

Republic. Thanks to these efforts, the *Enregistrement* still claimed over 14,000 *livres* in non-feudal ground rents in Paris, as well as 49,000 emphyteutic leases, even after passage of the law of 17 July 1793.[94]

Inflation, the Sale of *Biens Nationaux*, and the National Rents

The abolition in 1792-93 of entire categories of incorporeal property that had been maintained by the Constituent Assembly was not the only factor influencing the *Enregistrement*'s operations during the early years of the Republic. The collapse of the *assignat* may have even had a greater impact. Inflation disrupted broad areas of economic activity, including real estate sales, commerce, military supply contracts, and taxation, and also aspects of family life, such as inheritance and dowry arrangements. In general terms, it sparked a war throughout French society between creditors and debtors—including the creditors and debtors of rents.[95] The problem of balancing the respective claims of those who were owed against those who owed money was one of the most vexing challenges the post-Thermidorean legislatures faced.[96] The national rents were at the heart of the maelstrom.

Inflation sharply reduced the revenue generated by the national rents. This, in turn, slowed down and eventually halted the *Enregistrement*'s attempts to collect them. At first, the Thermidorean Convention tried to prevent people from paying their national dues in devalued assets by laws requiring payment in kind.[97] But of even more concern was the possibility that the debtors of national rents would try to liberate themselves entirely by effecting *rachats* with near-worthless paper. If this were allowed to occur, the national rents, which had promised so much in the early 1790s, faced the real prospect of being annihilated by a wave of *rachats* in *assignats*. There were signs that this was actually occurring. As inflation accelerated through the summer of 1795, so too did the pace of *rachat*. A surviving register of accounts from Marseille, covering the period 17 Frimaire II/7 December 1793 through 8 Thermidor III/26 July 1795 provides eloquent testimony.[98] In year II/1793-94, when the *assignat* was being propped up by the maximum and other measures, there were no *rachats* of national dues in the city and their collection continued at a slow, but steady pace. By the late summer of 1794, however, the Marseillais began to liberate their properties from national dues through *rachat*, instead of making their annual rent payments. By Messidor III/June-July 1795, the collection of national rents had all but ceased. It was replaced by *rachats* with now-worthless *assignats*. Facing the total evaporation of the national rents, the Thermidorean Convention took action. On 25 Messidor III/13 July 1795, it suspended all *rachats*. Although the suspension was lifted

in 15 Germinal IV/4 April 1796, and *rachats*, now with the rapidly depreciating and short-lived *mandats territoriaux* (a new kind of paper money briefly and
unsuccessfully introduced by the Directory) resumed, the definitive return of
metallic money in 1796 effectively halted the massive *rachat* of national incorporeal dues.[99]

The return of specie meant a return to the practices of 1792-94—including
the search for titles and collection of dues owed.[100] But to these were now added
a third activity, the collection of arrears. Many of the national dues had gone
uncollected for long periods, in some cases stretching back to before 1789. It had
not been uncommon for rents to lie dormant for years during the Old Regime,
but revolutionary disorders, the instability of law and administration, and, perhaps most of all, massive popular resistance, had exacerbated the problem.[101] In
addition, inflation may have discouraged the agents of the *Enregistrement* from
pressing too hard. Demands for payment would have produced only a meager
revenue in *assignats* or, worse, would have provoked *rachat* with worthless scrip.
With the withdrawal of paper money and the return of silver, however, these
years of unpaid dues could now be demanded in cold, hard cash. All that stood
between the *Enregistrement* and the collection of the delinquent dues was the
lack of regulations on how many back-years could be demanded and on how the
amounts due would be calculated—a vexing problem given the rampant inflation and changing currencies of the past decade. The material stakes in these
questions were great, both for individuals and for the state. Thus, as with the
question of the *rachat* of national rents, that of the collection of their arrears generated interminable, heated debate (and a succession of shifting laws), until the
Fructidor coup cleared the way for a definitive law, passed on 26 Brumaire VI/16
November 1797.[102] This ruled that arrears accrued up to 1 January1791, together
with those subsequent to the demonetization of the *assignat* on 29 Messidor IV/
17 July 1796, would be paid at their nominal value in silver. Those accrued in the
interval would also be paid in silver, but reduced to account for the depreciation
of the paper currency. The pursuit of arrears now began in earnest.[103]

The destruction of the Ministry of Finance's archives makes it impossible to
advance national figures. But departmental archives can give a sense of these
operations. Here is an example from Limoges. In 1746 the Augustins of Limoges
sold two houses on Rue des Soulles to the tailor Joseph Renaudin in exchange for
a 25-*livre* ground rent.[104] This was paid regularly through 1790, but after that payment stopped for several years, probably because the local *Enregistrement* agents,
overwhelmed as they were with the collection of the *droit d'enregistrement* and
sale of *biens nationaux*, made no attempt to collect it. In Frimaire VI (November-
December 1797), however, the *Enregistrement* summoned the property's new
owner, the carpenter Bertrand Bagnol, to pay the arrears that had accumulated
since 1791. Bagnol did not comply, so the *Enregistrement* took legal action

against him, ultimately placing a lien against his house. Bagnol responded by providing evidence that he had leased his property to Marie Ramiot, widow of the clothing-dealer Michel Courtier, and that, as a condition of the lease, she had assumed responsibility for paying the ground rent. The *Enregistrement* thus shifted its attention to Ramiot who eventually paid arrears of about 80 francs in silver after allowances for *assignat* depreciation had been made.

Despite the change of ownership and subsequent sub-lease to Ramiot, this rent's history was fairly easy for the *Enregistrement* to reconstitute. Given the facility with which these sorts of incorporeal properties could be fragmented and commercialized, however, this was not always the case. An example of a more complicated rent, again from Limoges, is the 50-*livre* ground rent imposed in 1767 by the Oratorians on a house in the Rue des Pousses that they had alienated to the woodworker Léonard Charpentier.[105] In 1782 Charpentier had transferred half of his property—and thus liability for half of the rent—to the baker Jacques Racaud. In 1793 Racaud resold his portion to the goldsmith and clockmaker Orry with a guarantee that he, Racaud, would pay whatever arrears he still owed. When the *Enregistrement* turned its attention to this rent in year VI/1797-98, it discovered that neither of the half rents of 25 *livres* each had been paid since mid-1792 and, moreover, that Racaud still owed arrears for the last six months of 1792. To collect these years of unpaid dues, the *Enregistrement* not only had to pursue the two current debtors of the original (but now divided) 50-*livre* rent, but also Racaud. By Brumaire VII/October-November 1798, both of the principal debtors had paid what they owed, and the following Ventôse Racaud complied as well. These three operations netted about 220 francs in silver. As these examples show, the collection of arrears was a wearying business that required a great deal of archival research and legal maneuvering for relatively little gain.

Moreover, debtors being pursued by the *Enregistrement* possessed a powerful means of resisting its demands: to claim that the rents in question were feudal and had thus been abolished. Some of these cases ended up in court, several even reaching the supreme appeals court in the land, the *Tribunal de Cassation*. These conflicts between the *Enregistrement* and debtors over the feudal status of contested rents thus added fuel to the larger debate over feudal abolition discussed in chapter 3.

The Brumairians and the *Rachat* and Sale of National Rents

One of the most pressing challenges facing the Brumairians after their seizure of power in November 1799 was France's desperate financial situation. Soon after the coup, the treasury informed Napoleon that it had only 167,000 francs on hand—and this when the cost of funding the government's basic operations exceeded 1 million a day![106] To deal with the crisis, the Consulate mobilized every resource it could. Although most of the physical *biens nationaux* had already been sold off during the previous decade, a mass of national rents remained in the hands of the state. According to the *Enregistrement*, these numbered over 300,000 and generated an annual revenue of over 6 million francs annually. They were distributed unevenly across France and varied in value from several francs to several thousand.[107] Nor were all the rents recoverable. According to one analyst in the Council of State, at least one-third of these rents was either contested or lacking titles.[108] Yet, despite these obstacles, the government concluded that, if capitalized by *rachat* or sale, the national rents presented a significant financial resource.

The government wasted no time in pursuing this aim. At the very first meeting of the new legislature on 12 Nivôse VIII/1 January 1800, it proposed a law on "the redemption of rents owed to the Republic."[109] Introducing the measure, councilor-of-state and soon-to-be head of the *Enregistrement*, Charles-Jacques Nicolas Duchatel, justified the measure in straightforward financial terms. The government needed money, and the Republic's rents were a valuable resource. "Despite the numerous reimbursements of rents, especially during the existence of paper money," they still offered a substantial annual revenue. Their collection, however, had proven costly, difficult, and slow. In contrast, *rachat* had the potential to allow the state to access their capital value quickly and with little effort. But the high rate at which *rachat* had been set in 1790 prevented the "numerous and valuable class of cultivators" from taking advantage of it. To revive the *rachat* operations and extend their benefit to this sector of society, Duchatel explained, the law under consideration would reduce the rate of *rachat* by 25 percent, from twenty to fifteen times the annual value. In practical terms, this meant that a 100-franc rent that could have previously been redeemed for 2,000 francs could now be extinguished for only 1,500. This reduction, Duchatel optimistically predicted, would lead debtors to reimburse most of the state's rents. To mop up the remainder, the government would offer them to individual buyers. Those who bought rents from the nation would be allowed to collect them, capitalize them by inciting a *rachat*, or even sell them to third parties.[110] The Tribunate approved the proposal unanimously, and the Legislative Body made it law on 21 Nivôse VIII/7 January 1800 by a vote of 224 to 3.

Initial results from the *rachat* and sale of the national rents seemed encouraging. The operation had, the Minister of Finance informed the Consuls a few months after the law's passage, improved the state's financial position. But more could be done. To this end, the Minister proposed revoking the law of 17 July 1793, which had suppressed ground rents stipulated in contracts with feudal provisions, and authorizing their *rachat* at the generous rate of ten times their annual value. Despite the steep discount, he assured, this would procure the government an additional 180 to 200 million francs.[111] His proposal seems to have inspired the unsuccessful attempt made by the Consulate the following Ventôse, discussed in chapter 3, to convince the legislature to revive the ground rents in question.

The *rachat* and sale of national rents thus proceeded without those established by feudally tainted contracts. A few departments experienced very good results. In the Vosges, for example, there were over 2,100 *rachats* of national rents in 1800.[112] But in the great majority of departments, the pace was slow. During the last months of the year, only twenty-eight people took advantage of the law of 21 Nivôse in the department of Vienne. Of these twenty-three effected a *rachat* and five a purchase.[113] The rents involved were of all types—ground rents, obituary rents, and others as well—and ranged in value from 5 to 125 francs annually. But all of the five rents purchased were ground rents, presumably because they were more secure (because backed by real estate) and easier to collect. Typical of these was the ground rent in grain purchased by the court clerk of Montmorillon, François Thomas. It had previously belonged to the Chapel of Pity which, in its turn, had depended on the Chapter of Our Lady of Montmorillon. The chapter had obtained it in 1545, as a pious bequest from Jean Giraud, former priest and canon of the chapter.

The *rachat* and sale of national rents in the poorer, mountainous department of the Aude proceeded somewhat differently.[114] There, forty-five operations took place: forty *rachats* and five sales. Nearly all the rents concerned were small ground rents, ranging from 1 to 33 francs annually. This suggests that most of these rents were the residue of small peasant property-ownership.

Given the loss of the archives of the *Enregistrement* and Ministry of Finance, it is impossible to know how much money these operations raised. But it soon became obvious to the government that the results were not brilliant. On 25 Brumaire IX/16 November 1800, Jean-Baptiste Lacoste reported to the Council that the 21 Nivôse law had had "little effect."[115] Ten years later, things had not markedly improved. At the beginning of 1810, it was estimated that the *rachat* and sale of national rents during the previous decade had raised only 5 million francs, a disappointing sum given that their total capital value was at least 45 million and quite possibly higher.[116] But it was clear to the Consular government long before this that something else needed to be done to capitalize the national rents.

Rescriptions and the War over the National Rents

On 25 Prairial VIII/16 June 1800, Napoleon approved a new method for converting the rents into capital.[117] By executive order, he authorized the Treasury to pay government contractors with certificates, called rescriptions, that they could exchange for national rents. In effect, this meant paying them with national rents. The purpose of this, his order stated, was to "place immediately at the government's disposition the important resources offered by the capital of the national rents, whose reimbursement can only be accomplished slowly and uncertainly." As a ministerial ruling made clear shortly after the executive order, contractors paid in rents could do what they liked with them—collect them, seek *rachats*, or sell them "without formality or fees."[118]

The payment of government contractors with national rents was far more effective than the *rachat*/sales operations.[119] One illustration comes from the department of the Indre-et-Loire.[120] There, more than 1,760 rents were eventually transferred to contractors, usually in great bundles, in eighty-one distinct payment operations. The total capital value of these rents exceeded 345,000 francs. Of the total, 744 rents worth over 105,000 francs went to a single individual, the merchant-banker of Blois, Norbert Lheritier-Vaugier. It is not clear from the records of the *Enregistrement*, which was only concerned with matching Lheritier-Vaugier's rescriptions to specific rents in its registers, what goods or services he had provided the government. Nor is it evident what the great merchant-banker felt about being paid in rents rather than cash. Nor is it known what he did with his rents.[121] But it is clear that operations of this sort, which took place in every department in France, went a long way toward getting the national rents out of the hands of the state. By 1810, the payment of government contractors with rescriptions had capitalized over 60 million francs worth of national rents.[122]

This practice, however, was not without its drawbacks. As had happened with the printing of *assignats* during the previous decade, the government found it hard to resist the temptation to issue more and more rescriptions. In year X/1801-2, it gave up trying to. In that year, the government took 6 million francs in valuable assets from the *Caisse d'amortissement* (a financial administration set up to help retire the debt) in exchange for 15 million francs worth of rescriptions for which national rents had not yet been found. Whatever concerns the government might have had that this would devalue the rescriptions, threaten the solvency of the *Caisse*, and put it on a collision course with contractors also seeking to identify rents to match to their rescriptions, all these concerns vanished before the allure of easy money. The *Caisse* thus found itself in desperate need of rents if it were to recoup its losses from what amounted to a 6-million-franc forced loan. At first, it sought to enlist the help of the *Enregistrement*, but these efforts produced scant results—in two years, only 400,000 francs worth of rents scattered across sixty-three departments.[123] And this in spite of the 5 percent commission on discoveries offered to the *Enregistrement* agents to stimulate their efforts.[124] Frustrated, the *Caisse* then sought to negotiate its rescriptions on the stock market, but their value plummeted to the prohibitively low rate of 36 to 45 percent of face value. Clearly, the rescriptions would be worthless unless national rents could be found for them. Frantic, the *Caisse's* director, François-Nicolas Mollien, began to hire private companies to sift through various archives to "discover" lost rents.[125]

It is difficult to get a clear picture of the chronology and extent of Mollien's recourse to private companies.[126] The first to be hired seems to have been the Dumarest company, which signed a contract on 21 Nivôse XIII/11 January 1805 giving it 8 percent of the value of the valid national rents it identified.[127] By early 1806, it claimed to have found 4 million francs in lost and dormant rents.[128] Encouraged by these results, Mollien extended these operations, ultimately contracting with six other companies—Godefroi and Cheron, Vanberchem and Leroux, Rouvin, Allard-Néoulle, Pezet-Corval, and Mariette—to cover the entire territory of the Empire.[129] The terms of their contracts were essentially the same as the original one signed with Dumarest.

The private companies seem to have been more successful than the over-burdened *Enregistrement* at discovering lost rents. By the beginning of 1810, they had found rents to match all but 2.5 million francs worth of the original 15 million in rescriptions.[130] But this very success led Duchatel, now head of the *Enregistrement*, to view the *Caisse's* contractors as interlopers whose very effectiveness posed an existential threat to his administration. In 1806, he launched a counterattack. First, he obtained permission from the Council of State to offer a much higher commission—25 percent as opposed to the *Caisse's* 8 percent—to anyone who brought their "discoveries" to the *Enregistrement*.[131] Second, he instituted legal proceedings against the head of one of the companies, Mariette, charging him with malfeasance.[132] It was alleged that he had stolen registers from local *Enregistrement* agents and taken for himself the money from the *rachat* of rents he had discovered. It was also alleged that his record-keeping was so shoddy that none of the rents he claimed to have discovered were actually useable. Although the government ultimately dropped the criminal charges against him, the damage was done—and not just to Mariette. Duchatel used the episode to cast aspersions on all the contractors, describing Leroux as a "poor moneychanger," Godefroy a mere "lottery administrator," and Vanberchem and Cheron as "wheelers and dealers" in a personal note to Napoleon. Their contracts were all revoked by Duchatel's ally, the Minister of Finance, in January 1808.[133] The *Enregistrement* had triumphed over the *Caisse* and its subcontractors.

The Hospitals Enter the Fray

The competition between the *Enregistrement* and *Caisse* was not the only conflict generated by the rescriptions. There was yet another party in the struggle, the hospitals, orphanages, and other charitable establishments of France. These became embroiled in the scramble for national rents in 1801 when the government decided to replace their physical properties (which had been sold as *biens nationaux*) with national rents.[134] This decision was overwhelmingly supported by the legislature and passed into law on 4 Ventôse IX/23 February 1801.[135] Henceforth, all "lost," "ignored," and "interrupted" national rents (the same ones sought by the *Enregistrement, Caisse*, and rescription-holders) were to form the endowment of the hospitals. Duchatel dutifully directed the local *Enregistrement* agents to comb through their records and provide the hospitals with titles to these dormant rents.[136] But again, results were disappointing. Perhaps because they were overworked, perhaps because they did not want to hand over their rents (on which their remuneration was partly based), the local agents do not seem to have put much effort into the task.

Given the lethargy, even passive resistance, of the *Enregistrement* agents, what were the hospitals to do? Like the *Caisse* when faced with similar inertia, they decided to turn to private companies to find rents for them. Taking advantage of a provision in the Ventôse law that encouraged "citizens" as well as public officials to bring national rents to the attention of the hospitals, individual establishments began to negotiate agreements directly with private contractors. Under this system, these people took their discoveries directly to the hospitals and were generally satisfied with taking arrears of these long-unpaid rents as their compensation. But once the *Enregistrement* began to offer a 25 percent commission for the discovery of lost national rents, they began to bypass the hospitals, instead going straight to Duchatel's administration.[137]

The result was the proliferation of companies which saw the search for national rents as a veritable El Dorado. According to Duchatel's account, the 1806 decision to offer 25 percent commissions had spawned a "multitude" of people who made a "business out of these sorts of affairs."[138] The names and numbers of these so-called "schemers" are unknown, although the two most prominent were the companies of Laraton and Montaiglon, both based in Paris. Although little is known about how this new crop of private companies operated, they probably employed the same strategies to capitalize "discovered" rents as had the *Caisse's* agents and those of the *Enregistrement*. For all of these agencies, the real purpose of identifying lost or concealed rents was to flush out their debtors and induce them to undertake a *rachat*. Once brought into the open, the delinquents would be given a choice: either pay the accumulated arrears (sometimes in excess of ten years) and make annual payments in the future or redeem it once and for all through *rachat*. From the agents' and government's perspective, this latter option was far preferable. Different means were employed to persuade the debtors to take it. One of these, recommended by Duchatel to his local bureaux chiefs, was to threaten to transfer the newly discovered rent to a rescription-holder. This would place the debtor at the mercy of the (presumably) more ruthless rescription-holder, but that was not all. It would also mean that the debtor must thereafter pay twenty times the annual value (per the existing legislation on privately held ground rents) rather than the special Brumairian rate of fifteen times the annual value (applicable only to national rents) if they wanted to effect a *rachat*.[139] A more common way of persuading the debtors was to forgive their arrears on condition that they effect a *rachat*. "It is necessary," one of the private companies' agents wrote, "to renounce the benefits of the past in order to obtain those of the future."[140] For a debtor who owed many years of arrears, this was an attractive option. But to make this system work, the agents charged with "discovering" lost rents also needed the authority to forgive arrears and, ideally, offer some flexibility on the rate of *rachat* itself.

When the power to discover rents and negotiate the terms of their *rachat* were vested in individual entrepreneurs, however, opportunities for abuse arose. Some observers believed that the private companies were particularly susceptible to this. Allegedly, they corrupted public officials, harassed the debtors of national rents, and profited shamelessly at the government's expense. There were certainly many illicit benefits unscrupulous agents could reap from this state of affairs. One was to bribe local *Enregistrement* officials to reclassify active rents as lost, thus allowing them to be claimed as "discoveries" for the 25 percent commission. Another was to steal or illegally purchase a national rent's title from the *Enregistrement*'s local office and treat directly with its debtor. In such instances, the debtor could either be made to pay a large sum for the title or might possibly even be blackmailed repeatedly with the threat of revelation.[141] By allowing unscrupulous profiteers to encroach upon the *Enregistrement*'s terrain, Duchatel fulminated, "outrage and corruption had spread everywhere."[142]

Matters came to a head in 1810. In a note dated 9 November 1810 Napoleon ordered a fundamental review.[143] His reason for doing so, however, was not the free-for-all between the *Enregistrement, Caisse*, hospitals, and the individual rescription-holders. Nor was it the alleged corruption of the private companies that had thrown themselves into the fray. Rather, what really seems to have prompted Napoleon's call for a review was the annexation in 1810 of new territories (Holland, much of Northern Germany, and large parts of Northern and Central Italy) which represented a potential windfall for imperial finances—if handled correctly. Chapter 3 has examined one result of the annexations: the recommendation drafted by Merlin and Cambacérès in early 1811 to roll-back the Convention's strict anti-feudal legislation. The other result was to provoke a general debate over how best to exploit the national rents.

Napoleon's request for an overhaul of domanial policy and practice was far from neutral. In his note, he expressed a preference for transferring responsibility for the national rents from the *Enregistrement* to a distinct administration or even a private company. "Everything leads me to believe," he wrote, "that we would achieve important results if an administration or special organization had a direct interest, thanks to big commissions, in procuring this revenue for the domain. There is no doubt that many millions can be discovered and that the moment has arrived to take steps in this regard."[144]

Working closely with Duchatel whose *Enregistrement* was part of his ministry, the Minister of Finances, Gaudin, prepared to defend his turf.[145] The two men argued that the *Enregistrement* was perfectly capable of administering the national rents. To create a new agency or, worse, authorize a self-interested company to handle them would be disastrous. Previous experience with such companies, both those employed by the *Caisse* and those which worked freelance for the hospitals, had demonstrated this beyond the shadow of a doubt. Because of their unscrupulous practices, the government had been deprived of resources, its administration had been penetrated and suborned, and innocent debtors of national rents had been harassed. The only thing the private companies had accomplished, Duchatel charged, was to hinder the operations of his administration.[146] Some changes were necessary, Gaudin and Duchatel conceded, but these—including once again the revival of the ground rents that had been suppressed in July 1793—could be implemented within the current administrative framework.

Against this, opposing position papers were printed and distributed to the Council of State. Although anonymous, the most forceful seems to have been written by one of the *Caisse*'s former contractors.[147] It began by savaging the *Enregistrement*'s performance during the past decade. Citing figures Duchatel himself had provided in an earlier statement, it noted that only 20 percent of the national rents recorded in its registers were actually viable. Many were feudal, others had already been redeemed, and still others lacked titles. This failure had two causes: the *Enregistrement* agents' lack of experience with difficult domanial issues and the incapacity of this single administration to perform all the tasks with which it had been charged. The solution was to shift responsibility for the national rents from the *Enregistrement* to a private company. This new company would have "no point of contact with the domain." Although it was to be supervised by commissioners delegated from the Council of State, its operations would be conducted in "secret," its true purpose concealed by the innocuous-sounding name "Archives Agency." This was necessary, the anonymous writer argued, to catch delinquents unaware. As compensation, the company would receive 25 percent of the capital value of rents it discovered and would also be allowed to negotiate *rachats* directly with their debtors. Finally, to provide legal rulings on rents whose non-feudal status was in dispute, a "consultative committee" would be set up under the direction of Merlin to "interpret the true meaning of the law of 17 July 1793." Given Merlin's well-known position on the matter, this would have effectively repealed the Convention's anti-feudal legislation. The payoff, claimed the writer, would be to increase the mass of national rents by 100 million francs.

Napoleon's call for a new look at the national rents thus revived competition between the *Enregistrement* and the private companies. It was, as one scholar has aptly put it, "the epilogue of a long struggle."[148] But there was a third position which also emerged during the course of the debate. This was articulated by Montaiglon, one of the most notorious of the "schemers" who had set up shop in 1806. His proposal was breathtaking in both its simplicity and its vast potential for corruption. Why not completely privatize the exploitation of the national rents? Why not let anyone who so desired engage in the discovery and negotiation of rents? Unbridled competition would be a spur to action. Only the "most diligent" would win, and the government would benefit.[149]

This debate took place in March 1811. But neither Napoleon nor the Council of State reached a decision. Instead, a commission was formed in January 1812 to study the matter further.[150] If it ever met, no record of its deliberations survives. It seems that the dramatic military and political events of 1813-14—which led, of course, to the loss of the newly annexed territories that had prompted Napoleon to undertake the review of feudal and domanial policy in the first place—so absorbed the government's attention, that it completely dropped the matter. In the end, all that this episode produced were papers.

The National Rents and the Feudal Question

Just like the issues of the mixed ground rents and feudal *engagement* rents, treated in chapters 3 and 5, respectively, that of the national rents intersected with the problem of feudal abolition and raised the question of whether the Convention's rigorous approach to it had infringed the rights of property. In considering how best to exploit the national rents, leading figures in Napoleon's regime repeatedly proposed abrogating the law of July 1793. Indeed, the potential windfall to be reaped by the state if it relaxed the anti-feudal legislation and collected national rents stipulated in contracts with feudal language was the principal argument for doing so. Ultimately the forces pushing for a relaxation prevailed, but only with the *Cour de Cassation*'s decision of 1834. But years before this, it seems that some of the Napoleonic *Enregistrement* offices in the provinces had quietly begun to collect feudally tinged national ground rents. Although the laws of the Council of State had repeatedly confirmed the Convention's anti-feudal legislation and even reinforced it, local agents still possessed a great deal of discretion when deciding whether or not a given rent was feudal. Since they received a percentage of the dues they collected, they clearly had an interest in preserving as many rents as possible.

In practice, therefore, if an agent called a rent non-feudal and the debtor was willing to pay it, then the rent was maintained. The registers of the local bureaux are thus full of rents that should have been suppressed in 1793, but that continued to be collected by the state well into the nineteenth century. Here is an example from the bureau of Marseille. It concerned an emphyteutic rent which had been established in favor of a convent in Marseille in 1612 and imposed on some of the land the convent had conceded. Although the rent was judged in 1813 to have been "created with a mix of feudality" and abolished, it had actually been paid through 1806. Another was the emphyteutic rent imposed in 1614 on a property conceded by the order of the Grands Carmes of Marseille. Although qualified in 1813 as an "emphyteutic rent mixed with feudality according to its title," it too had been paid well into the Napoleonic years (until 1805).[151] From these and many other examples, it is clear that the Napoleonic state itself, through the practice of its local agents, had some responsibility for prolonging the life of feudal property.

Although they did not scrupulously observe the national legislation, the agents of the Marseille bureau were at least consistent in their loose interpretation of it—an interpretation similar, if not identical, to Merlin's. In this, they sometimes received support from local tribunals. One illustration of this concerns the ground rent which had been imposed in 1724 by the order of Saint-Victor of Marseille on two parcels of farmland outside of the city. The debtor, Jean-Joseph Chaudony, was outraged and went to court. The local tribunal, however, upheld the legality of the rent and ordered him to pay it—which he did, through at least October 1806. Chaudony did not give up, however, and in 1813 the rent was finally deemed "feudal according to the titles."[152] The legal abolition of feudalism was thus not always taken on board or accepted by local tribunals. Together with the interpretative liberties taken by *Enregistrement* agents, nonchalance or ignorance on the part of the debtors, and the state's insatiable need for revenue, this ensured that feudally tinged national rents would persist for years—and in some cases decades—beyond their formal suppression.

The fall of Napoleon in 1815 did not end the ambiguity surrounding the national rents. Indeed, the return of the Bourbons inspired new fears of a revival of feudalism.[153] Although this proved illusory, the *Enregistrement* continued to grapple with the potentially feudal nature of the rents in its charge. In Marseille, for example, a systematic effort seems to have been made in 1816 and 1817 to distinguish between feudal and non-feudal ones.[154] Many of the former were thrown out, but others of dubious character were upheld and collected for decades. Possibly the most astonishing of the rents maintained as non-feudal was that imposed in 1714 by the Church of Saint-Martin of Marseille on a plot of land near the city. The original title described the property in question as "depending upon the *directe* of the aforesaid chapter" to which it owed an annual "*censive* of one *denier*." The rent's character appears even more questionable when one considers the ritual by which the chapter "bestowed the investiture" of the property on the purchaser, the gardener Etienne Nicholas. "By the touching of hands in the accustomed manner," Nicholas had recognized the chapter's "major direct domain and *seigneurie*," acknowledged its seigneurial right of first refusal *(droit de prélation)* and promised to pay "the *droit de lods* in case of alienation."[155] Despite all this, the rent—120 *livres* annually, representing a capital of 2,400 *livres*—was paid faithfully through the end of 1835 when the great-grandchildren of Etienne Nicholas finally effected a *rachat*.[156] Payments of such quasi-feudal national rents continued into the 1840s, and possibly beyond.[157] The persistence of these rents reinforces an argument developed throughout this book—that it was much harder to convert feudal into modern property than has generally been recognized. This was especially true when the rents in question belonged to the nation.

Conclusion

What was the significance of the national rents? Financially, they were negligible. Compared to the bulk of the *biens nationaux*, the Church, Crown, and émigré lands, they were obscure, marginal, and well deserving of the oblivion to which they have been consigned. But viewed from a constitutional perspective, the national rents were the most important of all the *biens nationaux*—because of the extraordinary range of challenges they posed to the revolutionary project of separating power and property. They were the mass of direct domain property the Revolution had acquired from the Crown, Church, and other similar institutions. Whether feudal or not, the national rents thus incarnated the very tenurial hierarchies of domination and dependence the Revolution sought to suppress. Too valuable to abandon, they were nonetheless totally antithetical to the Revolution's aim of independent, equal, and undivided property. By finally putting in place a mechanism to get rid of them, Napoleon scripted the last act in the great transformation of property begun in 1789.

That is significant, but there is more. The alienation of the national rents also completed the other operation required to realize the Great Demarcation—to remove property from the hands of the state. Although the revolutionaries had gone very far toward achieving this with the massive sale of physical *biens nationaux*, they had been stymied by the national rents. The problem of dealing with them thus passed to the Napoleonic regime. When it decided to reopen the sale and *rachat* of these incorporeal properties, it was completing the Revolution's unfinished business. In so doing, it consummated in a single action the two fundamental transformations the Revolution had sought to effect: the separation of property and power and the creation of a new order of equal and independent property. In this sense, Napoleon was very much heir to the Revolution.

Epilogue

It took many, many decades to realize in practice—and then only imperfectly—the Great Demarcation envisioned on the Night of August 4th. It would make for tedious reading indeed to follow this process to its bitter end, to the redemption of the last ground rent and *engagement*. Instead, this study concludes by examining the relationship between property and power as articulated in what many scholars take as the crowning achievement in the history of property in France—the Civil Code. Widely considered to be Napoleon's signal achievement, the Code (according to its makers) enshrined the fundamental principles of the French Revolution. Many commentators have agreed with them, but in recent decades a growing number have detected conservatism, backwardness, and even cynicism in the Code's provisions. Such critics have underlined some of its characteristics—the reinforcement of paternal authority, the disempowerment of women and children, and a general obsession with the absolute rights of property-holders—which fit uncomfortably with a certain vision of revolution.[1] But if assessed in relation to August 4th, the Code veritably breathed the principles pronounced on that Night. Those principles—the disentanglement of property and power and full property-ownership—pervade its articles.

This was no accident, for these fundamental aims were very much on the minds of its makers. Speaking of its approach to the issue of property, Treilhard promised that the Code presented "no vestige of the unsettled dispositions of feudal anarchy." It "ended the privileges of land just as much as those of birth . . . that is true equality."[2] As for the relationship between property and power, the Code confirmed their separation. "Property belongs to the citizen, empire to the sovereign," proclaimed Portalis. "Empire, which is the sovereign's share, contains no idea of domain . . . it consists solely in the power to govern."[3] Indeed, the very idea of a *civil* code reflected and reinforced the distinction made in 1789 between a public realm of power and a private realm of property. "The words *civil* law and *private* law are today synonyms," wrote the Council of State's secretary, Locré. "The Napoleonic Code is itself proof of it; all of its dispositions concern only particular interests."[4] The Code, Locré suggests, did not just consolidate the revolutionary remaking of property and power. It was itself made possible by their demarcation.

From the perspective of the transformations this book has explored, the makers of the Code were faithful to the principles of 1789. But, like their legislative predecessors, their attempts to translate those principles into workable law did not always go smoothly. At several points in their initial draft of the Code, they fell into the old confusion between property and power. One example comes from their treatment of the "different manners in which one acquires property." For reasons that are unclear, they resurrected a patriarchal conception of property rights by listing "paternal power" as the first way property could be acquired. The Paris appeals court, to which the draft was sent for comment, attacked this jarring provision.[5] It was omitted from the final version. The challenge of guaranteeing the independence of individual property from the state also proved daunting. The drafters realized that, in practice, collective needs sometimes had to trump the inviolability of individual property. To balance the rights of the property-owner with the needs of the polity, they were forced to define property in a way that many commentators have found unsatisfying, even self-contradictory. Property, stated article 544, was "the right to use and dispose of things *in the most absolute manner,*" but, it went on, that right was only absolute to the extent that the proprietor did "not use it in a way prohibited by laws or regulations."[6] This open-ended limitation of property rights has led one thoughtful but mistaken commentator to conclude that the Code was neither "individualistic" nor "modern," and that its reactionary makers wanted to preserve seigneurial property relations by renaming them.[7] This is going too far. Rather than interpret the Code's false steps and internal contradictions as evidence of bad faith, they should be seen as the byproducts of the makers' struggle with some of the same thorny questions—how to deal with the remnants of divided domain and where to trace the line between public and private property—that had bedeviled revolutionary legislators before them. By exploring the Code makers' efforts to resolve these issues, it becomes clear that they, like their predecessors, were consciously trying to realize in practice the principles crafted by the early modern jurists and proclaimed as the basis of the transformed polity by the revolutionaries on the Night of August 4th. In their attempts to do so, the makers of the Code would encounter the same problems of unifying divided domain and ensuring the demarcation between property and power.

In his famous Preliminary Discourse introducing the first draft of the Code to France, Jean-Etienne-Marie Portalis made this explicit. He began by insisting on the Code's revolutionary pedigree. It "maintained the salutary reforms enacted since the Revolution." Specifically, it abolished not only formal social distinctions but also the hierarchies of property entwined with those politically determined social categories.

> In the Old Regime, the distinction of privileged and non-privileged persons, of nobles and non-nobles, brought in its wake a crowd of property distinctions that have disappeared and cannot be revived. One might say that things were classed like persons. There were feudal properties and non-feudal, servile lands and free. All that exists no more.

But in the very same breath, Portalis admitted that this was just an ideal. Truly independent property was impossible to attain in a state of society. The "proximity of men" and their lands meant some degree of interdependence, and this would inevitably generate friction. Special laws on "urban and rural servitudes" (laws regulating the relations of real estate parcels to each other) were "indispensable."[8] Eliminating all traces of hierarchy and making all properties perfectly independent was thus impossible. Nor was it desirable in every circumstance. According to Portalis, the Revolution "had gone too far when, under pretext of erasing the smallest traces of feudalism, it had proscribed emphyteutic leases and perpetual ground rents." But rather than include a "particular and most complicated legislation" on these sorts of contracts in the Code, he announced, the drafting commission left the question of their reestablishment to the government's discretion.[9]

Before being submitted to the legislatures for approval, the draft of the Code was sent to the appellate courts of France for comment. Independently from one another, these courts zeroed in on the same set of articles—those related to proprietary independence and equality—at the heart of the revolutionary transformation of the polity. Portalis's ambiguous statement on ground rents was of particular concern. Some courts strongly supported their reestablishment and complained that an article to this effect should be placed in the Code.[10] The appellate court of Caen was insistent.

> We do not see why this contract, so useful and frequent, should be omitted from our code. Could it be because it has been assimilated to a feudal rent? Such an error could only gain credit at a time [the Terror] when all ideas were clouded.

The reestablishment of ground rents was thus "indispensable." But if it proved politically impossible to do so, the court suggested, perhaps it would be possible to stipulate that the *rachat* of such rents could only begin after a waiting period of twenty or thirty years.[11]

Other courts recoiled at the prospective return of ground rents. The most outspoken of these, the appeals court of Lyon, feared that Portalis's gesture in that direction presaged the return of feudalism itself. Going beyond the specific issue of ground rents, the Lyonnais magistrates issued a full-blown critique of the Code's suspicious silence on the absolute independence of individual properties.[12] They began by citing the law of 28 September 1791, which proclaimed that "the entire territory of France is free, just as the persons who inhabit it." This article, the magistrates lectured, "formally expressed the unanimous vow of the French nation for the fullness of property." But the draft code contained "not a single word about the liberty of the territory," nor any "precaution against the reestablishment of feudal servitudes." To remedy this, the court proposed a series of additional articles expressly prohibiting personal servitudes, property mutation fees, exclusive hunting rights, and other prerogatives formerly enjoyed by feudal lords. In essence, the Lyonnais magistrates wanted the Code to reiterate textually the many abolitions and prohibitions of August 4th.

When making their revisions, the Code's authors did not go this far. But they appended a new article, article 543, that reiterated in a subtle yet comprehensive fashion the abolition of divided domain in all of its forms. It stated that one could have "either a right of property over, or a simple right of use of, or the right to collect rent from" something. The terms "either . . . or . . . or" were inserted by the drafters to ensure that these various kinds of rights were exclusive of one another. One could not simultaneously hold two or three of these rights over something. This was intended to prevent a person from having both a property right in a thing and the right to collect dues from it—as was the case of lords who held the direct domain over a vassal's land while also levying various charges over it. By this elegant and entirely novel formulation, the makers of the Code had found a way to reaffirm the abolition of feudalism and divided domain without pronouncing the name of either, a kind of linguistic effacement even the members of the National Convention had been unable to achieve. But there could be no mistaking the drafters' intention. Treilhard spelled out its radical implications in a speech to the legislature. "The last article [543] . . . abolishes even the slightest trace of that domain of superiority formerly known by the names of feudal and *censuel seigneurie.*"[13] Théophile Berlier reassured the legislature on this score the following year, pronouncing that fiefs had been "abolished forever," as did Jean Albisson, who explicitly referenced the Night of August 4th.[14] Despite the fears of the appellate court of Lyon, it is certain that the makers of the Code had no second thoughts about the abolition of feudalism.

There still remained the question of perpetual ground rents. The Council of State seems to have been reluctant to deal with the issue, perhaps because opinions were sharply divided. These differences finally emerged into the open on 15 Ventôse XII/6 March 1804, after almost all the rest of the Code had been definitively drafted and approved by the legislature. Realizing that an explicit statement on ground rents was necessary, the Council finally resigned itself on that day to what its members surely knew would be a heated debate. Its membership was almost evenly divided, with Cambacérès, Jacques de Maleville, Jean Pelet, and Félix-Julien-Jean Bigot de Préamenu in favor of their reestablishment, and Tronchet, Jacques Defermon, Jean Bérenger, Emmanuel Crétet, and Regnaud Saint-Jean d'Angéley opposed. Portalis, who remained almost entirely silent, maneuvered—as he had done on prior occasions—to straddle both positions, trying not to offend his colleagues while at the same time attending closely to the way Napoleon (who was also in attendance) seemed to be leaning.

The session started with discussion of the economic ramifications of reviving ground rents. Those in favor rehashed arguments that had already been made in 1789, notably by Sieyès.[15] According to them, ground rents were the economic engine of the French countryside and the historic reason for its admirable development over the centuries. According to Maleville, they had "repopulated Gaul, devastated by barbarians and civil war" (57). Without them, France would still be covered by primeval forests. And they could still increase the amount of productive land. This is because property-holders unable to cultivate their lands personally would concede them under ground rents to peasant families who would clear them and make them fertile. Without ground rents, such property-owners would instead let their lands lie fallow, decreasing the amount of cultivated— and taxable—land in the country. They thus stimulated agriculture, increased tax revenue, and opened property-ownership to the poor, enhancing the stability of their families and of society as a whole. It would be better, Maleville admitted, if all properties could be held free and clear, but tolerating ground rents was clearly preferable to letting good land lie fallow.

Against this, the opponents of ground rents argued that they placed a crushing burden on the rural economy.[16] Far from encouraging poor peasants by the prospect of property-ownership, ground rents discouraged them by absorbing the fruits of their labor. The real way to spur agricultural production, Defermon argued, had been demonstrated by the Revolution—the "suppression of feudal rents and the possibility of redeeming ground rents" (61). Ground rents not only stifled production on individual fields but also dampened the rural land market in general. By "imprinting a perpetual stain" on properties, asserted Tronchet, ground rents "hindered the circulation of real estate; few people would consent to subject themselves to a charge from which they could never be freed" (57). In his only intervention in the debate, Portalis seemed at first to support ground rents, but ended up condemning them. He began by agreeing that they "multiplied the [number of] cultivators by making it possible for those without pecuniary means to make acquisitions." As such, they were appreciated, not resented as an unjust burden, by their debtors. But over time, a rent's "origin was forgotten," and it inevitably came to be seen as "a baseless servitude" (69). Despite their initial economic utility, ground rents inevitably evolved into sources of social tension and political liability.

The debate over the economics of ground rents thus raised political and constitutional issues that soon came to dominate the discussion. For the supporters of ground rents, the decisive consideration was to preserve the freedom of the proprietor to do as he liked with his property. For their opponents, what mattered most was the need to preserve the independence and equality of properties. Cambacérès spoke eloquently in favor of the former position. He began by noting that the sections of the Civil Code that had already been approved "authorized the most unlimited use, even abuse, of the right of property." Without violating this sacred principle, how could it be possible to prohibit a property-owner from alienating his property under a ground rent if neither "*moeurs* [moral norms] nor the interest of the state" were hurt by it (62)? Ground rents were not "essentially feudal" (56). So why had the Constituent Assembly abolished them? In Cambacérès's view, it had done so to "attack the privileged class" by going after "the property from which that class drew its force" while at the same time "attaching to itself the Third Estate." The Assembly's abolition of ground rents had "not been based on the principles of legislation," but had been motivated entirely by "politics" and "circumstance" (63). Many other revolutionary laws of circumstance, such as the institution of equal inheritance, had been revoked; there was no reason not to revoke the similarly circumstantial and equally ill-considered abolition of ground rents.

The opponents of ground rents argued that this form of contract created inequalities incompatible with liberty and equality. They were, according to Crétet, "a powerful means of holding [peasant] proprietors in [a state of] dependence." History had shown that ground rents always created "enormous inequalities." If they were reestablished, "the nation would be split into two classes." On one side would be those who "would enjoy the products of the earth without having to work." On the other would be "serfs, condemned to toil at the harshest labor just to pay their taxes and ground rent, without being able to obtain even basic subsistence for their families" (64-65). The revival of ground rents, chimed in Regnaud, would thus "create a new sort of supremacy in the village." Even if they did not "reestablish the diverse orders," they would nonetheless form "different classes of citizens" and the "drawbacks of feudalism" would return. Although a "purely civil" measure, the revival of ground rents would produce "great political effects" (68-69).

The supporters of the rents tried to counter these arguments by pointing out an awkward fact that probably no one on the Council wanted to hear, namely that the division of French society along class lines "already existed" even without ground rents (65). But it did not matter. At this point in the discussion,

Napoleon, who had not expressed the slightest interest in either the economic or constitutional implications of ground rents, redirected the conversation (66-67). What was "important above all else," he stated, was to determine "whether it was in the interest of the state" to reestablish ground rents. In his view, the matter was crystal clear. It was inconceivable that it could be beneficial to the state to set up a struggle between the tax collector and the owner of the ground rent over the peasant's surplus production. Moreover, as Bérenger had pointed out, properties burdened with ground rents generated less revenue in *droits d'enregistrement* because they changed hands less frequently and sold more cheaply than free properties. In all these ways, Napoleon concluded, it was the state that suffered most from ground rents. Under feudalism, when only a handful of great lords owned the land, they had been useful, for they had "softened the fate of the people" by giving them a property right (albeit subordinate) in their parcels. But with the end of feudalism, "this consideration had lost it force."

Ground rents, like all other rents, should thus be redeemable by their debtors. But, Napoleon continued, proprietors would not want to alienate their lands under redeemable ground rents if their debtors could reimburse the capital of the rent whenever they chose. The experience of the Thermidorean period had shown that, if allowed such an unlimited right of *rachat*, debtors would monitor fluctuations in inflation and the interest rate and wait until the former was high or the latter low to liberate themselves. Property-owners would foresee this and either leave their lands fallow or set their ground rents at prohibitively high rates to offset the risk of capital reimbursement in devalued currency. It was necessary, Napoleon concluded, to find a way of reconciling the legitimate interest of property-owners with the equally legitimate right of ground-rent debtors to effect a *rachat*. And he had a way. To square the circle, Napoleon proposed allowing proprietors who alienated their land under a ground rent to stipulate a period during which the rent would be irredeemable.[17] This compromise appealed to the Council. "Everything has been reconciled," exclaimed Pelet, with evident relief (67). Ground rents were thus declared essentially redeemable, albeit with the possibility of a thirty-year period in which redemption would be prohibited (76). The Council of State had remained faithful to the promise of the Night of August 4th by outlawing the perpetuity of rents—the source of divided domain—while at the same time making a pragmatic concession to the property-owning elite Napoleon wanted to attach to his rule.

The ambiguous hints about ground rents that Portalis had dropped in his Preliminary Discourse stoked the passions of the appeals courts and sparked debate within a divided Council of State. But the controversy over ground rents paled in comparison to that generated by the question of the relationship between individual property and the state. The first draft of the Civil Code contained a number of provisions which, in the view of the appeals courts, blurred the line between property and power. One of these provisions (Book II, Title 1, Article 1) seemed to classify the different categories of property according to the political status of their possessor. Properties, it read, belonged "either to the nation as a corps, or to public establishments, or to communes, or to individuals."[18] Of particular concern to the courts was that this article seemed to establish a distinct type of property right specific to public institutions. Even more threatening were articles 23 and 24. These not only appeared to reiterate the special property rights of public establishments, but worse, seemed to grant the state an open-ended authority to take the property of individuals. The first article stated that "the nation, public establishments, and communes" were bound by laws of property "specific to them," and that these distinct laws allowed them to "sell their properties and acquire new ones." The following article was even more troubling to the magistrates because it spoke of the nation's "right of recovering" properties it had alienated.[19] Taken together, these provisions gave the courts the impression that the Code was opening the way for the return of special laws for specific institutions, the revival of propertied political corps, and domanial exactions reminiscent of the Old Regime. They reacted with horror.

Leading the way again was the appeals court of Lyon.[20] It began with a sharp critique of the draft Code's implication of different kinds of property rights for the nation, public establishments, communes, and individuals. "The properties of the nation, communes, and public establishments," it asserted, "are governed by the same laws and the same forms as those of citizens."[21] Echoing these sentiments, the court of Paris focused particularly on the property rights the draft Code seemed to be affording public establishments. The various articles in question, it began, amounted to "a very formal recognition of a particular property right in public establishments." This was shocking, for "the question of whether these establishments are capable or not of possessing real estate as property was treated in great breadth and depth by the Constituent Assembly" during the debate over ecclesiastical property. That the drafting committee would include provisions "absolutely contrary" to the Assembly's decisions was astounding. That it had taken such a dramatic step without "even the slightest explanation in the Preliminary Discourse" was terrifying.[22] What was the government up to?

In fact, the makers had no secret intention of reviving propertied political corps. They had just been sloppy and subsequently rushed to correct their error. In their revised version of the Code, they erased all notion that the political status of the possessor somehow determined the nature of a property by deleting from Article 1 all reference to the "nation," "public establishments," "communes," and "individuals." Revised and renumbered as 516 in the definitive draft of the Code, the article simply stated that "all properties are moveable [*meubles*] or immovable [*immeubles*]." This implied that all property possessed the same, essential character, no matter to whom it belonged. Although seemingly minor, this change powerfully confirmed the Great Demarcation by establishing that property was defined by rules specific to itself, not by extraneous political factors. This, in short, confirmed the autonomy of the sphere of property. With this, the prospect of reviving proprietary corps vanished. Presenting the revised version of these articles to the legislature, Treilhard made it clear that they regarded only private, individual property, the "only type with which the Code is concerned." Things susceptible of private property could be "in the possession" of the nation or communes, but this did not change what Portalis described the following day as "their essential character."[23]

Of even more concern to the courts than the prospect of restoring special property rights to public establishments were the suggestions in the draft Code of a national domanial prerogative. While the former stirred memories of independent political corps, like the pre-1789 Church, the latter raised the specter of inquisitions, exactions, and extortions like those formerly conducted by the royal domain. The courts' fears centered on articles 23 and 24, which spoke of the nation not only buying and selling property, but, worse, recovering properties it had previously alienated.

The appeals court at Lyon led the protest yet again.[24] It began by criticizing the language of article 23—the one that spoke of the right of the nation, public establishments, and communes to buy and sell property. The article had to be replaced, it argued, because it involved those public instances too deeply in the realm of property, a realm that properly belonged to individuals. It proposed eliminating all reference to public establishments and replacing the existing formulation with the categorical statement that "the nation and communes can only acquire what is absolutely necessary and must sell everything that is not." Property had no place in the political sphere, except under exceptional circumstances; ideally, it should remain the exclusive preserve of the society of individuals.[25] Requiring that the state and communes alienate all but "absolutely necessary" properties amounted to a reaffirmation of the vision underlying the sale of *biens nationaux*, the vision of the Great Demarcation.

The court was even more troubled by article 24, which spoke of the nation's right to "recover" properties it had formerly alienated. The existence of such a right of recovery had never even been hinted at in the revolutionary debates over the national domain. But it was disturbingly familiar, for it had been the fundamental principle governing the former royal domain, that of inalienability, and enshrined in the Edict of Moulins. Did the makers of the Code hope to go back to the era of *engagements* and domanial extortion? The appeals court of Lyon certainly hoped not and lashed out at the article in a blistering attack that deserves to be quoted at length.

On seeing this article establish the principle that the nation has a right to recover its properties and rights, we bitterly recall the worry and expense, the harm and loss, even the ruin, that a great mass of citizens suffered in former times from inquisitions into domanial properties.

We ask ourselves what right the nation wants to reestablish or recover, over what properties it could have the right and intention to reclaim? . . .

The government's greatest interest, its first duty, is to ensure the stability of the citizens' properties. Their instability is a thousand times more dangerous, takes from the government a thousand times more revenue than it could possibly draw from the few properties it might recover. It is thus useful, even imperative, to suppress the end of this article and replace it with a disposition that assures that "the nation will never reclaim properties that it has alienated in proper legal form."

The shape of the polity envisioned by the Lyonnais magistrates emerges clearly from this criticism. On one side should be the sovereign state, divested of its holdings but guaranteeing the property of persons, while on the other should be society, defined by inviolable, individual property-holding. The continuity with the Night of August 4th—and the sixteenth-century jurists whose dream of demarcation informed it—is clear.

The enlarged committee charged with assimilating the magistrates' feedback and revising the original draft Code fundamentally rewrote the offending articles. There was no debate, no resistance to this within the committee. Louis-François-Antoine Goupil-Préfeln, the spokesman it chose to present the revised version to the legislature, portrayed it as an ironclad guarantee against future encroachment by the state upon an individual's private property. Thanks to it, he boasted, people would for the first time be able to obtain permanent legal injunctions against state claims to their property. As a result, private property would enjoy security to a degree it had never known before.

If this maxim had been consecrated by the ancient French legislation, if legitimate proprietors had been able to use it to oppose those men known under the name of *domanistes* or *feudistes*—men whose sole aim was . . . to despoil families who had possessed peacefully for many centuries—how many costly lawsuits mounted before distant tribunals would not have ruined those who defended themselves fruitlessly?

The Revolution's domanial reforms had "stopped these spoliations in their tracks." But the new disposition of the Code, permitting proprietors to prescribe against the nation in the same way they could against "particulars," would make "future and current property-holders [even] more confident."[26]

Speaking the same day, Portalis took great pains to reassure the legislators that he and his colleagues were utterly opposed to the notion of a proprietary state. When the "sovereign" levied taxes, it was not as a "superior and universal proprietor of the territory, but as supreme administrator of the public interest" that it did so. When it issued "civil laws to regulate the use of private property," it did so not as "master, but solely as arbitrator, as regulator, to maintain good order and peace." This had not always been the case. The "establishment of the feudal regime" had provoked a "strange revolution" through which "all ideas of the right of property were denatured . . . its true maxims obscured." It was because of this feudal revolution that the line between power and property had become blurred, that princes began to "arrogate property rights over the lands of particulars." But, he continued, the resulting confusion was never total. Neither in France nor anywhere else had "feudal lordship ever been seen as the necessary consequence of sovereignty." Even sovereign princes were considered to have two distinct qualities: that of "superior in the order of fiefs" and that of "political magistrate in the common order." The sixteenth-century jurists had clarified this distinction in theory, the Revolution had begun to carry out their vision in practice, and now the Code was enshrining the Great Demarcation permanently. Property was to be excluded forever from "the prerogatives of sovereign power."

In its silences, the language of the definitive version of the Code virtually screamed this demarcation. Its makers completely expunged those earlier provisions that spoke of the nation's right to acquire, sell, and recover property. Indeed, almost all references to the nation itself were deleted. When the drafters did mention the nation, it was to restrict its property rights. Thus, article 541 formally recognized the right of individuals to obtain injunctions against the state. And article 545 guaranteed that "no one can be forced to give up his property, except for the public utility and only after first receiving a just indemnity." In general, the Code limited the kinds of properties that could become "dependencies of the public domain" to those things "that are not susceptible of private property" such as rivers and ports.[27] The phrase "dependencies of the public domain" is significant because, like many other formulations in the Code, it is cast in such a way as to avoid the phrase "national property" or "property of the nation." Terms like "belonging to the nation," "in possession of the nation," or even "properties that do not belong to particulars" appear instead. This was no accident. The Code gives the nation a limited ability to possess, but never the right to own.[28] In contrast, the Code is full of references to "proprietors" and their "private property," The import of this is clear: individuals had a fundamental right to property, while the state could only dispose of things in exceptional circumstances. From its language, to its provisions, to its essential nature as a *civil*

Code, this legal monument confirmed and reinforced the distinction between property and power, confining each to its respective realm.

This brief look at the relationship between property and power in the Civil Code illustrates the extent to which legal personnel and their culture informed the revolutionary transformation of the polity. Its principal drafters were prominent jurists who had established their reputations well before the Revolution. They had thrown themselves into public affairs in 1789, serving as deputies and members of the government. One important finding of this book is that a distinct group of jurists (Cambacérès, Merlin, Treilhard, Tronchet, and several others) were instrumental in engineering the transformation of property that would make the Great Demarcation a reality. Historians have long recognized the role of lawyers in shaping eighteenth-century political culture and also their preponderance in the revolutionary assemblies.[29] But few scholars have considered how their professional culture helped define the Revolution's aims and policies.[30] The property reforms they enacted during the 1790s and enshrined by the Civil Code show the influence of sixteenth-century legal humanist thought. During the Restoration, the legal profession was proud of this filiation. Go back several centuries, the head of the Parisian bar urged his colleagues in 1829, "to the time when Bodin, Coquille, Loyseau, and Dumoulin were writing," for "mines of gold" could be found there.[31] Quietly, beneath the *sturm und drang* of the Revolution, the heirs of these early modern jurists steadily pursued their intellectual forebears' vision of a demarcation between property and power. They ultimately succeeded in making it the basis of the post-revolutionary polity.

This vein of continuity suggests that the French Revolution had a more deliberate, programmatic character than recent historical approaches allow for. Ever since the waning of the Marxist interpretation in the 1970s, historians have not emphasized the purposefulness of the revolutionary movement. This is in stark contrast to the Marxist interpretation, for which 1789 stood as the moment when a self-aware social class deliberately overturned the existing state of affairs and established a new order to suit its economic interests. This understanding of the Revolution rested on two notions: that objective socioeconomic factors determined revolutionary political aspirations and that the revolutionaries knew what they were aiming for when they overthrew the Old Regime. The collapse of the Marxist interpretation threw into question both of these notions.

The major historiographical trends that emerged in the wake of revisionism have articulated very different responses to the question of the relationship between social factors and political action. The discursive approach denies the existence of objective social reality behind political action. Instead, political action is impelled and given form by the discourses which structure a society's political culture. "Society" and the "social" are highly significant—but as discursive constructions which emerged (with fatal results for the old order) over the course of the eighteenth-century.[32] There is no objective social reality structuring action, only the internal logic of discourse itself.

Social historians have reacted against this position by focusing on instances where political actors, preferably from non-elite groups such as the peasantry or urban working class, inflected the course of revolutionary politics through their actions. To varying degrees, these historians acknowledge that "discourse" or "culture" mediated between the social realities that drove popular action and the forms and meanings that action assumed. But not infrequently, the role they allot to it is so secondary as to imply, like Marx did, a self-evident causal link between social reality and political action.

A third tendency, cultural history, has tried to bridge the gap between the two other approaches by showing how deep cultural shifts (which are increasingly being attributed to economic changes such as the rise of consumerism and the colonial economy) strained the political culture of the Old Regime to the breaking point and gave rise to new frames of meaning with radical political implications. The practitioners of cultural history recognize the importance of discourse, but they are equally concerned with the social forces that play upon and reshape it. It is the interaction between culture and society that produces political change.

In their very different ways, these approaches all provide new answers to the question of the relationship between the social and the political. But they share a common tendency to foreclose the possibility that the deputies self-consciously led the Revolution toward specific goals. The discursive approach leaves neither the revolutionaries nor anybody else with agency. Discourse structures their actions, discourse transforms occurrences into politically meaningful revolutionary events.[33] Paradoxically, the social approach also diminishes the agency of the revolutionary deputies. So intent is it upon highlighting popular action that it reduces the role of the legislators to insignificance. Like firemen rushing from one blaze to the next, they veer from crisis to crisis. In this view, people drive revolutionary politics, but this reduces the Revolution itself to a series of emergencies with no guiding purpose.[34] The cultural approach to the Revolution allows for both legislative and popular agency, but only within the cultural framework which defines the possibilities and meanings of action. Although individuals have choice and can act efficaciously, their choices and actions are constrained by the cultural grid within which they operate. Tectonic cultural shifts have already formed the channels through which revolutionary thought and action is compelled to flow.

Much can be said for and against each of these approaches. But none of them fits well with the story told in this book. The *Great Demarcation* has highlighted the importance of a compact group of lawyer-deputies who shared common social backgrounds, education, ideas, and aspirations. They seem to have been in control of the concepts furnished by their specific historio-legal milieu and to have used them purposefully to achieve their ends. They were doing more than articulating discourse, reacting to popular upheaval, and navigating culture. They were pursuing a program. That program, the Great Demarcation, was embedded within the legitimating discourses of the Revolution, resonated with revolutionary political culture, and contended with crises of all sorts. But to recognize these facts explains neither the substance of lawyer-deputies' overarching goal, nor the deliberate steps they took to realize it in practice.

Nothing better illustrates the clarity of their vision and the constancy with which they strove to attain it than their response to what was probably the most pressing and complex of all the contingencies faced by the Revolution—the debt. The national debt impinged on almost every aspect of political and social life during the Revolution. And in many ways it inhibited the revolutionary transformation of problematic properties. But at critical junctures, the revolutionaries shrugged off fiscal considerations in order to enact key constitutional reforms. Two striking instances of this were the decisions to abolish venal offices with full compensation for their owners (a commitment that added nearly a billion *livres* to the national debt) and to eliminate, rather than nationalize, the tithe (which, had it been treated like a feudal due and opened to *rachat*, would have easily provided for the reimbursement of those offices). Debt exerted a powerful influence, and that influence is at last being recognized by scholars.[35] But imperious as it could be, the debt took second stage to the Revolution's constitutional reforms. This is one of the reasons why the French Revolution was so radical and why contemporaries perceived it as such. When it mattered most, the revolutionaries pursued principle, even if that meant throwing pragmatism to the winds and bulling through contingencies. The issue of the debt—and the way the revolutionaries often set it aside in favor of their ideals—underlines the programmatic dimension of the Revolution.

There were many other revolutionary actors than Merlin and his like who were motivated by a conscious desire for change and pursued their aims with determination. Many of them were more visible and, in their moments of prominence, shone more brightly than the jurist-deputies. But most of them came to a bad end, and many of their aims remained unrealized—at least until 1848. Perhaps what helped Merlin and his kind to avoid the fate of Brissot, Danton, and Robespierre was that they were able to position themselves as technical experts above the fray. Whatever the reason for their survival and persistence, they were able to weather the storms of the Revolution and implement their program of demarcation. By recognizing that a core of revolutionary jurist-legislators successfully pursued a conscious vision of change with deep intellectual roots, we can restore the missing element of volition—and thus meaning—to historical understanding of the French Revolution. This perspective can help to explain why 1789 was significant and why contemporaries saw it as such a momentous event. Understood as the Great Demarcation, the Revolution was the moment when Europeans began a deliberate effort to break linguistically, legally, and institutionally with what had been the essence of their constitutional order— the confusion of property and power.

The revolutionaries' vision of a polity based on the separation of property and power was utopian. It not only sapped the conceptual foundation of the existing order, but also sought to make real what turned out to be an impossible distinction. *The Great Demarcation* has shown that the ideal of perfectly demarcated spheres of property and power proved stubbornly difficult to implement, not least because of the opposition it engendered. But the resistance of entrenched interests was eventually overcome. A more persistent—indeed, insurmountable—obstacle to the realization of the Great Demarcation was the inevitable friction of human interaction itself. The simple fact is that property-ownership (taken here in its broadest sense) conveys power over other people and their things. It could never be truly equal and absolutely independent. Yet, like all utopians, the revolutionaries attempted to realize the radical simplification of what existed—in their case, by trying to replace the interlocking webs of domination and dependence characteristic of early modern property relations with what the makers of the Code came to term "absolute" property. But despite their commitment to this ideal of hermetic property, they were forced to accept that, in the real world, properties, like the people who owned them, were entangled with other properties. And these entanglements were often hierarchical. Proprietary hierarchy could reemerge, they came to realize, in real-world situations, such as when water flowed from elevated terrain onto an adjacent land below (a case the makers of the Civil Code explicitly addressed) or when intellectual property is sold under a copyright (a case they did not consider). The history of property law since 1789 could be summed up as an ongoing attempt by jurists to construct new categories capable of comprehending the multiplicity of relationships generated by these entangled claims. Thus the proliferation of easements, servitudes, subsoil rights, condominium, and many others. Yet despite the messiness and complexity, the revolutionaries' impossible demarcation between pure power, on the one side, and absolute property, on the other, became the standard by which both are judged.

GLOSSARY

abbé: abbot

acte de reconaissance: legal document recognizing feudal overlordship

agrier: regional variant on the **champart**

albergement: the Dauphinois version of **emphyiteusis.** It was a type of non-feudal, hierarchical, divided-domain tenure and was generally accompanied by the **lods**.

allod: an independently owned property which depended upon no lord

antichrèse: a type of credit arrangement which assigned the lender of a capital the usufruct of a piece of real property in lieu of an interest payment

antiquaire: a scholar interested in ancient history

assignat: the paper money issued by the French government during the Revolution

augmentation des gages: fiscal maneuver to squeeze more money from venal officeholders

banalité: a milling, wine-pressing, bread-baking, or olive-pressing monopoly, often but not necessarily seigneurial

baron: baron

biens nationaux: the name given to former royal and ecclesiastical properties that were to be sold by the French nation to extricate it from its desperate fiscal straights. As the Revolution progressed, other confiscated properties, notably those of émigrés, were added to the **biens nationaux**.

bureau des trésoriers-généraux: a high financial court whose personnel had to purchase their offices. These offices were ennobling.

cahiers de doléances: list of grievances, aspirations, and instructions the electoral assemblies of 1789 provided to their deputies to the Estates-General

caisse d'amortissement: a financial administration set up to help retire the debt of the French state

cens: typically a small payment which signified the relationship of domination and dependence at the heart of the divided domain property arrangement. It generally indicated a land's dependence on a particular fief.

censive: a non-noble, dependent landholding under a feudal **directe**

centième denier: royal domanial sales tax

champart: an annual payment in kind representing a percentage of the harvest

ci-devant: literally "former"; used disparagingly during the Revolution to refer to nobles, fiefs, and other symbols of the Old Regime

comte: count

corps des arts et métiers: artisanal trade guild

corps politique: a corporate body entrusted with public authority and function

corvée: a seigneurial form of obligatory labor service under the Old Regime

cour (or tribunal) de cassation: the highest court in the French judicial system established after the French Revolution

cour des comptes: a sovereign financial court (the fiscal counterpart of the **parlements**) in which the magistrates were all venal officers. Their offices were ennobling.

dame: lady, used to refer to female lords

deniers: pence

directe: a form of incorporeal property consisting of the superior half of the two domains of the early modern French system of tenurial property-holding

domaniste: an expert in the law of the royal domain

droit d'amortissement: royal domanial tax imposed on the acquisition of sales by corporate bodies

droit de contrôle: royal domanial property sales tax, replaced by **droit d'enregistrement** after 1789

droit d'enregistrement: national property-sales tax instituted after 1789

droit de franc fief: an onerous indemnity non-nobles had to pay when they purchased fiefs

droit d'insinuation: royal domanial tax on inheritance arrangements

droit de prélation: the feudal right of first refusal on property transactions within a fief

droit de retour: the right of the Crown to reclaim fiefs left without a male heir

droit de retraite: the feudal right of first refusal on property transactions within a fief

droits casuels: property mutation fees

duc: duke

échanges: domanial properties transferred to individuals (known as *échangistes*) in exchange for equivalent properties transferred to the domain by those individuals

échevin, consul, capitoul, and jurat: various types of Old Regime municipal officers

emphytéose: **emphyteusis**

emphytéote: the holder of an **emphyteusis**

emphyteusis: a type of tenurial property-holding arrangement that, although non-feudal, produced a division of the domain of property and often stipulated a **cens** and **lods** as well as a perpetual ground rent

engagements: perpetually revocable grants of domanial property made to individuals (known as *engagistes*), in return for either a capital sum or an annual rent

état: formal personal standing within the Old Regime's society of orders

fermier: businessman who leases rights to collect taxes, feudal dues, etc.

feudiste: expert in the law of fiefs and their management

finance: capital sum paid to acquire a venal office or **engagement**

généralité: Old Regime administrative circumscription under a royal intendant

greffe: a record registration office

livelli: a type of perpetual ground rent common in Tuscany

livre: the pound of Old Regime France

lods et vente: mutation fees owed to the lord upon each sale of a property under his **directe**

mandats territoriaux: paper money that briefly replaced the **assignat** during the Directory

marquis: marquess

meier recht: German equivalent of the French **droit de retour**

notariat: a notarial practice

parlements: the highest provincial law courts in the Old Regime judicial system

péage: a toll to use a road, bridge, etc.

police: the regulatory powers of the lord over his tenants.

procureur-vendeur de meubles: public auctioneer of judicially seized goods

puissance publique: public power, often owned as private property before 1789

rachat: a repurchase system created by the Revolution to enable the holder of a useful domain to acquire the **directe** hanging over his land and thereby create a new type of complete, independent property. The system was meant to transform tenurial holding into property ownership.

ramhühner: a German equivalent of the French **champart**

Régie de l'Enregistrement: the Revolutionary administration responsible for the national domain

Régie des Domaines: the Old Regime administration responsible for the royal domain

rente convenancière: Breton feudal lease under which lord retained both domains of property

rente de fondation de messe: mass-endowing rent

rente emphytéotique: an emphyteutic rent

rente féodale: feudal rent

rente fieffée: Norman version of an **engagement** rent

rente obituaire: rent to fund prayers for the dead

rente seigneuriale: seigneurial rent

réunion: principle that prince's property becomes part of royal domain when he succeeds to the Throne

roturier: non-noble

seigneur: owner of a **seigneurie**, a lord

seigneur haut-jusiticer: a **seigneur** with the right of high justice

seigneurie: numbering about 70,000, **seigneuries** covered almost the entire surface of France. Although usually linked to a landed estate, called a fief, the **seigneurie** proper consisted in the right to exercise civil and criminal justice over the inhabitants of a specific area. This jurisdiction generally corresponded to the geographical boundaries of the fief with which the **seigneurie** was associated.

seigneurie directe (dominium directum): the jurist Loyseau's term for the superior property right in a hierarchical, divided-domain, tenurial arrangement. It was an abstract right that allowed its holder to demand certain dues and to exercise certain prerogatives over the subordinate property upon which it rested.

seigneurie utile (dominium utile): Loyseau's term for the subordinate property right in a hierarchical, divided-domain tenurial arrangement. It represented the actual possession and right to use a physical property, albeit subject to the **seigneurie directe**.

seigneurie privée: the jurist Loyseau's term for property rights

seigneurie publique: Loyseau's term for privately owned public power

sergenterie: office of sergeant

sieurie: archaic word for fully owned property

sous: shillings

supplément de finance: fiscal operation to squeeze more money from *engagistes*

surcens: a rent imposed on top of a **cens**

taille: the basic land tax under the Old Regime monarchy

tasque: regional variant of the **champart**

terrage: regional variant of the **champart**

treizième: Norman version of the **lods**

vicomte: viscount

NOTES

Introduction

1. Gérard Béaur, *Le Marché foncier à la veille de la Révolution: Les Mouvements de la propriété beauçerons dans les régions de Maintenon et de Janville de 1761 à 1790* (Paris: Editions de l'EHESS, 1989); Gérard Béaur, *L'Immobilier et la Révolution: Marché de la pierre et mutations urbaines, 1770-1810* (Paris: A. Collin, 1994); Jacques Dupâquier, *La Propriété et l'exploitation foncières à la fin de l'ancien régime dans la Gatinais septentrional* (Paris: Presses universitaires de France, 1956); Geneviève Koubi (ed.), *Propriété et révolution: Actes du colloque de Toulouse, 12–14 octobre 1989* (Paris: Editions du CNRS, 1990); Jean-Laurent Rosenthal, *The Fruits of Revolution: Property Rights, Litigation, and French Agriculture, 1700-1860* (Cambridge: Cambridge University Press, 1992); and Albert Soboul, *Les Campagnes montpeliéranes à la fin de l'ancien régime: Propriété et cultures d'après les compoix* (Paris: Presses universitaires de France, 1958). A notable exception is William H. Sewell Jr., *Work and Revolution in France: The Language of Labor from the Old Regime to 1848* (Cambridge: Cambridge University Press, 1980), chapter 6, "A Revolution in Property," 114–42.
2. Robert Descimon, "La Venalité des offices et la construction de l'Etat dans la France moderne: Des problèmes de la représentation symbolique aux problèmes du coût social du pouvoir," in Robert Descimon, Jean-Frédéric Schaub, and Bernard Vincent (eds.), *Les Figures de l'administrateur: Institutions, réseaux, pouvoirs en Espagne, en France et au Portugal* (Paris: Editions de l'EHESS, 1997), 77–93.
3. David D. Bien, "Offices, Corps, and a System of State Credit," in *The French Revolution and the Creation of Modern Political Culture*, vol. 1, *The Political Culture of the Old Regime*, ed. K. M. Baker (Oxford: Oxford University Press, 1987), 89–114; David D. Bien, "Les Offices, les corps et le crédit d'Etat: L'Utilisation des privilèges sous l'Ancien Régime," *Annales H.S.S.* 43, no. 2 (1988): 379–404; David D. Bien, "Manufacturing Nobles: The Chancelleries in France to 1789," *Journal of Modern History* 61, no. 3 (1989): 445–86; and Robert Descimon, "La Venalité des offices comme dette publique sous l'ancien régime français: Le Bien commun au pays des intérêts privés," in *La Dette publique dans l'histoire*, ed. Jean Andreau, Gérard Béaur, and Jean-Yves Grenier (Paris: Comité pour l'histoire économique et financière de la France, 2006), 175–240.
4. Guy Chaussinand-Nogaret, *La Noblesse au XVIIIè siècle: De la féodalité aux Lumières* (Paris: Hachette, 1976), 54.
5. François Bluche and Pierre Durye, *L'Anoblissement par charges avant 1789* (La Roche-sur-Yon: Imprimerie centrale de l'Ouest, 1962); William Doyle, *Venality: The Sale of Offices in 18th Century France* (Oxford: Clarendon Press, 1996); and Roland Mousnier, *La Venalité des offices sous Henri IV et Louis XIII*, 2nd ed. (Paris: Presses universitaires de France, 1971).
6. From the printed but unpublished inventory of Lyon's communal archives, 281–313.

7. Gail Bossenga, "Markets, the Patrimonial State, and the Origins of the French Revolution," *1650-1850: Ideas, Aesthetics, and Inquiries in the Early Modern Era* 11 (2005): 443–510.

8. Louis Ventre de la Touloubre, *Jurisprudence observée en Provence sur les matières féodales et les droits seigneuriaux divisée en deux parties* (Avignon: n.p., 1756), 117.

9. The term "social imaginary" is borrowed from Sarah Maza, *The Myth of the French Bourgeoisie: An Essay on the Social Imaginary, 1750-1850* (Cambridge, MA: Harvard University Press, 2005).

10. Tocqueville believed that "this impost was more responsible than any other for the great gulf that developed between the nobleman and the non-noble." Alexis de Tocqueville, *The Old Regime and the French Revolution*, trans. Stuart Gilbert (Garden City, NJ: Doubleday, 1955), 102.

11. This was the typical structure of property in Western Europe and the Americas until the eighteenth century, when it began to be rolled back. It still survives today in parts of Europe and its former colonies. It was particularly vigorous in Scotland where "the overwhelming majority of Scots lands [were] held . . . by a feudal title" within a complex "hierarchy of sovereign, superior, and vassal" until the Scottish Parliament passed the Abolition of Feudal Tenure Act in 2000. C. F. Kolbert and N. A. M. Mackay, *History of Scots and English Land Law* (The Keep, Berkhampsted, Herts: Geographical Publications Limited, 1977), 103 and 107. It still predominates in Brazil.

12. For a strong argument that a formal system of feudal government never actually existed during the Middle Ages, but was actually a creation of sixteenth-century jurists, see Elizabeth A. Brown, "The Tyranny of a Construct: Feudalism and the Historians of Medieval Europe," *American Historical Review* 79, no. 4 (October 1974): 1063–88. Brown's argument was further developed by Susan Reynolds, *Fiefs and Vassals: The Medieval Evidence Reinterpreted* (Oxford: Oxford University Press, 1994).

13. Bien, "Offices, Corps, and a System of State Credit," 89–114.

14. Figures from Paul Boiteau, *Etat de la France en 1789* (Paris: Perrotin, 1861), 339. On the high courts and magisterial elite of Aix, see Donna Bohanan, *Old and New Nobility in Aix-en-Provence, 1600-1695: Portrait of an Urban Elite* (Baton Rouge: Louisiana State University Press, 1992); and Monique Cubells, *La Provence des Lumières: Les Parlementaires d'Aix au 18è siècle* (Paris: Maloine, 1984).

15. Information on d'Albert, his family, and his *seigneurie* of Bormes is from Archives départementales (hereinafter, AD) du Var, 2 J 198 dossier l'Enfant and 4 E 14 Bormes. Further information is from Philemon Giraud, *Notes chronologiques pour servir à l'histoire de Bormes* (Hyerès: Cruves, 1859), and Louis Honoré, *Bormes au dix-huitième siècle* (Montauban: Orphelins imprimeurs, 1913).

16. Rafe Blaufarb, *The Politics of Fiscal Privilege in Provence, 1530s-1830s* (Washington, DC: Catholic University Press of America, 2012), 242–62.

17. Like the one in Bormes, it was empty and in an extreme state of disrepair, for Gautier de Girenton lived in Aix like d'Albert.

18. AD Bouches-du-Rhône, 1 Q 1025. He was the seventh (out of over 400) to do so.

19. By the Ordinance of 24 February 1645, confirmed after the restoration of the monarchy by act of Charles II in 1660.

20. America's path to the abolition of tenure was not straightforward. The New England colonies abolished feudal tenure before 1776. Eight states did so during or after the Revolution. But two (Pennsylvania and South Carolina) explicitly retained forms of proprietary tenure, and three others (Delaware, Georgia, and North Carolina) said nothing on the issue. See William R. Vance, "The Question for Tenure in the United States," *Yale Law Journal* 33, no. 3 (January 1924): 248–71.

21. On Tuscany, see Eric Cochrane, *Florence in the Forgotten Centuries, 1527-1800: A History of Florence and the Florentines in the Age of the Grand Dukes* (Chicago: University of Chicago Press, 1973), 428–91; Furio Diaz, *Francesco Maria Gianni: Dalla burocrazia alla politica sotto Pietro Leopoldo di Toscana* (Milan: R. Ricciardi, 1966); and Gavriele Turi, *"Viva Maria": La reazione alle riforme Leopoldine (1790-1799)* (Florence: L. S. Olschki, 1969). On Piedmont, see Max Bruchet, *L'Abolition des droits seigneuriaux en Savoie (1761-1793)* (Marseille: Lafitte reprints, [1908] 1979).

22. Cited in E. E. Rich and C. H. Wilson (eds.), *The Cambridge Economic History of Europe* (Cambridge: Cambridge University Press, 1977), 5:620.

23. For Marx, feudalism was primarily a mode of production "characterized by division of the soil amongst the greatest possible number of sub-feudatories." Karl Marx, *Capital: A Critique of Political Economy* (New York: Modern Library, 1936), 789. Decades before Marx, Adam Smith had focused on the economic ramifications of what he called "the feudal system." But unlike Marx, who believed that the economic structure of feudalism determined the feudal form of government, Smith believed that the economics of the "feudal system" were a consequence of "feudal government." Adam Smith, *An Inquiry into the Nature and Causes of the Wealth of Nations* (London: A. Strahan and T. Cadell, 1789), 1:376 and 422.

24. For a concise survey of this historiography, see William Doyle, *Origins of the French Revolution*, 3rd ed. (Oxford: Oxford University Press, 1999), 3–42.

25. Lauren R. Clay, "The Bourgeoisie, Capitalism, and the Origins of the French Revolution," in *The Oxford Handbook of the French Revolution*, ed. David Andress (Oxford: Oxford University Press, 2015), 21–39; Colin Jones, "The Great Chain of Buying: Medical Advertisement, the Bourgeois Public Sphere, and the Origins of the French Revolution," *American Historical Review* 101, no. 1 (1996): 13–40; Michael Kwass, *Contraband: Louis Mandrin and the Making of a Global Underground* (Cambridge, MA: Harvard University Press, 2014); Silvia Marzagalli, "Economic and Demographic Developments," in Andress (ed.), *Oxford Handbook*, 3–20; and William H. Sewell Jr., "Connecting Capitalism to the French Revolution: The Parisian Promenade and the Origins of Civic Equality in Eighteenth-Century France," *Critical Historical Studies* 1, no. 1 (Spring 2014): 5–46.

26. The term seems to have been coined in the 1720s by Henri de Boulainvilliers, who is discussed in the next chapter. Popularized by Montesquieu and Voltaire, it quickly passed into common usage.

27. The term is borrowed from J. G. A. Pocock, *The Ancient Constitution and the Feudal Law: English Historical Thought in the Seventeenth Century* (Cambridge: Cambridge University Press, 1957).

28. It was also an important way of talking about the self. See Charly Coleman, *The Virtues of Abandon: An Anti-Individualist History of the French Enlightenment* (Stanford, CA: Stanford University Press, 2014).

29. In a similar vein, Lucien Jaume traces the revolutionary conception of sovereignty to the sixteenth-century jurists. *Le Discours jacobin et la démocratie* (Paris: Fayard, 1989), 263–81.

30. Marcel Garaud, *Histoire générale du droit privé français*, vol. 2, *La Révolution et la propriété foncière* (Paris: Sirey, 1953).

31. In 2000 there were already more than 800 published studies of the nationalized properties. Eric Bodinier and Eric Teyssier, *L'Événement le plus important de la Révolution: La Vente des biens nationaux* (Paris: CTHS, 2000).

32. And, economic historians have argued in a vast literature, the essential precondition of capitalism. See Douglass C. North's classic *Structure and Change in Economic History* (New York: W. W. Norton, 1981) and the recent collection reassessing North's impact on the study of property rights and economic development edited by Sebastian Galiani, *Institutions, Property Right, and Economic Growth* (Cambridge: Cambridge University Press, 2014).

33. The term is from John Berger, *Ways of Seeing* (Harmondsworth, UK: Penguin, 1972).

Chapter 1

1. *AP*, 8:352. The phrase was dropped from the definitive decree, but reappeared in the rural code of 1791.

2. Daniel Edelstein, however, has recently questioned the centrality of Locke to eighteenth-century French thought in "Enlightenment Rights Talk," *Journal of Modern History* 84, no. 3 (September 2014): 530–65.

3. Thomas Kaiser, "Property, Sovereignty, the Declaration of the Rights of Man, and the Tradition of French Jurisprudence," in *The French Idea of Freedom: The Old Regime and the Declaration of Rights of 1789*, ed. Dale Van Kley (Stanford, CA: Stanford University Press, 1994), 301. Although it is not concerned with the eighteenth century, David Parker's

article on seventeenth-century conceptions of property provides essential background. See his "Absolutism, Feudalism, and Property Rights in the France of Louis XIV," *Past and Present*, no. 179 (May 2003): 60–96.

4. Kaiser, "Property, Sovereignty," 310–17. Although often translated by the common-law term "freehold," the *allod* was actually its antithesis. For unlike the English freeholds which were always held of some superior (as the name implies), *allods* were, by definition, *held* of nobody, but rather *owned* absolutely.

5. This point is made by Johnson Kent Wright, *A Classical Republican in Eighteenth-Century France: The Political Thought of Mably* (Palo Alto, CA: Stanford University Press, 1997), 125. A partial exception is J. Q. C. Mackrell, *The Attack on Feudalism in Eighteenth-Century France* (London: Routledge and Kegan Paul, 1973). Historians of the sixteenth century, however, have studied this subject in depth. In particular, see William Farr Church, *Constitutional Thought in Sixteenth-Century France: A Study in the Evolution of Ideas* (Cambridge, MA: Harvard University Press, 1941); Georges Huppert, "Naissance de l'histoire en France: Les 'Recherches' d'Estienne Pasquier," *Annales E.S.C.*, 23è année, no. 1 (1968): 69–105; Donald R. Kelley, "De Origine Feodorum: The Beginnings of a Historical Problem," *Speculum* 39, no. 2 (April 1964): 207–29; Donald R. Kelley, *Foundations of Modern Historical Scholarship: Language, Law, and History in the French Renaissance* (New York: Columbia University Press, 1970); Nannerl O. Keohane, *Philosophy and the State in France: The Renaissance to the Enlightenment* (Princeton, NJ: Princeton University Press, 1980); J. H. Salmon, "Renaissance Jurists and 'Enlightened' Magistrates: Perspectives on Feudalism in Eighteenth-Century France," *French History* 8, no. 4 (1994): 387–402; and Quentin Skinner, *The Foundations of Modern Political Thought*, 2 vols. (Cambridge: Cambridge University Press, 1978).

6. The foundational work is J. G. A. Pocock, *The Ancient Constitution and the Feudal Law: A Study of English Historical Thought in the Sixteenth Century* (Cambridge: Cambridge University Press, 1957).

7. A notable exception is Pocock, "Historical Introduction," in *The Political Works of James Harrington*, ed. J. G. A. Pocock (Cambridge: Cambridge University Press, 1977), 1–152.

8. Pocock, *Ancient Constitution*, 1. In Pocock's estimation, their study of the origins of fiefs was "the most remarkable historical work" the legal humanists undertook. J. G. A. Pocock, "The Origins of the Study of the Past: A Comparative Approach," in his *Political Thought and History: Essays on Theory and Method* (Cambridge: Cambridge University Press, 2009), 168.

9. The key Germanist work is François Hotman, *La Gaule françoise* (Cologne: Hierome Bertulphe, 1574).

10. Brown, "The Tyranny of a Construct"; and Reynolds, *Fiefs and Vassals*.

11. Antoine-Gaspard Boucher d'Argis, *Code rural, ou maximes et règlemens concernant les biens de campagne* (Paris: Prault, 1767), 1:29, italics added.

12. Pierre Bouquet, *Lettres provinciales, ou examen impartial de l'origine de la constitution et des révolutions de la monarchie françoise* (La Haye, Neutre, et Paris: Merlin, 1772), 16–17.

13. Lefevre de la Planche, *Mémoires sur les matières domaniales, ou traité du domaine* (Paris: Desaint and Saillant, 1764), 1:xliiii.

14. Abbé Fleury, *Droit public de France*, ed. J. B. Daragon (Paris: La Veuve Pierres, 1769), 1:5–9. Fleury noted several exceptions: (1) lords had retained the honorific marks of military power, (2) they continued to hold certain rights of taxation, and (3) they retained civil and criminal justice within their territories.

15. Bouquet, *Lettres provinciales*, 16–17.

16. Lefevre de la Planche, *Mémoires sur les matières domaniales*, 1:xxxvi.

17. "Dominium directum et jus regium universaliter in toto regne." Cited in Jean-Louis Thireau, *Charles Du Moulin (1500-1566): Etude sur les sources, la méthode, les idées politiques et économiques d'un juriste de la Renaissance* (Geneva: Droz, 1980), 232.

18. Ralph E. Giesey, "The Juristic Basis of Dynastic Right to the French Throne," *Transactions of the American Philosophical Society*, n.s., 51, no. 5 (1961): 3–47.

19. Skinner, *Foundations*, 2:264.

20. Cited in Thireau, *Charles Du Moulin*, 241.

21. Jean Bodin, *Les Six Livres de la République* (Paris: Jacques du Puis, 1583). Page references are in text.

22. Church, *Constitutional Thought*, 194–242; Julian Franklin, *Jean Bodin and the Rise of Absolutist Theory* (Cambridge: Cambridge University Press, 1973); Michael Sonenscher, *Before the Deluge: Public Debt, Inequality, and the Intellectual Origins of the French Revolution* (Princeton, NJ: Princeton University Press, 2007), 151–52; and Yves-Charles Zarka, "Constitution et souveraineté selon Bodin," *Il Pensiero Politico* 30, no. 2 (1997): 276–86.

23. Skinner, *Foundations*, 2:352 and 356.

24. From the journal Bodin kept while attending the Estates-General of Blois of 1576, cited by Robinet, *Dictionnaire universel des sciences morale, économique, politique, et diplomatique; ou Bibliothèque de l'homme d'état et citoyen* (Londres: Libraires associés, 1782), 22:33.

25. He did, however, allow for eminent domain: the appropriation of private property if neces- sary for the "conservation of the State." Bodin considered this right an attribute of pure sover- eignty, not a type of property right. And although he did not speak about the indemnities this might entail, the view that compensation was required in such cases was well established in jurisprudence. Old Regime jurists distinguished scrupulously between eminent domain and royal domanial property right. Napoleon's Civil Code would enshrine this distinction, along with the principle of indemnification.

26. Skinner, *Foundations*, 2:296–97.

27. Jean Bodin, *On Sovereignty*, ed. Julian H. Franklin (Cambridge: Cambridge University Press, 1992), xxii.

28. Herbert Rowen, *The King's State: Proprietary Dynasticism in Early Modern France* (New Brunswick, NJ: Rutgers University Press, 1980), 42.

29. The noun form of "*saisi de*" or "possessed of" was "*saisine*," the exact equivalent of "seisin," the common-law term for the legal act by which one formally entered into possession of a feudal property.

30. For an overview of his political thought, see Brigitte Basdevant-Gaudemet, *Aux origines de l'état moderne: Charles Loyseau, 1564-1627, théoricien de la puissance publique* (Paris: Economica, 1977); Jean Lelong, *La Vie et les oeuvres de Loyseau (1564-1627)* (Paris: LGDJ, 1909); and Howell A. Lloyd, "The Political Thought of Charles Loyseau (1564-1627)," *European History Quarterly* 111 (1981): 53–82.

31. This is the only one of his works to have been (partially) translated into English and published.

32. Loyseau's influence was immense. His works appeared in at least twenty editions over the course of the seventeenth century and directly influenced eighteenth-century theorists, such as Boucher d'Argis, whose *Encyclopédie* entry "Seigneurie" is nothing more than a summary of the theory Loyseau advanced in his *Treatise on Seigneuries*. *Encyclopédie*, 14:896–98.

33. Charles Loyseau, *Traité des seigneuries* (Paris: Abel L'Angelier, 1608). Page references are in text.

34. Rousseau borrows Loyseau's etymology of *seigneur* in his *Discourse on the Origins of Inequality*. See Jean-Jacques Rousseau, *Discourse on the Origins of Inequality (2nd Discourse), Polemics and Political Economy*, vol. 3, *Collected Writings of Rousseau*, ed. Roger D. Masters and Christopher Kelly, trans. Judith R. Bush, Roger D. Masters, Christopher Kelly, and Terrence Marshall (Hanover, NH and London: University Press of New England, 1992), 61.

35. This disparaging view of the origin of *seigneuries* was widely shared and even amplified in the eighteenth century. Thus, for the last royal historiographer of the Old Regime, Jacob-Nicolas Moreau, the usurpation as property of the sovereign right of justice transformed the "power of government" into the "power of property." With the transformation of "public power" into "a dependence and attribute of property," the kings found themselves "stripped of their author- ity." The entire work goes on in this vein, culminating in a call to recognize "the essential dif- ference" between "the power of property and the power of government." *Leçons de morale, de politique, et de droit pubic, puisées dans l'histoire de notre monarchie* (Versailles: Imprimerie du département des affaires étrangères, 1773), 81 and 179.

36. Loyseau was writing before the French acquired permanent overseas colonies and became involved in the transatlantic slave trade. Perhaps the explicit antislavery statements of Loyseau and other founders of the early modern French legal tradition can explain why no significant body of commentary on colonial law arose during the seventeenth and eighteenth centuries. Since it was impossible to reconcile the foundational principles of legal humanist jurispru- dence with chattel slavery, later generations of jurists kept silent and the French colonies

were allowed to develop in a virtual legal vacuum. On the absence of colonial law during the nineteenth century, see Miranda Frances Spieler, *Empire and Underworld: Captivity in French Guiana* (Cambridge, MA: Harvard University Press, 2012).

37. The paradoxical notion that property could originate from an act of nationalization finds an echo in the expropriation and sale of the *biens nationaux*. Might we think of the revolutionary nationalization in similar terms, as a moment when land redistribution accompanied the creation of a new polity?

38. For example, see Jacques Peissonel, *Traité de l'heredité des fiefs de Provence* (Aix: E. Roize, 1687).

39. Unlike some later writers, Loyseau did not view this as the source of the distinction between nobility and Third Estate.

40. Ed. Meynial, "Notes sur la formation de la théorie du domaine divisé (domaine direct et domaine utile) du XIIe au XIVe siècle dans les romanistes: Etude de dogmatique juridique," in *Melanges Fitting* (Montpellier: Société anonyme de l'imprimerie générale du midi, 1907), 410–61.

41. Others made this even more explicit. Pierre Jacquet wrote that it led to the "subjection of the tenant and the superiority of the lord." *Traité des fiefs* (Paris: Samson, 1763), 336. Charles de Lorry noted that "there remains in private *seigneurie* some mix of public *seigneurie*, the residue of the confusion of these two *seigneuries* over time." Lefevre de la Planche, *Mémoires sur les matières domaniales*, 1:lxxvii.

42. Boucher d'Argis expressed a similar sentiment in the eighteenth century. "The property that used to be called *sieurie*, from the pronoun '*sien*,' never partook of *seigneurie* or public power." "Seigneurie," *Encyclopédie*, 14:896–98.

43. The equation of proprietary kingship with despotism was widely held down to 1789 and even enjoyed something of a renaissance after 1750, in the context of resistance to the monarchy's unpopular tax increases.

44. The best summary is Margueritte Boulet-Sautel, "De Choppin à Proudhon: Naissance de la notion moderne de domaine public," *Droits* 22 (January 1994): 91–94.

45. René Choppin, *Trois livres du domaine de la Couronne de France* (Paris: Michel Sonnius, [orig. pub.1572] 1613), 12.

46. Ibid., 12 and 81.

47. Other important *domanistes* were Jehan Bacquet, *Quatrième traicté . . . des droits du domaine de la Couronne de France* (Paris: Nivelle, 1582); Pierre Cardin Le Bret, *De la souveraineté du Roi* (Paris: Toussaincts de Bray, 1632); Lefevre de la Planche, *Mémoires sur les matières domaniales*; and Bosquet, *Dictionnaire raisonné des domaines et droits domaniales*, 3 vols. (Rouen: J. J. Le Boullenger, 1762).

48. In its article on the "Domaine de la Couronne," the *Encyclopédie*, for example, listed no less than eleven separate domanial properties that "depended on [the King's] right of justice" (5:22).

49. Although jurists before and after 1789 often assumed that the Edict of Moulins established the doctrine of domanial inalienability, Guillaume Leyte has shown that it was actually the product of a historical evolution that began in the twelfth century. See his *Domaine et domanialité publique dans la France médiévale (XIIe-XVe siècles)*. Robert Descimon has shown that the definitive triumph of the doctrine of inalienability only came in 1607, with the reunion of Henri IV's Kingdom of Navarre to the royal domain of France. See his "L'Union au domaine royal et le principe d'inaliénabilité: La Construction d'une loi fondamentale au XVIe et XVIIe siècles," *Droits: Revue française de théorie juridique* 22 (1995): 81.

50. Sarah Hanley, *The Lit de Justice of the Kings of France: Constitutional Ideology in Legal Ritual and Discourse* (Princeton, NJ: Princeton, 1983), 174–82. See also Aurélie du Crest, *Modèle familial et pouvoir monarchique (XVIè-XVIIIè siècles)* (Aix-en-Provence: Presses universitaires d'Aix-Marseille, 2002); and Ralph E. Giesey, *Le Rôle méconnu de la loi salique: La Succession royale XIVè-XVIè siècles* (Paris: Les Belles Lettres, 2007).

51. Lefevre de la Planche, *Mémoires sur les matières domaniales*, 2:127. Lefevre's posthumous editor and commentator, the Inspector-General of the Royal Domain, Charles de Lorry, however, disagreed. Pointing out that, by definition, all fiefs depended upon a superior lordship, he argued that, since the monarchy had no feudal superior, it was a noble *allod*—a masterless property with superiority over dependent fiefs. Ibid., 2:85n1. Some jurists, however, argued that the King did have a feudal overlord: God. "The immortal" granted earth to man as a

fief, wrote Clément Vaillant, reserving "direct *seigneurie*" and establishing "charges," including "personal servitude, fidelity, [and] tributes." *De la source du fief* (Paris: Nicholas Buon, 1604), 1–2.

52. Ed. Andt, "Théorie de la directe universelle présentée d'après l'édit de 1692," *Revue historique de droit français et étranger*, 1922, 604–36; Robert Bautruche, *Une société en lutte contre le régime féodal: L'Alleu en Bordelais et en Bazadais du XIe au XVIIIe siècles* (Rodez: Imprimerie P. Carrère, 1947); E. Chénon, *Etude sur l'histoire des alleux en France* (Paris: Larose and Forcel, 1888); and Gérard Chianea, "Directe royale universelle et souveraineté royale en Dauphiné sous l'ancien régime," *Recueil de mémoires et travaux publié par la Société d'histoire du droit et des institutions des anciens pays de droit écrit, Fasc. IX, Melanges Roger Aubenas, Université de Montpellier I* (Montpellier: Faculté de droit et des sciences économiques, 1974), 142–56. The best (and only) treatment in English is Kaiser, "Property, Sovereignty."

53. Cited in Chénon, *Etude sur l'histoire des alleux*, 205.

54. Louis XIV certainly felt he had a seigneurial *directe* over all his kingdom. But it is an error to think that Louis XIV believed that his proprietary rights extended beyond this. Nanerl Keohane and Herbert Rowen have written that Louis XIV's claims went much further. Their interpretation, however, is based on a mistranslation of a phrase from his memoirs. "Les rois sont seigneurs absolus et ont naturellement la disposition pleine et libre de tous les biens, tant des seculiers que des ecclesiastiques." When asserting his right over "secular" properties, he was not (as they state) making a claim on non-ecclesiastical property. Rather, he was asserting the quite traditional royal right to use the resources of the *secular clergy* in case of national emergency. The Church never directly denied this right, even when it was invoked in 1789 to expropriate its properties. Keohane, *Philosophy and the State*, 248; and Rowen, *The King's State*, 80. The phrase in question is from Louis XIV, *Mémoires et divers écrits*, ed. Bernard Champigneulles (Paris: Club du livre, 1960), 150.

55. Cited in Chénon, *Etude sur les alleux*, 215.

56. Auguste Galland, *Contre le franc-alleu sans tiltre, pretendu par quelques provinces au préjudice du Roi* (np, 1629), 2.

57. *Du franc-aleu et origine des droicts seigneuriaux* (Paris: Estienne Richer, 1637), 3, 12.

58. Galland may have drawn on Jean de Basmaison Pougnet's account of the emergence of property in the aftermath of the Flood. *Sommaire, discours des fiefs et rierefiefs* (Paris: Guillaume Chaudière, 1579), 2. Jean-Jacques Rousseau borrowed this explanation of the origin of property and society for his *Discourse on the Origins of Inequality*.

59. The strength of the reaction is all the more remarkable when one considers that the King's claim to an universal *directe* still left the French monarchy with far more limited rights over the kingdom's property than those enjoyed by other European monarchs at the time. In seventeenth-century England, for example, the kings exercised immediate proprietary superiority over almost all the land in the country. This is because the statute Quia Emptores (1290) had abolished sub-infeudation (which continued in France until the Revolution). This had collapsed England's tenurial hierarchy, leaving the King as the immediate overlord of all but a handful of vestigial sub-tenures. The ultimate result, according to one of the most distinguished scholars of English land law, F. W. Maitland, was that "every acre of land is held of the King." Cited in William Searle Holdsworth, *An Historical Introduction to the Land Law* (Oxford: Oxford University Press, 1927), 21. On the statute Quia Emptores, see J. H. Baker, *An Introduction to English Legal History* (London: Butterworths, 1979), 208–9.

60. Kaiser, "Property, Sovereignty," 300–309.

61. The following paragraph summarizes the southern French argument, most cogently presented by Pierre de Caseneuve, *Instructions pour le franc-alleu de la province de Languedoc* (Toulouse: J. Boute, 1640); and Etienne Polverel, *Mémoire à consulter et consultation sur le franc-aleu du royaume de Navarre* (Paris: Knapen and fils, 1784).

62. This paragraph is based on M. F. I. Dunod de Charnage, *Observations sur les titres des droits de justice, des fiefs, des cens, des gens mariés, et des successions de la Coutume du Comté de Bourgogne* (Besançon: n.p., 1756), and Denis de Salvaing, *De l'usage des fiefs et autres droits seigneuriaux* (Grenoble: Robert Philippes, 1668).

63. Jean-Joseph-George de Leigonye, comte de Rangouse de la Bastide, *Essai sur l'origine des fiefs, de la noblesse de la Haute-Auvergne, et sur l'histoire naturelle de cette province* (Paris: Royez, 1784).

64. Cited in Andt, "Sur la théorie de la directe universelle," 613.

65. *Observations sommaires d'un citoyen de S.-Quentin en Vermandois, sur le franc-alleu de cette ville* (Paris: J. B. Brocas, 1769), 4; and Salvaing, *De l'usage des fiefs*, 271.

66. The remainder of this paragraph is based on Caseneuve, *Instructions pour le franc-alleu*, 68–70.

67. Lefevre de la Planche, *Mémoires sur les matières domaniales*, 1:119.

68. Ibid., 1:120–21.

69. Ibid., 1:153n4.

70. Edmé de la Poix de Fréminville, *Les Vrais Principes des fiefs en forme de dictionnaire*, 2 vols. (Paris: Valleyre père, 1769), references in text.

71. Baron de Puffendorf, *Le Droit de la nature et des gens*, trans. Jean Barbeyrac (Amsterdam: Henri Schelte, 1706), 1:408–20.

72. Mey et al., *Maximes du droit public françois*, 2nd ed., 2 vols. (Amsterdam: Marc Michel Rey, 1775), 1:41–43.

73. Marquis d'Argenson, *Considérations sur le gouvernement ancien et présent de la France* (Amsterdam: Marc Michel Rey, 1765), 2 and 285. In a brief, but suggestive reference, Sonenscher traces the origins of d'Argenson's distinction between dominion and empire to Bodin, Saint-Pierre, Dubos, and Voltaire. *Before the Deluge*, 162–63.

74. Polverel, *Mémoire à consulter*, 49 and 52.

75. Chianea, "Directe royale," 144–45.

76. For a comparison with Britain, where this realization dawned later, in the mid-seventeenth-century work of James Harrington, see Pocock, "Historical Introduction," 1–152.

77. Olivier Tholozan, *Henri de Boulainvilliers: L'Anti-absolutisme aristocratique légitimé par l'histoire* (Aix-en-Provence: PUAM, 1999), 83. See also Sylvana Tomaselli, "The Spirit of Nations," in *Cambridge History of Eighteenth-Century Political Thought*, ed. Mark Goldie and Richard Wokler (Cambridge: Cambridge University Press, 2006), 13. See also Phyllis K. Leffler, "French Historians and the Challenge to Louis XIV's Absolutism," *French Historical Studies* 14, no. 1 (Spring 1985): 1–22; and Lionel Rothkrug, *Opposition to Louis XIV: The Political and Social Origins of the French Enlightenment* (Princeton, NJ: Princeton University Press, 1965).

78. The standard biography is Renée Simon, *Henry de Boulainviller: Historien, politique, philosophe, astrologue, 1658-1722* (Paris: Boivin, n.d.).

79. The best overview is Harold A. Ellis, *Boulainvilliers and the French Monarchy: Aristocratic Politics in Early Eighteenth-Century France* (Ithaca, NY: Cornell University Press, 1988).

80. See Robin Price, "Boulainviller and the Myth of the Frankish Conquest of Gaul," *Studies in Voltaire and the Eighteenth Century* 199 (1987): 155–85.

81. *Abregé chronologique de l'histoire de France*, 3 vols. (La Haye, 1733).

82. The term is from Ellis, *Boulainvilliers and the French Monarchy*, 80.

83. *État de la France extrait des mémoires dressés par les intendants, avec des mémoires historiques sur l'ancien gouvernement de cette monarchie* (Londres: Palmer, 1727), 1:180.

84. Abbé Dubos, *Histoire critique de l'établissement de la monarchie françoise dans les Gaules*, 2 vols. (Amsterdam: François Changuin, 1734). Page references are in text.

85. Louis-Gabriel de Buat-Nançay, *Les Origines ou l'ancien gouvernement de la France, de l'Allemagne, et de l'Italie*, 2 vols. (La Haye, 1757); François de Paul Lagarde, *Traité historique de la souveraineté du Roi et des droits en dependant*, 2 vols. (Paris: Durand, 1754); and Gabriel Bonnot de Mably, *Observations sur l'histoire de France*, 2 vols. (Genève: Compagnie des libraires, 1765).

86. I have used the version in *Montesquieu: Oeuvres completes*, ed. Daniel Oster (Paris: Seuil, 1964), 528–795. Page references are in text.

87. On Montesquieu and feudalism, see Elisabeth Magnou-Nortier, "Les Lois féodales et la société d'après Montesquieu et Marc Bloch, ou la seigneurie banale reconsidérée," *Revue historique* 289, fasc. 22 (April-June 1993), 321–60; and Paul Ourliac, "Montesquieu, historien de la féodalité," in *Melanges Pierre Vellas: recherches et réalisations* (Paris: Pedone, 1995), 437–49.

88. Elie Carcassonne, *Montesquieu et le problème de la constitution française au XVIIIè siècle* (Geneva: Slatkine reprints, [1927] 1970), 103–77.

89. On contemporary critiques, see ibid., 125–42. For analysis of Montesquieu's historical craft, see Iris Cox, *Montesquieu and the History of French Laws* (Oxford: Voltaire Foundation, 1983). Needless to say, the concluding, historical chapters of *De l'Esprit des lois* are almost entirely passed over today.

90. Some have interpreted them as a defense of Montesquieu's class interests. See Louis Althusser, *Politics and History: Montesquieu, Rousseau, Hegel, and Marx*, trans. Ben Brewster (London: New Left Books, 1972).

91. Scholars used to identify Claude-Adrien Helvétius (1715-1771) as the sharpest critic of *De l'Esprit des lois*. But it is now thought that the comments once attributed to Helvétius were actually penned after his death by his executor, the future deputy Pierre-Louis Lefebvre-Laroche (dates of birth and death unknown). Whatever their author's true identity, they are worth quoting. "What the duce [*sic*] would he have us to understand by his treatise on fiefs?" "It is by these hereditary usurpations that we are [still] ruled. . . . It would require a more terrible remedy than conquest to release ourselves from them." Helvétius to M. Saurin in Antoine-Louis-Claude Destutt de Tracy, trans. Thomas Jefferson, *A Commentary and Review of Montesquieu's Spirit of Laws* (reprinted, New York: Burt Franklin, [1811] 1969), 291–92. On the controversy over the authorship of the comments, see Sophie Audidière's article "Claude-Adrien Helvétius," in the online *Montesquieu Dictionary*, published by the École Normale Supérieure de Lyon (dictionnaire-montesquieu.ens-lyon.fr). I thank Professor Audidière for guiding me through this controversy.

92. Published in *Oeuvres complètes de Voltaire* (Paris: P. Dupont, 1824), vol. 28. In his comments on venality, Voltaire actually proposed selling off Church property to reimburse the capital invested in the offices—a suggestion the French revolutionaries acted on. For a general treatment of Voltaire's reaction to Montesquieu, see Myrtille Méricam-Bourdet, "Voltaire contre Montesquieu? L'Apport des oeuvres historiques dans la controverse," *Revue française d'histoire des idées politiques: Débats et polémiques autour de L'Esprit des lois* 35, 1er semestre (2012): 25–36. I thank Professor Catherine Volpilhac-Auger for bringing this to my attention.

93. Keohane, *Philosophy and the State*, 418. For a more recent treatment emphasizing Montesquieu's monarchism, see Annalien de Dijn, "Montesquieu's Controversial Context: *The Spirit of the Laws* as a Monarchist Tract," *History of Political Thought* 34, no. 1 (2013): 66–88.

94. Carcassonne concluded it was "profound." *Montesquieu*, 674.

95. Critics like Veron de Forbonnais attacked him for providing no evidence for this assertion. Carcassonne, *Montesquieu*, 129.

96. For a comprehensive historiographical introduction, see Liana Vardi, *The Physiocrats and the World of the Enlightenment* (Cambridge: Cambridge University Press, 2012), 1–22.

97. Mirabeau, *L'Ami des hommes ou traité de la population* (Avignon, 1756), 31 and 50.

98. Gino Longhitano, "La Monarchie française entre la société des ordres et marché: Mirabeau, Quesnay, et le Traité de la monarchie," in Mirabeau and Quesnay, *Traité de la monarchie (1757-1759)*, ed. Gino Longhitano (Paris: Harmattan, 1999), xxxvii.

99. Ibid., 162. More democratic than Montesquieu, he had included "the popular multitude" among them. The others were the "sacredotal order," "the order of the rich and powerful," "the military order," and "the order of jurisprudence."

100. Ibid., 131–32.

101. Ibid., 29. The biblical reference to the story of Nabboth's vineyard was a common way to refer to the sanctity of property right. Its best-known use was by Boulainvilliers, who himself seems to have borrowed it from Cardin Lebret's *De la souveraineté du Roi* (1632).

102. Mirabeau and Quesnay, *Traité de la monarchie*, 131–32.

103. Ibid., 181 and 185. Paul Cheney has shown that Quesnay's notion of unitary sovereignty was derived from Bodin. *Revolutionary Commerce: Globalization and the French Monarchy* (Cambridge, MA: Harvard University Press, 2010), 149.

104. Mirabeau and Quesnay, *Traité de la Monarchie*, 131.

105. John Shovlin offers a nuanced analysis of their relationship, in which he notes some of the enduring differences between the men, despite Mirabeau's "conversion." *The Political Economy of Virtue: Language, Patriotism, and the Origins of the French Revolution* (Ithaca, NY: Cornell University Press, 2006), 105–7. For a book-length treatment, see Vardi, *The Physiocrats and the World of the Enlightenment*.

106. The following three paragraphs are based on Le Mercier's work (published in London, by Jean Nourse in 1767, page references are in text), but they could have just as well been based

on Pierre-Samuel Dupont de Nemours, whose *De l'origine et des progrès d'une science nouvelle* (Londres: Desaint, 1768) makes identical arguments in nearly the same language.

107. On the theme of morality, see Sonenscher, *Before the Deluge*, 189–222.

108. Vardi notes that Quesnay was very insistent about the language his followers used. *The Physiocrats and the World of the Enlightenment*, 128.

109. Published in Basle, 1779. Page references are in text except where noted.

110. Le Trosne, *Vues sur la justice criminelle* (Paris: Frères Debeire, 1777), 108–10.

111. Contemporaries certainly thought so. In fact, bad memories of the physiocrats' seeming insistence on a proprietary state remained so strong after 1789 that the makers of the Civil Code explicitly rejected the physiocrats' notion of co-property in their speeches to the Napoleonic legislatures.

112. For these reasons, Le Trosne went beyond calling for feudal abolition to demand the end of perpetual ground rents which, while not legally feudal, produced the same tenurial hierarchy as feudal dues (633–34). For the same reason, the issue of perpetual ground rents caused the revolutionaries more trouble than the better-known problem of feudal dues. Chapter 3 recounts the tortuous revolutionary approach to the rents.

113. *The Origins of Physiocracy: Economic Revolutions and Social Order in Eighteenth-Century France* (Ithaca, NY: Cornell University Press, 1977). For criticism, see Longhitano, "La Monarchie française," lxix (n. 157), in which he describes her conclusions as "fantastic."

114. De Stutt de Tracy, *A Commentary and Review of Montesquieu's Spirit of Laws*, 256 and 259.

Chapter 2

1. François Furet, "Night of August 4," in *A Critical Dictionary of the French Revolution*, ed. François Furet and Mona Ozouf, trans. Arthur Goldhammer (Cambridge, MA: Harvard University Press, 1989), 107 and 113. For a general treatment of the events of August 4th, see Michael P. Fitzsimmons, *The Night the Old Regime Ended: August 4, 1789, and the French Revolution* (University Park: Pennsylvania State University Press, 2003), 220.

2. I agree with the assessment of George V. Taylor, whose much-quoted phrase I am borrowing. I prefer the qualification "constitutional" to the one he used, "political," because it conveys the breadth of the changes envisioned. More important, it avoids reliance on the conceptual opposition of the "social" and the "political," which was crystallized by the abolitions of August 4th. George V. Taylor, "Noncapitalist Wealth and the Origins of the French Revolution," *American Historical Review* 72, no. 2 (January 1967): 491.

3. From the title of Fitzsimmons's book, *The Night the Old Regime Ended*.

4. For the Marxist interpretation, see Albert Soboul, *Précis historique de la Révolution française* (Paris: Editions sociales, 1962). Citation is from page 520. Although less doctrinaire in tone, the works of Jean-Pierre Hirsch and Patrick Kessel echo Soboul's basic analysis. Jean-Pierre Hirsch, *La Nuit du 4 août* (Paris: Gallimard/Julliard, 1978); and Patrick Kessel, *La Nuit du 4 août 1789* (Paris: Arthaud, 1969). See also Colin Jones, "Bourgeois Revolution Revivified: 1789 and Social Change," in *Rewriting the French Revolution*, ed. Colin Lucas (Oxford: Clarendon, 1991), 69–118.

5. The most sophisticated statement of this position is found in John Markoff, *The Abolition of Feudalism: Peasants, Lords, and Legislators in the French Revolution* (University Park: Pennsylvania State University Press, 1996).

6. Silvia Marzagalli, "Economic and Demographic Developments," in *The Oxford Handbook of the French Revolution*, ed. David Andress (Oxford: Oxford University Press, 2015), 13.

7. D. M. G. Sutherland claims that it is "common knowledge" that the abolition of feudalism in 1789 was "disengenuous." "Peasant, Lord, and Leviathan: Winners and Losers from the Abolition of French Feudalism, 1780-1820," *Journal of Economic History* 62, no. 1 (March 2002): 1.

8. The phrase is from Marshall Sahlins, cited in Keith Michael Baker, "Enlightenment Idioms, Old Regime Discourses, and Revolutionary Improvisations," in Thomas E. Kaiser and Dale K. Van Kley, *From Deficit to Deluge: The Origins of the French Revolution* (Stanford, CA: Stanford University Press, 2011), 184.

9. Gilbert Shapiro and John Markoff, *Revolutionary Demands: A Content Analysis of the Cahiers de Doléances of 1789* (Stanford, CA: Stanford University Press, 1998).

10. *AP*, 3:60.

11. *AP*, 3:66.

12. *AP*, 3:101–2. Logically consistent, it goes on to call for alienation of the royal domain.

13. Fitzsimmons, *The Night the Old Regime Ended*, 10–11. See *AP*, 8:283.

14. An exception is Keith Michael Baker, who has interpreted the Assembly's commitment to a declaration of rights as "the first step away from the idea of a constitution to be preserved and toward that of a constitution to be created." Keith Michael Baker, "Fixing the French Constitution," in *Inventing the French Revolution: Essays on French Political Culture in the Eighteenth Century*, ed. Keith Michael Baker (Cambridge: Cambridge University Press, 1990), 267.

15. *AP*, 8:261.

16. *AP*, 8:285.

17. *AP*, 8:288.

18. The term was popularized by Turgot, who used it in his *Encyclopédie* article, "Fondation." Turgot's arguments against the existence of *corps politiques* were recycled verbatim (indeed, quoted) in the debates over the nationalization of Church property.

19. *AP*, 8:382.

20. The Night of August 4th "stripped away the tangle of privileges that had defined a person's rights and duties under the Old Regime, leaving every man equal before the law." William H. Sewell Jr., "Connecting Capitalism to the French Revolution: The Parisian Promenade and the Origins of Civic Equality in Eighteenth-Century France," *Critical Historical Studies* 1, no. 1 (Spring 2014): 14.

21. Of course, he was to be a *he*, not a *she*, nor many other things (enslaved, poor, Jewish, foreign, etc.). There is a vast literature on the many types of people who were excluded in practice from the Revolution's theoretically universal category of citizenship.

22. Although one deputy proposed abolishing all corps on the Night of August 4th, the proposal did not make it into the decree of the 11th. This is because certain corps (notably that of the bakers, who supplied Paris with bread) were deemed essential to the maintenance of public order at that time. I thank Jeff Horn for sharing this insight. On the question of corps in August 1789, see Steven Laurence Kaplan, *La Fin des corporations* (Paris: Fayard, 2001), 422–58.

23. David D. Bien, "Property in Office under the Ancien Régime: The Case of the Stockbrokers," in *Early Modern Conceptions of Property (Consumption and Culture in the 17th and 18th Centuries)*, ed. John Brewer and Susan Staves. London: Routledge, 1996), 132. See also Doyle, *Venality*, 288–309.

24. Bruyère paid 371 *livres* at the end of 1790 to liberate his house from one of the many ecclesiastical *directes* scattered across his city. AD Rhône, 1 Q 48, "District de Lyon, Rachat des droits féodaux" (16 septembre 1790-9 juin 1791).

25. D. M. G. Sutherland offers a comprehensive analysis of the impact on rural France. See his, "Peasants, Lords, and Leviathan: Winners and Losers from the Abolition of French Feudalism, 1780-1820," *Journal of Economic History* 72, no. 1 (March 2002): 1–24.

26. Examples of scholars who have emphasized the Revolution's positive economic impact are Sutherland, "Peasants, Lords, and Leviathan," 18–19; and James Livesey, *Making Democracy in the French Revolution* (Cambridge, MA: Harvard University Press, 2001). Livesey is one of the few scholars to focus on ideas.

27. Anatoli Ado, *Paysans en révolution: Terre, pouvoir, et jacquerie, 1789-1794* (Paris: Société des Etudes Robespierristes, 1996); Florin Aftalion, *The French Revolution: An Economic Interpretation* (Cambridge: Cambridge University Press/Editions de la Maison des Sciences de l'Homme, 1990); François Crouzet, "Les Conséquences économiques de la Révolution française," *Révue économique* 40, no. 6 (1989): 1189-1203; and Peter McPhee, "The French Revolution, Peasants, and Capitalism," *American Historical Review* 94, no. 5 (December 1989): 1265–80.

28. Henri Marion, *La Dime écclésiastique en France au XVIIIè siècle et sa suppression* (Bordeaux: Imprimerie de l'université, 1912), 110–17.

29. Taylor, "Noncapitalist Wealth," 486.

30. Quoted in Hervé Leuwers, *Un jurist en politique: Merlin de Douai (1759-1838)* (Arras: Artois presses universitaires, 1996), 281.

31. M. Cicille, *Précis méthodique pour le rachat des droits féodaux* (Paris: Méquignon, 1790), 7.

32. *AP*, 8:345.

33. *AP*, 8:352.

34. *AP*, 26:760.

35. *AP*, 26:503.

36. Claude-Joseph de Ferrière, *Dictionnaire de droit et de pratique* (Paris: Saugrain, 1755), 1:710.

37. Ed. Meynial, "Notes sur la formation de la théorie du domaine divisé," 419.

38. Scipion du Perier, *Questions notables du droit* (Grenoble: Jean Nicolas, 1668), 142.

39. Robert-Joseph Pothier, *Traité du droit de domaine de propriété* (Paris: Debure, 1772), 5.

40. Unification of the domains of property could have been accomplished through the absorption of the useful domain by the *directe*. In fact, there was a type of tenure specific to Brittany, the *bail à covenant* or *domaine congéable* which assigned predominant property right to the *directe*. This type of tenure was so solidly grounded in law and practice that the revolutionaries declared it legitimate, despite the fact that the conditions it imposed on peasants were harsher than those of feudal leases. This prompted conflict between landlords and tenants which lasted until the *bail à covenant* was finally abolished in 1897. Auguste Chancerelle, *Etude sur le domaine congéable* (Quimper: Typographie Arsène de Kerangal, 1898); Léon Dubreuil, *Les Vicissitudes du domaine congéable en basse-Bretagne à l'époque de la Révolution*, 2 vols. (Rennes: Imprimerie Oberthur, 1915); and Hervé Le Lay, *Le Domaine congéable sous la Révolution* (Rennes: Imprimeries réunies, 1941).

41. Jean-Joseph Julien, *Nouveau commentaire sur les statuts de Provence* (Aix, 1778), 2:155.

42. James Q. Whitman, "The Seigneurs Descend to the Rank of Creditors: The Abolition of Respect," *Yale Journal of Law and Humanities* 6 (1994): 249–83.

43. In the Charente-Inférieure, for example, "fiefs almost totally lacked [landed] domains; they consist principally in *cens* and *rentes*." A.N. D XIV 2.

44. A.N. AF III 128.

45. On allodial property, see Claude-Joseph de Ferrière, *Dictionnaire de droit et de pratique, contenant l'explication des termes de droit, d'ordonnances, de coutumes, et de pratique, avec les jurisdictions de France* (Paris: Saugrain, 1755), 1:947–49; and M. Henrion de Pansey, *Traité des fiefs de Dumoulin, analysé et conferé avec les autres feudistes* (Paris: Valade, 1773), 685–86.

46. Billcocq, *Les Principes de droit françois sur les fiefs* (Paris: Louis Sevestre, 1729), 2; Claude de Ferrière, *Traité des fiefs, suivant les coutumes de France et l'usage des provinces de droit écrit* (Paris: Jean Cochart, 1680), 536; Henrion de Pansey, *Traité des fiefs*, 685–88; and Antoine Laplace, *Dictionnaire des fiefs et autres droits seigneuriaux* (Paris: Knappen, 1756), 47–48.

47. AD Bouches-du-Rhône, 301 E 414.

48. *Consolations au clergé et à la noblesse* (Versailles: Baudouin, 1789), 11. For comprehensive juridical analysis of these types of rents, see E. Garsonnet, *Histoire des locations perpétuelles et des baux à longue durée* (Paris: Larose, 1879); and Louis Vallée, *Le Bail à rente foncière dans l'ancien droit français et le droit intermédiaire* (Paris: V. Giard & E. Brière, 1900).

49. *AP*, 21:162; *AP*, 8:624; *AP*, 46:37; and *AP*, 30:162.

50. A.N. AF III 128.

51. "L'Acensement a rendu le peuple propriétaire." *AP*, 8:500. See also, *AP*, 11:687.

52. Ground rents were "the very staff of life in poor and isolated regions." P. M. Jones, *Politics and Rural Society: The Southern Massif Central, c.1750-1880* (Cambridge: Cambridge University Press, 1985), 168.

53. M. D. Dalloz, *Repertoire méthodique et alphabétique de législation, de doctrine, et de jurisprudence* (Paris: Bureau de jurisprudence générale, 1865), 38:373–87.

54. Max Bruchet, *L'Abolition des droits seigneuriaux en Savoie (1761-1793)* (Marseille: Lafitte reprints, [1908] 1979).

55. *AP*, 8:343–44.

56. *AP*, 11:499.

57. Merlin had been a lawyer in the *parlement* of Flanders before 1789. He served as a deputy in the National Assembly and Convention before holding a variety of high executive and judicial

positions (Director, Minister of Police, Minister of Justice, Councilor of State, Prosecutor of the *Cour de Cassation*) under the Directory and Napoleon. Before 1789 Tronchet was a consulting lawyer with the Paris bar. After serving in the National Assembly, he acted as one of Louis XVI's lawyers in his trial by the Convention in January 1793. He later returned to legislative office under the Directory. Napoleon appointed him to preside over the Civil Code committee.

58. *AP*, 8:621.
59. A.N. D XIV 3, "Villet Delandes to Feudal Committee" (6 March 1790), and A.N. D XIV 6, "Le Gorlier to Feudal Committee" (15 July 1790).
60. A.N. D XIV 1A, "Mimos and Ingrand to Feudal Committee" (12 January 1790).
61. *Lettre à mes vassaux* (Paris: Denné, 1790), 29; and *Réclamations des provinces contre les opérations de leurs députés* (1790).
62. *Des droits féodaux, ou délibération du conseil municipal de Tourves, du 8 décembre 1789* (Marseille: Pierre-Antoine Favet, 1789).
63. "We will always be slaves," wrote the municipal council of Saint-Martin de la Brasque in Provence, unless allowed to effect a *rachat* "as a corps." A.N. D XIV 2, "Saint-Martin de la Brasque to National Assembly" (14 October 1790).
64. A precedent for the collective approach was offered by the recent example of Savoy. The two most prominent participants in this debate, Sieyès and the *comte* d'Antraigues, both leaned heavily on the Savoyard model. Comte d'Antraigues, *Mémoire sur le rachat des droits féodaux declarés rachetables par l'arreté de l'Assemblée Nationale du 4 août* (Versailles: Baudouin, 1789). "Mémoire de M. l'abbé Sieyès sur le rachat des droits féodaux" (27 août 1789) in *AP*, 8:499–503.
65. Cicille, *Précis méthodique*, 1–2.
66. On the problems of communal property after 1789, see Caroline Gau-Cabée, *Droits d'usage et code civil: L'Invention d'un hybride juridique* (Paris: Librairie générale de droit et de jurisprudence, 2006).
67. Pierre-François Boncerf, *Moyens et méthodes pour éteindre les droits féodaux* (n.p., 1789).
68. Guillaume-François Le Trosne, *De l'administration provinciale et la réforme de l'impôt* (Basle: n.p., 1779).
69. *Précis d'une opération proposée par un patriote du district de l'Oratoire* (Paris: Desenne, 1790), 5.
70. M. Boudin, *Nouvelles réflexions sur le rachat des droits féodaux, pour servir de réponse aux rapports faits par M. Tronchet, au comité féodal de l'Assemblée Nationale; sur le mode & le prix du rachat des droits féodaux et censuels, non-supprimés sans indemnité* (Paris, Desenne, 1790), 9.
71. *AP*, 8:620–23.
72. All citations in this and the following three paragraphs are from this report. *AP*, 11:499–518.
73. *AP*, 12:389.
74. *AP*, 8:390.
75. *AP*, 12:390. Tronchet's belief that out-of-court settlements reflected the fact that this had been the traditional method for settling disputes between villages and their lords during the seventeenth and eighteenth centuries. See Rafe Blaufarb, "Conflict and Compromise: Communauté et Seigneurie in Early Modern Provence," *Journal of Modern History* 82, no. 3 (September 2010): 519–45.
76. This description is just a basic summary of the National Assembly's feudal legislation. There followed numerous technical modifications, often in response to regional particularities. For example, see *AP*, 23:435 for the law regulating the question of how to deal with a fief whose tenants have effected a *rachat*, but whose lord has not done so vis-à-vis his feudal superior.
77. Philippe Sagnac and Pierre Caron, *Les Comités des droits féodaux et de législation et l'abolition du régime seigneurial, 1789-1793* (Geneva: Mégariotis Reprints, [1907] n.d.).
78. A.N. D XIV 7B, "Le Chevalier de Saint-Vincent to Feudal Committee" (18 April 1790).
79. A typical call for the separate *rachat* of feudal dues is found in A.N. D XIV 5A, "Commune of Pralong en Forez to National Assembly" (30 June 1790). For an example of an appeal for collective *rachat*, see the petition of the inhabitants of the town of Cette, who demanded to "be allowed to free themselves together, as a *corps de commune*" from their feudal obligations. A.N. D XIV4, "Inhabitants of Cette to National Assembly" (2 September 1791).
80. A.N. D XIV 5B, "J. Tartivol to National Assembly, Department of the Loiret, and District of Pithiviers" (21 August 1791).

81. The contestation was over the so-called *rentes batardes*, a quasi-feudal annuity. For a description of this affair and how the revolutionary abolition of feudalism actually made the *rachat* of these *rentes* more difficult, see *Mémoire sur les rentes et les droits féodaux, contenant un projet pour effectuer l'amortissement, à l'avantage des créanciers & debiteurs présenté aux Etats-Généraux par un Dauphinois* (Paris: n.p., 1789).

82. AD Bouches-du-Rhône, C 1383, "Observations sur quelques parties du rapport du comité féodal" (30 April 1790). The Assembly corrected its error by its decree of 14 February 1791, which maintained in force all local pre-1789 anti-feudal laws more generous than those passed in 1790. *AP*, 23:172.

83. Noelle Plack, "Challenges in the Countryside, 1790-2," in *Oxford Handbook*, ed. Andress, 347–49.

84. For an overview of the pattern of resistance and violence, see Markoff, *The Abolition*, 337–426.

85. *Arrêt du conseil d'état du Roi, qui casse des délibérations prises par les municipalités de Marsagny, Termancy, Angely, & Buisson, concernant le payement des droits de champart, terrages, et autres* (11 July 1790). The royal *arrêt* was reprinted and circulated by local administrations across the country, as part of their attempt to induce peasant compliance.

86. *AP*, 19:15.

87. A.N. D XIV 5, *Proclamation du directoire du département du Lot* (30 August 1790).

88. A.N. D XIV 5B, "Septier, mayor of Brueyleroi, to National Assembly" (11 June 1790).

89. A.N. D XIV 7A, Untitled, printed circular from the intermediate commission of Lorraine and Barrois to parish priests (8 December 1789).

90. See n. 88.

91. Marcel Garaud, *La Révolution et la propriété foncière* (Paris: Sirey, 1958), 203.

92. *Projet d'instruction sur les droits de champart . . .* (Paris, 1790).

93. Timothy Tackett, *When the King Took Flight* (Cambridge, MA: Harvard University Press, 2004).

94. AD Gironde, 3 E 22409, notary Jean-Baptiste Dauche.

95. Sutherland, "Peasants, Lords, and Leviathan," 1.

96. AD Bouches-du-Rhône, 1 Q 1025 and 1027.

97. AD Bouches-du-Rhône, 1 Q 1095.

98. AD Rhône, 1 Q 43, 44, 45, and 48.

99. Archives de Paris, DQ 13 102.

100. AD Indre-et-Loire, 1 Q 1161.

101. This is perhaps one reason why the scale of *rachat* operations has been underestimated. The sample is from the departmental archives of the Gironde (AD Gironde). The three urban notaries were Jean-Baptiste-Anne Bouan (3 E 13180-13183), Bernard-Brice Darrieux (3 E 24724-24730), and Jean-Joseph-Louis Romegous (3 E 13080-13084). The three rural notaries were Jean-Baptiste Dauche of Cadillace (3 E 22407-22410), Antoine Cieux of Vayres (3 E 18717-18720), and Joseph La Valette of Saint-Emilion (3 E 28728-28731).

102. AD Isère, 9 J 243, Untitled act (Grenoble, 31 March 1791).

103. Ferradou, *Le Rachat*, 82–83.

104. AD Isère, 3 E 1434/18, Act of 8 August 1790.

105. See n. 101.

106. AD Indre-et-Loire, 1 Q 1161.

107. *AP*, 8:629.

108. *Second rapport du comité féodal, par M. Tronchet, Membre dudit Comité. Imprimé par ordre de l'Assemblée Nationale en date du 28 Mars 1790* (Paris: Imprimerie nationale, 1790), 40.

109. Garaud, *La Révolution et la propriété*, 209.

110. Dalloz, *Repertoire méthodique*, 38:339.

111. See n. 101.

112. Georges Lefebvre, *Les Paysans du Nord pendant la Révolution française* (Lille: Marquant, 1924), 1:210.

113. Garaud, *La Révolution et la propriété*, 102.

114. Ferradou, *Le Rachat*, 201–10.

115. AD Bouches-du-Rhône, 1 Q 1025 and 1027.

116. *Source*: AD Bouches-du-Rhône, 1 Q 1025 and 1027.

117. Indeed, *rachats* directed against the national *directe* were literally purchases of national property, albeit of the incorporeal, direct domain variety.

118. AD Bouches-du-Rhône, L 44, "Aix, Liquidation du sieur Clappier-Vauvenargues" (11 June 1791).

Chapter 3

1. Noting the "undeniable rarity of expropriation" during even the most radical phase of the Revolution, Jean-Pierre Hirsch has emphasized the revolutionaries' "remarkable" respect for property right. See Jean-Pierre Hirsch, "Terror and Property," in *The French Revolution and the Creation of Modern Political Culture*, vol. 4, *The Terror*, ed. Keith Michael Baker (Oxford: Pergamon, 1994), 211–22. Citations are from 211.

2. The most categorical statement is from Alphonse Aulard, who claimed that only with the passage of the July1793 law was the abolition of feudalism finally "complete." It was, he explained, "a revolution within the revolution." *La Révolution française et le régime féodal* (Paris: Alcan, 1919), 282, 252, and 283.

3. A.N. D XIV 7, "Petitioners of Heckling to National Assembly" (3 May 1792).

4. A.N. D XIV 5, "Addresse de la commune de La Capelle Biron" (20 March 1792).

5. Markoff, *The Abolition of Feudalism*, 464–65. On the disturbances, see Jean Boutier, *Campagnes en émoi: Révoltes et révolution en Bas-Limousin, 1789-1800* (Treignac: Les Monédières, 1987), esp. 109–72.

6. C. Michallet, *Le Mystère des droits féodaux dévoillés* (Trevoux: n.p., 1791). Page numbers are in the text.

7. *AP*, 39:194–96.

8. This kind of rhetoric supports the argument of David A. Bell, *The First Total War: Napoleon's Europe and the Birth of Warfare as We Know It* (Boston: Houghton-Mifflin, 2007).

9. *AP*, 39:196.

10. For an example, see A.N. D XIV 5B, "De la Vale Giblot, et. al. to National Assembly," (22 May 1792); and *Observations rapides présentées à l'Assemblée Nationale par M. Amyot* (n.p., 1792).

11. *AP*, 45:210.

12. *AP*, 45:16.

13. *AP*, 45:114.

14. *Lettre de M. Merlin, président du tribunal criminel du département du Nord* (Douai: n.p., 13 June 1792).

15. *AP*, 45:114.

16. *AP*, 45:347–48.

17. *AP*, 45:348.

18. *AP*, 45:16.

19. *AP*, 45:115–16.

20. *AP*, 45:209–10.

21. *AP*, 45:210.

22. *AP*, 45:17–18. Unless otherwise noted, all citations from this speech.

23. *AP*, 69:19–20.

24. *AP*, 69:98.

25. Philippe-Antoine Merlin, *Recueil alphabétique des questions de droit* (Paris: Garnery, 1810), 4:360.

26. *AP*, 69:98.

27. The same is true in other regions. See André Ferradou, *Le Rachat des droits féodaux dans la Gironde, 1790-1793* (Paris: Sirey, 1928).

28. AD Gironde, 3 E 22410, Contract of 2 November 1793.

29. AD Gironde, 3 E 13183, Contract of 23 September 1793. Perhaps this is related to Bordeaux's participation in the Federalist Revolt at this time.

30. AD Gironde, 3 E 13084, Contract of 22 August 1793.

31. AD Bouches-du-Rhône, 1 Q 1027.

32. "Adresse du directoire du département des Hautes-Alpes à la Convention Nationale" (4 September 1793), in Sagnac and Caron, *Les Comités des droits féodaux*, 783–84.

33. A.N. D III 358–359, "Goyau, procureur-général syndic du département de l'Allier aux citoyens députés composant le comité de legislation de la Convention Nationale" (10 September 1793).
34. For a selection of complaints, see Sagnac and Caron, *Les Comités des droits féodaux*, 783–811.
35. Ibid., 791–95.
36. A.N. D III 358–358, untitled, printed petition headed *Citoyens legislateurs* (Paris: Limodin, n.d.).
37. Caron and Sagnac, *Les Comités des droits féodaux*, 801–3.
38. Unless otherwise indicated, this and the following two paragraphs are based on A.N. D III, 358–359, "Résumé des opinions émises au comité de législation, en présence des commissaires du comité des domaines, séance du 7 septembre, soir."
39. This seems to have been the beginning of a partnership that lasted until the fall of Napoleon's Empire. The best-known law co-drafted by the two men was the notorious "Law of Suspects" (17 September 1793), but they also drew up important imperial feudal legislation that will be discussed later in this chapter.
40. The Committee's decision to use such positive language to describe the former lords is very surprising.
41. This was the bitter contemporary assessment of the Legislative Committee. See "Lettre du comité de législation au comité de salut public," in Caron and Sagnac, *Les Comités des droits féodaux*, 808.
42. *Décret de la Convention Nationale, du 2 Octobre 1793, l'an second de la république Françoise, une & indivisible, Relatif aux Actes de concession à titre d'inféodation, & au brûlement des titres féodaux mixtes.*
43. M. D. Dalloz, *Répertoire méthodique et alphabétique de legislation, de doctrine, et de jurisprudence* (Paris: Bureau de la jurisprudence générale, 1857), 38:350. Unless otherwise noted, this is the source of all citations in the paragraph.
44. For examples, see Caron and Sagnac, *Les Comités des droits féodaux*, 783–807.
45. In the department of the Vienne, the notary Gauvain was sent to the guillotine for having retained a register of feudal rents (which should have been turned over to local authorities and burned) and attempted to collect them. Pierre Massé, "Résistance aux rentes foncières dans la Vienne sous la Révolution," *Bulletin de la société des antiquaires de l'Ouest*, 4th series, 7 (1964): 370.
46. AD Vienne, 1 Q 307, Petition of Dumoustier (7 Fructidor XII).
47. Rebecca L. Spang, *Stuff and Money in the Time of the French Revolution* (Cambridge, MA: Harvard University Press, 2015), esp. chap. 6.
48. A.N. AF III 128, "Citoyen Boudier to Conseil des 500" (12 Messidor V).
49. For an insightful discussion of the war between creditors and debtors, see Judith A. Miller, "The Aftermath of the Assignat: Plaintiffs in the Age of Property, 1794-1804," in Howard G. Brown and Judith A. Miller, *Taking Liberties: Problems of a New Order from the French Revolution to Napoleon* (Manchester: Manchester University Press, 2002), 70–91.
50. A.N. AF III 128, "Plusieurs citoyens cultivateurs de la commune de Sainte-Soulle, canton de la Garrie, département de la Charente-Inférieure, au conseil des 500" (10 Messidor VI).
51. A.N. AF III 128, "Notables habitans du ci-devant district de Lamion, département des Cotes-du-Nord" (17 Ventôse V).
52. A.N. AF III 128, "Antoine-Nicholas Jaillant au conseil des 500" (17 Fructidor IV and Prairial V).
53. A.N. AF III 128, Judges of the Civil Tribunal of the Tarn to the Conseil of 500 (1er jour complémentaire IV).
54. A.N. AF III 128, "Lambert, homme de loi à Rouen aux citoyens représentants composant la commission pour le rétablissement des rentes foncières" (9 Messidor VI).
55. A.N. AF III 128, "Citoyen Lecoq au Corps Legislatif" (21 Vendémiaire VII).
56. A.N. AF III 128, "Lambert, homme de loi."
57. A.N. AF III 128, "Charles-François-Michel Préfosse" (3 Ventôse VII).
58. Although defenders of the law of 17 July 1793 often painted their opponents as counterrevolutionaries, returned émigrés, and ex-nobles, the example of Biré shows that this was not necessarily so.

59. A.N. AF III 128, "Guillaume Biré, captain des chasseurs de la Vendée, au 500" (26 Pluviôse V).
60. Again, terminology varied from province to province. In Provence, for example, the term *emphytéose* (emphyteusis) was employed, while in Dauphiné, such tenures were known as *albergements*. Both divided the domain of property and were generally accompanied by the *lods*. But neither was feudal.
61. A.N. AF III 128, "Citoyen Campoin au conseil des 500" (3 Messidor VI).
62. A.N. AF III 128, "Paul Julien au 500" (15 Frimaire V).
63. A.N. AF III 128, "Gaspard Bouvier, cultivateur, au 500" (4 Brumaire). The inhabitant of a village in the Isère, formerly part of Dauphiné, Bouvier had lost four ground rents as a result of the law of 17 July 1793.
64. A.N. AF III 128, "Citoyen Dehargne, commune de Vendôme" (22 Nivôse V).
65. A.N. AF III 128, "Citoyenne Jeanne Quenedy, veuve Oels, et ses enfans mineurs" (7 Pluviôse V).
66. A.N. AF III 126, "Citoyen-cultivateurs des cantons de la Javoues et la Rochelle aux 500" (28 Messidor VII).
67. A.N. AF III 128, "Habitants du canton de Collet, département de la Lozère, au 500" (13 Ventôse V).
68. Before the Revolution, Treilhard had been a prominent lawyer in the Paris *parlement*. Like many of his colleagues, he was a Jansenist.
69. A.N. AD XVIII^c 451, *Rapport fait par Ozun, aun nom de la commission des finances, sur les rentes foncières* (4 Thermidor V).
70. *PV, Thermidor V*, 39.
71. A.N. AD XVIII^c 451, *Opinion de Duchesne, député de la Drôme, sur le projet de résolution de la commission des finances, concernant les rentes foncières* (15 Thermidor V). Duchesne based his argument on the distinction between feudal and emphyteutic *directes*. This argument corresponded so closely to the one Merlin would articulate during the 1800s, that one wonders if the two men were linked in some way.
72. A.N. AD XVIII^c 451, *Opinion de Fabre (de l'Aude), sur le projet de résolution de la commission des finances, concernant les rentes foncières* (14 Germinal V, reprinted and redistributed on 15 Thermidor V).
73. A.N. AD XVIII^c 451, *Rapport fait par Ozun*.
74. A.N. AD XVIII^c 451, *Opinion de Duprat, sur les rentes foncières* (15 Thermidor V).
75. *Le Moniteur universel* (28 Fructidor V), 144.
76. A.N. AD XVIII^c 451, *Motion d'ordre de Gay-Vernon, relative au maintien des lois de la Convention Nationale, sur les rentes et droits féodaux* (21 Fructidor V), and *Motion d'ordre faite par Gay-Vernon, sur les rentes foncières et les droits féodaux* (3 jour complémentaire V).
77. A.N. AD XVIII^c 426, "Rapport au Directoire Exécutif" (Thermidor V). The minister estimated that the renewed collection of state-owned ground rents would raise 10 million *livres* per year, and that their *rachat* would reduce interest payments on the debt by 5 million *livres* per year.
78. *Le Moniteur universel* (19 Thermidor V), 1275. On the Commission's plan and the debate stirred by the article on ground rents, see *PV, Fructidor V*, 208–209.
79. A number of pamphlets calling for the revival of feudally tainted ground rents, possibly sponsored by the government, appeared at this time. See *Réflexions d'un ci-devant notaire de campagne, sur les injustices commises à l'égard d'une foule de républicains, par suite des fausses applications de la loi du 17 juillet 1793, présentées au premier consul de la République Française* (12 Ventôse VIII).
80. Chapter 6 addresses this law and its application.
81. A.N. AF IV 1248, "Rapport du ministre des finances aux consuls de la République" (25 Pluviôse VIII).
82. A.N. AF IV 1248, "De l'amélioration des finances" (Ventôse VIII).
83. *AP*, series 2, 1:328–29. On this legislative episode, see Geneviève Massa-Gille, "Les Rentes foncières sous le Consulat et l'Empire," *Bibliothèque de l'Ecole des Chartes* 133, no. 1 (1975): 76–77.
84. *AP*, series 2, 1:374–78. Page numbers are in parentheses.

85. Some deputies—among them Georges-Antoine Chabot—voted against the proposal for precisely this reason, because it did not go far enough. "I want us to return frankly to the decrees rendered by the Constituent and Legislative Assemblies, and that the iniquitous and confiscatory law of July 17, 1793, along with all those which form its worthy complement, be revoked." *AP*, series 2, 1:455.

86. *AP*, series 2, 1:457–60.

87. *AP*, series 2, 1:439–47. The speaker was Gillet.

88. The most philosophical mind in the legislature, Benjamin Constant, advanced the most concrete argument against the revival of ground rents. Suppose that a fief had generated an annual income of 25,000 francs in ground rents and 5,000 francs in other kinds of dues, he began. If acquired after July 1793—that is, after the abolition of ground rents—its price would have reflected the annual income it then produced: only 5,000 francs. What would happen if the ground rents were now reestablished? Who would own the 25,000 francs of annual income they generated? The buyer, who had only paid for land worth 5,000 francs annually? The original seller? What if the land had changed hands multiple times? These practical problems, Constant concluded, made it impossible to revive the ground rents. *AP*, series 2, 1:460–62.

89. *AP*, series 2, 1:438.

90. *AP*, series 2, 1:447.

91. *AP*, series 2, 1:435.

92. *AP*, series 2, 1:446.

93. *AP*, series 2, 1:439. Italics in original.

94. *AP*, series 2, 1:435–36.

95. A.N. AF IV 1077 "Note pour les consuls" (1801 or 1802), and "Sur les rentes dues a l'état" (n.d.). See also A.N. AF 1249, "Rapport sur l'amélioration du domaine de l'état" (25 Brumaire IX). Massa-Gille mentions that a commission consisting of Defermon, Regnault, and Treilhard was also formed to study the question of ground rents, but none of its papers survive. See Massa-Gille, "Les Rentes foncières," 78–81.

96. Unless otherwise noted, descriptions of cases and quotes from rulings are from Henri-Jean-Baptiste Dard's magisterial *Du rétablissement des rentes foncières melangées de féodalité* (Paris: Le Normant, 1814). Page numbers given in parentheses.

97. From *Journal des audiences de la cour de cassation* (1808), cited in Patault, "Un conflit," 442.

98. Marquiset, *Napoléon sténographié*, 75.

99. "Note dictée par Napoléon au ministre secrétaire d'Etat le 9 novembre 1810." The full text is reproduced in Massa-Gille, *Les Rentes foncières*, 333–36.

100. *Rapport et projet de décret sur le mode d'application des lois françaises concernant l'abolition de la féodalité aux départemens nouvellement réunis à l'Empire* (Paris, 2 February 1811). Unless otherwise noted, the citations in the remainder of this section are from this source.

101. With some minor adjustments to account for local variations, this was the direction adopted by Imperial policy. On these modifications, see M. le chevalier Faure, *Observations et projet de décret concernant l'abolition de la féodalité dans les départemens de la Hollande* (Paris, 2 February 1813).

102. On these anti-feudal reforms, see Eric Cochrane, *Florence in the Forgotten Centuries, 1527-1800: A History of Florence and the Florentines in the Age of the Grand Dukes* (Chicago: University of Chicago Press, 1973), 428–91.

103. These lands included the Rhineland, Piedmont, the part of Liguria known as the Imperial Fiefs, Parma and Plaisance, Tuscany, the Roman states, and the lands under the jurisdiction of the imperial courts of the Hague and Hamburg.

104. On these debates, see the *Rapport et projet d'avis sur la suppression des droits féodaux dans le ci-devant Piémont* (Paris, 12 Messidor XIII).

105. *Décret qui nomme le comte de Chabran et le chevalier Faure membres de la commission de gouvernement de l'Ems-Supérieur, des Bouches-du-Weser, et des Bouches-de-l'Elbe, et le sieur Petit de Veauverger secrétaire général de ladite commission* (Paris, 18 December 1810).

106. *Rapports et projets de décret sur l'abolition de la féodalité dans les départemens de l'Ems-Supérieur, des Bouches-du-Wesser et des Bouches-de-l'Elbe* (25 novembre 1811). The remainder of this paragraph is based on this document.

107. The *Acte constitutionnel* (15 November 1807) and decrees of 23 January 1808, 28 March 1809, 27 July 1809, 18 August 1809, 20 April 1810, 7 September 1810, and 1 December 1810. Faure also considered that an eighth decree (that of 13 April 1811) should also be considered as having taken effect in the former Westphalian territories, even though it had been promulgated after the annexation of the new departments.

108. The decrees of 12 December 1808 and 11 January 1809.

109. They did, however, recognize the emphyteutic *directe.*

110. For a full account of this session, see Jean Bourdon, *Napoléon au Conseil d'Etat* (Paris: Berger-Levrault, 1963), 264–74.

111. *Rapport et projets de décrets sur les modifications que les lois françaises, relatives à l'abolition de la féodalité, sont susceptibles de recevoir dans quelques-uns des pays réunis à l'Empire* (Paris, 21 June 1813).

112. Massa-Gille, "Les Rentes foncières," 81 and 321–22.

113. For example, Dard, *Du rétablissement* and *De la féodalité* (Gand: Imprimerie royale, 1815). Each subsequent revolution seemed to rekindle these fears. For example, see a curious pamphlet that appeared soon after the July 1830 revolution. M. Le Beschu de Champsavin, *La Peur des revenants* (Paris: n.p., October 1831).

114. Anne-Marie Patault, "Un conflict entre la court de cassation et le conseil d'état," *Revue historique de droit français et étranger* 56 (1978): 443–44.

115. Dalloz, *Répertoire méthodique*, 38:369–70.

Chapter 4

1. For an overview of this vast literature, see Bodinier and Teyssier, *L'Événement le plus important.*

2. For example, *Requête d'un cultivateur au Roi, après la retraite des notables* (n.p., n.d.), and *Ressource immense et légitime pour la libération des dettes de l'Etat* (n.p., 22 April 1789).

3. Gilbert Shapiro and John Markoff, *Revolutionary Demands: A Content Analysis of the Cahiers de Doléances of 1789* (Stanford, CA: Stanford University Press, 1998), 603.

4. Citation is from the title of Bodinier and Teyssier, *L'Événement le plus important.*

5. Louis XIV, *Mémoires*, 150.

6. *AP*, 9:455.

7. *AP*, 8:364.

8. *AP*, 9:369.

9. *AP*, 8:370.

10. *AP*, 8:383.

11. *AP*, 8:385.

12. *AP*, 8:385–86.

13. *AP*, 8:387.

14. *AP*, 8:387.

15. *AP*, 8:394.

16. *AP*, 8:354.

17. *AP*, 9:103–4.

18. *AP*, 9:125.

19. *AP*, 9:139.

20. *AP*, 9:193.

21. Armand-Benoît-Joseph Guffroy, *Offrande à la nation, 11 août* (Paris: Deray, 1789), 8–9. All citations in this paragraph are from this document.

22. See especially, Lenglet, *Du domaine national, ou réponse à M. l'abbé Sieyes, sur les biens ecclesiastiques* (n.p., September 1789); and Joseph-Michel-Antoine Servan, *Refutation de l'ouvrage de M. l'abbé Sieyes sur les biens ecclesiastiques* (Paris: Desray, 1789).

23. Some contemporaries suggested a causal link between the government's forced relocation to Paris and the proposal to expropriate the Church. See *Lettre d'un député à ses commettans* (n.p., n.d.), 5.

24. All Talleyrand citations in this paragraph are from *AP*, 9:398–99.

25. *AP*, 9:607.

26. For example, Jean-Louis de Viefville des Essarts, who warned that the *biens nationaux* would be sold at "a vile price." *AP*, 9:514.

27. *Lettre de M***, sur la conduite du clergé dans l'Assemblée nationale, ou histoire fidele et raisonée des décrets de l'Assemblée, relativement aux biens écclésiastiques et à la réligion* (Paris: n.p., 1791), 13.

28. *AP*, 9:639.

29. *AP*, 9:635.

30. *AP*, 9:423.

31. *AP*, 9:484.

32. *AP*, 9:609.

33. *AP*, 9:606.

34. *AP*, 9:619–20.

35. *AP*, 9:420.

36. *AP*, 9:429.

37. *AP*, 9:632.

38. *AP*, 9:614.

39. *AP*, 9:428, 518, and 634.

40. *AP*, 9:619.

41. *AP*, 9:610.

42. *AP*, 9:428–29.

43. *AP*, 9:484.

44. Citations in this and following paragraph are from *AP*, 9:485–87.

45. Turgot, "Fondation" in *Encyclopédie*, 7:72–75; and John Locke, *Second Treatise of Government*.

46. *AP*, 9:416–18.

47. *AP*, 9:607.

48. *AP*, 9:641–45. Mirabeau's notion of property as a product of society was restated by Maximillien Robespierre in his famous speech of 24 April 1793, in which he described property as a "social institution." *AP*, 62:197.

49. *AP*, 9:649.

50. *AP*, 10:681.

51. *Abbé* Arthur Dillon, *Appel à la commune, aux districts de Paris, aux futurs départemens, et généralement à tout le peuple françois, sous le jugement de l'Europe et de la posterité* (Paris: n.p., 1790), 7. Italics in the original. See also *Les Veritables Interets de la nation* (Paris: n.p., 1789), 3; *Idées sur la vente de portion des biens du clergé* (Paris: Veuve Dessaint, n.d.), 1; and *Mémoire sur la vente des biens nationaux* (Paris: Girouard, n.d.), 2.

52. *La Ressurection du clergé* (Paris: L. Jorry, 1789), 8.

53. *Lettre de M***, sur la conduite du clergé dans l'Assemblée nationale, ou histoire fidele et raisonée des decrets de l'Assemblée, relativement aux biens ecclesiastiques et à la religion* (Paris: n.p., 1791), 13.

54. *AP*, 9:491.

55. For an overview of early modern French domanial jurisprudence, see Guillaume Leyte, *Domaine et domanialité publique dans la France médiévale (XIIe-Xve siècles)* (Strasbourg: Presses universitaires de Strasbourg, 1996).

56. *AP*, 10:49; Ferrière, *Dictionnaire de droit*, 1:711; and *Encyclopédie*, 5:21–28.

57. Ferrière, *Dictionnaire de droit*, 1:710.

58. *AP*, 10:52.

59. Edict of July 1607, in *AP*, series 2, 12:404.

60. André-Marie-Jean-Jacques Dupin, *Des apanages en général et en particulier de l'apanage d'Orléans* (Paris: Everat, 1827).

61. On the doctrine of inalienability, see Anne Rousselet, *La Règle de l'inaliénabilité du domaine de la Couronne: Etude doctrinale de 1556 à la fin de l'Ancien Régime* (Paris: L.G.D.J, 1997).

62. *AP*, 9:240 and 246.

63. *AP*, 9:247.

64. *AP*, 9:46–54.

65. The Committee's subsequent reports also invoked Auguesseau, Choppin, Le Bret, Lefevre de la Planche, Loyseau, Montesquieu, and other authoritative jurists.

66. *AP*, 10:49.

67. This was very similar to the way the Crown used venal offices to shore up its credit.

68. *AP*, 10:50–51.
69. *AP*, 11:62 and 68.
70. *AP*, 26:470.
71. *AP*, 12:633–60.
72. Most pamphlets and projects produced at this time display a similar hesitation or lack of clarity. They generally claimed that the nation was the true proprietor of the royal domain, but did not go so far as to assert either the nonexistence of the royal domain or the existence of a national one. See the various materials in A.N. D VI 2 for examples.
73. *AP*, 15:451.
74. *AP*, 15:452.
75. *AP*, 13:47 and 50.
76. *AP*, 20:323.
77. *AP*, 20:319.
78. *AP*, 20:324. Additional articles of the decree stipulated that pre-1566 exchanges with the domain conducted without fraud would be confirmed, but that pre-1566 alienations whose contracts contained reversion clauses would be perpetually revocable.
79. A.N. AD X 22, *Analyse critique du projet de décret proposé à l'assemblée nationale, par le comité des domaines, au rapport de M. Enjubault de la Roche* (n.p., 1790).
80. On Babeuf's communal notion of property, see William H. Sewell Jr., "Beyond 1793: Babeuf, Louis Blanc, and the Genealogy of 'Social Revolution,'" in *The French Revolution and the Creation of Modern Political Culture*, vol. 3, *The Transformation of Political Culture, 1789-1848*, ed. François Furet and Mona Ozouf (Oxford: Pergamon, 1989), 509–26. On Linguet, see Darline Gay Levy, *The Ideas and Careers of Simon-Nicolas-Henri Linguet: A Study in Eighteenth-Century French Politics* (Urbana: University of Illinois Press, 1980).
81. It is not clear exactly when the term *"biens nationaux"* replaced the terms *"biens écclésiastiques"* and *"domaines de la Couronne"* in the revolutionaries' vocabulary. This linguistic and conceptual shift seems to have taken place over the course of 1790, in conjunction with the emergence of the concept of a national domain. It is significant that the term *"biens nationaux"* did not figure in the crucial laws of December 1789 and April 1790 that initiated their sale.
82. *AP*, 12:633.
83. *AP*, 20:323. As with Bodin's discussion of sovereignty two centuries before, confusion between the concepts of sovereignty and property rights creeps into Barère's discourse at the very point where he attempts most decisively to separate them.
84. *AP*, 20:323.
85. *AP*, 20:322.
86. *AP*, 12:636–37.
87. *AP*, 12:659.
88. *AP*, 12:636.
89. *AP*, 20:317.
90. *AP*, 12:636.
91. *AP*, 12:637.
92. *AP*, 20:322.
93. The term is from Enjubault's definitive report, *AP*, 20:317. The second quote in the sentence is from *AP*, 12:659.
94. *AP*, 12:655.
95. *AP*, 12:659.
96. The *droit d'aubaine* was abolished shortly thereafter by a separate decree.
97. The term "public property" is from *AP*, 20:317. The term "public domain" is from *AP*, 20:317.

Chapter 5

1. Bodinier and Teyssier, *L'Événement le plus important*, 33.
2. A.N. AF III 125, "Mémoire pour Maximillien-Louis Béthune-Sully" (IV).
3. AD Isère, 2 C 651.
4. AD Loir-et-Cher, Q 1613, 1631, and 1657, respectively.
5. A.N. Q3 328, "Domaines aliénés, généralité de Caen" (n.d.).

6. All these examples are from AD Isère, 2 C 651.

7. AD Isère, 7 C 853. The similarity between the mode of selling these (public posters, the form of the posters themselves, and sale at public auction) and that of *biens nationaux* suggests that the revolutionary practice owed something to the Old Regime precedent.

8. A.N. AD X 22, Legras, *Réflexions sur les domaines engagés concédés et aliénés par l'ancien gouvernement*, 11–12.

9. A.N. AD X 20, *Opinion de Garat, sur la résolution du 17 thermidor an 6, relative aux domaines engagés* (5 Vendémiaire an 7), 8.

10. Cited in Merlin, *Recueil alphabétique des questions de droit*, 2:395.

11. Ferrière, *Dictionnaire de droit*, 1:129–30. See also, A.N. AD X 17, *Observations a l'Assemblée Nationale, pour les engagistes des Greffes, et autres Offices domaniaux* (n.p., n.d.), 1–2. which, after having cited Domat's definition of *antichrèse*, noted that it amounted to "the exact definition of the nature of the agreement between the state and the *engagistes*." "In relation to one another, the prince and the *engagiste* are in the same situation as borrower and lender."

12. A.N. AD X 19, *Opinion de Laumond, sur les domaines engagés* (6 Messidor VI), 2.

13. Although the resemblance between the two is very strong, no Old Regime jurist ever commented on this. In strictly legal terms, it would appear that venal offices were actually a type of *engagement*.

14. This was identical to the procedure known as *"augmentation des gages,"* a procedure by which the Crown squeezed money out of bodies of officeholders. See Bien, "Offices, Corps, and a System of State Credit."

15. *AP*, 12:635.

16. *AP*, series 2, 26:166.

17. A.N. AD X 18, *Rapport fait par Blutel, au nom d'une commission spéciale* (6 Frimaire V), 4.

18. *AP*, 9:240–47.

19. A.N. AD X 15, 16, 17, and 19.

20. A number of these proposals are found in the records of the Committee of Finances, A.N. D VI 2.

21. *AP*, 12:637–42.

22. *AP*, 20:319; 10:655; 20:319.

23. *AP*, 31:236–38.

24. *AP*, 49:267–70.

25. A.N. AD X 18, *Rapport fait par Salligny, député par le département de la Marne, sur la résolution relative aux ventes sur soumission des domaines engagés* (12 Thermidor, an V), 2.

26. *Enregistrement* circular, 2:42–49, 109–11, 126, 107.

27. AD Isère, 1 Q 556, "Receveur de l'enregistrement au bureau de Tullies aux citoyens administrateurs du district de Saint Marcellin" (24 Nivôse II). The letter describes the dispossession of three *engagistes* between July 1793 and Frimaire II/November-December 1793. This is the only evidence I have found of the execution of the law of 3 September 1792.

28. A.N. AD X 22, Legras, *Réflexions sur les domaines engagés*, 8.

29. A.N. AD X 17, *Rapport fait à la Convention Nationale, Dans la séance du 1er frimaire de la deuxième année Républicaine, au nom de la commission des finances, des comités des domaines, de législation et des finances réunis; sur les domaines aliénés, par CAMBON, Député par le Département de l'Hérault* (Paris: Imprimerie nationale, II), 8.

30. Ibid., 9. All subsequent citations are from this report.

31. A.N. AD X 18, *Rapport fait par Salligny*, 3.

32. AD Aude, 1 Q 787; and AD Loir-et-Cher, Q 1593.

33. For examples, see the correspondence in AD Calvados, 1 Q 980; and AD Vienne, 1 Q 402 and 564.

34. AD Aude, 1 Q 787.

35. AD Vienne, 1 Q 564.

36. AD Isère, 1 Q 555, "Declarations relatives aux domaines nationaux engagés ou aliénés conformement à loi du 10 Frimaire an 2nd."

37. AD Isère, 1 Q 555, "Copie de la lettre écrite par la commission des revenus nationaux aux administrateurs du département de l'Isère" (7 Messidor II).

38. A.N. AF III 123, Petition from Jean-Olivier Marmion (17 Ventôse VI), Petition from Citizen Michallet (Ventôse IV), Petition from Veuve Dupré (8 Fructidor IV), and AF III 125, Petition from Citizen Douroure (Prairial V).

39. A.N. AD X 22, Legras, *Réflexions sur les domaines engagés*.

40. A.N. AD X 22, *Rapport fait au nom des comités des domaines et des finances, sur les réclamations faites contre la loi du 10 frimaire, concernant les domaines aliénés; par Ch. Delacroix*.

41. A.N. AD X 17, *Rapport fait au nom du comité des finances, sur les réclamations contre la loi du 10 frimaire concernant les domaines aliénés, & sur les changemens additions au rapport fait par Ch. Delacroix, sur le même objet, par P.A. Lozeau, De la Charente-Inférieure* (Frimaire III).

42. It did, however, succeed in having a law passed on 7 Nivôse V returning their original properties to *échangistes* who had been dispossessed by the law of 10 Frimaire II.

43. A.N. AF III 127, Cottinet to Council of 500 (28 Thermidor V).

44. A.N. AF III 125, Minister of Finances Ramel to Citizen Bauldry (3 Brumaire V).

45. A.N. AD X 18, *Observations sur le rapport fait par le représentant du peuple Saligny, au Consiel des Anciens, dans la séance du 12 Thermidor, an V, concernant la Résolution prise par le Conseil des Cinq-cents, le 20 Frimaire de la même année* (Rouen, V), 4.

46. A.N. AF III 123, "Petition Père Pillet, ci-devant propriétaire, au 500" (Pluviôse VI).

47. For an example, see AD Calvados, 1 Q 979, "Directoire du département du Calvados [to unnamed recipients in Paris, presumably the domanial committee of the National Assembly]" (7 February 1791).

48. A.N. AD X 18, *Observations sur le rapport fait par le représentant du peuple Saligny*, 1.

49. A.N. AF III 123, Petition of Citoyenne veuve Tingry (Thermidor IV).

50. A.N. AF III 123, Petition from Jean-Olivier Marmion to 500 (17 Ventôse VI).

51. A.N. AD X 22, Legras, *Réflexions sur les domaines engagés*.

52. A.N. AF III 123, "Objets à examiner."

53. A.N. AD X 18, *Rapport fait par Blutel, au nom d'une commission spéciale, séance du 6 Frimaire, an 5*.

54. AD Calvados, "Directoire du département du Calvados to the Conseil des Anciens" (28 Frimaire V).

55. A.N. AD X 18, *Rapport fait par Saligny*, 9.

56. A.N. AD X 19, *Opinion de Laumond, sur les domaines engagés, séance du 6 Messidor an 6*, 4.

57. A.N. AD X 19, "Aux citoyens, membres du conseil des cinq-cents" (n.p., n.d.), 6.

58. The first epithet is from A.N. AF III 127, "Charles to Lamarque" (24 Brumaire V); and the second from A.N. AD X 18, Vimar, *Observations*, 21.

59. A.N. AD X 18, *Rapport et projets de résolution dans les formes constitutionnelles, présentés par Bergier, au nom de la commission spéciale des domaines engagés, composée des représentans du peuple Leclerc (de Loir-et-Cher), Baucheton, Rouzet, Laloi, Duchatel (de la Gironde), et Bergier. Première lecture faite à la séance du 16 brumaire an 5*, 5.

60. There were at least thirty speeches made in the course of the debate which were printed and can be consulted in A.N. AD X 19 and 20.

61. A.N. AD X 19, *Opinion de Bertrand (du Calvados), sur le mode d'aliénation des domaines engagés, proposé par la commission des finances, séance du 5 Messidor an 6*, 4.

62. A.N. AD X 20, *Rapport fait par Régnier, sur la résolution du 22 frimaire, concernant les domaines engagés par l'ancien gouvernement. Séance du 13 ventose an 7*, 2.

63. One of the speakers in the debate, whose name is more readily associated with the abolition of slavery in Saint-Domingue than the reform of property law, Léger-Félicité Sonthonax (1763-1813), had pleaded successfully to reserve consideration of colonial property holdings, all of which originated from domanial alienations, for special legislation. Is there any significance to the fact that the two legislators most closely associated with the legal abolition of slavery in Saint-Domingue, Sonthonax and Polverel, also intervened publicly in debates over the domain? This aspect of these two lawyer/politicians' careers has not been considered by colonial historians. A.N. AD X 20, *Motion d'ordre faite par Sonthonax, sur la résolution du 27 thermidor dernier, relative aux domaines engagés. Séance du 2 vendémiaire an 7*.

64. This begged the question of how, in the absence of a declaration, these delinquent *engagements* would be discovered. What became of undeclared and undetected *engagements*? Might some have quietly assumed the character of private property and survived to the present day?

65. A.N. AD X 20, *Loi relative aux domaines engagés par l'ancien gouvernement* (14 Ventôse VII), article 29.

66. A.N. AD X 19, *Opinion de Duchatel (de la Gironde), sur les domaines engagés, séance du 7 messidor an 6, 6; Opinion de J. Duffau, sur la résolution du 27 thermidor an 6, concernant les domaines engagés, séance du troisième jour complémentaire an 6, 5;* and *Opinion de Cornudet, sur la résolution du 27 thermidor an 6, concernant les domaines engagés. Séance du 4 vendémiaire an 7, 5.*

67. A.N. AD X 20, *Rapport fait par Régnier,* 11–12.

68. A.N. AD X 21, *Rapport fait par Portiez, au nom de la commission chargée de l'examen du projet de loi tenant à accorder un nouveau délai aux engagistes et échangistes, pour faire leurs déclarations en exécution de la loi du 14 ventose an 7 sur les domaines engagés par l'ancien gouvernement* (11 Pluviôse VIII), 4.

69. A.N. AD X 21, *Loi qui proroge le délai accordé aux engagistes et échangistes non maintenus, pour faire la déclaration prescrite par la loi du 14 Ventose an VII* (16 Pluviôse VIII).

70. AD Loir-et-Cher, Q 248.

71. A.N. Q3 239. I have chosen this sample of his work because of the (relative) legibility of the page on which it was recorded.

72. The royal government had often subcontracted the work of the financial administration. This practice returned under the Empire and Restoration.

73. *Rapport et projet de décret sur la requête du sieur Sevestre. Rapport de la commission du contentieux* (Paris, 7 May 1812).

74. Ibid.

75. *AP,* series 2, 26:166.

76. This estimate is based on Pierre Branda, *Le Prix de la gloire: Napoléon et l'argent* (Paris: Fayard, 2007), 254. Generally, the revenue generated by the *Régie de l'Enregistrement* was about two-thirds of the revenue raised by direct taxation.

77. AD Isère, 1 Q 556, Director of Domaines at Grenoble to the Prefect of the Isère (17 June 1843).

78. AD Aude, 1 Q 756, Unsigned letter, probably addressed to director of the domanial administration in the Aude (22 March 1829).

79. *AP,* series 2, 26:22. In this and the following paragraph, page numbers for citations (all from this volume of *AP*) will be in parentheses.

80. The reference is to the ordinance of 31 March 1819.

81. *AP,* series 2, 59:469.

82. For example, see AD Isère 1 Q 555, *Sommation aux detenteurs des propriétés engagées, situées dans le département de l'Isère.* Emphasizing that the flood of summonses was the result of local initiative, the Minister of Finances assured the legislature in June 1829 that "no order had been given to the domanial administration to issue the summonses which are being complained of." *AP,* series 2, 60:241.

83. AD Loir-et-Cher, Q 1591.

84. Numerous examples of this practice exist in every departmental archive in France. For one of them, see the summons issued against the *seigneurie* of Mazerolles in March 1828 and annulled the following May. AD Aude, 1 Q 763, dossier on *seigneurie* of Mazerolles.

85. AD Isère, 1 Q 555, "Faure, Ducoin, and Champel to Prefect" (20 December 1812). In this case, the property in question had originally been part of the ancient riverbed of the Isère. The exemption claim was upheld.

86. AD Isère, 1 Q 555, Dossier Durey de Moinville.

87. AD Isère, 1 Q 556, Dossier Le Marchand.

88. AD Isère, 1 Q 557, "Rapport sur la terre de Morestel, dont M. de Quinsonas est engagiste" (16 December 1817).

89. AD Vosges, 17 Q 2, "Direction générale de l'Enregistrement, des domaines, et du timbre au préfet des Vosges" (Epinal, 2 janvier 1877).

90. *AP,* series 2, 59:466–67 (25 May 1829).

91. The terms are from the *baron* de Glandevès, scion of an ancient Provençal family, who spoke in support of Daru, but interestingly invoked the ancient privileges of Provence (confirmed in treaties and charters dating back to the fifteenth century) guaranteeing the inherent alienability of the comtal domain against the last-minute pretentions of the *Enregistrement.*

He claimed that, until the recent offensive, the *Enregistrement* had respected these ancient rights and abstained from conducting investigations in the five departments composing the former province since March 1821. *AP*, series 2, 59:469.

92. *AP*, series 2, 60:225–26.
93. For example, the case of the *comtesse* de Sardis, who was still being hounded in 1845. AD Loir-et-Cher, Q 260, Dossier on the "Affaire de Sourdis."
94. Merlin, *Recueil alphabétique des questions de droit*, vol. 2, "Engagement," 394–98.
95. Ibid., vol. 3, "Emphytéose," 374.
96. Quoted in Jean-Baptiste Sirey, *Recueil des lois et des arrêts en matière civile, criminelle, commerciale, et de droit public, depuis l'avénement de Napoléon. 1re partie. Jurisprudence de la Cour de Cassation* (Paris: n.p., 1810), 10:7–8.
97. AD Calvados, 1 Q 1100.
98. AD Isère, 1 Q 556, Petition of the Vachon children and heirs (1812).
99. AD Isère, Decision of prefect of Isère (28 June 1812).
100. *AP*, series 2, 60:234.

Chapter 6

1. AD Bouches-du-Rhône, 1 Q 1009-1024.
2. AD Bouches-du-Rhône, 1 Q 1285. The capital value of the cash payments alone exceeded 1.5 million *livres*.
3. From the typescript catalog of the 1 G series at AD Haute-Vienne.
4. *Observations sur les justices possédées par l'église* (Paris: Desprez, 1786), 3–4.
5. AD Haute-Vienne, 1 Q 17.
6. AD Seine-Maritime, 1 QP 965.
7. AD Seine-Maritime, 1 QP 687.
8. AD Seine-Maritime, 1 QP 540. These consisted in seigneurial jurisdiction, homages, feudal rents, a pigeon-breeding monopoly, *treizièmes*, and many more of the "rights of noble fiefs."
9. Both references are from AD Haute-Vienne, L 632, "Declaration des biens écclésiastiques du district de Dorat" (1790).
10. A.N. Q2 222.
11. The fact that the *rentes de fondation de messe* were renamed *fondations nationales* probably did nothing to soothe their feelings. For the name change, see AD Bouches-du-Rhône, 1 Q 1274.
12. The low estimate (which includes only the revenues of the ex-royal domain) was offered by Tronchet in September 1789. The high estimate was provided by the domanial committee, which broke down the annual revenue of the national rents in this way: 4.5 million for those formerly belonging to the royal domain and 18 million for those of the Church. The sources are *AP*, 8:623 and 19:481.
13. The low estimate is from A.N. AD IX 555, "Tableau des besoins et des ressources de la nation, presentée à l'Assemblée Nationale, séance du 3 avril 1792, par J. Cambon, député de l'Hérault." The high estimate is from *Aperçu estimatif de la valeur capitale des Droits incorporels-casuels, nationaux, par M. Belle, Vice-Président du Comité de l'Ordinaire des Finances* (Paris: Imprimerie nationale, 1792).
14. Pierre-François Boncerf, *Moyens et methodes pour éteindre les droits féodaux* (1789).
15. Boudin, *Nouvelles réflexions sur le rachat des droits féodaux* (Paris: Desene, 1790), 16.
16. *AP*, 8:623.
17. *AP*, 9:269–313. See also A.N. D VI 2, M. Caseneuve, "Moyen prompt et solide pour fournir à tous les besoins du gouvernement et pour ranimer la circulation" (n.d.), and C. N. Roland, "Projet pour la liberation des dettes de l'état" (n.d.).
18. *AP*, 9:156.
19. *AP*, 9:500.
20. *AP*, 8:346.
21. A.N. D XIV 5A, "Guion to the National Assembly" (13 November 1789).
22. *AP*, 11:438.

23. Text of law in *AP*, 15:506–8.
24. AC Grenoble CC 1314, "Registre pour la perception des lods"; and AC Bordeaux CC 1087, "Register on the "fiefs et seigneuries de la ville."
25. A.N. BB 30 127. Access to these documents is restricted because they bear the signatures of revolutionary celebrities. I wish to thank Madame Rouge-Ducos for making an exception on my behalf.
26. A.N. D XIV 5B, "Chauston, Desnoyers, Girard, Ducloux, and La Guerenne to National Assembly" (12 October 1791).
27. AD Isère, 1 Q 129, Poster (3 February 1791).
28. A.N. D III, "Rapport sur les droits féodaux" (late 1792 or 1793).
29. AD Seine Maritime, 1 QP 477, "Acte d'adjudication de domaines nationaux" (14 April 1791).
30. AD Aude, 1 Q 241, "Alienation des biens nationaux" (3 May 1791).
31. AD Haute-Vienne, 1 Q 17, "Illegible name to departmental administration" (1 April 1791).
32. A.N. D XIV5A, Delarozière to Feudal Committee (17 April 1792).
33. The time was spring 1791, and the committees were Alienation, Domains, Ecclesiastic, Extraordinary, Feudal, Finance, and Taxation.
34. *AP*, 12:633–59.
35. *AP*, 16:677.
36. *AP*, 20:424–25.
37. AD Bouches-du-Rhône, 1 Q 1025 ad 1027.
38. AD Bouches-du-Rhône, 1 Q 1095. In Marseille, there were only fifteen *rachats* of non-national dues. These targeted *directes* (most likely non-feudal) held by the *corps* of notaries (3), guilds (2), and ten others with no indication of the owner.
39. A.N. Q2 222.
40. AD Seine Maritime, 1 QP 1232, "Etat des requetes qui se trouvent actuellement au directoire du district de Rouen" (20 June 1791).
41. AD Rhône, 1 Q 43, 44, and 45.
42. AD Bouches-du-Rhône, 1 Q 1174, "Registre pour inscrire les actes de rachat des droits féodaux et leurs receptes."
43. AD Bouches-du-Rhône, 1 Q 1167, "Quittances de rachat, bureau de Gardanne."
44. Robert Garaud, *Le Rachat des droits féodaux et des dîmes inféodées en Haute-Vienne* (Limoges: Dupuy-Moulinier, 1939), 102.
45. AD Bouches-du-Rhône, L 55.
46. AD Bouches-du-Rhône, 1 Q 743.
47. AD Bouches-du-Rhône, 1 Q 744, "Administrators of the department of the Bouches-du-Rhône to the administrators of the district of Aix" (17 January 1791).
48. The Old Regime domanial administration, the *Régie des Domaines*, continued to function through spring 1791 and, in some former provinces where special arrangements had been made, even longer. The former Duchy of Loraine provides many illustrations of this. For example, in 1784 a financier named Jean Lacroix had signed a nine-year lease to exploit the domanial rights over the district of Neufchateau. His lease was allowed to run its course, and Lacroix continued to collect various domanial dues—including the *cens* on the banal ovens of Neufchateau, fishing rights over the La Monyon River, and others through 1793. AD Vosges, 1 C 130.
49. *AP*, 19:489.
50. *AP*, 19:489–91.
51. The definitive law was passed on 23 October 1790. *AP*, 20:7.
52. AD Seine Maritime, 1 QP 966, 1 QP 528, 1 QP 539, and 1 QP 965.
53. AD Bouches-du-Rhône, 1 Q 762.
54. AD Bouches-du-Rhône, 1 Q 759.
55. For an example, see A.N. D XIV 4, Department of the Gironde to the Domanial Committee, (16 November 1790).
56. Complicating matters further, a third agency concerned with the *biens nationaux* was created in 1790 within the *caisse d'amortissement*. It often clashed with the departmental administrations and was finally suppressed in 1794. For a summary of this shifting administrative

landscape, see *Mémoire concernant les recherches et les découvertes à faire dans toute la France sur les domaines corporels et incorporels* (Paris, 12 March 1811), 3–12.

57. This paragraph is based on de Visme's report of 9 March 1791. *AP*, 23:760–65. The quotation is from 762.

58. The sole work on the *Régie de l'Enregistrement* is Jean-Paul Massaloux, *La Régie de l'enregistrement et des domaines aux XVIIIè et XIXè siècles: Étude historique* (Geneva: Droz, 1989). Because of the destruction of the Finance Ministry's archives in 1870, it is impossible to identify its personnel. There are indications that some were former members of the Old Regime royal-domanial administration. For an example, see the letter from a regional royal-domanial official in the Burgundian countryside to his boss in Dijon, trying to explain the unauthorized leave he had taken to seek a new job in the nascent *Enregistrement*. AD Côte d'Or, C 7563, "Lettre du contrôleur des domaines, Duparc, au breau d'Avallon, à Monsieur Campan, directeur des domaines à Dijon" (17 juin 1790).

59. *AP*, 23:762.

60. On the possible political reasons behind the transfer of responsibility for the former ecclesiastical dues from local administrations to the *Enregistrement*, see Philippe Goujard, "L'Abolition de la féodalité dans le district de Neufchâtel (Seine-Inférieure)," in *Contributions à l'histoire paysanne de la révolution française*, ed. Albert Soboul (Paris: Editions sociales, 1977), 370.

61. The text of these laws may be found in A.N. AD X 16.

62. *Mémoire concernant les recherches et découvertes*, 8–9.

63. AD Aude, 1 Q 1539, "Bureau d'Alzonne, régistre de recette des lods et ventes, le 12 septembre 1791, et suiv."

64. AD Var, 1 C 237, "Registre de recettes pour les droits seigneuriaux, casules, lods. Généralité de Provence, bureau de Correns, de 1778 à 1792 inclusivement."

65. Archives de Paris, DQ 13 101, "Registre no.1. Registre de recette des droits seigneuriaux casuels, commencé le 17 novembre 1791 et fini le 29 septembre 1792."

66. AD Côte d'Or, C 7564, "Lambert, directeur du breau de Seyssel, à Monsieur Campan, à Dijon" (7 octobre 1790).

67. AD Bouches-du-Rhône, 302 E 1337. Acts of 25 April 1792 and 28 April 1792.

68. *AP*, 23:763. All citations in the paragraph are from this.

69. A.N. D III 358, J. G. Geoffroy, "Dissertation" (8 November 1792).

70. *AP*, 23:763.

71. A.N. D III 358, Geoffroy, "Dissertation." Marginal note by anonymous committee member.

72. There is evidence that the sale of national dues actually continued for months after its prohibition. A.N. D VI 58, "Amelot, directeur de la caisse de l'extraordinaire au président de l'assemblée nationale" (13 January 1792).

73. AD Seine Maritime, 1 QP 966.

74. AD Loir-et-Cher, Q 112, "Petition" (23 April 1792).

75. *AP*, 22:721–22.

76. All examples from AD Isère, 1 Q 399. Complicating this situation was the fact that many of these individuals did not hold their fiefs as private property, but rather as *engagements*.

77. AD Seine Maritime, 1 QP 500.

78. Example is from AD Seine Maritime, 1 QP 539. For the Colberts and Penthievres, see AD Seine Maritime, 1 QP 1232.

79. AD Seine Maritime, 1 QP 364, "Administrateur des domaines nationaux aux administrateurs du département de la Seine inférieure" (12 July 1793).

80. A.N. Q2 222, "Commissaire des droits nationaux dans Paris au citoyen directeur de la Régie nationale de l'Enregistrement des domaines et droits y réunis" (26 February and 18 June 1793).

81. A.N. Q2 222, "Etat des glebes ou maisons dont dépendent les droits nationaux à faire reconnoitre dans Paris et nouvelle enclave de cette ville" (10 April 1793).

82. A.N. Q2 222, "Lettre Ponsao, directeur du bureau de Saint-Esprit" (16 Ventôse II).

83. *Observations présentées au Comité de Législation, sur les pertes immenses de propriétés foncières, résultantes, soit pour la Nation, soit pour le particulier, de la Loi du 17 Juillet dernier* (30 1er mois II).

84. *Enregistrement* circular no. 450, of 17 September 1793. In *Circulaires de la Régie de l'Enregistrement et du Domaine National* (Paris: an I), 2:177–81.

85. *Enregistrement* circular no. 560, of 12 Ventôse II. In *Circulaires*, 2:330–31.

86. Decree of 18 June 1792, in *AP*, 45:336–37. Law of 6 July 1792 in A.N. AD IV 24.

87. *Décret de la Convention Nationale . . . relatif à la faculté accordée à des Acquéreurs de Biens nationaux dans lesquels étoient compris des Droits supprimés, de renoncer à leurs Adjudications* (19 Ventôse II). The other extensions were granted by the laws of 25 July 1792 and 17 July 1793.

88. AD Vienne, 1 Q 578.

89. AD Loir-et-Cher, Q 118, Petition of Jean-François Riffault, citoyen notaire à Blois (undated, but probably November 1792).

90. AD Isère, 1 Q 13.

91. AD Seine Maritime, 1 QP 500, "Barrois to Directoire of Rouen" (1 January 1793).

92. For the copious correspondence on his complex case, see AD Haute-Vienne, 1 Q 8 and 13.

93. A.N. Q2 222. The earlier version employed the "vous" form, the latter the "tu."

94. A.N. Q2 222, "Notes des rentes foncières concernées par l'article 2 de la loi du 17 juillet 1793."

95. For a typical statement of the creditors' position, see A.N. AD II 32, "La verité." For the debtors, see "Sur le project" in A.N. AD II 32.

96. Although expressed in myriad ways, the debate centered on the question of how contracts could be cancelled. The key interventions in the debate are found in A.N. XVIIIc 369 and 435. For analysis of the debate, see Miller, "The Aftermath of the Assignat," 70–91.

97. These were the laws of 2 Thermidor III/20 July 1795 and 3 Brumaire IV/25 October 1794, requiring that half of annual dues and arrears, respectively, be paid in kind.

98. AD Bouches-du-Rhône, 1 Q 1274.

99. From Messidor IV (June-July 1796) through Vendémiaire V (September-October 1796), nearly 37,000 *livres* worth of national ground rents were reimbursed by property-holders in Marseille with *assignats*. AD Bouches-du-Rhône, 1 Q 1275.

100. Examples may be found in A.N. Q3 239.

101. On the non-payment of arrears, see A.N. D XIV 5b.

102. For the speeches and laws, see A.N. AD II 31.

103. *Enregistrement* circular no. 1475, 1 Pluviôse VII, *Circulaires de la Régie*, 6:44–47.

104. AD Haute-Vienne, 1 Q 917, "Rentes constituées, District de Limoges," article 215.

105. AD Haute-Vienne, 1 Q 917, article 208.

106. Martin-Michel-Charles Gaudin, *Mémoires, souvenirs, opinions, et écrits du duc de Gaëte, ancien ministre des finances* (Paris: Armand Colin, 1926), 134.

107. The department with the fewest rents was the Hautes-Alpes (147 rents producing only 2,743 francs annually); that with the most was the Seine-et-Oise (25,157 rents generating 225,920 francs annually). For a department-by-department breakdown, as well as national totals, see A.N. AF IV 1249, "Etat général des rentes foncières et constituées qui, au 1er Messidor an VIII, se percevoient au profit de la République" (15 Vendémiaire IX).

108. A.N. AF IV 1249, "Rapport sur l'administration du domaine de l'état" (25 Brumaire IX).

109. Paragraph based on *AP*, series 2, 1:13–14, 43–45, and 56–57. For a summary, see René Stourm, *Les Finances du Consulat* (Paris: Guillaumin, 1902), 63–69.

110. This was made explicit by *Enregistrement* circular no. 1849, 23 Messidor VIII.

111. A.N. AF IV 1248, "Rapport du ministre des finances aux consuls de la République" (25 Pluviôse VIII).

112. AD Vosges, 1 Q 17.

113. AD Vienne, 1 Q 1095, Register of *rachats* (24 Germinal VIII-15 Thermidor VIII).

114. AD Aude, 1 Q 720, Register of *rachats* (begun 12 Floréal VIII).

115. A.N. AF IV 1249, Lacoste "Rapport sur l'amélioration du domaine de l'état."

116. Geneviève Massa-Gille, "Les Rentes foncières sous le Consulat et l'Empire," *Bibliotheque de l'école des chartes* 133, no. 2 (1975): 325.

117. *Enregistrement* circular no. 1845, 14 Messidor VIII, on implementation of arreté of 24 Prairial VIII.

118. *Enregistrement* circular no. 1912, 19 Brumaire IX.

119. Stourm, *Les Finances du Consulat*, 69–70.

120. AD Indre-et-Loire, 1 Q 657, "Enregistrement des transfers des capitaux des rentes nation-ales données en payement des créances des ministres, échangées contre des rescriptions de la Trésorerie en execution de l'arrêt des consuls du 27 Prairial VIII."

121. In the case of *cultivateur* Martin Brousteau, of the village of Taussigny, we know that he was able to exchange a 1,000-franc rescription against a ground rent that had formerly been lev-ied by the priest of the village on his own property! By acquiring it with his rescription, Brousteau extinguished it. In his and several other cases, rescriptions and transfers thus amounted to *rachats*. Brousteau's case is detailed in AD Indre-et-Loire, 1 Q 657.

122. Massa-Gille, "Rentes foncières," 325.

123. Ibid., 259.

124. AD Indre-et-Loire, 1 Q 658, *Enregistrement* circular (25 Floréal XI).

125. *Enregistrement* circular of 22 Fructidor XI. See also A.N. AF IV 1292.

126. For Mollien's recollections of how these operations proceeded, see François-Nicolas Mollien, *Mémoires d'un ministre du trésor public, 1780-1815* (Paris: Guillaumin, 1898), 287–91.

127. Dumarest contract of 21 Nivôse XIII/11 January 1805 in the *Régie* circular of 29 January 1808. Massa-Gille has found some indications that private companies may have been employed as much as two years earlier. See her "Rentes foncières," 261.

128. *Correspondence du dépôt des lois avec les fonctionnaires publics, ou compte rendu de l'état de la législation, de la jurisprudence, et de l'administration de l'Empire français* (Paris: Rondondeau, n.d.), 405.

129. Letter of 14 June 1806, *Circulaires de la Régie*, 185–86, containing the Gaudin's decision of 24 April 1806. For the geographical distribution of these companies, see AD Haute-Vienne, 1 Q 913, "Etat nominatif des agens avec lesquels la caisse d'amortissement a conclu des trai-tés pour la recherche des rentes ignorées."

130. Massa-Gille, "Rentes foncières," 268.

131. This was the decree of 23 January 1806, giving former clergy a 25 percent commission for revealing former ecclesiastic (now national) rents, and the avis of 7 June 1806, which extended the commission to all informers. Massa-Gille, "Rentes foncières," 256.

132. Because of these legal proceedings and the papers they generated, we know much more about Jean-Victor-Gabriel-Benjamin Mariette than any other contractor. Sometimes calling himself Mariette de Wauville, he was a lawyer, former artillery officer, son of a receiver of the former royal domain, and had himself served as receiver at Valognes before going into busi-ness for himself. Massa-Gille, "Rentes foncières," 273.

133. Contractors working in the four Rhenish "reunified departments," as well as the depart-ments of the Ourthe and Forêts (in present-day Belgium) were exempted, although their contracts would ultimately be revoked in 1810. Massa-Gille, "Rentes foncièrese," 277.

134. A.N. AF IV 1249 Conseil extraordinaire des finances (5 Brumaire IX).

135. *AP*, series 2, 2:350, 363, 389–95, 401–2.

136. Régie circular of 18 Thermidor IX.

137. A.N. AF IV 1294, "Observations sur le tableau des decrets rendus depuis 1806 jusqu'au novembre 1811, relativement aux domaines usurrpés et célés, soit qu'ils ayent été décou-verts par les hospices, soit qu'ils l'ayent été par des anonymes appliquant leurs découvertes aux hospices" (November 1811).

138. A.N. AF IV 1292, Duchatel, *Mémoire redigé sur la demande de Son Excellence le ministre des finances, par le conseiller d'état, directeur général de l'administration de l'enregistrement et des domaines, touchant les rentes et biens domaniaux à recouvrer par l'état* (Paris, late 1810), 28.

139. AD Indre-et-Loire, 1 Q 658, Circular (25 Floréal XI).

140. A.N. AF IV 1292, *Mémoire concernant les recherches et les découvertes à faire dans toute la France . . .*, 34; and "Notte pour Son Excellence, le ministre sécrétaire d'état" (n.d.).

141. These are detailed in A.N. AF IV 1294, "Observations sur le tableau"; A.N. AF IV 1292, Duchatel, *Mémoire redigé*; and Massa-Gille, "Rentes foncières," 287–88.

142. A.N. AF IV 1077, "Duchatel to Napoleon" (12 February 1812).

143. The text of Napoleon's note is reproduced in Massa-Gille, "Rentes foncières," 333–36.

144. Ibid., 336.

145. Unless otherwise indicated, this paragraph is based on the printed materials submitted by Gaudin to Napoleon on 9 January 1811. They are in A.N. AF IV 1292.

146. A.N. AF IV 1077, "Duchatel to Napoleon" (12 February 1812).
147. A.N. AF IV 1292, *Mémoire concernant les recherches et les découvertes à faire dans toute la France* ... (printed on 12 March 1811). This document is the basis of this paragraph.
148. Massa-Gille, "Rentes foncières," 270.
149. A.N. AF IV 1292, untitled, unsigned mémoire (26 September 1810). Attributed by Massa-Gille to Montaiglon, "Rentes foncières," 297.
150. Massa-Gille, "Rentes foncières," 297–98.
151. AD Bouches-du-Rhône, 1 Q 1292, "Sommier des droits incorporels, verifié le 20 avril 1813."
152. AD Bouches-du-Rhône, 1 Q 1292, "Sommier des droits incorporels, verifié le 20 avril 1813."
153. For example, see *De la féodalité ou mémoire sur cette question: Le Rétablissement de la Féodalité étoit-il plus à craindre sous le gouvernement du Roi que sous l'empire de Buonaparte?* (Gand: Imprimerie Royale, 1815). The fear of the rebirth of feudalism continued well into the 1830s. See, for example, the aptly titled *La Peur des revenants* (October 1831).
154. AD Bouches-du-Rhône, 1 Q 1291, "Sommier de consistance de rentes nationales."
155. AD Bouches-du-Rhône, 357 E 199, Notarized act of notary Natoire (24 March 1714).
156. AD Bouches-du-Rhône, 1 Q 1293, "Sommier certain des rentes."
157. For example, AD Vienne, 1 Q 308, petition of P. G. Mireau to the Prefect (27 May 1840), requesting a *rachat* of a similar national ground rent. The longest-lived national rent I have identified was a formerly ecclesiastical ground rent, that of the Sardou and Garoute heirs. It was regularly paid through 18 May 1843. Bouches-du-Rhône, 1 Q 1293, "Sommier certain des rentes."

Epilogue

1. For example, Suzanne Desan, *The Family on Trial in Revolutionary France* (Berkeley: University of California Press, 2004); and Jennifer Ngaire Heuer, *The Family and the Nation: Gender and Citizenship in Revolutionary France, 1789-1830* (Ithaca, NY: Cornell University Press, 2005).
2. *AP*, series 2, 4:587.
3. *AP*, series 2, 4:14. In a subsequent speech, Portalis stated that "empire" and "sovereignty" were synonyms. *AP*, series 2, 5:208.
4. Jean-Guillaume Locré, *Esprit du Code Napoléon* (Paris: Imprimerie impériale, 1807), 24.
5. For first draft of Code containing the offending expression "puissance paternelle," see Pierre-Antoine Fenet, *Recueil complet des travaux préparatoires du code civil* (Paris: Videcoq, 1836), 2:123. For the critique of the Paris appellate court, see ibid., 5:211.
6. Article 544.
7. James Gordley, "Myths of the French Civil Code," *American Journal of Comparative Law* 42, no. 3 (Summer 1994): 462. Gordley claims that neither the revolutionary abolition of feudalism nor the Code's anti-feudal provisions had any "practical [i.e., economic] consequences" and challenges scholars to name them. This is easily done: the end of property mutation fees (the *droit de lods*), the abolition of the seigneurial right of first refusal (the *droit de re traite*), and the prohibition on entailments, to name a few.
8. Fenet, *Recueil*, 1:508–9. The Code ultimately included an entire section of servitudes.
9. Ibid., 1:516–17.
10. Ibid., 5:205 (Paris) and 315 (Poitiers).
11. Ibid., 3:396–97.
12. Ibid., 4:93–108.
13. *AP*, series 2, 5:203.
14. *AP*, series 2, 5:220 and 238.
15. Fenet, *Recueil*, vol. 11. Especially Maleville (57–59 and 64), but also Cambacérès (56), Pelet (60–61), and Bigot (66). Pages numbers in parentheses in text.
16. Ibid. Especially Tronchet (57 and 60) and Defermon (61).
17. This was the fall-back position suggested by the appellate court of Caen.
18. Fenet, *Recueil*, 2:97.
19. Ibid., 2:100.
20. The appeals courts of Paris and Rennes also expressed concern at this. Ibid., 5:205–7 (Paris) and 350–51 (Rennes).

21. Ibid., 4:93.
22. Ibid., 5:205–6.
23. Treilhard in *AP*, series 2, 5:203, and Portalis in *AP*, series 2, 5:206. The revised, definitive version of the Code expunged all reference to public establishments, thus implicitly denying their right to own property.
24. And again, Paris echoed the opinions of the Lyonnais magistrates. See Fenet, *Recueil*, 5:205–7.
25. Ibid., 4:93.
26. Ibid., 11:48–49.
27. Article 538.
28. This is significant when considered in the context of the principle, put succinctly by Portalis, that "property is a right, simple possession is just a fact." *AP*, series 2, 5:209.
29. David A. Bell, *Lawyers and Citizens: The Making of a Political Elite in Old Regime France* (New York: Oxford University Press, 1994); Lenard R. Berlanstein, *The Barristers of Toulouse in the Eighteenth Century (1740-1793)* (Baltimore, MD: Johns Hopkins University Press, 1975); Philip Dawson, *Provincial Magistrates in Revolutionary Politics in France, 1789-1795* (Cambridge, MA: Harvard University Press, 1972); and Michael P. Fitzsimmons, *The Parisian Order of Barristers and the French Revolution* (Cambridge, MA: Harvard University Press, 1987).
30. An exception is Donald R. Kelley, "Men of Law and the French Revolution," in *Politics, Ideology, and the Law in Early Modern Europe: Essays in Honor of J. H. M. Salmon*, ed. Adrianna E. Bakos (Rochester, NY: University of Rochester Press, 1994), 127–46. Also helpful is Kelley's *Historians and the Law in Postrevolutionary France* (Princeton, NJ: Princeton University Press, 1984), as well as Jean-Louis Halpérin, *L'Impossible Code civil* (Paris: Presses universitaires de France, 1992), which examines the unsuccessful attempts by Cambacérès to push through a civil code during the 1790s.
31. M. Dupin, aîné, *Profession d'avocat* (Paris: Alex-Gobelet, 1832), 1:6. Speech delivered on 1 December 1829.
32. Keith Michael Baker, "Enlightenment Idioms, Old Regime Discourses, and Revolutionary Improvisation," in *From Deficit to Deluge: The Origins of the French Revolution*, ed. Thomas Kaiser and Dale Van Kley (Palo Alto, CA: Stanford University Press, 1994), 165–97; and Daniel Gordon, *Citizens Without Sovereignty: Equality and Sociability in French Thought, 1670-1789* (Princeton, NJ: Princeton University Press, 1994).
33. Keith Michael Bakers gives the wonderful example of the King's Flight to Varennes. It was revolutionary discourse, he observes, that transformed the "glimpse of a fat man heading toward the French border in a lumbering carriage" into the politically significant event it immediately became. Baker, "Enlightenment Idioms," 167.
34. John Markoff gives much consideration to the dialogue between the National Assembly and peasantry, but concludes that it was peasant pressure that drove forward the revolutionary abolition of feudalism. In contrast, both Peter McPhee and Noelle Plack assign responsibility for revolutionary change almost exclusively to the peasantry. See Markoff, *Abolition of Feudalism*; Peter McPhee, "A Social Revolution: Rethinking Popular Insurrection in 1789," in *Oxford Handbook*, ed. Andress, 164–79; and Noelle Plack, "Challenges in the Countryside, 1790-2," in *Oxford Handbook*, ed. Andress, 346–61.
35. Clare Haru Crowston, *Credit, Fashion, Sex: Economics of Regard in Old Regime France* (Durham, NC: Duke University Press, 2013); Michael Sonenscher, *Before the Deluge: Public Debt, Inequality, and the Intellectual Origins of the French Revolution* (Princeton, NJ: Princeton University Press, 2007); Spang, *Stuff and Money*; and Erika M. Vause, "In the Red and in the Black: Bankruptcy, Debt Imprisonment, and the Culture of Credit in Post-Revolutionary France" (Ph.D. dissertation, University of Chicago, 2012).

BIBLIOGRAPHY

Archives and Libraries Consulted

Archives nationales, Paris
Archives communales, Bordeaux
Archives communales, Grenoble
Archives communales, Lyon
Archives de Paris
Archives départementales de l'Aude, Carcassonne
Archives départementales des Bouches-du-Rhône, Aix-en-Provence
Archives départementales des Bouches-du-Rhône, Marseille
Archives départementales du Calvados, Caen
Archives départementales de la Côte d'Or, Dijon
Archives départementales de la Gironde, Bordeaux
Archives départementales de la Haute-Vienne, Limoges
Archives départementales d'Indre et Loire, Tours
Archives départementales de l'Isère, Grenoble
Archives départementales du Loir-et-Cher, Blois
Archives départementales du Rhône, Lyon
Archives départementales de la Seine-Maritime, Rouen
Archives départementales du Var, Draguignan
Archives départementales de la Vienne, Poitiers
Archives départementales des Vosges, Épinal
Bibliothèque Méjanes, Aix-en-Provence
Bibliothèque nationale de France, Paris
The British Library, London

Published Primary Sources

Abregé chronologique de l'histoire de France. 3 vols. La Haye, 1733.

Analyse critique du projet de décret proposé à l'assemblée nationale, par le comité des domaines, au rapport de M. Enjubault de la Roche. n.p., 1790.

Aperçu estimatif de la valeur capitale des Droits incorporels-casuels, nationaux, par M. Belle, Vice-Président du Comité de l'Ordinaire des Finances. Paris: Imprimerie nationale, 1792.

Archives parlementaires de 1787–1860. Edited by J. Mavidal and E. Laurent et al., 100 vols. Paris: Dupont et al., 1867–2000.

Argenson, Marquis de. *Considérations sur le gouvernement ancien et présent de la France.* Amsterdam: Marc Michel Rey, 1765.

Argis, Antoine-Gaspard Boucher de. *Code rural, ou maximes et règlemens concernant les biens de campagne.* Vol. 1. Paris: Prault, 1767.

Arouet, François-Marie. *Oeuvres complètes de Voltaire.* Vol. 28. Paris: P. Dupont, 1824.

Arrêt du conseil d'état du Roi, qui casse des délibérations prises par les municipalités de Marsagny, Termancy, Angely, & Buisson, concernant le payement des droits de champart, terrages, et autres. 11 July 1790.

Bacquet, Jehan. *Quatrième traicté ... des droits du domaine de la Couronne de France.* Paris: Nivelle, 1582.

Billcocq. *Les Principes de droit françois sur les fiefs.* Paris: Louis Sevestre, 1729.

Bodin, Jean. *Les Six Livres de la République.* Paris: Jacques du Puis, 1583.

Bodin, Jean. *On Sovereignty.* Edited by Julian H. Franklin. Cambridge: Cambridge University Press, 1992.

Boncerf, Pierre-François. *Moyens et méthodes pour éteindre les droits féodaux.* n.p., 1789.

Bosquet, *Dictionnaire raisonné des domaines et droits domaniales.* 3 vols. Rouen: J. J. Le Boullenger, 1762.

Boudin, M. *Nouvelles réflexions sur le rachat des droits féodaux, pour servir de réponse aux rapports faits par M. Tronchet, au comité féodal de l'Assemblée Nationale; sur le mode & le prix du rachat des droits féodaux et censuels, non-supprimés sans indemnité.* Paris: Desene, 1790.

Bouquet, Pierre. *Lettres provinciales, ou examen impartial de l'origine de la constitution et des révolutions de la monarchie françoise.* La Haye, Neutre, et Paris: Merlin, 1772.

Buat-Nançay, Louis-Gabriel de. *Les Origines ou l'ancien gouvernement de la France, de l'Allemagne, et de l'Italie.* 2 vols. La Haye, 1757.

Caseneuve, Pierre de. *Instructions pour le franc-alleu de la province de Languedoc.* Toulouse: J. Boute, 1640.

Charnage, M. F. I. Dunod de. *Observations sur les titres des droits de justice, des fiefs, des cens, des gens mariés, et des successions de la Coutume du Comté de Bourgogne.* Besançon: n.p., 1756.

Choppin, René. *Trois livres du domaine de la Couronne de France.* Paris: Michel Sonnius, 1613.

Cicille, M. *Précis méthodique pour le rachat des droits féodaux.* Paris: Méquignon, 1790.

Circulaires de la Régie de l'Enregistrement et du Domaine National. Vol. 2. Paris: an I.

Citoyens legislateurs. Paris: Limodin, n.d.

Consolations au clergé et à la noblesse. Versailles: Baudouin, 1789.

Correspondence du dépôt des lois avec les fonctionnaires publics, ou compte rendu de l'état de la législation, de la jurisprudence, et de l'administration de l'Empire français. Paris: Rondondeau, n.d.

Dalloz, M. D. *Repertoire méthodique et alphabétique de législation, de doctrine, et de jurisprudence.* Vol. 38. Paris: Bureau de jurisprudence générale, 1865.

Dard, Henri-Jean-Baptiste. *Du rétablissement* and *De la féodalité.* Gand: Imprimerie royale, 1815.

Dard, Henri-Jean-Baptiste. *Du rétablissement des rentes foncières melangées de féodalité.* Paris: Le Normant, 1814.

De la féodalité ou mémoire sur cette question: Le Rétablissement de la Féodalité étoit-il plus à craindre sous le gouvernement du Roi que sous l'empire de Buonaparte? Gand: Imprimerie Royale, 1815.

Décret de la Convention Nationale, du 2 Octobre 1793, l'an second de la république Françoise, une & indivisible, Relatif aux Actes de concession à titre d'inféodation, & au brûlement des titres féodaux mixtes.

Décret de la Convention Nationale ... relatif à la faculté accordée à des Acquéreurs de Biens nationaux dans lesquels étoient compris des Droits supprimés, de renoncer à leurs Adjudications. 19 Ventôse II.

Décret qui nomme le comte de Chabran et le chevalier Faure membres de la commission de gouvernement de l'Ems-Supérieur, des Bouches-du-Weser, et des Bouches-de-l'Elbe, et le sieur Petit de Veauverger secrétaire général de ladite commission. Paris, 18 December 1810.

Des droits féodaux, ou délibération du conseil municipal de Tourves, du 8 décembre 1789. Marseille: Pierre-Antoine Favet, 1789.

Destutt de Tracy, Antoine-Louis-Claude. *A Commentary and Review of Montesquieu's Spirit of Laws.* Translated by Thomas Jefferson. Reprint, New York: Burt Franklin, 1969.

Diderot, Denis, and Jean le Rond d'Alembert, eds. *Encyclopédie, ou dictionnaire raisonné des sciences, des arts et des métiers, etc.* Paris, 1755.

Dillon, *Abbé* Arthur. *Appel à la commune, aux districts de Paris, aux futurs départemens, et généralement à tout le peuple françois, sous le jugement de l'Europe et de la posterité.* Paris: n.p., 1790.

Du franc-aleu et origine des droicts seigneuriaux. Paris: Estienne Richer, 1637.

Dubos, Abbé. *Histoire critique de l'établissement de la monarchie françoise dans les Gaules.* 2 vols. Amsterdam: François Changuin, 1734.

Dupin, André-Marie-Jean-Jacques. *Des apanages en général et en particulier de l'apanage d'Orléans.* Paris: Everat, 1827.

Dupin, André-Marie-Jean-Jacques. *Profession d'avocat.* Vol. 1. Paris: Alex-Gobelet, 1832.

Dupont de Nemours, Pierre-Samuel. *De l'origine et des progrès d'une science nouvelle.* Londres: Desaint, 1768.

Etat de la France extrait des mémoires dressés par les intendants, avec des mémoires historiques sur l'ancien gouvernement de cette monarchie. Vol. 1. Londres: Palmer, 1727.

Faure, M. le chevalier. *Observations et projet de décret concernant l'abolition de la féodalité dans les départemens de la Hollande.* Paris, 2 February 1813.

Fenet, Pierre-Antoine. *Recueil complet des travaux préparatoires du code civil.* Vol. 2. Paris: Videcoq, 1836.

Ferrière, Claude-Joseph de. *Dictionnaire de droit et de pratique, contenant l'explication des termes de droit, d'ordonnances, de coutumes, et de pratique, avec les jurisdictions de France.* Vol. 1. Paris: Saugrain, 1755.

Ferrière, Claude-Joseph de. *Traité des fiefs, suivant les coutumes de France et l'usage des provinces de droit écrit.* Paris: Jean Cochart, 1680.

Fleury, Abbé. *Droit public de France.* Edited by J. B. Daragon. Vol. 1. Paris: La Veuve Pierres, 1769.

Fréminville, Edmé de la Poix de. *Les Vrais Principes des fiefs en forme de dictionnaire.* 2 vols. Paris: Valleyre père, 1769.

Galland, Auguste. *Contre le franc-alleu sans tiltre, pretendu par quelques provinces au préjudice du Roi.* n.p., 1629.

Gazette Nationale ou le Moniteur Universel. A Paris, de l'imprimerie du citoyen Agasse propriétaire du Moniteur, rue des Poitevins, n° 18.

Guffroy, Armand-Benoît-Joseph. *Offrande à la nation, 11 août.* Paris: Deray, 1789.

Hotman, François. *La Gaule Françoise.* Cologne: Hierome Bertulphe, 1574.

Idées sur la vente de portion des biens du clergé. Paris: Veuve Dessaint, n.d.

Jacquet, Pierre. *Traité des fiefs.* Paris: Samson, 1763.

Julien, Jean-Joseph. *Nouveau commentaire sur les statuts de Provence.* Vol. 2. Aix, 1778.

La Peur des revenants. October 1831.

La Planche, Lefevre de. *Mémoires sur les matières domaniales, ou traité du domaine.* 2 vols. Paris: Desaint and Saillant, 1764.

La Ressurection du clergé. Paris: L. Jorry, 1789.

La Touloubre, Christophe Félix Louis Ventre de. *Jurisprudence observée en Provence sur les matières féodales et les droits seigneuriaux divisée en deux parties.* Avignon, 1756.

Laplace, Antoine. *Dictionnaire des fiefs et autres droits seigneuriaux.* Paris: Knappen, 1756.

Launay, Emmanuel Henri Louis Alexandre de, comte d'Antraigues. *Mémoire sur le rachat des droits féodaux declarés rachetables par l'arreté de l'Assemblée Nationale du 4 août.* Versailles: Baudouin, 1789.

Le Bret, Pierre Cardin. *De la souveraineté du Roi.* Paris: Toussaincts de Bray, 1632.

Le Mercier de la Rivière, Pierre-Paul. *L'Ordre naturel et éssentiel des sociétés politiques.* London: Jean Nourse, 1767.

Le Trosne, Guillaume-François. *De l'administration provinciale et la réforme de l'impôt.* Basle, 1779.

Le Trosne, Guillaume-François. *Vues sur la justice criminelle.* Paris: Frères Debeire, 1777.

Leigonye, Jean-Joseph-George de, comte de Rangouse de la Bastide. *Essai sur l'origine des fiefs, de la noblesse de la Haute-Auvergne, et sur l'histoire naturelle de cette province.* Paris: Royez, 1784.

Lenglet, *Du domaine national, ou réponse à M. l'abbé Sieyes, sur les biens ecclesiastiques.* n.p., September 1789.

Les Veritables Interets de la nation. Paris: n.p., 1789.

Lettre à mes vassaux. Paris: Denné, 1790.

Lettre de M***, sur la conduite du clergé dans l'Assemblée nationale, ou histoire fidele et raisonée des décrets de l'Assemblée, relativement aux biens écclésiastiques et à la réligion. Paris: n.p., 1791.

Lettre de M. Merlin, président du tribunal criminel du département du Nord. Douai: n.p., 13 June 1792.

Lettre d'un député à ses commettans. n.p., n.d.

Locke, John. *Second Treatise of Government.* London: Awnsham Churchill, 1690.

Locré, Jean-Guillaume. *Esprit du Code Napoléon.* Paris: Imprimerie impériale, 1807.

Louis XIV. *Mémoires et divers écrits.* Edited by Bernard Champigneulle. Paris: Le Club Français du Livre, 1960.

Loyseau, Charles. *Traité des seigneuries.* Paris: Abel L'Angelier, 1608.

Mably, Gabriel Bonnot de. *Observations sur l'histoire de France.* 2 vols. Genève: Compagnie des libraires, 1765.

Mémoire sur la vente des biens nationaux. Paris: Girouard, n.d.

Mémoire sur les rentes et les droits féodaux, contenant un projet pour effectuer l'amortissement, à l'avantage des créanciers & debiteurs présenté aux Etats-Généraux par un Dauphinois. Paris: n.p., 1789.

Merlin, Philippe-Antoine. *Recueil alphabétique des questions de droit.* Vol. 4. Paris: Garnery, 1810.

Mey et al. *Maximes du droit public françois.* 2 vols. Amsterdam, Marc Michel Rey, 1775.

Michallet, C. *Le Mystère des droits féodaux dévoillés.* Trevoux: n.p., 1791.

Mirabeau, Victor Riqueti de. *L'Ami des hommes ou traité de la population.* Avignon, 1756.

Mollien, François-Nicolas. *Mémoires d'un ministre du trésor public, 1780–1815.* Paris: Guillaumin, 1898.

Moreau, Jacob-Nicolas. *Leçons de morale, de politique, et de droit pubic, puisées dans l'histoire de notre monarchie.* Versailles: Imprimerie du département des affaires étrangères, 1773.

Observations présentées au Comité de Législation, sur les pertes immenses de propriétés foncières, résultantes, soit pour la Nation, soit pour le particulier, de la Loi du 17 Juillet dernier. 30 1er mois II.

Observations rapides présentées à l'Assemblée Nationale par M. Amyot. n.p., 1792.

Observations sommaires d'un citoyen de S.-Quentin en Vermandois, sur le franc-alleu de cette ville. Paris: J. B. Brocas, 1769.

Observations sur les justices possédées par l'église. Paris: Desprez, 1786.

Pansey, M. Henrion de. *Traité des fiefs de Dumoulin, analysé et conferé avec les autres feudistes.* Paris: Valade, 1773.

Paul Lagarde, François de. *Traité historique de la souveraineté du Roi et des droits en dependant.* 2 vols. Paris: Durand, 1754.

Peissonel, Jacques. *Traité de l'heredité des fiefs de Provence.* Aix: E. Roize, 1687.

Perier, Scipion du. *Questions notables du droit.* Grenoble: Jean Nicolas, 1668.

Polverel, Etienne. *Mémoire à consulter et consultation sur le franc-aleu du royaume de Navarre.* Paris: Knapen and fils, 1784.

Pothier, Robert-Joseph. *Traité du droit de domaine de propriété.* Vol. 1. Paris: Debure, 1772.

Pougnet, Jean de Basmaison. *Sommaire, discours des fiefs et rierefiefs.* Paris: Guillaume Chaudière, 1579.

Précis d'une opération proposée par un patriote du district de l'Oratoire. Paris: Desenne, 1790.

Projet d'instruction sur les droits de champart. Paris, 1790.

Puffendorf, Baron de. *Le Droit de la nature et des gens.* Translated by Jean Barbeyrac. Vol. 1. Amsterdam: Henri Schelte, 1706.

Rapport et projet d'avis sur la suppression des droits féodaux dans le ci-devant Piémont. Paris, 12 Messidor XIII.

Rapport et projet de décret sur la requête du sieur Sevestre. Rapport de la commission du contentieux. Paris, 7 May 1812.

Rapport et projet de décret sur le mode d'application des lois françaises concernant l'abolition de la féodalité aux départemens nouvellement réunis à l'Empire. Paris, 2 February 1811.

Rapports et projets de décret sur l'abolition de la féodalité dans les départemens de l'Ems-Supérieur, des Bouches-du-Wesser et des Bouches-de-l'Elbe. 25 novembre 1811.

Réclamations des provinces contre les opérations de leurs députés. 1790.

Reflexions d'un ci-devant notaire de campagne, sur les injustices commises à l'égard d'une foule de républicains, par suite des fausses applications de la loi du 17 juillet 1793, présentées au premier consul de la République Française. 12 Ventôse VIII.

Requête d'un cultivateur au Roi, après la retraite des notables. n.p., n.d.

Ressource immense et légitime pour la libération des dettes de l'Etat. n.p., 22 April 1789.

Robinet, Jean-Baptiste-René. *Dictionnaire universel des sciences morale, économique, politique, et diplomatique; ou Bibliothèque de l'homme d'état et citoyen.* Vol. 22. Londres: Libraires associés, 1782.

Rousseau, Jean-Jacques. *Discourse on the Origins of Inequality (2nd Discourse), Polemics and Political Economy.* In *Collected Writings of Rousseau,* edited by Roger D. Masters and Christopher Kelly, translated by Judith R. Bush, Roger D. Masters, Christopher Kelly, and Terrence Marshall. Vol. 3. Hanover, NH and London: University Press of New England, 1992.

Salvaing, Denis de. *De l'usage des fiefs et autres droits seigneuriaux.* Grenoble: Robert Philippes, 1668.

Second rapport du comité féodal, par M. Tronchet, Membre dudit Comité. Imprimé par ordre de l'Assemblée Nationale en date du 28 Mars 1790. Paris: Imprimerie nationale, 1790.

Secondat, Charles Louis de, baron de La Brède et de *Montesquieu. Montesquieu: Oeuvres completes.* Edited by Daniel Oster. Paris: Seuil, 1964.

Servan, Joseph-Michel-Antoine. *Refutation de l'ouvrage de M. l'abbé Sieyes sur les biens ecclesiastiques.* Paris: Desray, 1789.

Simon, Renée. *Henry de Boulainviller: Historien, politique, philosophe, astrologue, 1658–1722.* Paris, Boivin, n.d.

Sirey, Jean-Baptiste. *Recueil des lois et des arrêts en matière civile, criminelle, commerciale, et de droit public, depuis l'avénement de Napoléon. 1re partie. Jurisprudence de la Cour de Cassation.* Vol. 10. Paris: n.p., 1810.

Smith, Adam. *An Inquiry into the Nature and Causes of the Wealth of Nations.* Vol. 1. London: A. Strahan and T. Cadell, 1789.

Vaillant, Clément. *De la source du fief.* Paris: Nicholas Buon, 1604.

Secondary Sources

Ado, Anatoli. *Paysans en révolution: Terre, pouvoir, et jacquerie, 1789-1794.* Paris: Société des études robespierristes, 1996.

Aftalion, Florin. *The French Revolution: An Economic Interpretation.* Cambridge: Cambridge University Press, 1990.

Althusser, Louis. *Politics and History: Montesquieu, Rousseau, Hegel, and Marx.* Translated by Ben Brewster. London: New Left Books, 1972.

Andt, Ed. "Théorie de la directe universelle présentée d'après l'édit de 1692." *Revue historique de droit français et étranger,* 1922.

Audidière, Sophie. "Claude-Adrien Helvétius." In the online *Montesquieu Dictionary.* École Normale Supérieure de Lyon. http://dictionnaire-montesquieu.ens-lyon.fr.

Aulard, Alphonse. *La Révolution française et le régime féodal.* Paris: Alcan, 1919.

Baker, J. H. *An Introduction to English Legal History.* London: Butterworths, 1979.

Baker, Keith Michael. "Enlightenment Idioms, Old Regime Discourses, and Revolutionary Improvisations." In *From Deficit to Deluge: The Origins of the French Revolution,* edited by Thomas E. Kaiser and Dale K. Van Kley. Stanford, CA: Stanford University Press, 2011.

Baker, Keith Michael. "Fixing the French Constitution." In *Inventing the French Revolution: Essays on French Political Culture in the Eighteenth Century,* edited by Keith Michael Baker. Cambridge: Cambridge University Press, 1990.

Basdevant-Gaudemet, Brigitte. *Aux origines de l'état moderne: Charles Loyseau, 1564–1627, théoricien de la puissance publique.* Paris: Economica, 1977.

Bautruche, Robert. *Une société en lutte contre le régime féodal: L'Alleu en Bordelais et en Bazadais du XIe au XVIIIe siècles*. Rodez: Imprimerie P. Carrère, 1947.

Béaur, Gérard. *Le Marché foncier à la veille de la Révolution: Les Mouvements de la propriété beauçerons dans les régions de Maintenon et de Janville de 1761 à 1790*. Paris: Editions de l'EHESS, 1989.

Béaur, Gérard. *L'Immobilier et la Révolution: Marché de la pierre et mutations urbaines, 1770-1810*. Paris: A. Collin, 1994.

Bell, David A. *The First Total War: Napoleon's Europe and the Birth of Warfare as We Know It*. Boston: Houghton-Mifflin, 2007.

Bell, David A. *Lawyers and Citizens: The Making of a Political Elite in Old Regime France*. New York: Oxford University Press, 1994.

Berger, John. *Ways of Seeing*. Harmondsworth, UK: Penguin, 1972.

Berlanstein, Lenard R. *The Barristers of Toulouse in the Eighteenth Century*. Baltimore, MD: Johns Hopkins University Press, 1975.

Bien, David D. "Manufacturing Nobles: The Chancelleries in France to 1789." *Journal of Modern History* 61, no. 3 (1989): 445–86.

Bien, David D. "Offices, Corps, and a System of State Credit: The Uses of Privilege under the Ancien Régime." In *The Political Culture of the Old Regime*, vol. 1 of *The French Revolution and the Creation of Modern Political Culture*, edited by Keith Michael Baker. Oxford: Oxford University Press, 1987.

Bien, David D. "Les Offices, les corps et le crédit d'Etat: L'Utilisation des privilèges sous l'Ancien Régime." *Annales H.S.S.* 43, no. 2 (1988): 379–404.

Bien, David D. "Property in Office under the Ancien Régime: The Case of the Stockbrokers." In *Early Modern Conceptions of Property (Consumption and Culture in the 17th and 18th Centuries)*, edited by John Brewer and Susan Staves. London: Routledge, 1996.

Blaufarb, Rafe. "Conflict and Compromise: Communauté et Seigneurie in Early Modern Provence." *Journal of Modern History* 82, no. 3 (September 2010): 519–45.

Blaufarb, Rafe. "Nobles, Aristocrats, and the Origins of the French Revolution." In *Tocqueville & Beyond: Essays on the Old Regime in Honor of David D. Bien*, edited by Robert M. Schwartz and Robert A. Schneider. Newark: University of Delaware Press, 2003.

Blaufarb, Rafe. *The Politics of Fiscal Privilege in Provence, 1530s-1830s*. Washington, DC: Catholic University Press of America, 2012.

Bluche, François, and Pierre Durye. *L'Anoblissement par charges avant 1789*. La Roche-sur-Yon: Imprimerie centrale de l'Ouest, 1962.

Bodinier, Eric, and Eric Teyssier. *L'Événement le plus important de la Révolution: La Vente des biens nationaux*. Paris: CTHS, 2000.

Bohanan, Donna. *Old and New Nobility in Aix-en-Provence, 1600-1695: Portrait of an Urban Elite*. Baton Rouge: Louisiana State University Press, 1992.

Boiteau, Paul. *État de la France en 1789*. Paris: Perrotin, 1861.

Bossenga, Gail. "Markets, the Patrimonial State, and the Origins of the French Revolution." *1650-1850: Ideas, Aesthetics, and Inquiries in the Early Modern Era* 11 (2005): 443–510.

Boulet-Sautel, Margueritte. "De Choppin à Proudhon: Naissance de la notion moderne de domaine public." *Droits* 22 (January 1994): 91–102.

Boutier, Jean. *Campagnes en émoi: Révoltes et révolution en Bas-Limousin, 1789-1800*. Treignac: Les Monédières, 1987.

Branda, Pierre. *Le Prix de la gloire: Napoléon et l'argent*. Paris: Fayard, 2007.

Brown, Elizabeth A. "The Tyranny of a Construct: Feudalism and the Historians of Medieval Europe." *American Historical Review* 79, no. 4 (October 1974): 1063–88.

Bruchet, Max. *L'Abolition des droits seigneuriaux en Savoie (1761-1793)*. Marseille: Lafitte reprints, [1908] 1979.

Carcassonne, Elie. *Montesquieu et le problème de la constitution française au XVIIIè siècle*. Geneva: Slatkine reprints, 1970.

Chancerelle, Auguste. *Étude sur le domaine congéable*. Quimper: Typographie Arsène de Kerangal, 1898.

Chaussinand-Nogaret, Guy. *La Noblesse au XVIIIè siècle: de la féodalité aux Lumières.* Paris: Hachette, 1976.

Cheney, Paul. *Revolutionary Commerce: Globalization and the French Monarchy.* Cambridge, MA: Harvard University Press, 2010.

Chénon, E. *Étude sur l'histoire des alleux en France.* Paris: Larose and Forcel, 1888.

Chianea, Gérard. "Directe royale universelle et souveraineté royale en Dauphiné sous l'ancien régime." *Recueil de mémoires et travaux publié par la Société d'histoire du droit et des institutions des anciens pays de droit écrit, Fasc. IX, Melanges Roger Aubenas, Université de Montpellier I.* Montpellier: Faculté de droit et des sciences économiques, 1974.

Church, William Farr. *Constitutional Thought in Sixteenth-Century France: A Study in the Evolution of Ideas.* Cambridge, MA: Harvard University Press, 1941.

Clay, Lauren R. "The Bourgeoisie, Capitalism, and the Origins of the French Revolution," In *The Oxford Handbook of the French Revolution,* edited by David Andress. Oxford: Oxford University Press, 2015.

Cochrane, Eric. *Florence in the Forgotten Centuries, 1527–1800: A History of Florence and the Florentines in the Age of the Grand Dukes.* Chicago: University of Chicago Press, 1973.

Coleman, Charly. *The Virtues of Abandon: An Anti-Individualist History of the French Enlightenment.* Stanford, CA: Stanford University Press, 2014.

Cox, Iris. *Montesquieu and the History of French Laws.* Oxford: Voltaire Foundation, 1983.

Crest, Aurélie du. *Modèle familial et pouvoir monarchique (XVIè–XVIIIè siècles).* Aix-en-Provence: Presses universitaires d'Aix-Marseille, 2002.

Crouzet, François. "Les Conséquences économiques de la Révolution française." *Révue économique* 40, no. 6 (November 1989): 1189–1203.

Cubells, Monique. *La Provence des Lumières: Les Parlementaires d'Aix au 18è siècle.* Paris: Maloine, 1984.

Dawson, Philip. "The Bourgeoisie de Robe in 1789." *French Historical Studies* 4 (1965): 1–21.

Desan, Suzanne. *The Family on Trial in Revolutionary France.* Berkeley: University of California Press, 2004.

Descimon, Robert. "La Venalité des offices comme dette publique sous l'ancien régime français: Le Bien commun au pays des intérêts privés." In *La Dette publique dans l'histoire,* edited by Jean Andreau, Gérard Béaur, and Jean-Yves Grenier. Paris: Comité pour l'histoire économique et financière de la France, 2006.

Descimon, Robert. "La Venalité des offices et la construction de l'Etat dans la France moderne: Des problèmes de la représentation symbolique aux problèmes du coût social du pouvoir." In *Les Figures de l'administrateur: Institutions, réseaux, pouvoirs en Espagne, en France et au Portugal,* edited by Descimon, Jean-Frédéric Schaub, and Bernard Vincent. Paris: Editions de l'EHESS, 1997.

Descimon, Robert. "L'Union au domaine royal et le principe d'inaliénabilité: La Construction d'une loi fondamentale au XVIe et XVIIe siècles." *Droits: Revue française de théorie juridique* 22 (1995): 79–90.

Diaz, Furio. *Francesco Maria Gianni: Dalla burocrazia alla politica sotto Pietro Leopoldo di Toscana.* Milan: R. Ricciardi, 1966.

Dijn, Annalien de. "Montesquieu's Controversial Context: *The Spirit of the Laws* as a Monarchist Tract." *History of Political Thought* 34, no. 1 (2013): 66–88.

Doyle, William. *Origins of the French Revolution.* 3rd ed. Oxford: Oxford University Press, 1999.

Doyle, William. *Venality: The Sale of Offices in 18th Century France.* Oxford: Clarendon Press, 1996.

Dubreuil, Léon. *Les Vicissitudes du domaine congéable en basse-Bretagne à l'époque de la Révolution.* 2 vols. Rennes: Imprimerie Oberthur, 1915.

Dupâquier, Jacques. *La Propriété et l'exploitation foncières à la fin de l'ancien régime dans la Gatinais septentrional.* Paris: Presses universitaires de France, 1956.

Edelstein, Daniel. "Enlightenment Rights Talk." *Journal of Modern History* 84, no. 3 (September 2014): 530–65.

Ellis, Harold A. *Boulainvilliers and the French Monarchy: Aristocratic Politics in Early Eighteenth-Century France.* Ithaca, NY: Cornell University Press, 1988.

Ferradou, André. *Le Rachat des droits féodaux dans la Gironde, 1790-1793*. Paris: Sirey, 1928.

Fitzsimmons, Michael P. *The Night the Old Regime Ended: August 4, 1789 and the French Revolution*. University Park: Pennsylvania State University Press, 2003.

Fitzsimmons, Michael P. *The Parisian Order of Barristers and the French Revolution*. Cambridge, MA: Harvard University Press, 1987.

Fox-Genovese, Elizabeth. *The Origins of Physiocracy: Economic Revolutions and Social Order in Eighteenth-Century France*. Ithaca, NY: Cornell University Press, 1977.

Franklin, Julian. *Jean Bodin and the Rise of Absolutist Theory*. Cambridge: Cambridge University Press, 1973.

Furet, François. *Marx and the French Revolution*. Translated by Deborah Kan Furet. Chicago: University of Chicago Press, 1988.

Furet, François. "Night of August 4." In *A Critical Dictionary of the French Revolution*, edited by François Furet and Mona Ozouf, translated by Arthur Goldhammer. Cambridge, MA: Harvard University Press, 1989.

Galiani, Sebastian, and Itai Sened, eds. *Institutions, Property Rights, and Economic Growth: The Legacy of Douglass North*. Cambridge: Cambridge University Press, 2014.

Garaud, Marcel. *Histoire générale du droit privé français*, vol. 2, *La Révolution et la propriété foncière*. Paris: Sirey, 1953.

Garaud, Marcel. *La Révolution et la propriété foncière*. Paris: Sirey, 1958.

Garaud, Robert. *Le Rachat des droits féodaux et des dîmes inféodées en Haute-Vienne*. Limoges: Dupuy-Moulinier, 1939.

Garsonnet, E. *Histoire des locations perpétuelles et des baux à longue durée*. Paris: Larose, 1879.

Gau-Cabée, Caroline. *Droits d'usage et code civil: L'Invention d'un hybride juridique*. Paris: Librairie générale de droit et de jurisprudence, 2006.

Gaudin, Martin-Michel-Charles. *Mémoires, souvenirs, opinions, et écrits du duc de Gaëte, ancien ministre des finances*. Paris: Armand Colin, 1926.

Giesey, Ralph E. "The Juristic Basis of Dynastic Right to the French Throne." *Transactions of the American Philosophical Society*, n.s., 51, no. 5 (1961): 3–47.

Giesey, Ralph E. *Le Rôle méconnu de la loi salique: La Succession royale XIVè–XVIè siècles*. Paris: Les Belles Lettres, 2007.

Giraud, Philemon. *Notes chronologiques pour servir à l'histoire de Bormes*. Hyerès: Cruves, 1859.

Gordley, James. "Myths of the French Civil Code." *American Journal of Comparative Law* 42, no. 3 (Summer 1994): 459–505.

Goujard, Philippe. "L'Abolition de la féodalité dans le district de Neufchâtel (Seine-Inférieure)." In *Contributions à l'histoire paysanne de la révolution française*, edited by Albert Soboul. Paris: Editions sociales, 1977.

Halpérin, Jean-Louis. *L'Impossible code civil*. Paris: Presses universitaires de France, 1992.

Hanley, Sarah. *The Lit de Justice of the Kings of France: Constitutional Ideology in Legal Ritual and Discourse*. Princeton, NJ: Princeton, 1983.

Heuer, Jennifer Ngaire. *The Family and the Nation: Gender and Citizenship in Revolutionary France, 1789-1830*. Ithaca, NY: Cornell University Press, 2005.

Hirsch, Jean-Pierre. *La Nuit du 4 août*. Paris: Gallimard/Julliard, 1978.

Hirsch, Jean-Pierre. "Terror and Property." In *The French Revolution and the Creation of Modern Political Culture*, vol. 4, *The Terror*, edited by Keith Michael Baker. Oxford: Pergamon, 1994.

Holdsworth, William Searle. *An Historical Introduction to the Land Law*. Oxford: Oxford University Press, 1927.

Honoré, Louis. *Bormes au dix-huitième siècle*. Montauban: Orphelins imprimeurs, 1913.

Hunt, Lynn. *Politics, Culture, and Class in the French Revolution*. Berkeley: University of California Press, 2004.

Huppert, Georges. "Naissance de l'histoire en France: Les 'Recherches' d'Estienne Pasquier." *Annales E.S.C.*, 23è année, no. 1 (1968): 69–105.

Jaume, Lucien. *Le Discours jacobin et la démocratie*. Paris: Fayard, 1989.

Jones, Colin. "Bourgeois Revolution Revivified: 1789 and Social Change." In *Rewriting the French Revolution*, edited by Colin Lucas. Oxford: Clarendon, 1991.

Jones, Colin. "The Great Chain of Buying: Medical Advertisement, the Bourgeois Public Sphere, and the Origins of the French Revolution." *American Historical Review* 101, no. 1 (1996): 13–40.

Jones, P. M. *Politics and Rural Society. The Southern Massif Central, c.1750-1880.* Cambridge: Cambridge University Press, 1985.

Kaiser, Thomas. "Property, Sovereignty, the Declaration of the Rights of Man, and the Tradition of French Jurisprudence." In *The French Idea of Freedom: The Old Regime and the Declaration of Rights of 1789*, edited by Dale Van Kley. Stanford, CA: Stanford University Press, 1994.

Kaplan, Steven Laurence. *La Fin des corporations*. Paris: Fayard, 2001.

Kelley, Donald R. "De Origine Feodorum: The Beginnings of a Historical Problem." *Speculum* 39, no. 2 (April 1964): 207–29.

Kelley, Donald R. *Foundations of Modern Historical Scholarship: Language, Law, and History in the French Renaissance*. New York: Columbia University Press, 1970.

Kelley, Donald R. *Historians and the Law in Postrevolutionary France*. Princeton, NJ: Princeton University Press, 1984.

Kelley, Donald R. "Men of Law and the French Revolution." In *Politics, Ideology, and the Law in Early Modern Europe: Essays in Honor of J. H. M. Salmon*, edited by Adrianna E. Bakos. Rochester, NY: University of Rochester Press, 1994.

Keohane, Nannerl O. *Philosophy and the State in France: The Renaissance to the Enlightenment*. Princeton, NJ: Princeton University Press, 1980.

Kessel, Patrick. *La Nuit du 4 août 1789*. Paris: Arthaud, 1969.

Kolbert, C. F., and N. A. M. Mackay. *History of Scots and English Land Law*. The Keep, Berkhampsted, Herts: Geographical Publications Limited, 1977.

Koubi, Geneviève, ed. *Propriété et révolution: Actes du colloque de Toulouse, 12–14 octobre 1989*. Paris: Editions du CNRS, 1990.

Le Lay, Hervé. *Le Domaine congéable sous la Révolution*. Rennes: Imprimeries réunies, 1941.

Lefebvre, Georges. *Les Paysans du Nord pendant la Révolution française*. Vol. 1. Lille: Marquant, 1924.

Leffler, Phyllis K. "French Historians and the Challenge to Louis XIV's Absolutism." *French Historical Studies* 14, no. 1 (Spring 1985): 1–22.

Lelong, Jean. *La Vie et les oeuvres de Loyseau (1564–1627)*. Paris: LGDJ, 1909.

Levy, Darline Gay. *The Ideas and Careers of Simon-Nicolas-Henri Linguet: A Study in Eighteenth-Century French Politics*. Urbana: University of Illinois Press, 1980.

Leyte, Guillaume. *Domaine et domanialité publique dans la France médiévale (XIIe–XVe siècles)*. Strasbourg: Presses universitaires de Strasbourg, 1996.

Livesey, James. *Making Democracy in the French Revolution*. Cambridge, MA: Harvard University Press, 2001.

Lloyd, Howell A. "The Political Thought of Charles Loyseau (1564-1627)." *European History Quarterly* 111 (1981): 53–82.

Longhitano, Gino. "La Monarchie française entre la société des ordres et marché: Mirabeau, Quesnay, et le Traité de la monarchie." In Mirabeau and Quesnay, *Traité de la monarchie (1757–1759)*, edited by Gino Longhitano. Paris: Harmattan, 1999.

Mackrell, J. Q. C. *The Attack on Feudalism in Eighteenth-Century France*. London: Routledge and Kegan Paul, 1973.

Magnou-Nortier, Elisabeth. "Les Lois féodales et la société d'après Montesquieu et Marc Bloch, ou la seigneurie banale reconsidérée." *Revue historique* 89, fasc. 22 (April-June 1993): 321–60.

Marion, Henri. *La Dime écclésiastique en France au XVIIIè siècle et sa suppression*. Bordeaux: Imprimerie de l'université, 1912.

Markoff, John. *The Abolition of Feudalism: Peasants, Lords, and Legislators in the French Revolution*. University Park: Pennsylvania State University Press, 1996.

Marquiset, Alfred. *Napoléon sténographié au conseil d'état, 1804–1805*. Paris: Champion, 1913.

Marx, Karl. *Capital: A Critique of Political Economy*. New York: Modern Library, 1936.

Marzagalli, Silvia. "Economic and Demographic Developments." In *The Oxford Handbook of the French Revolution*, edited by David Andress. Oxford: Oxford University Press, 2015.

Massa-Gille, Geneviève. "Les Rentes foncières sous le Consulat et l'Empire." *Bibliothèque de l'École des Chartes* 133, no. 2 (July-December 1975): 247–337.

Massaloux, Jean-Paul. *La Régie de l'enregistrement et des domaines aux XVIIIè et XIXè siècles: Étude historique*. Geneva: Droz, 1989.

Massé, Pierre. "Résistance aux rentes foncières dans la Vienne sous la Révolution." *Bulletin de la société des antiquaires de l'Ouest*, 4th series, 7 (1964): 363–84.

Maza, Sarah. *The Myth of the French Bourgeoisie: An Essay on the Social Imaginary, 1750-1850.* Cambridge, MA: Harvard University Press, 2005.

McPhee, Peter. "The French Revolution, Peasants, and Capitalism." *American Historical Review* 94, no. 5 (December 1989): 1265–80.

Méricam-Bourdet, Myrtille. "Voltaire contre Montesquieu? L'Apport des oeuvres historiques dans la controverse." *Revue française d'histoire des idées politiques: Débats et polémiques autour de L'Esprit des lois* 35, 1er semestre (2012): 25–36.

Meynial, Edmond. "Notes sur la formation de la théorie du domaine divisé (domaine direct et domaine utile) du XIIe au XIVe siècle dans les romanistes: Étude de dogmatique juridique." In *Melanges Fitting*. Montpellier: Société anonyme de l'imprimerie générale du midi, 1907.

Miller, Judith A. "The Aftermath of the Assignat: Plaintiffs in the Age of Property, 1794–1804." In *Taking Liberties: Problems of a New Order from the French Revolution to Napoleon*, edited by Howard G. Brown and Judith A. Miller. Manchester: Manchester University Press, 2002.

Mousnier, Roland. *La Venalité des offices sous Henri IV et Louis XIII*. 2nd ed. Paris: Presses universitaires de France, 1971.

North, Douglass C. *Structure and Change in Economic History*. New York: W. W. Norton, 1981.

Ourliac, Paul. "Montesquieu, historien de la féodalité." In *Melanges Pierre Vellas: recherches et réalisations*. Paris: Pedone, 1995.

Parker, David. "Absolutism, Feudalism, and Property Rights in the France of Louis XIV." *Past and Present*, no. 179 (May 2003): 60–96.

Patault, Anne-Marie. "Un conflit entre la cour de cassation et le conseil d'état: L'Abolition des droits féodaux et le droit de propriété." *Revue historique de droit français et étranger* 56 (1978): 427–44.

Plack, Noelle. "Challenges in the Countryside, 1790–2." In *The Oxford Handbook of the French Revolution*, edited by David Andress. Oxford: Oxford University Press, 2015.

Pocock, J. G. A. *The Ancient Constitution and the Feudal Law: English Historical Thought in the Seventeenth Century*. Cambridge: Cambridge University Press, 1957.

Pocock, J. G. A. "Historical Introduction." In *The Political Works of James Harrington*, edited by J. G. A. Pocock. Cambridge: Cambridge University Press, 1977.

Pocock, J. G. A. "The Origins of the Study of the Past: A Comparative Approach." In *Political Thought and History: Essays on Theory and Method*. Cambridge: Cambridge University Press, 2009.

Price, Robin. "Boulainviller and the Myth of the Frankish Conquest of Gaul." *Studies in Voltaire and the Eighteenth Century* 199 (1987): 155–85.

Reynolds, Susan. *Fiefs and Vassals: The Medieval Evidence Reinterpreted*. Oxford: Oxford University Press, 1994.

Rich, E. E., and C. H. Wilson, eds. *The Cambridge Economic History of Europe*. Vol. 5. Cambridge: Cambridge University Press, 1977.

Rosenthal, Jean-Laurent. *The Fruits of Revolution: Property Rights, Litigation, and French Agriculture, 1700-1860*. Cambridge: Cambridge University Press, 1992.

Rothkrug, Lionel. *Opposition to Louis XIV: The Political and Social Origins of the French Enlightenment*. Princeton, NJ: Princeton University Press, 1965.

Rousselet, Anne. *La Règle de l'inaliénabilité du domaine de la Couronne: Étude doctrinale de 1556 à la fin de l'Ancien Régime*. Paris: L.G.D.J, 1997.

Bibliography

269

Rowen, Herbert. *The King's State: Proprietary Dynasticism in Early Modern France*. New Brunswick, NJ: Rutgers University Press, 1980.

Sagnac, Ph., and P. Caron, eds. *Les Comités des droits féodaux et de législation et l'abolition du régime seigneurial, 1789–1793*. Geneva: Mégariotis Reprints, [1907] n.d.

Salmon, J. H. "Renaissance Jurists and 'Enlightened' Magistrates: Perspectives on Feudalism in Eighteenth-Century France." *French History* 8, no. 4 (1994): 387–402.

Sewell, William H. "Beyond 1793: Babeuf, Louis Blanc, and the Genealogy of 'Social Revolution.'" In *The French Revolution and the Creation of Modern Political Culture*, vol. 3, *The Transformation of Political Culture, 1789–1848*, edited by François Furet and Mona Ozouf. Oxford: Pergamon, 1989.

Sewell, William H. "Connecting Capitalism to the French Revolution: The Parisian Promenade and the Origins of Civic Equality in Eighteenth-Century France." *Critical Historical Studies* 1, no. 1 (Spring 2014): 5–46.

Sewell, William H. *Work and Revolution in France: The Language of Labor from the Old Regime to 1848*. Cambridge: Cambridge University Press, 1980.

Shapiro, Gilbert, and John Markoff. *Revolutionary Demands: A Content Analysis of the Cahiers de Doléances of 1789*. Stanford, CA: Stanford University Press, 1998.

Shovlin, John. *The Political Economy of Virtue: Language, Patriotism, and the Origins of the French Revolution*. Ithaca, NY: Cornell University Press, 2006.

Skinner, Quentin. *The Foundations of Modern Political Thought*. 2 vols. Cambridge: Cambridge University Press, 1978.

Soboul, Albert. *Les Campagnes montpeliéranes à la fin de l'ancien régime: propriété et cultures d'après les compoix*. Paris: Presses universitaires de France, 1958.

Soboul, Albert. *Précis historique de la Révolution française*. Paris: Editions sociales, 1962.

Sonenscher, Michael. *Before the Deluge: Public Debt, Inequality, and the Intellectual Origins of the French Revolution*. Princeton, NJ: Princeton University Press, 2007.

Spang, Rebecca L. *Stuff and Money in the Time of the French Revolution*. Cambridge, MA: Harvard University Press, 2015.

Spieler, Miranda Frances. *Empire and Underworld: Captivity in French Guiana*. Cambridge, MA: Harvard University Press, 2012.

Stourm, René. *Les Finances du Consulat*. Paris: Guillaumin, 1902.

Sutherland, D. M. G. "Peasant, Lord, and Leviathan: Winners and Losers from the Abolition of French Feudalism, 1780–1820." *Journal of Economic History* 62, no. 1 (March 2002): 1–24.

Tackett, Timothy. *When the King Took Flight*. Cambridge, MA: Harvard University Press, 2004.

Taylor, George V. "Noncapitalist Wealth and the Origins of the French Revolution." *American Historical Review* 72, no. 2 (January 1967): 469–96.

Thireau, Jean-Louis. *Charles Du Moulin (1500–1566): Étude sur les sources, la méthode, les idées politiques et économiques d'un juriste de la Renaissance*. Geneva: Droz, 1980.

Tholozan, Olivier. *Henri de Boulainvilliers: L'Anti-absolutisme aristocratique légitimé par l'histoire*. Aix-en-Provence: PUAM, 1999.

Tocqueville, Alexis de. *The Ancien Régime and the Revolution*. Translated by Gerald Bevan. London: Penguin, 2008.

Tocqueville, Alexis de. *L'ancien régime et la Révolution*. 2nd Edition. Paris: Michel Lévy frères, 1856.

Tocqueville, Alexis de. *The Old Regime and the French Revolution*. Translated by Stuart Gilbert. Garden City, NJ: Doubleday, 1955.

Tomaselli, Sylvana. "The Spirit of Nations." In *Cambridge History of Eighteenth-Century Political Thought*, edited by Mark Goldie and Richard Wokler. Cambridge: Cambridge University Press, 2006.

Turi, Gavriele. *'Viva Maria': La reazione alle riforme Leopoldine (1790–1799)*. Florence: L. S. Olschki, 1969.

Vallée, Louis. *Le Bail à rente foncière dans l'ancien droit français et le droit intermédiaire*. Paris: V. Giard & E. Brière, 1900.

Vardi, Liana. *The Physiocrats and the World of the Enlightenment*. Cambridge: Cambridge University Press, 2012.

Whitman, James Q. "The Seigneurs Descend to the Rank of Creditors: The Abolition of Respect." *Yale Journal of Law and Humanities* 6 (1994): 249–83.

Wright, Johnson Kent. *A Classical Republican in Eighteenth-Century France: The Political Thought of Mably*. Palo Alto, CA: Stanford University Press, 1997.

Zarka, Yves-Charles. "Constitution et souveraineté selon Bodin." *Il Pensiero Politico* 30, no. 2 (1997): 276–86.

INDEX

Abbey of Du Vallasse, 185
Abbey of Fécamp, 177, 185
Abbey of Longueville, 181, 185
Abbey of Montivilliers, 185
Abbey of Sainte-Geneviève, 182
Abbey of Saint-Georges de Bocherville, 177
Abbey of Saint-Germain des Près, 164
Abbey of the Virginity (Loir-et-Cher), 99
Aguesseau, Henri François, 150
Aix-en-Provence
  guild offices in, 5
  municipal offices in, 5
  nobles in, 6–7
  notarial registers of, 65
  rachat payments in, 76, 79, 91, 182–183, 188
  Roman Catholic Church in, 7–8, 129, 176
  sovereign courts in, 6
  venal offices in, 5–6
Albisson, Jean, 211
Alciato, André, 16
Allarde, baron d', 179
Allard-Néoulle, 200
Allein, marquis d', 183
allodiality. *See also seigneuries*
  defenses of, 19, 31–35, 64
  French Revolution's challenge to,
    51–52, 58–59
  heritability and, 65
  hierarchical division and, 64–65
  lack of feudal superiority in, 65, 99
  Merlin on, 110
  Michallet on, 85
  Montesquieu's account of, 39–40
  National Convention regulations
    regarding, 99–100
  Roman law and, 31, 33, 39
  royal challenges to principle of, 30–32
  royal claims of fees for, 30, 35

seventeenth-century debates regarding, 15
  usurping of, 33
Alsace, 114
antichrèse credit arrangements, 150
Antonin religious order, 122
apanages (princely grants), 137
Aquitaine, 31
Arbois commune, 108
Archbishop of Arles, 185
Arian heresy, 31
assignat (French Revolution currency), 96–97,
  194–195
Aude department, 198
Augustin family (Limoges), 195
Aurillac, 32
Aurons, *seigneur* of, 183
Auvergne, 110
Aveyron region, 99

Babeuf, François-Noël, 143
Bagnol, Bertrand, 195–196
bail à covenant (tenure in Brittany), 238n40
banalités (service monopolies in *seigneuries*),
  7, 70, 74
Barbé-Marbois, François, 31, 167
Barère, Bertrand
  on alienability and inalienability of national
    domain, 143–145
  Domanial Committee leadership of, 137
  expropriation of royal property and, 139–141,
    152–154, 159
  on local administration of *rachat*
    collection, 181
Barony of Bormes, 6
Barony of Saint-Sulpice et Villelongue, 166
Bérenger, Jean, 212, 214
Berlier, Théophile, 116–117, 211
Béthune-Sully courtier dynasty, 152

Bezard, Francois-Simeon, 105
biens nationaux (properties confiscated in French
    Revolution). *See also* national domain
  alienability and inalienability principles
      regarding, 143–145, 216
  concerns regarding viability of, 105
  criticism of sellers of, 161
  engagements and, 153, 155–156, 158–163,
      165–166, 172–173
  faith in the French Revolution expressed
      through purchase of, 99, 105
  law establishing (1790), 179–180
  Law of 28 Ventôse IV reactivating sale of,
      158–159, 162
  national rents and, 178, 183, 188–190, 192,
      194–195, 197, 201, 206
  national rents as, 176
  rachat payments and, 190
  Roman Catholic Church properties sold as,
      178, 180–181
  sale to individuals of, 180
  as source of national revenue, 120, 144
Bigot de Préamenu, Félix-Julien-Jean, 212
Billon village, 180
Biré, Guillaume, 98
Blaswai (citizen in Orléans), 92
Blois, 155
Bodin, Jean
  eminent domain and, 231n25
  property rights in the theories of, 20–23, 35,
      44, 129, 231n25
  royal power in the theories of, 19, 21–23, 28
  on *seigneuries*, 21–22
  sovereignty in the theories of, 21–23
  on venal offices, 22, 43
Boisbelle and Henchmont (échange), 149
Boisgelin de Cicé, Jean de Dieu-Raymond,
      129–130
Bonaparte, Louis, 112
Bonaparte, Napoleon. *See* Napoleon Bonaparte
Boncerf, Pierre-François, 68, 178
Bonnal, François de, 131
Bonnet, Jean-Baptiste, 65
Bordeaux
  Edict of 1692 protested in, 31
  national rents and, 180
  rachat (redemption payments) in, 76,
      78–79, 90–91
Bormes, 6–7
Boucher d'Argis, Antoine-Gaspard, 17
Bouches-de-l'Elbe, 115
Bouches-du-Rhône, 185
Bouches-du-Weser, 115
Boudier (citizen of Normandy in ground rent
      dispute), 96
Boudin, M. (pamphleteer), 175, 178
Boulainviliers, Henry de, 17, 36–38

Boulard, Jean-Joseph, 188
Bouquet, Pierre, 18
Bourbon-Penthièvre, House of, 164, 189
Bremen, 115
Breton Club, 49
Brissot, Jacques Pierre, 221
Brittany, 238n40
Brou village, 180
Brueyleroi (Loiret), 75
Brumairians, 102–106, 163, 196–198
Brunache, Pierre, 185
Buat, comte de, 37
Burgundy, 31, 99
Buzot, François-Nicolas-Léonard, 125

Cadillac (village), 75
Caesar, Julius, 24
cahiers de doléances, 51–52, 67, 122
Caisse d'amortissement (financial administration
        for retiring national debt), 199–203,
        252–253n56
Calonne, Charles Alexandre de, 152
Calvados, 155
Cambacérès, Jean-Jacques-Régis
    Domanial Committee of National Convention
        and, 93
    feudal abolition in imperial territories and,
        112–116
    Great Demarcation and, 219
    Merlin-Cambacérès report and, 114–116, 202
    restoration of ground rents and, 212–213
Cambon, Pierre-Joseph, 154–155
Cambridge School of historians, 16
Campoin (Burgundian involved in ground rent
        dispute), 98–99
Camus, Armand-Gaston, 132–133, 140
Capet, Hugues, 37, 138
Carolingian Dynasty, 138
Caseneuve, Pierre de, 31–32
Caussat, Jacquette, 156
Caussat, Margueritte, 156
Célestin religious order, 122
censives (land grants in exchange for rents)
    definition of, 26
    divided domain and, 65
    French Revolution and changes to, 58, 74
    lords' exploiting of, 30
    no feudal concessions for, 107
    payments for, 64
    rachat and the termination of, 58
Chabot, Georges-Antoine, 244n85
Chamber of Deputies, 167, 169
Chamber of Peers, 167, 169
Champagne, 31, 165
Chapel of Notre Dame de Lorrette, 177
Chapel of Saint-Chef (Isère), 193
Chapter of Romartin, 179

Chapter of Saint-Cerneuf de Billon, 180
Charles Martel (Frankish prince), 37
Charlier, Louis-Joseph, 90
Charpentier, Léonard, 196
Chasset, Charles-Antoine, 184
Chaudony, Jean-Joseph, 205
Chazal, Jean-Pierre, 104–105
Cheron, 200
Choppin, René, 29
The Church. *See* Roman Catholic Church
Church of Saint-Martin of Marseille, 205–206
Civil Code
    abolition of social distinctions in, 210
    appellate courts' review of the text of,
        209–210, 215–217
    article 23 of, 215–216
    article 24 of, 215–217
    article 516 of, 215–216
    article 543 of, 211
    article 544 in, 209
    article 545 of, 218
    criticisms of, 208
    on divided domain, 211
    ground rents and, 210–214
    paternal power and, 208–209
    property rights in, 3, 11, 208–211,
        214–219, 222
Clappiers-Vauvengargues, 80, 95
Clerc, Jean, 185
Cloppenburg, 115
Clovis, 17–18, 32, 37
Code Michau, 30
Colberts, 189–190
Commentaires sur l'Esprit des lois (Voltaire), 38
Committee of Public Safety, 94–95
Committee of the Constitution (National
    Assembly), 52
Committee on Alienation (National
    Assembly), 184
Committee on Feudal Rights. *See* Feudal
    Committee
Condé courtier dynasty, 152
Constant, Benjamin, 244n88
Constituent Assembly
    abolition of feudalism and, 75, 103–104, 113
    Civil Code and, 215
    Couthon's critique of, 86
    engagements and, 153–154
    Feudal Committee of, 86–87, 89
    ground rents and, 103–104, 213
    Legislative Assembly as successor to, 83
    rachat (redemption payment) system and,
        75–76, 80–84, 86–90, 95, 99, 191–192
    rural code established by, 61
Consulate government, 83, 106, 163–164,
    197–198
Convention. *See* National Convention

corps des arts et métiers (trade guilds), 134
Costil, Pierre, 172
Council of 500
    domanial commission of, 153, 155, 160
    engagement legislation and, 162
    ground rents and, 97, 100–102
Council of Elders, 160, 162
Council of State
    engagement claim cases and, 165
    ground rents and, 107–112, 116, 211–214
    imperial annexation questions and, 112, 116
    national rents debate and, 203–204
Cour de Cassation (supreme appeals court),
    106–108, 110–111, 117, 171–172, 204
Courren, Gayetan, 188
Courtier, Michel, 196
Couthon, Georges, 86–87
Crétet, Emmanuel, 212–213
the Crown
    allodiality challenged by, 30–32
    Bodin's theories regarding, 19, 21–23, 28
    Clovis's annexation of power to, 18
    concession of domanial properties by, 139
    Dumoulin's theories on, 19–20, 32
    ecclesiastical property claimed by, 122–123
    engagements (revocable grants of property)
        from, 148–173
    financial needs of, 30, 35
    Loyseau's theories regarding, 28–29
    nationalization of property of, 11–12,
        119–122, 132, 134–135, 137–141,
        143–145, 173, 175–176, 178, 183, 188, 206
    physiocrats' theories regarding, 42–45
    proprietary superiority asserted by, 4,
        18–22, 27–35, 39, 43–44, 122, 136–137,
        142, 233n54
    royal domain and, 29–30, 34–35
    seigneuries and, 3, 136
    succession rules and, 29, 42, 45
    taxation and, 34, 42
Cuges, 7
Custom of Paris, 20

d'Aiguillon, duc, 49, 66
d'Albert, Esprit-Hiacinthe-Bernard, 6, 8, 57–58
Danton, Georges, 221
Dard, Henri-Jean-Baptiste, 108
D'Argenson, marquis, 34
Darracq, François-Balthazar, 101
Daru, Pierre-Antoine-Noël-Bruno de, 169,
    173–174
d'Auberville, 185
Dauche, Jean-Baptiste, 90–91
Dauphiné
    allodiality in, 31–32, 110
    engagement grants in, 149–150
    rachat (redemption) system debates in, 74

Declaration of Rights, 52, 93
Decree of August 11th (1789)
  ground rents abolished by, 54, 56, 58–59, 65,
    73, 210
  language on abolishing feudalism in,
    49–51, 66
  national domain and, 136
  property and power separated through,
    52–53, 55–57
  redemption measures outlined in, 50–51, 60
  Roman Catholic Church independence
    curtailed by, 50, 53–55, 60
  seigneurial justice abolished by, 50–51, 53,
    55–56, 58, 60
  venal offices abolished by, 50–51, 53, 55–57,
    60, 221
de Fayac, 76
Defermon, Jacques, 212
Dehargne (citizen involved in ground rent
    dispute in Vendôme), 99
de la Borderie, Gentry, 193
Delacroix, Charles-François, 157
de la Croix de Pisançon, Jean-François, 190
*De l'Administration provinciale et la réforme de
    l'impôt* (Le Trosne), 43
Delarozière, Monsieur, 181
De l'Esprit des lois (Montesquieu),
    38–40, 235n91
de Pons, dame, 165–166
Deslandes, Villet, 67
d'Espagnac, comte, 152
Destutt de Tracy, Antoine-Louis-Claude, 46–47
Deusy, François-Joseph-Sixte, 87–88
Devolx, Monsieur, 185
Dijon, 31
Dillon, *abbé* Arthur, 135
direct domain
  abolition (1793) of, 83
  allodiality and, 110
  cens payments within, 63
  Civil Code and, 211
  Council of State's abolition of, 109–111
  hierarchy of multiple owners under, 62–63
  National Assembly's recognition of, 66
  National Convention's recognition of, 90
  nationalization of ecclesiastical property and,
    118–119
  rachat payments and, 80
  seigneurs' jurisdiction and, 62, 206
Directory period, 83, 96, 100–102, 156, 195
Domanial Committee (National Assembly)
  administration of expropriated royal property
    and, 139–141
  administration of feudal abolition and, 93
  on alienability and inalienability of the
    national domain, 143–146
  engagements examined by, 152–153
  fraud investigations by, 137–138

  leaders of, 137
  national *versus* individual property debates
    and, 130
  royal concession of domanial properties
    and, 139
droit de franc fief (indemnity for *seigneuries*), 3, 65
droit d'enregistrement tax, 165, 167, 186, 195, 214
Drôme, 156
Dubos, Abbé, 17, 37–39, 138
Duchatel, Charles-Jacques Nicolas, 197, 200–203
Duchesne, Pierre-François, 101, 103–104
Duchy of Aremberg, 115
Duchy of Loraine, 252n48
Duchy of Oldenburg, 115
Dumarest, 200
Dumolard, Joseph-Vincent, 88
Dumoulin, Charles
  property rights in theories of, 19–20, 22, 32,
    35, 39, 70
  royal power in theories of, 19–20, 32
  on *seigneuries*, 20, 22, 32
Dumoustier (citizen of Loudon in ground rent
    dispute), 96
Dupont, Pierre-Samuel, 179
Duport, Jean-François-Adrien, 128
Duprat, Pierre-Louis, 101–102
Dupré, Denis, 190
Durand de Maillane, Pierre-Toussaint, 179
Duroure (citizen in Maine-et-Loire), 157

Ecclesiastical Committee (National Assembly),
    125, 140, 179
échanges (domanial properties transfered to
    individuals), 148–150, 152, 162
Edict of August 1692, 30–31
Edict of Moulins
  engagements created by, 171
  inalienability principle established by,
    142–143, 149, 173, 216
  proprietary character of monarchy affirmed by,
    29, 42, 137–138
  Salic Law of succession affirmed by, 42, 45
Émile (Rousseau), 132
Empire. *See also* Brumairians; Napoleon
    Bonaparte
  collapse of, 107, 117
  feudalism debates and, 83
  ground rent questions in, 111–117
  military crisis of 1813-1814 and, 117, 204
  private companies as rent collectors in, 200
Ems-Supérieur, 115
engagements (revocable grants of domanial
    property)
  antichrèse credit arrangements and, 150
  archival research for the recovery of, 166
  Civil Code and, 216
  complicated legal status of, 150–151
  composite public-private nature of, 148

Cour de Cassation ruling (1805) on, 171–172
debates regarding revocation of, 153–154
definition of, 137, 149
feudal considerations regarding, 170–172
"Great Push of 1828-129" regarding, 167–170,
   173–174
hierarchical division of, 150
inalienability and, 149, 173–174
Law of 10 Frimaire II revoking, 154–158, 169
Law of 14 Ventôse VII (on resale to original
   holders), 160–170, 172
Law of Ventôse IV and, 158–159, 162
Louis XIV and, 139
property rights regarding, 151–152
reclassification of land as, 143
reimbursement for revocation of, 155
as source of income, 139, 153
supplément de finance payments for, 151,
   161–163, 165, 169
venal offices compared to, 151
English Civil War, 8
Enjubault de la Roche,
   René-Urbain-Pierre-Charles-Félix
on alienability and inalienability of national
   domain, 141–142, 144–145
on *biens nationaux,* 144
on challenges of implementing domanial
   matters, 148
on "domain in its proper sense," 145
Domanial Committee leadership of, 137
expropriation of royal property and, 139–141,
   152–154, 159
on Frankish kings' monarchical powers, 138
on "goods without a master," 146
on local administration of *rachat*
   collection, 181
on royal concession of domanial
   properties, 139
on royal powers, 138–139
royal property fraud investigations of, 138
Estates-General, 51–52, 144
Eymar, Esprit-Hiacinthe-Bernard d',
   129–130, 132

Falcoz de la Blache, Alexandre-Joseph, 190
Faure, Louis-Joseph, 115
Faye, Jean, 91
Fayolle, André, 156
Ferradou, André, 78–79
Feudal Committee (Constituent Assembly),
   86–87, 89
Feudal Committee (National Assembly)
contractual dues approved by, 71
domanial abolition approach to ending
   feudalism debated at, 68–69
national rents system and, 179, 181–182
petitions to, 73–74
rachat collection and, 77–78

rachat system established by, 66–68,
   71–74, 86–88
feudalism
abolition in Napoleonic Empire territories of,
   111–117
ceremonies of, 4
engagements (revocable grants of domanial
   property) and, 170–172
European decline in, 8
fears regarding the restoration of, 100–103,
   105–106
French Revolution's abolition of, 8–10, 12–13,
   15, 48–62, 64–84, 86–100, 103–104, 109,
   111–112, 117–119, 170, 191–194, 210
hierarchy of, 4–5, 8
Marx on, 8–9
national rents replacement of, 176, 188–189,
   191, 193, 205
origins of, 16–18, 31–33, 36–38, 46, 84–86
pre-French Revolution calls to abolish, 34
Quesnay's critique of, 41
"Second Feudal Abolition" (July 1793) and,
   191–194
tenurial system as defining feature of, 4
Fiévée, Joseph, 164
Filmer, Robert, 15
Fitzsimmons, Michael, 48
Fleury, Abbé de, 18
Fox-Genovese, Elizabeth, 45
Franche-Comté, 31
François of Lorraine, 113
Francus (founder of Aurillac), 32
Franks
Church properties in Gaul and, 37, 130
Gaul conquered by, 16–17, 31–32, 36–37, 39,
   46, 84–85, 88, 130
monarchical power asserted by, 21, 33, 37,
   85, 138
property system under, 17–18, 24–26,
   28–29, 31–32, 36–39, 46–47, 84–85, 88,
   138, 143
Roman Empire and, 37, 39
seigneuries under, 24–25, 28
French Revolution
allodiality challenged by, 51–52, 58–59
Crown land nationalized during, 11–12,
   119–122, 132, 134–135, 137–141,
   143–145, 173, 175–176, 178, 183,
   188, 206
ecclesiastical property nationalized during, 3,
   11–13, 53–54, 78, 118–125, 128–129, 137,
   140, 143, 146, 173, 175–179, 185–186,
   188–190, 206
feudalism abolished by, 8–10, 12–13, 15,
   48–62, 64–84, 86–100, 103–104, 109,
   111–112, 117–119, 170, 191–194, 210
legitimating discourses of, 221
Marxist interpretations of, 9, 49–50, 59, 219

French Revolution (*Cont.*)
  Marx on, 8–9
  seigneuries abolished by, 12–13, 50–53, 55–60,
    175–176
  Tocqueville on, 1, 15
  venal offices abolished by, 12, 50–51, 53,
    55–57, 60, 175, 221
Furet, François, 48

Galissonnière, comte de la, 128, 130
Galland, Auguste, 30
Gallic Wars, 24
Gap (village in Dauphiné), 91
Garaud, Marcel, 12
Gaudin, Martin-Michel-Charles, 103, 203
Gaul
  Frankish conquest of, 16–17, 31–32, 36–37,
    39, 46, 84–85, 88, 130
  Frankish property system in, 17–18, 24–26,
    28–29, 32, 37–39, 46–47, 85, 88, 130
  Roman rule of, 16, 37, 84–85
Gautier de Girenton, Gabrielle-Charlotte de, 7
Gay-Vernon, Léonard-Honoré, 102
General Hospital of Saint John the Baptist
    of Le Havre, 190
Gennelais fief, 177
Gerle, Dom, 135
Germanist theory of feudal origins, 16–17, 36
Germany, 111, 115, 202
Gillet, Jean-Claude, 105
Giraud, Jean, 198
Girenton, Gautier de, 7
Girondins, 88, 90
Godefroi, 200
Goths, 31
Goujoun, Jean-Marie-Claude, 87
Goupil-Préfeln, Louis-François-Antoine, 217
Grand Duchy of Berg, 115
Grand Mill of Saint-Etienne, 171
Grands Carmes of Marseille, 205
Grasse, Henry de, 7
Great Demarcation
  Civil Code's enshrining of, 218–219
  extrication of property from the state and,
    147, 206
  French Revolution's legitimating discourses
    and, 221
  legacy of, 11, 14
  property and power separated in, 57, 136, 173,
    219, 222
Great Fear, 10, 49
Grenoble, 31, 180, 190
ground rents
  as agent of democratization of property
    ownership, 65
  burden of proof regarding legitimacy of, 87
  Civil Code and, 210–214

Constituent Assembly and, 103–104, 213
continuation after French Revolution of,
  67, 93–98
Council of 500 and, 97, 100–102
Council of State and, 107–112, 116, 211–214
Cour de Cassation ruling (1838) on, 117
Decree of August 11 (1789) and the abolition
  of, 54, 56, 58–59, 65, 73, 210
Directory legislature debates on, 100–102
divided dominality and, 66
efforts to revive, 102–110, 117, 197–198, 203,
  210–214
engagements and, 149, 172
hospitals and, 202
in imperial territories, 111–117
legal status of, 63, 72
Merlin's effort to revive, 106–110
Napoleonic Era collection of, 204
National Convention laws on, 90, 92–95,
  97–101, 103–104, 109, 113–114
nationalized Church property and, 124–125
national rent system and, 175–178
nineteenth century appeals to restore, 117
perpetual nature of, 45, 56, 58, 65–66, 72
rachat (redemption) system and, 74, 90
royal revenue from, 69
as source of national income, 93, 101–106, 117
tithes as, 54
in Tuscany, 111, 114
Guffroy, Armand-Benoît-Joseph, 125–126
Guien, André, 185
Guion, 179

Hamburg, 115
Hanseatic lands, 115
Hautes-Alpes, 156
Haute-Vienne, 78, 182–183
Helvétius, Claude-Adrien, 235n91
Henri IV (king of France), 136–137
Henrique, Germain, 185
Heurtevent, 63
Histoire critique de l'établissement de la monarchie
    françoise dans les Gaules (Dubos), 37
Holland, 111–113, 202
Holy Roman Empire, 17
hospitals, 200–203
Huet, Monsieur, 181
Hungarian incursions (medieval France), 37
Huns, 21
hunting rights, 48, 56, 211

Inconveniens des droits féodaux (Boncerf), 68
Indre-et-Loire, 199
inflation, 72, 96, 194–196, 214
Instruction (Merlin), 75
Isoré, Jacques, 89
Italy, 111, 113–114, 202. *See also specific locations*

Jacobins, 88
Jaillant, Antoine, 97
Jallet, Jacques, 130
Jesuits, 122
Joint Committee of Domains and Finance
    (National Convention), 157
Journu-Auber, Bernard, 87–88
Julien, Paul, 99
Julien, Pierre, 65
Justinian (Roman emperor), 37

Kaiser, Thomas, 15
King's Secretaries, 2

Lacoste, Benjamin-Eléonor-Louis de, 123
Lacoste, Jean-Baptiste, 198
La Croix de Sayre d'Ornacieux,
    Barthélemy-Artus de, 76
Lafare, Bishop, 179
Lafayette, Marquis de, 88
Lagarde, François de Paule, 37
Lagrévol, Jean-Baptiste, 88
Lamaure, 185
Lameth, Alexandre-Théodore-Victor de, 123
L'Ami des hommes (Mirabeau), 40
Langon, Nicholas-François de, 190
Languedoc, 31, 110
Latour-Duchâtel, Gaspard-Séverin, 87–88
Lauenberg, 115
Law of 10 Frimaire II/30 November 1793,
    154–158, 169
Law of 14 Ventôse VII/4 March 1799,
    160–170, 172
Law of 28 Ventôse IV/18 March 1796,
    158–159, 162
Laxaque, Pierre, 107
Le Bienvenu, Pierre, 63
Lebret, Paul-Charles-Cardin, 189–190
Le Carpentier (widow), 172
Le Chapelier, Isaac-René-Guy, 127–129
Le Chateau (fief in Normandy), 177
Leclerc de Juigné, Antoine-Eléonor-Léon,
    124–125
Le Cousteiler, Louis-Gaspard, 172
Le Dauphin (legal official in Mayenne), 92
Lefebvre, Georges, 78
Lefebvre-Laroche, Pierre-Louis, 235n91
Lefevre de la Planche, 18, 29, 33, 232–233n51
legal humanism, 9, 16–18
Legislation Committee (National Convention),
    92–95, 188, 192
Legislative Assembly
    engagements and, 153
    feudal abolition and, 191–192
    feudal property and, 61
    lods abolished by, 192
    rachat system amended by, 80, 82–84

as successor to Constituent Assembly, 83
Le Gorlier, Monsieur, 67
Lemaillaud, Joseph-François, 89
Le Mercier de la Rivière, Pierre-Paul, 41–43
Le Mystère des droits féodaux dévoilé
    (Michallet), 84–88
l'Enfant de la Patriere, Suzanne de, 6
le Noble, Jean-Charles, 177
Leopold (Grand Duke of Tuscany), 113
Leroux, 200
Le Trosne, Guillaume-François, 43–45, 68,
    236n112
Lezourmel (inspector of domains), 164
Lheritier-Vaugier, Norbert, 199
Libri Feudis (Book of Fiefs), 16
Liguria, 114, 116
Limoges, 176, 193, 195–196
Limoux, 181
Linguet, Simon-Nicolas-Henri, 143
livelli (ground rent in Tuscany), 111, 114
Locke, John, 15, 131, 133–134
Locré Roissy, Jean Guillaume, 208–209
Lombard monarchs, 21
L'Ordre naturel et éssentiel des sociétés politiques
    (Le Mercier de la Rivière), 41
Lot-et-Garonne, 84
Louis XIV (king of France)
    assertion of feudal superiority by, 30,
        233n54, 233n59
    on Crown's right to use ecclesiastical
        property, 122
    engagements (concession of domanial
        properties) and, 139, 151, 170
    negative responses to absolutism of, 37
Louis XVI (king of France), 88, 139
Loyseau, Charles
    anti-slavery sentiments of, 231n36
    on Frankish conquest of Gaul, 31, 33, 36
    intellectual influences on, 19
    property rights in the theories of, 23–29, 35,
        39–40, 44, 46, 69, 129
    Roman law and, 26–27
    royal power in the theories of, 28–29
    on *seigneuries*, 23–28, 32, 51, 56, 69, 113
    venal offices criticized by, 43
Lübeck, 115
Lyon
    appeals court in, 171, 211, 215–217
    rachat payments in, 182
    sale of public offices in, 2
Lyon, Pierre, 185

Mably, Abbé, 17, 37, 138
Mailhe, Jean-Baptiste, 88–89
Maleville, Jacques de, 212
Mante, Jacques, 190
Mariette, Jean-Victor-Gabriel, 200, 255n132

Marmion, Jean-Olivier, 157
Marseille
    inflation in, 194
    mercantile families in, 6
    national rents payments in, 182, 185, 194,
        205–206
    Roman Catholic Church in, 176, 205–206
Marx, Karl, 8–9, 48, 220
Marxist interpretations of the French Revolution,
    9, 49–50, 59, 219
Marzagalli, Silvia, 49
Maury, Abbé Jean-Siffrein, 74, 129–132
Medard (widow of Bordeaux), 91
Meffray, François-Joseph de, 190
Merlin-Cambacérès report, 114–116, 202
Merlin de Douai, Philipe-Antoine
    on abolition of feudal regime, 66
    on *banalités* (service monopolies in
        seigneuries), 70
    contractual feudalism and, 85–86, 89, 103
    Domanial Committee of National Convention
        and, 93
    on engagements (revocable grants of domanial
        property), 171–172
    feudal abolition in imperial territories and,
        112–117
    Great Demarcation facilitated by, 219, 221
    ground rent revival campaign of, 106–110
    Instruction by, 75
    National Convention's feudal abolition law
        and, 90
    national rents for disputed territories and,
        203–204
    on *rachat* enforcement, 75
    on *rachat* system burden of proof, 87
    rachat system design and, 66, 69–73, 79–80,
        83–84, 86, 89
    seigneurial justice criticized by, 60
Merovingian Dynasty, 138
Mey, Abbé, 34
Michallet, C., 84–88
Mirabeau, Honoré-Gabriel Riqueti de
    ecclesiastical property debates and, 127–129,
        133–134, 146
    physiocracy of, 40
    property rights in the theories of, 41
Mollien, François-Nicolas, 200
Montaiglon (private collector of national
    rents), 204
Montesquieu (Charles-Louis de Secondat)
    Boulainviliers critiqued by, 37–38
    feudalism defended by, 38–41, 46–47
    French Revolution influenced by, 38–39
    on the interdependence of monarchy and
        nobility, 18
    monarchical power in the theories of, 39
    property rights in the theories of, 39–40, 46
    seigneuries defended by, 38–41

    on separation of powers, 38
    venal offices defended by, 38
Montivilliers district, 185
Montmorency, M. Anne-Léon, 190
Montmorencys, 189–190
Moreau, Jacob-Nicolas, 231n35
Mounier, Jean-Joseph, 52

Napoleon Bonaparte
    on the abolition of feudal duties, 82
    coup (1798) by, 102
    fall (1815) of, 205
    ground rent revival proposals and, 102–108,
        111–117, 212, 214
    imperial annexations of, 111–117
    national rents and, 177, 197–199, 202–204,
        206–207
    political liberty diminished under, 11
    property law reform under, 11
    rachat payments reduced under, 197–198
    rescriptions and, 198–199
Napoleonic Code. *See* Civil Code
Napoleonic Empire. *See* Empire
National Assembly. *See also* Decree of August 11
        (1789); Night of August 4 (1789)
    Committee on Alienation and, 184
    Committee on the Constitution and, 52
    direct domain recognized by, 66
    Domanial Committee and, 93, 130, 137,
        139–141, 143–146, 152, 184
    Ecclesiastical Committee and, 125, 140, 179
    ecclesiastical property expropriation and,
        122–128, 135, 140, 177, 189
    engagements and, 152–153
    expropriation of royal property and,
        137–141, 144
    Feudal Committee of, 66–69, 71–74, 77,
        86–87, 89, 179, 181–182
    feudal order abolished by, 48–50, 61, 68–71
    inalienability principle and, 144
    national rent system and, 178–179, 181–182,
        184–185, 187–190
    peasant revolts (1789) and, 50, 52
    property rights debates at, 61, 123–124
    rachat (redemption) system and, 66–68,
        71–74, 77–78, 80, 179
    taxation issues and, 55–56
    venal offices abolished by, 50–51
National Convention
    on allodiality, 99–100
    direct domain recognized by, 90
    engagements revoked by, 153–159
    feudalism abolished without compensation
        by, 76, 80–83, 89–102, 104–105, 109,
        111–112, 117, 170–171, 191–192,
        204, 211
    on ground rents, 90, 92–95, 97–101, 103–104,
        109, 113–114

Joint Committee of Domains and Finance
and, 157
Legislation Committee of, 92–95, 188, 192
national rent system and, 188
opposition to feudal abolition law of, 96–100
order to burn feudal titles by, 91
Paris demonstrations suppressed by, 93
petitions to, 92–94, 98–100, 191–192
rachat payments suspended (1795-96) by,
194–195
Ventôse Laws and, 94
national domain. *See also biens nationaux*
alienability *versus* inalienability of,
141–147, 173
engagements and, 153, 172–173
establishment of, 12, 121, 126, 135–136, 216
national rents and, 176–177, 184, 187
property rights and, 121, 135–141
public property/particular property
distinction and, 128, 146–147
sale of land from, 12–13, 121, 146, 148, 153,
155–163, 165–166, 172–173
national rents
Catholic Church property converted into,
176–180, 185–186, 188, 206
collection of, 184–189
Crown property converted into, 176, 178, 183,
188, 206
disputed territories and, 203–204
establishment of, 175–176
feudal questions regarding, 204–206
hospitals and, 200–203
inflationary concerns regarding, 194–196
legal status of, 176
the nation as vassal under, 189–191
private companies as collectors of, 200,
202, 204
rachat payments and, 181–190, 197
rescriptions and, 198–200
search for original titles and, 191–192
"Second Feudal Abolition" (July 1793) and,
191–194
as source of national income, 178, 182, 189,
197–199
towns and villages' purchasing of, 180
Navarre, 31, 34
Necker, Jacques, 122–123, 125
Nicholas, Etienne, 206
Niel, Monsieur, 185
Night of August 4th 1789
abolition of colonial slavery proposed on, 50
abolition of feudalism proposed on, 10,
48–49, 61, 66–67, 86, 208
abolition of trade guilds proposed on, 50
demarcation of property and sovereignty
discussed at, 173
ecclesiastic property discussed during,
122–123, 127–128, 179

implementation of reforms made on, 11, 120,
208–209, 214
Lyonnais appellate court reference to,
211, 217
Marxist interpretations of, 49–50
peasant revolts preceding, 48–50
rachat (redemption) system proposed
during, 66
Noailles, vicomte de, 49, 66
nobility
allodiality and, 58–59, 65
Civil Code's abolition of status of, 210
Decree of August 11 (1789) and the abolition
of special land rights for, 53–54, 56
Montesquieu's defense of, 38
popular sentiment against, 86
sale of prerogatives for annuities by, 7
seigneuries as basis of, 3, 28, 40
venal offices and, 2–3, 6–7
Normandy
engagement grants in, 149–150
ground rents in, 98
rachat payments in, 185
Roman Catholic Church lands in, 122, 177,
189–190
Norman incursion (medieval France), 37
Notre Dame de Paris, 180
Nouvelles reflexions sur le rachat des droits féodaux
(Boudin), 175
nulle terre sans seigneur ("no land without a lord")
principle, 30, 71
nul seigneur sans titre (no lord without title), 30,
71, 110

Observations sommaires sur les biens ecclésiastiques
(Sieyès), 126
Order of Malta at Saint-Antoine, 190
Order of Saint-Jean of Malta, 65
Order of the Bonne Nouvelle of Rouen, 177
Orival fief, 189
Orléans, 92, 180
Orléans, duc d', 92
Ottoman Empire, 39
Ozun, Antoine-Joseph, 101–102

Paix-la-Quertier (property in Normandy), 63–64
Paris
appeals court in, 209, 215
Custom of Paris and, 20
Edict of 1692 protested in, 31
engagements in, 157
ground rents in, 194
National Convention's suppression of
protests in, 93
rachat payments in, 182, 187
search for original land titles in, 191
Paris Commune, 164
Parma, 114

Peixoto, Charles, 76
Pelet, Jean, 212, 214
Pelisanne farm, 185
Pénières-Delors, Jean-Augustin, 105–106
Percy, Domaine du, 76
Perrier, Claude, 190
Pezet-Corval, 200
physiocrats
    abstract terminology of, 45
    on hereditary monarchy, 42, 45
    property rights in the theories of, 41–46, 50,
        120, 236n11
    royal power in the theories of, 42–45
    seigneuries criticized by, 43, 45–46
    taxation in the theories of, 42–44
    venal offices criticized by, 43
    willingness to abandon tradition by, 45
Piedmont, 8, 111, 114
Pinon (citizen of Orléans), 92, 95
Plaine de Voye engagement, 172
Plaisance, 114
Pocock, J.G.A., 16
Poix de Fréminville, Edmé de la, 33, 40
Polignac courtier dynasty, 152
Polverel, Etienne, 31, 34–35, 249n63
Portalis, Jean-Etienne-Marie
    on abolition of social distinctions, 210
    Civil Code and, 209–211, 214, 216, 218
    ground rents and, 210–214
    on property and citizenship, 208
    proprietary state opposed by, 218
Portiez, Louis, 163
Pothier, Robert-Joseph, 62
Préfosse, Charles-François-Michel, 63–64, 98
Priory of Chastaing, 193
Priory of Saint-Avertin, 192–193
Provençe, 74, 110, 185. *See also specific towns*
Prunier, Françoise, 190
Puffendorf, Samuel von, 34

Quenedy, Jeanne, 99–100
Quesnay, François, 40–41
Racaud, Jacques, 196
rachat (redemption payments)
    abandonment (1793) of, 73–74, 76, 80–82
    burden of proof for legitimacy on lords
        for, 85–89
    Constituent Assembly and, 75–76, 80–84,
        86–90, 95, 99, 191–192
    enforcement problems regarding, 75
    hospitals and, 201–202
    inflationary concerns regarding,
        194–196, 214
    Napoleon's reduction of, 197–198
    National Assembly and, 66–68, 71–74, 77–78,
        80, 179

nationalized Church property and, 124–125
negotiations between lords and tenants
    regarding, 72
peasants' resistance toward, 74–75, 80, 86
political debates regarding design of, 67–68,
    71–73, 86–87
private arrangements regarding, 76
private companies as collectors of, 200,
    202, 204
real estate market and, 77, 89–91
social composition of participants in, 79
as source of national revenue, 101, 182,
    197–199
successes of, 76–77
suspension (1795-1796) of, 194–195
Ramel-Nogaret, Dominique-Vincent, 102
Ramiot, Marie, 196
Régie de l'Enregistrement, 93, 152–154,
    182, 186
Régie des Domaines, 182
Regnier, Claude-Ambroise, 103, 105
Renaudin, Joseph, 195
rents. *See* ground rents; national rents
rescriptions, 198–200
The Restoration, 117, 173, 219
Ricard, Marie, 188
Riffault, Jean-François, 192–193
Ritterbüttel, 115
Robert, Jean, 190
Robespierre, Maximilien, 221
Roederer, Pierre-Louis, 140
Rohan-Guémenée courtier dynasty, 152
Roland, Jean-Marie, 179
Roman Catholic Church
    the Crown's use of property of, 122–123
    Decree of August 11 (1789) and changes to,
        50, 53–55, 60
    extent of property owned by, 3, 7–8, 32, 56,
        118–119, 176–178
    in Frank-controlled Gaul, 37, 130
    Frankish appropriation of lands of, 37
    as largest owner of *seigneuries*, 3
    nationalization of property of, 3, 11–13,
        53–54, 78, 118–125, 128–129, 137,
        140, 143, 146, 173, 175–179, 185–186,
        188–190, 206
    property rights questions regarding, 125–135,
        137, 146
    proposal to make state religion
        of France, 135
    public mission of, 128
    sovereignty of, 54–55, 119
    tithes and, 54, 60, 122–125, 221
Roman Empire, 16, 37, 84–85. *See also*
    Roman Law
Romanist theory of feudal origins, 16–17, 37

Roman law
  allodiality and, 31, 33, 39
  emphyteutic leases and, 109–110
  ground rents and, 112, 114
  seigneuries and, 23–24, 26–27
  southern French provinces influenced by, 62,
    95, 109
Rome, French imperial department of, 113
Rouen, 182, 193
Rousseau, Jean-Jacques, 132–134
Roussillon, 31, 110
Rouvin, 200
Roux, Simon, 185
Rowen, Herbert, 22–23
Roy, Antoine, 167
Ruan village, 180
Rungis village, 180

Sacristy of La Chatte, 180
Saint-Barthélemy of Aix monastery, 188
Saint-Chamas (town in Provençe), 185
Saint-Domingue, 249n63
Saint-Jean d'Angéley, Regnaud, 212
Saint-Priest le Betoux, 177
Saint-Quentin-en-Vermandois, 32
Saint-Victor of Marseille order, 205
Salic Law, 29, 42, 45
Sancerre, County of, 152
Saniée, Madeleine-Henriette-Celestine-Mélanie
    Baillard, 189
Savoy, 66, 239n64
Secondat, Charles-Louis de. *See* Montesquieu
Second Treatise (Locke), 15
Seignelay, Colbert de, 124
seigneuries (jurisdictional lordships)
  banalités (service monopolies) and, 7, 70, 74
  Bodin's theories regarding, 21–22
  the Crown's ownership of, 3, 136
  Dumoulin's theories regarding, 20, 22, 32
  échanges and, 149
  engagements (revocable grants of domanial
    property) and, 150–151, 168
  etymology of, 24
  Frankish rule and, 24–25, 28
  French Revolution's abolition of, 12–13,
    50–53, 55–60, 175–176
  heritability of, 24–26, 39–40, 51
  hierarchical division of, 3, 82
  lords' jurisdiction over, 2–3, 9, 26, 28, 39, 41,
    50–51, 53, 55, 57–59
  Loyseau's theories regarding, 23–28, 32, 51,
    56, 69, 113
  military service obligations and, 26, 39–40
  Mirabeau on, 41
  Montesquieu's defense of, 38–41
  Moreau's criticism of, 231n35

nobility conferred by ownership of, 3, 28, 40
  origins of, 2, 17, 24–25, 36
  physiocrats' views of, 43, 45–46
  public-private distinction in, 24–28, 32,
    46, 113
  right of first refusal (*droit de prélation*)
    and, 206
  Roman Catholic Church ownership of, 3
  Roman law and, 23–24, 26–27
  seigneurie directe (tenurial superiority), 25–27,
    35, 45, 55–56, 58, 60, 62, 64–66, 69, 82,
    110–111
  seigneurie privée (private property), 24, 27, 69
  seigneuries utiles (possession and use rights),
    25–27, 45, 55–56, 58, 62, 69
  service-based awards of, 25
  state's superior right over, 25
  subaltern public power annexed to, 18
seigneurs hauts-justiciers, 3
sieurie ("full property of something"), 27, 56
Sieyès, Abbé Emanuel-Joseph
  on the abolition of public *seigneuries*, 52
  on the abolition of tithes, 124
  on ground rents' democratization of
    property, 59, 65
  on legitimate property and independence, 61
  on restoration of ground rents, 212
  on the Roman Catholic Church and property
    rights, 126
Six Books of the Republic (Bodin), 20–23
Skinner, Quentin, 19, 21
Smith, Adam, 229n23
Social Contract (Rousseau), 132–133
Sonthonax, Léger-Félicité, 249n63
The Spirit of the Laws (Montesquieu), 38–40

Talleyrand-Périgord, Charles-Maurice de, 121,
    126–127
Talon, Louis, 183
Target, Guy-Jean-Baptiste, 52
tenurial system. *See* feudalism
the Terror, 137, 169, 210
Tête-Noire-Lafayette, Claude-Philippe, 171–172
thèse nobiliaire, 36
thèse seigneuriale, 36, 38
Third Estate, 38, 58, 74, 213
Thouret, Jacques-Guillaume, 119, 131–133
Tingry (widow of Caen), 159
tithes, 54, 60, 122–125, 221
Tocqueville, Alexis de, 1, 15
Toulouse, 31
Tournon military school, 190
Traité de la monarchie (Mirabeau), 40–41
Traité du domaine de droit de propriété
    (Pothier), 62
Trasimène, 113

Treatise of Orders and Plain Dignities
    (Loyseau), 23
Treatise on Offices (Loyseau), 23
Treatise on Seigneuries (Loyseau), 23–25, 28
Treilhard, Jean-Baptiste
    Civil Code and, 208, 211, 216
    on feudal dues and ecclesiastical
        properties, 179
    Great Demarcation facilitated by, 219
    ground rent proposals of, 100–101
    on national domain, 135
The Tribunate, 103, 105–106, 197
Tronchet, François-Denis
    domanial abolition denounced by, 68–69
    Grand Demarcation facilitated by, 219
    on maintaining feudal dues system, 179
    rachat collection and, 77
    rachat (redemption) system design and,
        66–67, 71–73, 79–80, 83–84, 86, 89
    on restoring ground rents, 212
Turgot, Anne Robert Joseph, 123, 126,
    131–134
Tuscany, 8, 111, 113–114, 116

United States, 8, 61, 228n20

Vachon, Louis-François de, 172
Vanberchem, 200
Vautier, 63
Vauvenargues, Lord, 183
Vechte, 115
venal offices
    Bodin on, 22, 43
    French Revolution's abolition of, 12, 50–51,
        53, 55–57, 60, 175, 221
    Loyseau on, 38
    Montesquieu's defense of, 38
    noble status acquired through, 2–3, 6–7
    Old Regime's reliance on, 2–8
Ventôse Laws, 94
Verden, 115
Vienne, 155–156, 192
Vimar, Nicholas, 158–159
Viscounty of Landes, 149
Visme, Jacques-François-Laurent de, 184
Vitecoq, 185
Voltaire, 38, 235n92

Westphalia, 115

Yonne village councils, 74–75